Praise for *Game of Shadows*:

"The best-made case that performance-enhancing drugs played a major role in baseball's inflated homer totals."
—*Sports Illustrated*

"The evidence is detailed, damning, and overwhelming. . . . It's a growing bonfire of controversy. This book is one of the matches."
—*The Philadelphia Inquirer*

"A compelling narrative that outlines the crimes committed by BALCO officials and elite athletes. . . . Anyone who wants to discuss or debate baseball's steroids problems—and the investigation spawned by *Game of Shadows*—should read this book."
—*San Jose Mercury News*

"Scorching. . . . A testament to baseball's failure." —*Newsweek*

"[Fainaru-Wada and Williams] have got the goods and they reveal them methodically. Everything is well-sourced and meticulously step-by-step."
—*Chicago Tribune*

"Finally, there is substantial, documented, hard-to-refute evidence. What all of baseball's drug testing could not prove has instead been proven by Mark Fainaru-Wada and Lance Williams."
York *Daily News*

"Damning."
—*New York Post*

"Explosive."
—*Newsday*

"A book-length exposé . . . [*Game of Shadows*] has received so much news coverage already that some may think they already know enough. The news coverage, however, does not begin to capture the breadth and depth of the documentation provided by Fainaru-Wada and Williams about drug cheating. . . . An intellectual home run."
—*The Denver Post*

Mark Fainaru-Wada and **Lance Williams** are investigative reporters for *The San Francisco Chronicle*. Fainaru-Wada and Williams won the Dick Schaap Excellence in Sports Journalism Award, the George Polk Award, and the Edgar A. Poe Award for their reporting. They live in San Francisco.

GAME OF SHADOWS

Barry Bonds, BALCO, and the Steroids Scandal That Rocked Professional Sports

Mark Fainaru-Wada
and
Lance Williams

GOTHAM BOOKS

GOTHAM BOOKS
Published by Penguin Group (USA) Inc.
375 Hudson Street, New York, New York 10014, U.S.A.
Penguin Group (Canada), 90 Eglinton Avenue East, Suite 700, Toronto, Ontario, Canada
M4P 2Y3 (a division of Pearson Penguin Canada Inc.); Penguin Books Ltd, 80 Strand,
London WC2R 0RL, England; Penguin Ireland, 25 St Stephen's Green, Dublin 2, Ireland
(a division of Penguin Books Ltd); Penguin Group (Australia), 250 Camberwell Road,
Camberwell, Victoria 3124, Australia (a division of Pearson Australia Group Pty Ltd);
Penguin Books India Pvt Ltd, 11 Community Centre, Panchsheel Park, New Delhi–
110 017, India; Penguin Group (NZ), 67 Apollo Drive, Mairangi Bay, Albany 1311,
Auckland, New Zealand (a division of Pearson New Zealand Ltd); Penguin Books
(South Africa) (Pty) Ltd, 24 Sturdee Avenue, Rosebank, Johannesburg 2196, South Africa

Penguin Books Ltd, Registered Offices: 80 Strand, London WC2R 0RL, England

Published by Gotham Books, a division of Penguin Group (USA) Inc.

Previously published as a Gotham Books hardcover edition, March 2006

First trade paperback printing, March 2007

5 7 9 10 8 6 4

Copyright © 2006 by Mark Fainaru-Wada and Lance Williams
Afterword copyright © 2007 by Mark Fainaru-Wada and Lance Williams

Gotham Books and the skyscraper logo are trademarks of Penguin Group (USA) Inc.

The Library of Congress has catalogued the hardcover edition of this book as follows:
Fainaru-Wada, Mark.
Game of Shadows : Barry Bonds, BALCO, and the steroids scandal that rocked
professional sports / Mark Fainaru-Wada and Lance Williams.
p. cm.
Includes bibliographical references.
ISBN 1-592-40199-6 (hardcover)   ISBN 978-1-592-40268-7 (paperback)
1. Anabolic steroids—Health aspects.   2. Doping in sports.   3. Steroids.   I. Williams,
Lance, 1950–   II. Title.
RC1230 . F35 2006
362.29—dc22   2005037750

Printed in the United States of America
Set in Berkeley Book • Designed by Elke Sigal

To Max and Ella
—MFW

To Barbara
—LW

Contents

Prologue

On May 22, 1998, the San Francisco Giants arrived in St. Louis for a three-game series with the Cardinals. That weekend, Giants All-Star left fielder Barry Bonds got a firsthand look at the frenzied excitement surrounding Mark McGwire, baseball's emerging Home Run King.

Bonds had recently remarried, but on this trip he was accompanied by his girlfriend, Kimberly Bell, a slender, attractive woman with long brown hair and brown eyes whom he had met four years earlier in the players' parking lot at Candlestick Park. Bell had been looking forward to the trip, and it was pleasant in many ways—a big hotel room with a view of St. Louis's famous arch; a wonderful seat eight rows behind home plate; and even tornado warnings, which were exotic to a California girl. But Bonds was sulky and brooding. A three-time winner of the National League Most Valuable Player award, he was one of the most prideful stars in baseball. All that weekend, though, he was overshadowed by McGwire.

Even by the standards of the modern game, the Cardinals' first baseman was a player of exceptional size and power. That summer the 6-foot-5 McGwire weighed 260 muscular pounds and was hitting balls that traveled in long, soaring arcs. The season was less than two months old, but he already had hit 20 home runs. McGwire's pace was ahead of Babe Ruth when he hit 60 home runs in 1927, and also ahead of Roger Maris when he hit 61 to break Ruth's record in 1961. Players, fans, and the media were already anticipating that McGwire could break baseball's most storied record, and the noisy attention he received as a result was impossible to ignore.

Before Friday night's game, even the Giants' coaches acted like fans, gathering behind the batting cage and watching as McGwire hit 10 batting practice pitches into the stands. During the game itself, McGwire crushed a home run into an area of Busch Stadium's upper deck called "Big Mac Land." The home run entitled everyone in the sellout crowd of 43,000 to a free hamburger. For the Giants, Bonds went 1 for 4 with a double. The Cardinals won 4–3.

On Saturday night, McGwire singled in the first inning and scored from second when Bonds made a poor throw on a hit to left field. Then McGwire hit two more home runs, the second one bouncing off the Chevrolet sign on the left-field scoreboard. The Cards won 11–10.

On Sunday, Bonds himself hit a dramatic two-run homer, his 11th of the season, to tie the game in the ninth inning. But in the 12th, after the Giants had pulled ahead 6–4, McGwire hit an equally dramatic shot to tie the game again. It was his fourth home run of the series, and his 24th of the young season. The Giants finally won in 17, but Bonds's mood remained irretrievably foul.

On that trip, Bonds began making racial remarks about McGwire to Kimberly Bell. According to Bell, he would repeat them throughout the summer, as McGwire and Sammy Sosa, the buff, fan-friendly Chicago Cubs slugger who also was hitting home runs at an amazing rate, became the talk of the nation.

"They're just letting him do it because he's a white boy," Bonds said of McGwire and his chase of Maris's record. The pursuit by Sosa, a Latino player from the Dominican Republic, was entertaining but doomed, Bonds declared. As a matter of policy, "They'll never let him win," he said.

As he sometimes did when he was in a particularly bleak mood, Bonds was channeling racial attitudes picked up from his father, the former Giants star Bobby Bonds, and his godfather, the great Willie Mays, both African-American ballplayers who had experienced virulent racism while starting their professional careers in the Jim Crow South. Barry Bonds himself had never seen anything remotely like that: He had grown up in an affluent white suburb on the San Francisco Peninsula, and his best boyhood friend, his first wife, and his present girlfriend all were white. When Bonds railed about McGwire, he didn't articulate who "they" were, or how the supposed conspiracy to rig the home run record was being carried out. But his brooding anger was real enough, and it continued throughout a year in which he batted .303, hit 37 home runs, made the All-Star team for the eighth time, and was almost completely ignored. For, as the 1998 season unfolded, the attention of all baseball focused on McGwire's home run chase and on his gentlemanly rivalry with Sosa. The quest to hit 61 home runs transfixed even casual fans, in the way that a great pennant race used to do in the old days.

Something about McGwire's appearance—the red hair and the freckled, craggy face that sometimes burst into a winning smile—seemed to invite affectionate hyperbole. The sportswriters who covered him wrote that McGwire had Popeye's forearms and shoulders as broad as Paul Bunyan's. The nature of his quest was also expressed in hyperbolic terms: McGwire's home run chase was "a metaphor for the best in America," a newspaper editor told an Iowa professor who was studying the chase as a cultural phenomenon. It was more significant than "the ascent on Mount Everest," as San Francisco Giants marketing man Pat Gallagher proclaimed. And from acting baseball commissioner Bud Selig down to its ordinary fans—anybody who cared about the game and worried about its future—all agreed that McGwire's pursuit of the home run record was hugely important. It had made watching the sport of baseball enjoyable again, for the first time in quite a while.

Baseball's fans are among the most forgiving in all sports, but the toxic relations between team owners and the players union had put the fans' patience to the test for a generation. From 1971 through 1990, seven baseball seasons had been interrupted by labor disputes. The eighth interruption, which began in August 1994, lasted 234 days and led to the only cancellation of the World Series since World War I. It also nearly killed the game.

As always, both the union and the owners claimed the dispute was about baseball's future. Actually, it was just another fight about money. For fans, the dispute was dispiriting and pointless, an argument between millionaires and billionaires.

The owners finally reopened the ballparks, and the players slunk back into them two weeks after the 1995 season had been scheduled to start. In park after park they were greeted with a cascade of boos. Many fans just stayed away. Attendance in 1995 was down 28 percent, nearly 20 million, from 1993, the last pre-strike season. It crept back in the following seasons, but in 1997, attendance was still down 10 percent, or more than 7 million fans, from the pre-strike high. By some estimates the lockout had cost the owners $500 million in lost revenues in 1994, and $800 million more in 1995. More worrisome still were the many signs that interest in the game might have permanently ebbed.

Then, in 1998, McGwire's assault on Maris's record brought the fans back to baseball in droves. The Cardinals' home attendance, which had languished since the lockout, would top 3.1 million, a club record, and other National League clubs saw big gains as well. For fans, McGwire's escalating home run totals became a daily reminder of the game's underlying drama and intensity—and its history, for the ghosts of Ruth and Maris hovered about all summer long. And if McGwire's chase of the home run record evoked baseball's past, Sosa was a charming connection to its future, one of a stream of talented Latino players who were flooding into the game. Fans were drawn to Sosa, McGwire's friendly rival, and the complex ritual he went through each time he crossed home plate after a homer, including the blown kiss and the tap of his heart to honor his mother.

By mid-summer the home run chase took on a traveling circus atmosphere. One night in Phoenix, 25,000 people showed up to watch McGwire take his hacks in batting practice, while a TV station provided pitch-by-pitch commentary and the scoreboard registered the distance of each practice home run. A media pack worthy of a presidential candidate on election night tailed McGwire across the country, recording his every word and action.

In August, when McGwire had already hit 43 bombs, a veteran Associated Press writer named Steve Wilstein stopped by the big Cardinal's locker in Busch Stadium. As he waited for McGwire to emerge from the shower, Wilstein noted items in plain view on a locker shelf: a photo of McGwire with his 10-year-old son; a can of Popeye-brand spinach; a bottle of a product called androstenedione. Wilstein assumed it was some sort of vitamin.

But Andro was more than that. The product was a testosterone booster marketed by Patrick Arnold, a renegade chemist who was pioneering the development of steroids that would be undetectable by the most sophisticated laboratory tests. Andro was legal. But it had been banned by the International Olympic Committee, the National Collegiate Athletic Association, and the National Football League. Olympic doping experts told Wilstein that Andro had the same muscle-building effects as anabolic steroids, which Congress had outlawed in 1991. Andro was a steroid by another name. In the Olympics, using Andro was considered cheating. Users who got caught were banned.

Baseball, however, had no rules against steroid use, and a different attitude about cheating. From corking bats to doctoring balls to hiding a coach with binoculars in the scoreboard to steal signs, the impulse to cut corners was almost as old as the game itself. Players did what they could to get an edge, without shame or serious consequence. Performance-enhancing drugs had become another way to accomplish that. For decades, the game's drug of choice was not steroids but "greenies," or amphetamines, which were popped by players seeking to kick their performance up a notch, hoping to overcome fatigue, aches and pains, hangovers, even boredom.

Perhaps because of the sport's antipathy to weight lifting, steroids were slow to catch on. For much of the game's history, players were discouraged from pumping iron, lest they lose the flexibility and quick wrists needed to get around on the pitched ball.

That began to change in the mid-to-late 1980s. By his own account, the Typhoid Mary of steroid use in the big leagues was the Cuban slugger Jose Canseco, the first player to hit 40 home runs and steal 40 bases in the same season. Canseco was also McGwire's teammate on the dominating Oakland Athletics clubs of the 1980s. In 2005, out of baseball, financially strapped, and on probation for assault, Canseco would write a confessional memoir, claiming to have "single handedly changed the game of baseball" by popularizing weight training and performance-enhancing drugs. Canseco said his own career proved that strength conditioning, when combined with steroids and human growth hormone, translated into a higher batting average and more power. He claimed that the drugs could transform a good player into a great one. After his Rookie of the Year season in 1986, when he hit 33 home runs, Canseco claimed other players began to emulate him, and weight training and juicing swept the game.

In the book's most enduring image, Canseco described going into the bathroom at the Oakland Coliseum with McGwire before A's games. There, he wrote, the two sluggers would inject themselves with the steroid Deca-Durabolin, then take the field.

But in 1998, Canseco's disclosures about his famous teammate were far in the unanticipated future. And in 1998, McGwire had been caught only with Andro, not with Growth or Deca. Still, the AP's revelation that McGwire was using a drug that would have gotten him banned from the Olympic Games pushed its way into the headlines. Many in baseball's establishment reacted with outrage—not at McGwire, but at Wilstein, the writer who broke the story.

Leading the attack was Tony LaRussa, the Cardinals' tightly wound manager. He lashed out at the media, agitating to ban the Associated Press from the Cards' clubhouse on the spurious grounds that Wilstein had violated an unwritten baseball rule by looking in McGwire's locker.

Acting commissioner Bud Selig promised baseball would commission a scientific study about the health effects of performance-enhancing drugs. But he made it clear he would take no action regarding McGwire and Andro.

Selig's deepest fear was that the Andro story would develop into a scandal that would ruin McGwire and kill baseball's lucrative renaissance just as it was beginning. Fans loved the long ball; crowds were packing the parks; the rancor of the strike was being forgotten; McGwire and Sosa were bringing baseball back from oblivion's edge. And if it sometimes seemed that baseball was devolving into an arcade game, with double-digit scores resembling those in football, and if players were showing up at spring training 15 pounds heavier and displaying the physiques of bodybuilders, those were concerns for another time.

Soon, the Andro story faded. Stubborn pitchers continued to challenge McGwire, and he continued to drive the ball. The rate at which he hit homers was unprecedented—once every 7.27 at bats, far above Ruth's career average of 11.76—and the distances they traveled inspired awe. At Busch Stadium, where the center field fence was 402 feet from home plate, he hit a 545-foot shot that slammed into a seat in the second deck. The club marked the spot by painting a big picture of a Band-Aid there. A home run in the thin air of Denver sailed out of Coors Field, bounced through the players' parking lot, and finally came to rest against a fence 700 feet from the plate.

McGwire hit number 62 on September 8 in St. Louis, amidst a wild celebration and before a national TV audience, and then continued hitting bombs: five of them in his final 11 at-bats, including two on the last day of the season, to finish with 70, four ahead of Sosa. In 36 seasons, no baseball player had topped the 61 home run mark—and now two players had blown past it in the same year. Many at the time said McGwire's 1998 season was the greatest offensive performance in the history of the sport.

On the West Coast, Barry Bonds was astounded and aggrieved by the outpouring of hero worship for McGwire, a hitter whom he regarded as obviously inferior to himself. Bonds was 33 years old, had played in the big leagues for 12 years, and was known for an unusual combination of speed and power. In 1993, when he joined the Giants, Bonds had signed what was then the richest contract in the game: $43.75 million for six years. In 1996 he had become the second player in history, after Canseco, to hit 40 home runs and steal 40 bases in the same season. Bonds knew he was on his way to the Hall of Fame. For as long as he had played baseball, Bonds had regarded himself as better than every other player he encountered, and he almost always was right.

But as the 1998 season ended, Bonds's elite status had slipped a notch. The game and its fans were less interested in the complete player who could hit for average and power, and who had great speed and an excellent glove. The emphasis was shifting to pure slugging. From now on, the biggest contracts and the most adulation would go to big, muscular players who could put up home run numbers unlike anything the game had ever seen: players like Mark McGwire. As McGwire's pursuit of the home run record became the constant topic of the nation's media, and as McGwire was celebrated as the best slugger of the modern era and perhaps the greatest slugger who had ever lived, Bonds became more jealous than people who knew him well had ever seen.

To Bonds, it was a joke. He had been around enough gyms to recognize that McGwire was a juicer. Bonds himself had never used anything more performance enhancing than a protein shake from the health-food store. But as the 1998 season unfolded, and as he watched Mark McGwire take over the game—his game—Barry Bonds decided that he, too, would begin using what he called "the shit."

Game of Shadows

Part I

Cheat or Lose

Chapter 1

On a steamy May morning in 2001, at North Carolina State University, Victor Conte could see it all coming together. The years of scraping and scheming and networking finally were about to pay off. Playing multiple roles—benevolent pitchman, self-taught scientist, schmoozer extraordinaire—Conte had orchestrated the ultimate marketing moment. Fame and glory and riches were all now within reach.

Conte had arrived in Raleigh from the West Coast only the day before. There, he owned and operated BALCO, the Bay Area Laboratory Co-Operative, a little-known distributor of nutritional supplements that was located in a suburban strip mall not far from San Francisco International Airport. He had created a surefire nutritional supplement, a tiny pill called ZMA, which, according to Conte, not only would make you stronger, but would enable you to run faster, jump higher, hit harder, swim better, sleep sounder, and even have better sex. Now, just off the plane from Los Angeles, was a writer for *FLEX* magazine, the bodybuilders' bible, whom Conte had handpicked to deliver a story that would drive sales of ZMA through the roof.

The protagonist for Conte's miracle story was track-and-field superstar Marion Jones, the most famous female athlete in the world. Jones had won five medals—three gold—at the Sydney Olympics the previous summer, becoming the newly crowned "world's fastest woman."

Since her triumphant performance, Jones had been catapulted to global superstardom. She was on the covers of *Vogue, Time, Newsweek,* and *Sports Illustrated for Women*. Buff and beautiful, Jones was the ultimate cover girl, an ultra-fit athlete whom millions of fans had come to know intimately through NBC's extensive coverage of the Summer Games.

Jones was in great demand as a pitchwoman, and under ordinary circumstances it might cost a company millions to induce her to endorse its products. But this was not the case for Conte. Jones had started doing business with Conte and his BALCO lab in the months leading up to Sydney, and their bond was so strong that when Conte asked, Jones graciously agreed to be featured in a muscle magazine, even though the story and the photo spread would not benefit her at all. In fact, the writer, Jim Schmaltz, didn't have to go through any of the grief, hassles, and likely rejection that faced writers for even the biggest magazines who wanted an exclusive interview with Marion Jones. Conte just called him one day and said, "Hey, you want an exclusive with Marion Jones?" "Sure," Schmaltz replied, and he was soon on a plane to Raleigh.

Schmaltz was expected to produce an elaborately staged advertorial to promote Conte and his supplement, not Jones. That was the way it worked at *FLEX*. The worlds of bodybuilding magazines and the dietary supplement business were intertwined, feeding off one another while selling better bodies, better health, better sex. *FLEX* was part of a $1 billion media empire built by Joe and Ben Weider, the brother tandem considered the godfathers of bodybuilding. Their magazines featured chiseled, updated versions of Charles Atlas and extolled the benefits of working out like Mr. Olympia. Each issue featured a scantily clad "fitness" model: a woman surely attainable if only a man trained determinedly and used all the vitamins and powders advertised. Page after page of ads hawked products that promised DEFINED FREAKY MASS, ROCK-HARD MUSCLES, BIONIC STRENGTH & COLOSSAL MUSCLE GAINS. One product promised to deliver ORGASMIC THRUST ACTIVATION.

It was big business—a largely unregulated, $17 billion industry that produced drinkable, chewable, injectable "supplements," substances sold as the scientifically designed, essential components of every athlete's training regimen. As with any other highly competitive business, the key to success was finding a way to make your products stand out.

Conte said ZMA was short for either "zinc magnesium aspartate" or "zinc monomethionine aspartate." The vitamin was supposed to correct deficiencies in zinc and magnesium, and Conte maintained that every athlete—indeed, every person—was deficient in those trace minerals. ZMA had reached the marketplace in 1999, and now Conte was using the tried-and-true method of celebrity endorsement to market his supplement, enlisting a clientele of athletic superstars who could attest to the values of his pill. In promotional materials, he would insist that "many 1988, 1992, 1996, and 2000 U.S. Olympic medalists achieved their success utilizing the ingredients in ZMA."

As Schmaltz and a freelance photographer arrived to work up a feature on Marion Jones's supposed passion for bodybuilding, the writer knew the critical subtext: He would chronicle Jones's endorsements for Victor Conte of BALCO Labs and his fantastic ZMA supplement. In other words, Marion Jones wasn't Marion Jones without Victor Conte.

Schmaltz watched as Jones lifted weights under the supervision of her then-husband C. J. Hunter, the disgraced world-champion shot-putter who had tested positive for steroids on the eve of the Sydney Games the previous September. Conte also had brought along his pal Milos "The Mind" Sarcev, a Yugoslavian bodybuilding legend, personal trainer, and self-described "anabolic expert." Sarcev had nearly died a year earlier when he struck a vein in one of his triceps while injecting a drug known as "synthol," popular among bodybuilders because it expands the muscles. He was creating a weight-lifting program for another BALCO client, the Olympic sprinter Tim Montgomery. Montgomery and Jones were training partners—soon to be lovers—and Montgomery, then known as "Tiny Tim," was working out in Raleigh that day as well.

Sarcev, his muscled chest bursting out of a red tank top bearing the letters ZMA, watched Jones's workout at the gym on the North Carolina State campus, spotting for her as she did some front squats. Afterward, the two modeled for photos, at one point playfully competing in a pose down. "I could turn you into a physique champion, no doubt about it," Sarcev told Jones.

As the FLEX photographer snapped shots, Sarcev and Jones compared their chiseled stomachs, and then crouched in the starting blocks on the track. At one point, everyone posed for a group shot:

Sarcev, Jones, the burly Hunter, and Conte, the mastermind, peering out from behind wire-rim glasses, a thin mustache giving him the look of a carnival barker. Everyone wore ZMA gear except Jones. Conte believed Jones should be wearing the ZMA logo, too, as compensation for his "nutritional consultation," but Jones and Hunter feared the consequences of being seen as too closely aligned with BALCO. Jones had a multimillion-dollar endorsement deal with Nike, and the sports apparel giant might interpret her wearing anything other than its famous Swoosh logo as a breach of the contract. Besides, they knew that certain aspects of Conte's business could never stand the light of day.

Schmaltz spent about 15 minutes interviewing Jones in the stands overlooking the N.C. State track. She praised Conte and BALCO, claiming ZMA gave her a better night's sleep and more effective morning workouts. The writer and the Olympian didn't discuss the fact that there was no scientific basis to Conte's claims about ZMA, or that Conte was a junior college dropout with no background in medicine or health.

Four months later, a picture of Jones adorned the cover of the September 2001 issue of *FLEX*, accompanied by the words: MARION JONES EXCLUSIVE! "Bodybuilding should be in the Olympics." The eight-page spread ran with the headline "A Jones for Bodybuilding."

"One look at the curves and indentations of Marion Jones' extraordinary musculature proves that the world's top female athlete has applied the highest quality of training and nutrition science to take advantage of her natural gifts," Schmaltz wrote. He also wrote that Jones hoped to break the world records in the 100- and 200-meter dashes, thus passing her idol, the flamboyant sprinter Florence Griffith Joyner. The story did not mention that Griffith Joyner had died prematurely at the age of 38 from an apparent heart seizure, an event widely speculated to have been brought on by steroid abuse.

A second story in the issue, titled, "Fuel for the Fire: Marion Jones' Supplement Program," described Jones as "part of a growing number of sports superstars who work with Victor Conte of Balco Labs." Conte, the story said, was "best known as the architect of the popular ZMA supplement, which is becoming a staple of many athletic regimens."

A sidebar headlined "What's Inside Marion?" laid out the "current supplement regimen" Conte had designed for Jones. Listed were 33 items she supposedly ingested daily, including a special whey-protein blend, creatine monohydrate, vitamins A, C, E, D, B_1, B_2, B_6, and B_{12}, omega-3 fatty acids, dextrose, tyrosine, folic acid, and, of course, three capsules of ZMA before bedtime.

But the real story lay in the substances that were *not* listed as being "inside Marion." Jones was getting more than just legal nutritional supplements in exchange for her willingness to endorse Conte's business and products. Although Jones denied it, Conte provided her with an array of undetectable, banned performance-enhancing drugs that she used before, during, and after her triumphs at the Sydney Olympics, according to statements made later by Conte and Hunter. The drugs included human growth hormone, the endurance-booster EPO, insulin, and "The Clear," the designer steroid administered by placing a couple drops under the tongue.

Hunter would later say that he himself injected his wife with EPO, inserting the syringe just under the skin near her front waistline. He also said he witnessed her injecting herself with EPO and growth hormone. And he said Jones's Olympic entourage had smuggled growth hormone and The Clear through Australian customs in September 2000. Conte eventually told a national television audience that he had taught Jones how to inject herself with human growth hormone using a new device, describing a time in April 2001—one month before the interview with Schmaltz—when he sat a foot away from her in a California hotel room and watched her shoot growth hormone into her quadriceps.

Throughout her career, Jones has steadfastly denied ever using banned drugs.

The *FLEX* article, with its cheery pictures of Jones side by side with the husky anabolic expert Sarcev, all but revealed one of the dirty little secrets of American sports in the 21st century: that top-level athletes had become as enmeshed in the steroid culture as bodybuilders. The drugs were illegal, and users faced serious health risks. But even baseball players, whose unimposing physiques once could have led them to be mistaken for insurance salesman or PE teachers, had come to resemble NFL linebackers.

It was surprising—yet telling—that the paths of Jones and Sarcev had crossed. Jones's sport boasted the most stringent drug-testing policy in the world: An athlete could be disqualified from competition for two years if caught just once, and then banned for life if nabbed a second time. Bodybuilders, meanwhile, were human lab rats, swallowing and injecting and rubbing on anything and everything to compete in a sport that was essentially a muscle-bound freak show. These were the converging worlds of Victor Conte, a man who hoped to engineer the perfect athlete to prove he could create superstardom. Conte wanted the world to know that he was the man pulling the strings, creating the superstars who would set world records, hit mammoth home runs, and sack countless quarterbacks.

The *FLEX* article would get that message out. Conte needed to be part of the story, as much to gratify his own outsized ego as to sell ZMA. He wasn't satisfied simply with standing in the shadows while his athletes shattered records and won glory. Conte wanted to be famous himself. He wanted to be celebrated as the bold scientist who was transforming the world of sports, and whose critically important work was acknowledged by great athletes. Of course, there was a secret that couldn't be revealed in any story about Victor Conte or Marion Jones or BALCO labs.

Unfortunately, Conte wasn't the kind of person who was good at keeping secrets.

Victor Conte Jr. grew up midway between San Francisco and Los Angeles, in the heart of California's Central Valley, the most productive agricultural region in the world. He was born in 1950 to Victor Conte Sr., a sturdy construction supervisor who loved to hunt and fish, and to Shirley Conte, a homemaker who was the glue of the family. Victor Sr. was a well-built, beer-drinking U.S. Navy veteran reared in the Depression era, with a plain sense of what it meant to work for a living.

Unlike his father, Victor Conte Jr.—the oldest of three siblings—was lithe and wiry, standing 5 feet 10 but weighing just 145 pounds by the time he was attending McLane High in Fresno in 1967. Victor wasn't much for fishing with his dad during the Conte family's annual treks to Shaver Lake, the big reservoir on the western edge of the High Sierra. He preferred water skiing. "He could go on a single ski for nine hours straight and never fall down," marvels his cousin Bruce Conte. Victor was a jumper, and he tried the long jump, the high jump, and even the triple jump, an event in which he set a school record at McLane by leaping 46 feet, 1 1/2 inches. He also found a way to make a quick buck with his talents down at the Cedar Lanes bowling alley. Nearby was a pond maybe 15 feet across. Conte and his pals would make modest wagers with unsuspecting kids that he could take a couple steps and leap across the pond. He always made it. "It blew everybody's mind," Bruce says.

Victor's athletic skills and outgoing personality made him a magnet for other kids. He particularly had a way with girls, driven by a self-confidence that belied his ordinary appearance. If he saw a girl he liked, sometimes he would simply walk over and pick her up. Literally. He would just snatch her up in his arms and sweep her off her feet. "He wasn't a shy type," Bruce says of his cousin.

After high school, Victor enrolled at Fresno City College. He competed on the track team and considered a career as an accountant, mainly to placate his dad, but his real passion was music. Victor, Bruce, and another cousin, Michael, were each self-taught on the guitar or bass, and on family camping trips, the three boys would play surf tunes around the campfire.

For a time, Victor Sr. was able to dismiss his son's music as a kid's whimsy. But in the fall of 1969, Bruce Conte persuaded his cousin to drop out of junior college to form a group called Common Ground. For the next decade, as Conte hopped from band to band, trying to make it as a professional musician, his father would introduce him by saying, "This is my son Victor. He's never worked a day in his life."

In fact, Victor Conte Jr. was an operator in ways his father could not have imagined. He often ended up managing the bands he played in, finding the gigs, booking studio time, hiring and firing. He could listen to a record once and memorize it, almost note for note. He was versatile, able to play jazz, funk, or rock. And he worked hard at his craft, practicing as much as five hours a day. Conte also was a showman. Languid and slithery as he played his bass across the stage, Conte came to be known as the Walkin' Fish. "He had this funny way of moving on the stage," says a guitarist known as "Dulo," who played for a time with Conte. "It was kind of like a fish walking on its tail. He kind of shuffled."

Before long, Conte had broken from his father's working-class, Italian Catholic ethos. He studied Eastern philosophy. He read the Bhagavad Gita, the sacred Hindu scripture, and recited it to his friends with the same uncanny memory he had for music. Dulo thought Conte was a man with a strong moral compass, a follower of the Golden Rule who believed in Karma. He would say things like, "If you left $1,000 in a wallet on a park bench, if you had your shit together, you could go away and come back twenty-four hours later and it would be there."

Conte was the most loyal, caring, and spiritual man he'd ever met, Dulo thought.

In 1970, the 20-year-old Conte quit Common Ground and moved to Los Angeles to join a band with Don "Sugarcane" Harris, the blues violinist. That band ultimately became Pure Food and Drug Act (an irony noted in many news stories after the BALCO scandal erupted 30 years later). In 1972, the band delivered its only album, *Choice Cuts*.

By then, cousin Bruce had moved to the San Francisco Bay Area and landed his dream job as guitarist for Tower of Power, a hot funk band noted for its big horn section. Bill Graham, San Francisco's famed concert promoter, signed TOP in 1970, and the group had several hits, including "You're Still a Young Man" and "So Very Hard to Go."

TOP was reaching its zenith when Bruce joined, but drug problems caused constant turnover. In October 1977, bassist Francis "Rocco" Prestia, the innovator of a technique known as "Fingerstyle Funk," left the band. Victor Conte, who by then had left Pure Food and Drug Act and was living with Bruce, tried out. Band leader Emilio Castillo initially didn't want to mix "family" with the band, Conte told *The Fresno Bee* at the time. But Conte said that after nine bass players had tried out, he was given a shot and Castillo "stopped the band in the middle of the second tune and said I was hired if I wanted it."

Later, Castillo and sax player Steve "Doc" Kupka recalled the hiring differently: Conte got the job basically because he was Bruce's cousin.

Conte joined Tower of Power in late 1977. The band was between managers, and Conte saw this as an opportunity. He studied the band's financial records, he spoke up in meetings, he acted like a guy who had been around for years rather than a newcomer. "Victor was a natural leader, so it made him hard to follow [others] and keep his mouth shut," says Bruce Conte, who thought his cousin was merely trying to help the group through a rough spell.

While on the road with the band early in 1979, Victor and Bruce called drummer Dave Garibaldi to their hotel room and laid out a new plan for TOP. Victor Conte had big ideas: a new manager and new material that could turn the band into a national sensation. Garibaldi was a legend in TOP, and a lifelong friend of Castillo, the group's leader. The drummer left the room and told Castillo the Contes were trying to hijack the band. After TOP returned to the Bay Area, Castillo picked up Bruce and Victor Conte in his old Chevy, then parked at the end of a cul-de-sac and lit a joint before breaking the news.

"I'm replacing you guys in the band," Castillo said.

The Contes were shocked.

"Can't we even talk about it?" said Bruce. He had been with TOP six years, and had planned to be with the band for life.

"No, we're not gonna talk, there's no reason to. We need new blood in the band."

Years later, Emilio Castillo would say, "Victor is kind of a power-driven guy, he gets in there and likes to stir the pot. Victor was always the go-getter, it was always one scam or another. He was one of those guys who liked to play the angles, and he was good at it."

Just before he joined Tower of Power in late 1977, Conte had married Audrey Stein after a brief courtship. In Audrey, Conte found his kindred spirit, a stunning and intense 22-year-old San Franciscan who shared his passion for music, was articulate, and had a growing interest in health. Even amidst the drugged-out world of TOP, Conte had worked out with weights and taken vitamin pills, preaching a spiritually healthy existence.

That Audrey and Conte would view themselves as advocates of a healthier lifestyle represented a contradiction. Audrey struggled with drugs most of her life. Conte smoked marijuana regularly and was dealing drugs, too, according to Audrey and a person who knew the family.

In hindsight, the tried-and-true vows were never more apt: The couple was together for better *and* for worse. Like so many Northern Californians of the era, they became New Age devotees who ate bland, healthy foods, practiced yoga, and went on religious retreats. In the years before her drug problems got out of hand, Audrey rejected traditional American medicine in favor of herbalism, acupuncture, and homeopathy. She championed the healing powers of love and spirituality, seeking a "wellness" that mere doctors couldn't understand or provide.

Conte bounced around for the next few years. He played for a time with jazz pianist Herbie Hancock. He and Bruce formed a group called Jump Street. But Tower of Power had been his best shot, and Conte had blown that. In 1982, now with two young daughters, Conte decided to set aside his bass and join the working world. Maybe he'd even find a job his father might respect.

In 1983, Victor and Audrey opened the Millbrae Holistic Health Center, a clinic that promoted natural healing. The Contes sold vitamins out of the small storefront in Millbrae, a middle-class suburb on the San Francisco Peninsula, 15 miles south of the city and just a few minutes' drive from the airport. At the same time Conte was selling vitamins at the health food store, he also was dealing pot out of his house, according to Audrey and a source close to the family at the time.

One evening in 1983, two masked men with guns kicked in the door and demanded a $100,000 stash of marijuana. Conte refused, and the gunmen—Hells Angels, Audrey Conte later claimed—tied him up and ransacked the house. Finally, after the bikers threatened Audrey and the couple's daughters, then ages five and three, Conte gave them the drugs. Afterward, Conte filed a police report claiming the home had been burglarized while nobody was home. His daughter Alicia recounted a different story: Her grandmother claimed that when Conte wasn't home, a former high school friend of Audrey's had broken into the place, tied everybody up, and stolen some cash and credit cards.

Meanwhile, Conte hoped to turn the couple's legitimate business into a moneymaker. He settled on a plan to strike it rich in the nutrition business, though it's not clear how or where he dreamed it up. Conte decided that he could make a scientific breakthrough in sports medicine. It didn't matter to him that he was neither a scientist nor even a med student. Conte spent hours at the medical library at nearby Stanford University, reading about nutrition and biochemistry. Ever the quick study, he sought to absorb everything he could get his hands on so the information would be ready when an opportunity arose to make his sales pitch. Just like that, Victor Conte the bass player had become Victor Conte the nutritionist.

It was an improbable conversion, but Conte possessed a reptilian facility for changing his skin. He viewed whatever business he chose as merely a forum for his rise to greatness. Less than a year after Millbrae Holistic opened its doors, Conte would shut it down in favor of a new venture called the Bay Area Laboratory Co-Operative.

BALCO, for short.

Chapter 2

Willy Cahill lived a life steeped in judo. His father, John Cahill, had learned the ancient Japanese martial arts on the Big Island of Hawaii in the 1930s, under Grandmaster Henry Seishiro Okazaki, who was said to have turned to the discipline after he contracted tuberculosis at age 19. Okazaki threw himself into judo with such zeal that he supposedly fought off the disease, telling others that he became the "owner of a body as if made of iron."

Cahill's father had opened a dojo, a martial arts training hall, in the San Francisco suburb of Daly City in 1948, when Cahill was a teenager. Willy mastered the sport, eventually becoming a 10th Dan in jujitsu, the highest black belt rank, and a seventh Dan in judo. When his father died in 1962, Cahill took over the family business and the next year built a new dojo in suburban San Bruno, near the San Francisco International Airport. By the 1970s, when the sport was gaining in popularity, Cahill was one of the country's preeminent coaches. Several of his students won national championships, and he represented the United States as a coach at international competitions.

In the early 1980s, Cahill read a newspaper article about a local nutrition company supposedly on the cutting edge of optimizing athletic performance. What was to become the nation's multibillion-dollar nutritional supplement industry was in its infancy at the time, and the company's program of detecting athletes' mineral deficiencies through clinical tests and correcting them through supplements seemed unusual and innovative. The judo master made an appointment to see what might be in it for his students.

At BALCO's tiny, trailer-like offices in San Mateo, just a few miles down Highway 101 from his dojo, Cahill was greeted by Victor Conte. In fact, he was bowled over by Conte. Nothing stood out about the man. Now in his early 30s, Conte was of average build and wore big, round glasses, had curly black hair, and sported a thin mustache that looked a bit cheesy. But when Conte opened his mouth, he was more impressive. The two men chatted for about 45 minutes, with Conte doing most of the talking. He described his successful music career with Tower of Power and explained how he had moved on to focus on athletes' nutrition. A concept called trace mineral testing was very important, he claimed. Even the world's most finely tuned athletes were supposedly deficient in crucial elements like zinc, chromium, and copper.

BALCO's practice was cutting edge, Conte said: Samples of an athlete's blood, urine, and hair were analyzed using a high-tech device called the inductively coupled plasma spectrometer—the ICP. The ICP was the size of a pickup truck. It was invented for industrial jobs: to analyze the welds on the casings of atomic bombs and identify defects; to examine jet engines and determine when parts needed replacing; to study the chemical composition of soil samples at dumps and detect levels of toxicity.

But Conte said BALCO had realized a clinical application for the machine, and he claimed it had enormous implications for sports medicine. When athletes engage in high-intensity workouts, Conte told Cahill, those training sessions leave them depleted in minerals vital to their success. The ICP could evaluate the chemical makeup of hair, urine, and blood and pinpoint precisely which minerals an athlete lacked. BALCO then could correct the deficiencies with the precise minerals that were needed. It was far more scientific than simply tossing a bunch of pills and powders at the athlete and saying, "Here, this ought to help." It's a brand-new science, Conte told Cahill, and it will revolutionize the way athletes tend to their bodies and enhance their performances.

To scientists and physicians with credentials and expertise in nutrition, the BALCO theory was pseudoscience, a joke. Dr. Gary Wadler, the internationally recognized steroid expert from New York University's School of Medicine, would later describe it as little more than a marketing ploy, "the world of hocus pocus." Actually, experts said, Americans had so much good, vitamin-enriched food available to them that significant nutritional deficiencies were rare in the United States, confined to members of the underclass, drug addicts, and people with specific medical conditions. Mineral deficiencies also were rare. For most Americans, including elite athletes, a One-A-Day multivitamin was more than enough to take care of any deficiency that might occur. Conte's theory about trace mineral deficiency and sports "is completely bogus," as Dr. Candy Tsourounis, the director of the UC–San Francisco School of Pharmacy's Drug Information Analysis Service, put it.

Conte claimed such criticism simply proved the worth of his ideas. He said the entire medical profession was ignorant about nutrition, and it plotted and schemed to prevent patients from getting too healthy lest doctors have fewer hours to bill. "Doctors go to medical school and study nutrition for maybe one day," Conte told Cahill. "Nutrition is not important to them. Doctors, they want to keep you sick. They're gonna help you, but they don't want to get you well real quick."

Cahill became a believer. He got himself tested, and he brought his judo athletes to BALCO. Many were already taking pills and supplements of some sort; the first thing Conte did with Cahill's judo students was to gather all the substances they were ingesting, all the supplements and powders, and toss the stuff in the garbage. They would start from scratch, with the supplements Conte supplied, according to Conte's plan.

Cahill's teams continued their successes on the national and international level, and he would remain a friend and supporter of Conte for the next two decades. Years later, he would say: "He should have been a salesman. He can really talk. I listen to him and I listen to my doctor, he knew more about nutrition than my doctor. . . . When he talks, whether he knows what he's talking about or not, he makes you believe he knows what he's talking about."

Conte began to style himself as a "nutritionist/scientist/inventor." As he would put it in an e-mail he sent years later: "I am the guy that has always tried to think outside the box for new ways to accomplish things."

About the time Cahill discovered Victor Conte, so, too, did Dr. Brian Halevie-Goldman, a South African psychiatrist who had just obtained his California medical license. The young doctor, a quirky, talkative sort himself, would say he had already met one mesmerizing figure since his graduation from the University of Witwatersrand in 1977. Goldman claimed he had volunteered for a year at a hospital in Calcutta, where he worked at times alongside Mother Teresa. They didn't really get along.

"We had different goals," Goldman said. "I'm a doctor, we're not taught how to deal with death, we want to save everybody. She wasn't as concerned about them living as making sure they were comfortable and treated like Jesus Christ themselves."

A few years later, Goldman landed in Northern California in need of a job. He answered a newspaper ad: A San Mateo lab was looking for a medical director.

Goldman would play a pivotal role in the process of remaking Audrey Conte's health food store into BALCO. He became close to the Contes and, like so many others, would say he was awed by Victor's personality and intelligence.

Goldman thought Conte had the kind of seductive patter that comes naturally to street preachers. He would liken his boss to Al Sharpton and the Reverend Jesse Jackson. Because his gift for gab was meshed with a capacity to memorize and recite mass amounts of information, Conte was an overwhelming presence. He could—and would—convince you anything was possible, opportunities were everywhere, success was just around the corner. People would spontaneously materialize at the office, Goldman said, just to listen to Conte's motivational fervor.

Arguing a point with Conte was often a losing proposition. "He has this kind of way of building," Goldman says, "of having a bunch of facts and presenting them like a musician would, building to a climax and then coming to an elegant conclusion."

Conte adopted different personas for different audiences. For a marketing photo, he could make himself look like a scientist, wearing a white lab coat and posing beside his giant ICP spectrometer. He could sound like a scientist, too. As he later wrote in an e-mail explaining aspects of trace mineral testing: "The reason that we test multiple compartments is because each compartment provides a different type of clinical information. For example, whole blood (red blood cells, plasma, and white cells combined) represents the 'retention' of elements and urine represents the 'acute excretion or clearance' of elements."

But around athletes, he might shift his persona. His language became crass and expletive-laced, the kind of talk that resonated in the locker rooms of the macho world of sports. His ability to alter his presentation helped lure athletes straining to reach the next level, as well as prospective investors.

In 1989, Conte created 50 shares of BALCO stock, keeping half for himself and selling the rest at $2,500 each. Years later, he sought to explain BALCO's chronic financial problems by saying promotional costs were steep in the early years. He would offer his services gratis to many college and Olympic-level athletes and coaches who found their way to BALCO. The plan was to create a database of world-class athletes using ICP analysis, and then use performance data to prove his novel approach. Conte was sure the endeavor would work—he had an abiding belief in the power of positive thinking. In addition to dabbling in Eastern philosophy, Conte subscribed to the teachings of the late Reverend Ernest Holmes, founder of the Los Angeles–based Church of Religious Science, whose book *The Science of Mind* espoused upbeat metaphysical ideas.

Among the first athletes to walk through the doors of BALCO was Greg Tafralis, then 25, a local shot-putter struggling to become an Olympian. He was ranked 10th nationally at the time and had to improve his performance dramatically to make it among the top three who would qualify for a spot on the U.S. Olympic team.

Tafralis was impressed with Conte, and he became an eager participant in BALCO's unusual testing program. Conte was "the smartest son of a bitch" he'd ever met, Tafralis later said. He took to calling the self-made scientist "Tennessee Tuxedo"—after the scheming, wisecracking, and rebellious penguin in the television cartoon of the 1960s. In addition to bringing other athletes to BALCO, Tafralis would introduce Conte to his boyhood friend Jim Valente. Valente had worked on the San Francisco Peninsula as a dry cleaner and in a grocery store. He spent the next 20 years alongside Conte, investing in BALCO and later becoming its vice president.

As for Tafralis, he quickly rose up the ranks of American shot-putters, finishing fourth at the national championships in 1984, second over the next three years, and first in 1988, the year of the Seoul Olympics. Tafralis then took second at the U.S. Trials in 1988, and he'd finally made it: He was an Olympian.

One of his training and BALCO mates, shot-putter Jim Doehring, also made the U.S. team. Seven years earlier, Doehring had nearly been killed in a motorcycle accident in Southern California; he had been hurled about 100 feet through the air, landing bloody and barely conscious, with several broken vertebrae and a shattered jaw. A man who witnessed the crash ran to Doehring, found him bleeding from the mouth and ears, and figured he was looking at a dead man. After five hours of surgery, Doehring pulled through. But he lost 60 pounds while on a liquid diet because of the jaw injury, dropping from 250-plus to 190. Somehow, he managed to put his body and his life back together and to resume his athletic career.

The year 1988 was a high time for Victor Conte. He was sponsoring 25 "BALCO Olympians," athletes he had taken under his wing and given the full BALCO treatment. By this point, Conte had started an ancillary business called SNAC System Inc., Scientific Nutrition for Advanced Conditioning, which created and sold the supplements his athletes supposedly lacked. On the eve of the Seoul Games, the *San Francisco Examiner* ran a story on the cover of its sports section trumpeting Conte's unique approach to nutrition, with testimonials from some of his clients.

Conte claimed he had offered to help all U.S. athletes, but his offer was lost in the Olympic bureaucracy: "We sent a proposal to the chief medical officer of the United States Olympic Committee to prove this in fact works, but there's so much red tape." The story ran with a large picture of several husky athletes hoisting Conte above their heads, as if he himself had just won a gold medal. Among them were Tafralis and Doehring.

Tafralis finished ninth at the Seoul Olympics, and Doehring finished

11th, well behind gold medalist Ulf Timmerman, who later would be revealed as a product of East Germany's methodical and successful Olympic doping machine. The 1988 Summer Games, though, would be infamously remembered as the Ben Johnson Games, for the Canadian sprinter who broke the world record in the 100 meters—only to have his record erased two days later when he tested positive for the bodybuilder's steroid stanozolol.

Johnson's ignominious fall represented the biggest doping scandal in Olympic history. Although steroid use had been suspected among athletes behind the Iron Curtain for years, for the first time the public was forced to confront the reality that the world's greatest athletes were using chemicals to enhance their performances. The scandal became the lead story on television newscasts and in newspapers around the world, a morality play of epic proportions. "The world's fastest human has been convicted of speeding on steroids," Dave Anderson wrote in *The New York Times*. "And the Olympics has been smeared by drugs as never before."

Johnson's coach was Charlie Francis, a former sprinter at Stanford University in California, who had competed for his native Canada at the 1972 Olympics. He would later be called "Charlie the Chemist" for his doping expertise. As the Johnson scandal unfolded, Francis emerged as a drug cheat of unflinching honesty and broad perspective. In his testimony before a Canadian government committee a few months after Johnson was unmasked, and in articles and interviews over the following decades, Francis declared that steroid abuse was so pervasive in Olympic sports that it had become impossible to succeed without drugs. Of course he had provided steroids to Johnson, Francis testified: "We had no reason to believe that anyone at the highest levels was not using performance-enhancing drugs." That, in a nutshell, was Francis's thesis: Cheat or lose.

It had always been that way, he believed. Francis traced the use of performance-enhancing drugs in sports to 776 BC, when by his account the ancient Greek Olympians ate sheep's testicles to spike their testosterone levels before competing. In the modern era, the government of Communist East Germany had doped its athletes en masse for more than two decades in hopes of winning international prestige through Olympic success. Beginning in the 1960s, under a program titled "State Planning Theme," more than 10,000 young athletes were given powerful steroids, and the side effects were horrific: severe heart and liver damage—even birth defects in children born to doped athletes. The 1986 women's shot-put champion, Heidi Kreiger, said she ultimately had to have a sex change operation—becoming Andreas Kreiger—as a result of the huge doses of steroids she took during the seventies and eighties.

But in competition, the program worked. At the 1976 Montreal Olympics, East German women won gold medals in 11 of the 13 swimming events, and the country of just 17 million remained an Olympic powerhouse until the Iron Curtain came down.

Francis declared that the East Germans were not alone. He claimed that at the 1984 Olympics in Los Angeles, American officials headed off a steroids scandal by suppressing test results that revealed doping on the U.S. Olympic team. By the 2000 Games, Francis asserted that the doping of elite athletes had become extraordinarily sophisticated: One group of sprinters in Sydney was using the oral steroids anavar and halostin, along with injections of human growth hormone, insulin, and EPO, a prescription drug that increases endurance by stimulating production of red blood cells. "The systematic use of performance-enhancing drugs in sports for more than 50 years has punted performance standards clear out of sight," Francis wrote, "so far out of sight that no human can attain them without chemical assistance."

Canadian sports officials banned Francis from coaching on any national team for life for his role in the Johnson scandal. Many critics dismissed his sweeping accusations about sports doping, calling Francis a sore loser, a promoter of conspiracy theories. Even as the Olympic movement devised more stringent and sophisticated tests to catch drug cheats, it was reluctant to acknowledge that the problem was as pervasive as Francis had claimed.

Less than a year after the Ben Johnson scandal, Jim Doehring, the Olympic shot-putter who had worked with Conte and BALCO labs, admitted to the *Los Angeles Times* that he, too, was a steroid user. Like

Francis, Doehring said athletes had no choice but to take drugs. They were pervasive in world-class track and field and always would be.

"There's no way that the testing is going to catch up to the athletes," Doehring told the *Times*. "The athletes are too far ahead. They've got blocking agents, masking agents . . . you've got all kinds of things helping the athletes out. . . . I'd have to say everyone's using something and I'm not excluding myself from that."

Besides, he told the paper, if somehow they actually rid the sport of juicing, nobody would want to watch.

"It's going to be a dying sport if they finally clean it up," Doehring said. "You'll have guys running the 100 [meter] in 11 flat, throwing the javelin 220 feet, throwing [the shot put] 65 feet. Who's gonna come to see that?"

It was an exceptional admission: an active athlete confessing that he was dirty, acknowledging he cheated, and asserting that everybody in his sport was doing it, too.

The story ran on page 16 of the sports section.

A year and a half later, Doehring was hit with a two-year suspension for failing a drug test. Several years later, in 1995, Tafralis also was nailed for using steroids. Conte was never accused of supplying drugs to Doehring and Tafralis, and other BALCO Olympians who worked with him during that period have said Conte didn't offer them steroids. Conte would claim he didn't become a steroid dealer until years later. Regardless, by the time of the Seoul Games, he had learned about drug use at the highest levels of sport. One family acquaintance recalled an afternoon at Conte's San Mateo home during the 1980s, when the two men were smoking pot and watching football on TV. "Most of those guys are on steroids," Conte told him. "And the best ones you can bet are on steroids."

Conte had been exposed to the world of big-time sports, and he liked it. He especially appreciated hanging out with the athletes, feeling as if he had contributed to their success.

Conte's database of world-class athletes continued to grow. Olympic discus great Mac Wilkins came on board and told the *San Mateo Times* that the results of BALCO's regimen were "so dramatic, I'm amazed it's legal." Swimming superstar Matt Biondi was directed to BALCO by Karl Mohr, an assistant coach at UC–Berkeley who specialized in training. Mohr had met Conte at a trade fair called Whole Earth Expo, and he thought Conte fascinating and sincere, and his work important. With Biondi and Wilkins affiliated with BALCO, Conte could say he had worked with one of the world's greatest swimmers and one of the world's greatest discus throwers. Over the course of three Olympics, Biondi would win 11 medals, eight of them gold. Wilkins would compete in four Olympics, win a gold and a silver medal, and set the world record four times during his career.

To promote his businesses, Conte claimed credit for the successes of his star clients. To spread the word, he applied the method he would use often over the next 15 years: He found a friendly writer to present Conte's spin while making it appear as if the article were objective. In late 1990, a freelancer named Richard Goodman wrote a piece for the magazine *Health World* in which he championed BALCO's innovative use of the ICP, the company's swelling list of devotees, and its brilliant founder, Victor Conte.

Goodman wrote that although Conte's science was ignored by the U.S. Olympic Committee, many top-level athletes were turning to BALCO, including Biondi. According to Goodman, Biondi was struggling in the 200-meter freestyle but "improved significantly" after Conte diagnosed and corrected a magnesium deficiency.

It wasn't long before Goodman was a full-time BALCO employee.

Even as more athletes were turning to BALCO in search of the elusive edge, Conte's business difficulties were mounting. In 1992, leading up to the Summer Games in Barcelona, he spent whatever cash he had supporting yet another set of BALCO Olympians. He brainstormed other ways to make money from BALCO, but none of them panned out. For example, Conte thought he was on to something when a swimmer he was testing said his chronic acne decreased after he took a supplement containing zinc. Conte envisioned a vast market and wrote a scientific paper, "Zap Your Zits with Zinc," but the idea never got off the ground.

Conte claimed he had discovered another use for BALCO's ICP machine: It could test women's silicone breast implants to determine whether they had leaked or were making the women ill. Some of Conte's friends and colleagues insisted he was genuinely interested in helping the women. But he had also seized on an opportunity: The $95 BALCO implant test was offered at a time when thousands of lawsuits were being filed by women claiming breast implants had caused them serious health problems. In 1993, the California State Health Department investigated complaints that the BALCO test was bogus and ruled it to be "false and misleading." The state ordered BALCO to stop its testing.

By the 1990s, Conte's businesses had begun falling into financial disarray, and he had an unpaid balance of $85,400 on his credit cards. Conte and BALCO also were slow to pay bills, and creditors became increasingly impatient. He and his companies ultimately were hit with 19 different lawsuits. The Internal Revenue Service and the state Franchise Tax Board filed 12 liens seeking unpaid taxes, the biggest for $33,000. The county filed eight actions in an effort to collect unpaid local business taxes. Creditors' claims topped $300,000.

Conte's marriage also was failing. The Contes' relationship had deteriorated to the point that one person who knew the family well suggested that Conte had slept on the couch for 10 years.

The final breakup came after a mysterious house fire in 1994. To Audrey, it was Victor at his worst: a combination murder plot and insurance scam. She told friends she awoke from a sound sleep to find the entire wall of her bedroom ablaze. The Contes' middle daughter, Alicia, who was 14 at the time, said the fire had started by accident when a cat knocked over a burning candle. Alicia said the fire pushed her mother over the edge—"My mom was on a rampage for a good year," she later recalled.

The couple filed for divorce in 1995, and the court papers contained wild accusations. Conte claimed Audrey had tried to run him over with the family car. She also tore out a clump of his hair and threatened to put a bullet in his head, he told the court. He obtained a restraining order against Audrey, citing harassing phone calls ("Victor, you are a motherfucker and I hope everyone at BALCO hears this message.") and coded death threats left on his pager ("43 187," Conte believed, translated to "Fuck you, I'm going to kill you."). He had her arrested for allegedly taking their pet Rottweiler from his apartment and refusing to give it back.

Audrey acknowledged that her behavior left "much to be desired," but she blamed drug abuse and mental illness, for which she said she was seeking help. She also claimed years of mistreatment from Conte, and she alleged that he had tried to kill her by burning the family home down with her in it. She complained that he had swindled her out of her rightful share of the business because the health food store that became BALCO had originally been hers. He also hid his income to avoid paying alimony, she claimed.

Conte won custody of the couples' three daughters by convincing the court their mother was a hopeless drug addict.

After the girls were grown, Alicia would portray Conte as the tough, caring father who kept his family together during the difficult divorce, who intervened to try to keep his girls off drugs and out of trouble. "Through all the madness, my dad has been the one that stressed to us not to do drugs," Alicia says.

But a court filing from the era suggests a father overwhelmed. In 1995, Conte asked a judge in San Mateo for a protective order against Alicia's 18-year-old boyfriend. He claimed his daughter and the boyfriend were using drugs and had stolen a car. The boyfriend accused Conte of calling the police on Alicia and getting her arrested, Conte said. Conte told the court he was afraid the boy was going to hurt him.

With the divorce, the financial problems, the business concerns, and raising three daughters, Conte by the mid-1990s was teetering on the edge of failure, though the power of positive thinking never would allow him to admit it. Instead, he expressed confidence that he would get past these difficult times, just as he had gotten past his father's disapproval of his musical ambitions, just as he had found another gig when he was fired from Tower of Power.

In many ways, the next few years would be pivotal. They would bring him new opportunities to make money and would give him new and important contacts in the world of sports. Indeed, many athletes would find themselves seeking his nutritional guidance, believing he could take them where they dreamed to go.

But these years were also the beginning of Victor Conte's undoing.

Chapter 3

From the first time he stepped onto a playing field, it was apparent he would become one of the greatest baseball players of his generation. As he reached manhood, he grew rangy, muscular, and fast, with a keen batting eye, the ability to hit to all fields, and an extraordinary knowledge of the game. He also presented one of the most difficult personalities in the history of a sport that had produced such impossible characters as Ty Cobb and Billy Martin. Barry Lamar Bonds, the San Francisco Giants' marquee player of the 1990s, was a narcissistic yet deeply insecure man, often surly and rude, always self-absorbed. Driven by hubris, he was offended by the idea that anyone in baseball was greater than he. Some who were close to Bonds thought his drive to be acknowledged as the game's premier player flowed from an intense sense of rivalry with his father, a baseball player whom Bonds seemed to emulate and resent in equal measure. Indeed, many of the quirks in Bonds's complicated personality—including the impulse that led him to use the banned drugs that would transform him, late in his career, into a record-breaking home run hitter—seemed related to his troubled relationship with Bobby Bonds, the former Giants star.

Bobby Bonds grew up in Riverside, 60 miles east of Los Angeles, and he was perhaps the greatest high school athlete California's vast Inland Empire region had ever produced. He starred in football, basketball, and track, and he was an extraordinary baseball player: a speedster with excellent power. He signed with the San Francisco Giants out of high school, and in 1966 they sent him to the Western Carolina League. There, the free-spirited youth from California would confront old-style Southern racism, and more than 30 years later, he still seemed stunned and scarred by what he encountered. "They just used to call you a nigger," he would tell a television interviewer in 1999.

After only two years in the minors, he was called up to the Giants, and in his first game he hit a grand slam. Soon, 22-year-old Bobby Bonds was the Giants' starting right fielder, playing alongside the great center fielder Willie Mays, then 38 years old and nearing the end of his career. The Giants persuaded themselves that the young slugger was the solution to what had seemed an insoluble personnel problem: how to replace Mays, one of the greatest players ever. Like Mays when he was younger (and indeed, like his son would someday be), Bobby Bonds was a power hitter with great speed. When Mays needed a day off, the Giants began moving Bonds over to center field. After the club traded Mays to the New York Mets in 1972, Bobby Bonds got the job full time. He emerged as a slugging lead-off man, averaging 30 home runs and 30 stolen bases every year. He made the All-Star team twice and won three Gold Gloves. But by the time Mays departed, the club was in decline. It soon became clear that Bobby Bonds really wasn't another Willie Mays—who was?—and the pressures of living up to that impossible task may have exacerbated other problems Bobby faced.

One was alcoholism, manifested by separate arrests for drunken driving and resisting arrest in 1973. Another was a moody, standoffish manner that suggested to the white executives who ran the game that Bobby had developed a chip on his shoulder. Certainly he was no longer the happy-go-lucky kid whom the Giants had shipped off to the Jim Crow South. In those days, the proprietors of American sports were still rattled by the memory of Tommie Smith and John Carlos, the African-American Olympians who had raised their fists in a Black Power salute while "The Star-Spangled Banner" played at the 1968 Olympics in Mexico City. A black athlete who was even slightly assertive might be labeled a black militant. The Giants grew increasingly worried about Bonds's drinking and his attitude. When he had an off year in 1974, they traded him to the Yankees for another player who had failed to meet impossible expectations: Bobby Murcer, Mickey Mantle's successor in center field.

Bobby Bonds hit 32 home runs for the Yankees, but they traded him to the California Angels. He hit 37 home runs for them, but the Angels traded him, too, and after that no club wanted him for very long. In the five years that followed, he played for the White Sox, Rangers, Indians, Cardinals, and Cubs. Embittered, he retired after the 1981 season, when his oldest son was entering his senior year in high school. Young Barry Bonds had become quite a ballplayer.

While he was still with the Giants, Bobby Bonds had settled his family in San Carlos, a San Francisco Peninsula suburb 15 miles south of Candlestick Park. It was an unusual choice for a man regarded by baseball as a black militant: San Carlos's population was 98 percent white. The suburb had near-perfect weather, good schools, and excellent youth sports programs centered at Burton Park, a complex with two baseball diamonds. Of Bobby Bonds's three sons, Barry had the most passion for the game. As a five-year-old, he liked going with his father to Candlestick, putting on his little Giants uniform, and running around the outfield before games. He also liked hanging around Willie Mays's locker, trying to swipe the great player's glove or play some other prank. Mays was delighted by the child and agreed to become his godfather.

Bobby Bonds had hoped his oldest son would be a ballplayer. And from his earliest days in San Carlos Little League, young Barry was the best player on the field, much like his father had been as a boy. The father was pleased with the son's ability, but there was growing tension between them. After he grew up to become a baseball star in his own right, Barry Bonds complained bitterly about his father, sometimes to reporters. In interviews, Bonds said that when he was a boy, he hadn't liked his father. He told friends that his father beat him and psychologically dominated his mother. He claimed his father had ignored his achievements and refused to attend his games and other school events. He said that in college he discouraged his father from coming to watch him play because he feared he would show up drunk.

After Barry signed with the Giants and the club hired Bobby as hitting coach, Barry told friends, "He wouldn't have his job if it wasn't for me." Barry was critical even during Bobby's exhausting fight with the cancer that finally killed him, when he fell asleep on the couch after chemotherapy. This was the time of life when his mother should be getting out and traveling and enjoying herself, he told a friend, "and he's there sitting on his ass."

The problems between son and father were rooted in Bobby's frequent separations from the family. He had been away every summer of his son's life. But there was another source of friction. No matter how much Barry excelled at baseball, he couldn't escape feeling that people discounted his achievements because of his father. Outstanding play was expected of him because of who he was. Other kids would rag on Barry or talk behind his back, saying that no coach would ever cut him from a team or bench him from a game because he was Bobby Bonds's son. As a result, when people tried to befriend or praise him, Barry became suspicious, doubting their sincerity. Were people nice to him because they liked him? Or was it because they wanted something from his famous dad? Was Barry playing ball because he wanted to? Or was baseball simply something everyone expected of Bobby Bonds's son?

Bonds would later try to describe the feeling of being pushed into a baseball career. "I was a celebrity child, not just in baseball by my own instincts," is how he put it. The pressure changed the way he related to people and made him more withdrawn. A growing racial consciousness added to his sense of isolation: "I was the only black kid at parties," he would say.

Even as a multimillionaire athlete, Bonds still chafed over memories of his senior year at Junipero Serra High School in San Mateo, when he batted nearly .500, hit a series of tape-measure home runs, and believed his achievements were discounted because of his famous father. "What bat did he swing for me?" he said to *Playboy* magazine in 1993, after he signed with the Giants. "You get tired of hearing, 'Oh, it's because of your Dad.' "

But to an extent, what the other kids said was true. Most high school baseball players have to work hard for playing time. They must show up early to practice, perform all the drills and run all the sprints the coach assigns, cheer and give high-fives when somebody scores. Barry Bonds didn't have to do any of that because of his talent, and because of who he was. Few youth baseball coaches would put Bobby

Bonds's son on the bench for very long; instead, they cut him slack and listened to backtalk they wouldn't have tolerated from anyone else. However much he resented his father, Bonds took advantage of the special status he derived from him. With Bonds, there was always an attitude. When the Serra team took the field, the other players would come hustling out of the dugout and sprint into position, just the way coaches like. Barry would saunter out to center field, fiddling with his glove or sunglasses.

"Everything was easy for me, all sports, when I was a kid," he would say. "I'd work half as hard as other kids did and I was better. Why work when I had so much ability?"

After high school, the Giants drafted Barry Bonds and offered a $70,000 signing bonus. Advised by his father and Mays, Bonds went to Arizona State instead. Once again he was a dominating player, batting .347 with 45 home runs in a three-year career. As a junior, he rapped seven consecutive hits in the Sun Devils' losing effort in the College World Series tournament. Once again, he had trouble making friends.

"I never saw a teammate care about him," his coach, the late Jim Brock, told *Sports Illustrated* in 1990. "Part of it would be his being rude, inconsiderate, and self-centered. He bragged about the money he had turned down, and he popped off about his Dad. I don't think he ever figured out what to do to get people to like him."

Brock was considered tough, demanding, and distant. But even he found himself making a different set of rules for Bonds, excusing his objectionable behavior because of his tremendous talent. The coddling started from the day Bonds arrived on campus driving a new Pontiac Trans Am. When his teammates first saw the shiny black car, it was parked in the coach's parking space.

In 1984, Bonds and some teammates were caught breaking curfew, and Bonds mouthed off when the coach confronted them. Momentarily pushed past his limit, Brock blew up and kicked Bonds off the team. After he calmed down, the coach told the other players he had suspended Bonds and asked them to vote on whether to let him return; Brock was confident they would want their best player back. But Bonds was so unpopular that his teammates voted to kick him off the team for good. Before the incident spun further out of control, the coach ordered a second vote, and Bonds was reinstated.

The Pittsburgh Pirates drafted Bonds in the first round of the 1985 draft, and he skipped his senior year in college. He played only 115 minor-league games over parts of two seasons before he was called up. Pirates manager Jim Leyland put Bonds in the lineup in center field on May 30, 1986, six weeks before his 22nd birthday. Like other coaches before him, Leyland babied Bonds. The young player quickly got a reputation for having great potential and a bad attitude. Writers said he refused to run out ground balls. Fans and teammates alike said he refused to sign autographs. He became surly with writers who asked him about his father. If a writer thoughtlessly addressed him as "Bobby," he would stop the interview: "First of all, you better get my name right," he would scold. He seemed to care only about his stats. In 1989, when he batted .248, Leyland observed that Bonds's average had gone to hell because he had spent the final six weeks of the season in a stubborn, failed attempt to hit his 20th home run.

Bonds had an epiphany that off season: "I realized what I'd been doing—walking off the field thinking I could have done better, cutting myself short—was wrong." Bonds took the Pirates to salary arbitration in 1989, the first in a series of bitter wrangles over money that would turn the Pittsburgh fans against him. Although Bonds eventually developed into an outstanding player in Pittsburgh, the only player in the club's history to win two National League MVP awards, the fans came to regard him as greedy, unpleasant, and a choke artist. Actually, beginning in 1989, the Pirates' front office had promoted the view of Bonds as a failure in the clutch to beat him in arbitration. The club commissioned an Elias Sports Bureau study showing that in "late inning pressure situations" Bonds batted only .103, perhaps the worst clutch performance by a star player in the history of the game. Because of his complaints about money and his demands to be traded, the Pittsburgh writers awarded Bonds their "MDP" award, for "Most Despised Pirate."

Bonds was angry and resentful at his treatment in Pittsburgh. At first it affected his play, but eventually he began to develop a final important component to his complicated adult personality. When he returned to the club for spring training in 1990, he seemed far more thick-skinned, better able to block out the criticism from the press and the booing from the fans and play well despite it. Actually, it was more that that, people close to him believed. Not only could he block out all the negativity, Bonds now actually seemed to play better when the world was angry at him, when the clubhouse, the press box, and the stands were in an uproar because of something outrageous he had said or done. It was as though he had learned how to tap into negative energy and channel it to his advantage, to propel his game to a higher level.

By the time Bonds got to San Francisco, people close to him swore he would deliberately say horrible things to the press, hoping to provoke outrage and kick his game up a notch. "My grandmother wants me to get her some wheelchair that drives like a car," he told *The New York Times Magazine* in one such over-the-top remark. "Why do I need to get her some wheelchair when she's gonna die anyway?" Starting in spring training with the Pirates in 1990, Bonds began telling writers and photographers to stay out of his face, and he used the same line with autograph-seeking fans. Rude, sulking, doing all he could to live up to his MDP status, he also had a career year: .301 average, 34 home runs, 103 RBI, and the National League Most Valuable Player award, an honor that had eluded his father. After the season, he again took the Pirates to salary arbitration and lost.

The arbitrator's ruling was still eating at him when he got to Bradenton, Florida, for spring training in 1991. Angered by the news coverage of the salary dispute, he declared he wouldn't speak to the media all year. Then, on a single morning of practice, he alienated the organization, the fans, and the press by having serial on-the-field blowups, with the action recorded by television crews.

Bonds was loosening up when he noticed two TV cameramen and a freelance photographer preparing to take his picture. Bonds was friendly with the still photographer, but the TV crews made him agitated. "Get out of my face!" he shouted, and brandished a ball as though he was going to throw it at them.

The altercation brought over the Pirates' press secretary, Jim

Lachima, who tried to calm the angry star. "I'll make my own rules here!" Bonds shouted, as the TV crews videotaped the action.

The racket attracted coach Bill Virdon, the bespectacled center fielder on the Pirates 1960 World Series team and a former Pirates manager, who was running outfielder's drills. Virdon tried to break up the dispute and get Bonds to join the workout. Bonds said Virdon made a crack about his salary dispute. Virdon said Bonds declared, "Nobody's going to tell me what to do."

Whatever the provocation, Bonds was suddenly in the face of the old Pirates star, yelling and cursing.

And that brought over Jim Leyland, neck veins bulging, shouting and raging like a man who had been pushed too far. "I've kissed your butt for three years. No one player is going to ruin this camp!" Leyland cried. When Bonds came back at him, Leyland erupted in a long, obscenity-laced outburst. "Don't fuck with me!" Leyland yelled. "I'm the manager of this fucking team!" Finally, Bobby Bonilla, Bonds's only friend on the club, intervened and led him away. The video, with much of Leyland's tirade bleeped out, was broadcast and rebroadcast back home. After it was over, a contrite Bonds gave his first interview of the spring, saying, "Everybody keeps making me out to be the bad guy." But later, he accused the club of inviting the TV crews to the workout in a deliberate attempt to set him up.

In 1992, the final year of his contract with the Pirates, Bonds won his second MVP award, batting .311 with 34 home runs. He was finally a free agent, but Pirates fans were indifferent. Not only had they been turned off by his difficult personality, but they were convinced Bonds had choked in three consecutive National League playoffs. In 1990, when the Pirates lost to the Reds four games to two, Bonds batted .167 and drove in a single run. In 1991, when they lost to the Braves in seven games, he batted .148 with no RBI at all. But worst of all was the excruciating loss in 1992, again to Atlanta. Bonds hit reasonably well this time: .261, with a home run. But his performance in left field in the seventh game, when the Pirates were only one out away from a victory that would put them in the World Series, made Bonds's batting line meaningless.

With two outs in the bottom of the ninth, bases loaded, and the

Pirates leading by a run, the Braves sent up pinch hitter Francisco Cabrera. As the Braves fans hooted and did the "Tomahawk Chop," Andy Van Slyke, the Pirates' center fielder, whistled to Bonds, then signalled with his glove for him to move in and to his left. Bonds looked at Van Slyke, but didn't move. Instead, he stayed just where he was, deep, guarding the left-field line. Until he won his first MVP in 1990, Bonds had been paid less than Van Slyke, and he still resented it. Bonds called him "the Great White Hope."

Cabrera slapped a base hit to left field, about where Van Slyke had tried to get Bonds to play. The runner on third, David Justice, trotted home with the tying run. On second for the Braves was the slow-footed Sid Bream, a former Pirate who once said that everybody in the Pittsburgh clubhouse had wanted to punch Barry out at one time or another. As Bonds played the ball, Bream rounded third and lumbered home. Bonds's throw was strong, but it was up the first base line. Bream scored, and the Braves were in the World Series. Later in the clubhouse, Bonds burst into tears, but Pittsburgh had seen enough. After the series, Leyland told Bonds there was no way the small-market Pirates could afford to sign him. Eventually, the club offered Bonds a five-year, $25 million contract. Bonds spurned it. Instead, he went home to California to earn more money than any baseball player had ever been paid.

Chapter 4

T he man who lured Barry Bonds to the Giants was Peter Magowan, lead investor for the latest local effort to keep major-league baseball in San Francisco. The blond, boyish-looking Magowan had no background in sports, but he had proved himself an extraordinarily tough businessman. Magowan had majored in literature at Stanford and studied economics at Oxford, and in 1980, he had become CEO of Safeway Stores, succeeding his father, who had built the supermarket chain. The company had a history of easy, paternalistic relations with employees. "Safeway Offers Security" was its motto.

But in 1986, Safeway was threatened with a hostile takeover at the hands of the corporate raiders Herbert and Robert Haft. Magowan vowed to fight, to take the publicly traded company private through a leveraged buyout. He brought in Kohlberg Kravis Roberts (KKR), the private equity firm whose $25 billion takeover of RJR Nabisco in 1988 was made famous in the book *Barbarians at the Gate*. Safeway and KKR borrowed huge sums to buy up the company's stock. The maneuver fended off the raiders and made millions for shareholders, including Magowan himself. But the carnage among Safeway employees was extraordinary: In the four years after the LBO, 63,000 Safeway workers lost their jobs as Magowan spun off entire divisions, closed or sold 1,200 stores, and laid off longtime employees en masse to raise money to pay down the debt.

Magowan was unapologetic. He had done what was necessary to save the company. Six years later, he decided to leave the supermarket business. His next challenge would be to confront what for 25 years had proved among the most intractable business problems in professional sports: saving the San Francisco Giants.

The Giants' underlying problem was their ballpark, the worst in baseball. Candlestick Park was built on the shore of San Francisco Bay, south of the city. It stood in a natural wind tunnel, due east of a notch in the mountains that walled off the Bay from the Pacific. On summer afternoons, cold ocean air poured through the notch at 15 miles per hour, propelling banks of fog directly at Candlestick Point.

There were few places in the Bay Area—indeed, few places south of Alaska—with worse summer weather. On a sunny day, watching a game at Candlestick could be exhausting, as the wind swirled dirt, hot dog wrappers, and other baseball detritus across the playing field and into the stands. At night, when temperatures dropped into the 40s, games could be otherworldly. Sometimes great creamy globs of fog would spill over the lip of the stadium, obscuring the lights and the left-field stands. On nights like that only a few thousand fans would show up in the 62,000-seat stadium, wearing stocking caps and parkas, huddling under blankets, and swigging liquor to stay warm.

Even when the Giants had good teams, the park's weather cut deeply into attendance. Two owners in succession gave up on the team because of Candlestick. In 1976, Horace Stoneham, who had brought the Giants west from New York after the 1957 season, sold the franchise to the Labatt Breweries of Canada, which intended to move the team to Toronto. But the city tied the deal up in court, and at the last moment, Robert Lurie, a San Francisco real estate investor and socialite, agreed to buy the team.

For 15 years, Lurie doggedly lobbied the city to replace Candlestick with a modern stadium in a locale with better weather—a rail yard along the Bay in China Basin, just south of downtown, was the favored site. Two San Francisco mayors tried to accommodate him. But Lurie's blustering threats to move the team if the taxpayers didn't build him a new ballpark played poorly in a city known for left-liberal progressivism. Opponents portrayed him as a spoiled multimillionaire looking for a government handout, and in four elections voters rejected spending tax money on a new ballpark. In August 1992, as the team was stumbling to a fifth-place finish, Lurie sold the Giants to a Florida combine for $110 million. They planned to move the team into the meat locker–like confines of St. Petersburg's Suncoast Dome, an indoor stadium built for baseball but at that point only the venue for ice hockey games and tractor pulls. Before the sale was complete, however, San Francisco's moneyed elite decided they wanted to keep the Giants after all. A group of local developers and financiers offered Lurie $10 million less than the Florida combine, and the league pressured him to accept.

Magowan emerged as the Giants' president and managing partner. A local business newspaper soon dubbed him "St. Peter," savior of San Francisco baseball, and he won civic awards for his efforts to keep the team. Magowan basked in the praise. And when it came to the business of baseball, he wasn't nearly so cold-blooded as he had been when he was facing down the corporate raiders and laying off employees by the thousands. Instead, Magowan turned out to be an enthusiastic fan. He had grown up in New York City rooting for the Giants. He could recite, batter by batter, the ninth inning of the famous 1951 playoff between the Giants and the Brooklyn Dodgers, which ended with the Giants' Bobby Thomson's thrilling home run. Now, as the 1993 season approached, he was eager to be known as the man who had saved the Giants for San Francisco. He was so eager that he was willing to accept a cost structure that every other major league owner would have rejected as untenable.

For 25 years, new ballparks in the U.S. had been built with public funds. Baseball behaved as though it were a municipality's duty to provide a stadium at taxpayers' expense for the team's profitable use. But from watching Lurie's maneuvers, Magowan had concluded that San Francisco voters would never approve public subsidies for a new park in China Basin. Rather than playing tough with the elected officials to extract financial concessions, Magowan announced the Giants would pay for the project. The result would be the 41,000-seat Pac Bell Park, which would open in 2000 at a cost of $350 million. Magowan had offset some of the financing problems by selling naming rights to the telephone company for $50 million. Still, construction of the park put the Giants at a long-term competitive disadvantage, saddling the team with about $150 million of debt. There was no way to do an LBO or order mass layoffs or sell off assets to raise quick cash that would pay the debt down. Instead, the Giants would start each year needing $20 million to pay the stadium mortgage, a cost borne by no other major-league club. To break even, the Giants calculated the team would need to sell three million tickets per year for the 20-year life of the loan on Pac Bell Park.

Looking forward in 1993, Magowan knew the Giants needed to start winning immediately, and beyond that he believed they needed a marquee player, a star who would attract fans to Candlestick now and bring them to the new park when it was finished. He settled on Barry Bonds, who was not only an MVP free agent but the son of a Giants star and Willie Mays's godson. In 1993, Magowan signed him to baseball's biggest contract: six years guaranteed at $43.75 million, with two option years as well.

Magowan was convinced that Bonds's problems in Pittsburgh were caused by the Pirates' insensitivity. Magowan would show him the Giants were different. To make the star more comfortable, Magowan agreed to hire Dusty Baker, a boyhood friend of Bonds's father, as manager. Further demonstrating his desire to please—and his cluelessness regarding the complexities of Bonds's relationships—Magowan hired Bonds's father as hitting coach. Bonds had heard that Cal Ripken, the Baltimore Orioles star, got a private hotel suite on road trips, so the Giants wrote a hotel suite into Bonds's contract, too. Even before he arrived, Bonds saw how much power he could exert over the ball club.

Bonds responded to his new contract with yet another MVP year in 1993. He batted .336 with 46 home runs, 123 RBI, 129 runs, 126 walks, and an on-base percentage of .458—career highs in all those categories. Better still, he led the Giants in a rousing, down-to-the-wire pennant race that they lost to the Braves on the final day of the season.

Bonds had done everything the Giants had hoped, and in the years that followed he would continue to play excellent baseball. In his first six years in San Francisco, he batted .307 and averaged 39 home runs and 100 RBI. His performance was even more remarkable when you considered that throughout the entire period, one person or another whose opinion should have mattered to Bonds—teammates, fans, the press, his manager, his father, his wife—was angry with him.

The deportment issues that Magowan had blamed on Pittsburgh's insensitivity flared soon after Bonds joined the team. Early in his first season with the club, Bonds walked into a meeting of Giants pitchers and began pointing at the ones he had tagged for home runs, saying, "I got you, and I got you, and you."

The honeymoon with the Bay Area press was over within six weeks of his arrival. "I don't like the media, I don't like to deal with the media, and I'm not obligated to deal with the media," the *San Francisco Examiner* magazine quoted him as saying on May 16, 1993. "If they don't stop printing lies, I won't talk to them at all . . . I don't care."

Bonds also did his best to alienate the admiring Magowan, who was paying him $8 million a year. He gave the owner problems over autographs, according to a source familiar with Bonds. The owner would call Giants equipment manager Mike Murphy and tell him he wanted Bonds to sign some balls. According to the source, Murphy would relay the message to Bonds, but the star would say, "I ain't gonna sign no fucking balls." That left Murphy with the awkward task of coming up with an excuse that Magowan would accept. It was Bonds's way of demonstrating that he was running the team. Magowan bit his tongue, a sign of times to come.

Bonds's marriage also collapsed. He had met Sun, a lovely Swedish woman, in 1987 in a club in Montreal, where she was working as a bartender, but it was a bad match. Bonds wanted someone who would do what she was told; Sun wasn't submissive. She pushed back at Barry, challenged him, persisted in trying to force him to keep his promises and treat her with respect. Bonds told *Playboy* in 1993: "Sun has more patience than toilet paper. I tell her, 'Toilet paper just sits there and waits. It sits there and waits, just like you.'" Within a year, Sun filed for divorce and sued to overturn their prenuptial agreement, saying she had signed it without an attorney's advice and at a time when she didn't understand English. The expensive legal fight dragged on for years and went all the way to the California Supreme Court before Bonds was upheld.

None of that seemed to bother Bonds. He thrived on the chaos that so often swirled around him: It distracted everyone else, but made him more focused. He continued piling up All-Star appearances—six in his first six years in San Francisco—and won four Silver Slugger awards and five Gold Gloves during that time. Still, as the years went by, Bonds sometimes thought he had made a mistake coming to San Francisco. After the near-miss in 1993, the Giants had three losing seasons, and when they got to the playoffs in 1997, they were swept by the Florida Marlins, who went on to win the World Series. Bonds fretted that he might never play in the Series himself, would never have a champion's ring. In 1998, he decided he wanted to be traded to Atlanta; at the All-Star game, he asked Braves ace Tom Glavine to speak to his front office about it. The idea went nowhere. He continued to sulk, and as McGwire broke Maris's record and was honored as the savior of baseball, Bonds's mood grew worse.

Bonds thought it was absurd. McGwire was a pure slugger and nothing more: He was slow on the bases, mediocre defensively, and his lifetime batting average was .265. Besides, Bonds was convinced McGwire was on steroids. Bonds had never been interested in them, and had become less diligent about weight training the longer he stayed in the game. At 33, it was increasingly difficult to pump iron, especially during the season, when you had little time or energy to begin with. Like many players, Bonds ended each year beaten down and out of shape.

After the 1997 season, Bonds had tried to get more serious about lifting weights. He hired a coach named Raymond Farris for both strength training and running. At the track at Menlo College near Stanford University, Farris supervised a speed camp—workouts intended to make football players faster. The camp was popular with college players hoping to be selected in the NFL draft and NFL journeymen trying to stay in shape and catch on with another team. For a time, Jerry Rice, the great 49ers receiver, worked out with Farris.

Bonds took the program seriously. He was convinced he needed to train to prolong his career and win one more big contract. But soon he began complaining that Farris was a football guy who didn't know how to work with baseball players. Farris had him doing squats like a linebacker, and his back hurt all the time. Bonds later accused Farris of trying to trade on their relationship to make money, calling him "kind of a little shark. He wants to do card shows for you."

The dissatisfaction with Farris, frustration with the Giants, and jealousy of McGwire put Bonds in a foul temper. He pondered what steroids might do for his game, especially his power hitting. The home run totals of McGwire and Sosa had set the bar extremely high. From now on, to make the really big money and be counted among the game's elite, a hitter would be required to hit home runs at an unprecedented rate.

The Giants' 1998 season ended with more disappointment as the team lost a one-game playoff for the wild-card slot to Sosa's Cubs. In the off-season, Bonds made his move. He began working out with a real gym rat, a trainer who spent 12 hours a day pumping iron in a gym on the San Francisco Peninsula. Bonds's new workout partner called himself the "Weight Guru," and he had a sophisticated approach to training. He prescribed specific, intense workouts for individual muscle groups and he tailored the program for baseball to maximize hitting power while maintaining agility. He could talk about nutrition and blood tests and body fat percentages with such authority that you might mistake him for a doctor.

Not incidentally, the Weight Guru was a longtime steroid user and dealer. He had expertise with drugs ranging from old reliables like Deca-Durabolin and Winstrol to more exotic substances like human growth hormone. The drugs could quicken recovery after workouts, build stamina, add muscle. They could eliminate that slump in August, when the minor injuries and fatigue of the long season would otherwise wear a ballplayer down. Beyond that, for a player with the natural ability of Bonds, the sky was the limit as far as what the drugs might do. The Weight Guru told Bonds all of this, and Bonds decided to go for it. The Weight Guru's name was Greg Anderson.

Chapter 5

I n 1995, BALCO was awash in debt. The "Zap Your Zits with Zinc" idea had gone nowhere, and the breast implant testing plan had been exposed by state authorities as a sham.

Then the solution to Victor Conte's financial problems materialized, in the form of Michael Conte, the cousin who had once joined Victor and Bruce in playing surfer tunes by the campfire on boyhood vacations. Some who knew the Contes would say that Michael was the family's black sheep, the man who corrupted Victor and led him to a life of wrongdoing. Whatever the dynamic of their relationship, it is indisputable that, in 1995, the year that Michael Conte arrived at BALCO, the little company had its highest-grossing year so far: $926,000, according to tax records. Victor paid himself a salary of $150,000; he soon wore a Rolex watch, drove a Mercedes, and was living in a home with a pool not far from the Peninsula Golf and Country Club in San Mateo.

The spike in business came because of a Medicare billing scam. Victor Conte, with the help of his cousin, struck a deal to perform trace-element tests on the blood and urine of geriatric patients in Florida. BALCO's partner was a Miami company called Franklin Laboratories, which collected the samples, shipped them cross-country to BALCO, and billed Medicare more than $200 per test. But some doctors whose names appeared on Franklin Labs's billings said they had never ordered any trace-mineral tests, and some patients appeared to have had the same expensive tests run multiple times. Soon, a federal investigation was underway.

In 1996, a Miami prosecutor sued BALCO, Conte, and Franklin

Labs, accusing them of fraud. The FBI showed up at BALCO and froze the company's bank accounts, according to Richard Goodman, the writer whom Conte had hired. Franklin Labs paid $4.8 million to settle the case and went out of business. The government dropped the lawsuit against BALCO and Conte, but that was only a reprieve. Soon a new federal probe of BALCO was underway, with the help of a well-placed informant: Michael Conte.

After BALCO was accused of fraud, Michael Conte had left to set up his own lab. He returned to the business of bilking the federal government, and was indicted on Medicare fraud and money-laundering charges. Michael Conte pleaded guilty and agreed to testify against his cousin in hopes of gaining a reduced sentence. In a letter to a federal prosecutor, his lawyer wrote that Michael Conte had "provided the government with substantial information regarding BALCO's operation" and had "identified the transactions used to hide the kickbacks BALCO fraudulently provided." Michael Conte served 14 months in prison. After his release, he was contacted by the *Chicago Tribune* and was asked to discuss his cousin, who was by then facing steroids conspiracy charges. "The only Victor Conte I know is dead," Michael said.

Federal prosecutors in San Francisco eventually sued BALCO, alleging $1.8 million in fraudulent Medicare billings. Though the lawsuit wasn't filed until several years later, the lucrative business of running tests on senior citizens came to an abrupt end. "We immediately went from feast to absolutely nothing," Goodman said. "We were stuck with the idea that we had to develop another product to somehow make money."

Perhaps it was inevitable that Randy Huntington would cross paths with Victor Conte and BALCO. Huntington was a successful coach who had trained NFL players, a tennis champion, and two Olympic jumpers who had set world records. But in the world of sports, Huntington was also considered something of an oddball. He had an enthusiastic faith in innovation as the key to improving athletic performance, and he seemed perpetually in search of some new technique, procedure, or substance that might give one of his athletes an edge. He was called

"Mr. Gizmo" for his willingness to experiment and for his quest for scientific solutions to the challenge of training athletes.

"If you want to push toward the envelope of human performance, you have to lean on science," he once told a reporter.

Some of the innovations Huntington embraced seemed a little silly. In 1988, he marketed an athletic training aid called Music-in-Sync, 64 audiotapes created by an Oregon composer who liked to run for fun. Each tape featured the sound of a runner's feet hitting the ground over and over, along with music described as a "combination of triumphant Olympic and Wimbledon horn, New Age electronics, jazz fusion, and avant-garde classical." The tapes were a "music pharmacy" for athletes, composer James Sundquist claimed. Huntington said they were ideal training devices.

Huntington's methods got results, as the experience of his prize pupil, long jumper Mike Powell, proved. Powell's successes—two Olympic silver medals, and the stunning leap of 29 feet, 4 1/2 inches that shattered the long jump World Record in 1991—were a testament to Mr. Gizmo and his commitment to innovation. To maximize the jumper's performance, Huntington set him up with two massage therapists, a physical therapist, a water therapist, a chiropractor, a sports psychologist, a biomechanics specialist, and an orthopedic surgeon. To build leg strength, Huntington had Powell sprint while tied to an open parachute. To stimulate Powell's muscles, Huntington used a battery-powered appliance that produced electric current. For mental conditioning, Huntington sent Powell to an Oregon doctor named Herman Frankel, who introduced the idea of visualization. Powell was instructed to imagine not only his soaring jumps, but also "what it would feel like on the victory stand and what the first interview after the jump would be like." When Powell broke the record at the World Championships in Tokyo, he credited Huntington for his success.

Like judo coach Willy Cahill, Huntington learned of Conte through a newspaper article in a local paper. That was in the 1980s, when Huntington was a track coach at UC–Berkeley. Mr. Gizmo went to BALCO, listened to Conte, and came away convinced he had found something worth trying. Huntington ordered blood and urine tests for everybody he knew: his mother, his grandmother, his friends, and the athletes he trained. From Powell to Los Angeles Rams receiver

Henry Ellard, from tennis champion Michael Chang to World Record triple-jumper Willie Banks, Huntington sent a procession of elite athletes to Conte.

Among them, in the summer of 1996, was William Thomas Romanowski, perhaps the toughest, most durable pro football player of his era. "Romo" (love him or hate him, few called him by his surname) played with wild abandon the NFL's fiercest position, linebacker, for 16 violent years, with the 49ers, Eagles, Broncos, and Raiders. He won four Super Bowl rings and, before a series of concussions ended his career in 2003, competed in an astounding 243 consecutive games. In a sport that left men crippled for life, Romo's coaches never had to worry about whether he'd be ready come Sunday.

Teammates loved Romo. Opponents hated him. He was violent and emotional—a potent mix that led to an extensive NFL rap sheet. He became known for late hits and cheap shots, for which the league disciplined and fined him repeatedly. He spit in the face of 49ers wide receiver J. J. Stokes and threw a football at the crotch of New York Jets linebacker Brian Cox. He broke Carolina Panthers quarterback Kerry Collins's jaw and kicked Arizona Cardinals running back Larry Centers in the head. He ended the career of Raiders tight end Marcus Williams during a scuffle in practice, sucker punching his teammate and shattering his eye socket, resulting in a civil lawsuit that ended with Romo paying Williams $415,000.

Victor Conte was delighted by Romo's arrival. It gave him somebody truly famous to brag about. Those who worked around Conte increasingly viewed him as a jock-sniffer—"Victor was very impressed by star athletes," Goodman said—and Romo was the biggest star yet to become a customer. Romo was also intensely interested in what BALCO could do for him. The linebacker was a Huntington disciple, open to any theory or remedy that would help him thrive in the cutthroat world of professional football. With Romo—as with many elite athletes—recovery was the key to his training. The sooner his body could bounce back from the stress of an intense workout or a particularly painful game, the sooner he could return to the weight room or the practice field. This was also the greatest but least-known value of using steroids.

Romo had assembled an entourage that was even bigger than

Mike Powell's: five chiropractors, four acupuncturists, three nutritionists, two massage therapists, a speed coach, and a high-performance trainer. Romo said he paid them a collective $200,000 annually. He bought a portable hyperbaric chamber to increase oxygen delivery to his muscles and aid recovery from strenuous workouts. He drank at least one gallon of ionized water each day. And it wasn't enough to have his urine and blood and hair tested regularly; Romo had his stool analyzed, too.

Romo called himself a supplement "guru" and he carried a big black tackle box with him everywhere. In it were dozens of compartments for all the pills he took daily. Huntington had bought Romo his first pill box, but it was just a small container, with maybe eight sections.

"I opened his mind to alternative therapies, but then he went nuts," Huntington says. "He was like, 'What about this, what about that?' . . . He was willing to try anything without being willing to discriminate."

Steroids were part of Romo's regimen by the time he met Conte in 1996. Huntington had suspected Romo was juicing, and he asked Conte to check the linebacker for low copper levels—a telltale sign of steroid use. When the tests showed Romo was, indeed, deficient in copper, Huntington confronted his client, who admitted to taking a "little testosterone."

In fact, teammates knew they could turn to Romo if they wanted performance-enhancing drugs. Colorado sheriff's deputies who investigated him in 1999 for allegedly misusing prescription diet pills turned up evidence that Romo distributed drugs. Former 49ers defensive lineman Martin Harrison told officers that Romo regularly doled out amphetamines to his San Francisco teammates in the early 1990s. Harrison said a steady stream of 49ers came by Romo's locker before games in search of the little white pills.

Before a game in 1992, Harrison said Romo offered him some speed. Harrison refused, but Romo persisted, explaining that it would get him hyped up and provide that extra edge. "It's no big deal, I take it, everybody takes it," Romo told Harrison. Harrison passed.

Years later, when the two men were reunited as teammates on the

Denver Broncos, Harrison and his wife, Debbie, lived in an exclusive, gated community near Romo and his wife, Julie. The couples had dinner together sometimes, and Romo continued to press Harrison to use drugs. According to Harrison, Romo put it in racial terms: Romo and Harrison were white players in a black man's game. They needed to get an edge so they could compete with the black players who dominated the NFL. Romo admitted using steroids and growth hormone, and he offered to get the drugs for Harrison. When Debbie Harrison told Romo to stop pushing drugs on her husband, Romo called her "Mother Teresa."

Romanowski and Conte quickly bonded. Conte saw tremendous promotional opportunities in his relationship with the NFL star. So whenever Romo called, Conte jumped. He would get the pro football star whatever he needed, whenever he needed it. For his part, Romo opened doors for BALCO.

In 1997, Conte and Jim Valente flew to Denver to collect test samples from most of the Broncos. They did the same with the Miami Dolphins, whose strength and conditioning coach was a friend of Randy Huntington. Conte hoped the football players would endorse a new product he had created: ZMA.

Conte gave away six-month supplies of ZMA pills to NFL players and other elite athletes long before the product ever made it to the marketplace. He encouraged local pro teams and college programs to try ZMA, but they weren't interested. By then, General Nutrition Center stores across the country were carrying many products that promised increased muscle mass, just like ZMA. Conte decided he needed some scientific research to give his product credibility and help him pitch ZMA to the big supplement manufacturers and distributors.

At a sports medicine conference in 1997, Conte had met Lorrie Brilla, an associate professor of physical education at Western Washington University in Bellingham. Conte impressed Brilla as knowledgeable about mineral deficiencies. She assumed he was a scientist of some sort. Not long after they met, Conte asked Brilla to conduct a research study on SNAC's zinc-magnesium supplement, and she agreed.

In November 1998, Brilla presented her findings on a poster board at a meeting of the Southwest Chapter of the American College of Sports Medicine, in Las Vegas. They also were trumpeted in an unusual press release issued by SNAC System of Burlingame, California: "NCAA football players who took ZMA nightly during an 8-week spring training program had 2.5 times greater strength gains than a placebo group." The ZMA users experienced "anabolic hormone increases," the press release quoted Brilla as saying, and it cited John Gamble, the Dolphins' strength coach, as reporting that his players slept better and had fewer cramps because of ZMA. And there was a quote from Victor Conte, identified only as Brilla's "co-investigator": "ZMA is the only all-natural product that has been clinically proven to increase anabolic hormone levels and strength in trained athletes."

What the press release didn't say was that Conte owned SNAC and it was simply an affiliate of BALCO. Nor did it reveal that Conte's SNAC had helped pay for the study or that Brilla had been aided by Jim Valente and Dr. Brian Goldman, BALCO's vice president and medical director, respectively. It also didn't report that of the 57 Western Washington University football players who signed up for the study, 30 quit. By the end, only a dozen players were using ZMA while 15 took the placebo.

But the results were all that Conte thought he needed. He set out to leverage Brilla's ZMA study into a manufacturing and distribution contract with a big vitamin company. He was rebuffed by executives at Long Island–based Country Life Vitamins, which had a sports and fitness division known as Biochem. Will Brink, a consultant knowledgeable about supplements, was asked by Biochem to attend the meeting and assess Conte's pitch. Brink knew the business was significant parts smoke, mirrors, and showmanship, and he saw all that in Conte. He sat and listened to the fast-talking, energetic BALCO owner but quickly dismissed ZMA as "a bit of a yawn."

Undeterred, Conte pressed on and negotiated a modest contract with the king of supplement distributors, Experimental and Applied Sciences, Inc. (EAS), of Golden, Colorado. The firm's CEO was Bill Phillips, a former Mr. Teen Colorado bodybuilder and author of *The Anabolic Reference Guide*, considered the bible for steroid users. EAS had recently turned Creatine into the hottest-selling supplement on the market and had obtained endorsements from many players on the 1998 Super Bowl champion Denver Broncos, including quarterback

John Elway, tight end Shannon Sharpe and, of course, linebacker Bill Romanowski.

At EAS, Phillips employed two convicted steroid dealers, including one who wrote a regular column for a Phillips bodybuilding magazine. When the NFL got wind of Phillips's background, the league announced it was reviewing a variety of matters connected to EAS.

None of this concerned Victor Conte. In the supplement business, almost anything that generated publicity was good for business. EAS paid Conte a $75,000 advance for the exclusive distribution rights to ZMA. The relationship started poorly, with EAS officials accusing SNAC of breach of contract for allegedly failing to present evidence that ZMA actually worked the way Conte promised it did. Ultimately, the contract was replaced by an agreement that allowed EAS to continue selling ZMA, but not as an exclusive distributor.

Soon, other sports nutrition companies were selling ZMA under a variety of names: ZMA Fuel, Recovery Stack with ZMA, Pro ZMA, and Z-Mass PM. Conte threatened to sue businesses that tried to use his trademarked ZMA name without paying. Once ZMA was finally on the market, Conte began his campaign to drum up sales by getting ZMA touted in the muscle magazines. That would be made easier by his recent entrée into the world of bodybuilding, and by his growing association with elite athletes like Bill Romanowski.

Richard Goodman, the freelance writer whom Conte had hired, had once owned a gym and was familiar with the bodybuilding scene. In 1998, on behalf of BALCO, Goodman sent out marketing packets to about two dozen big-name bodybuilders. He included the 1990 article he had written, "The Atomic Level Athletic Frontier," which touted BALCO and Conte. And he offered the bodybuilders free tests of their blood and urine. The mailing generated one response. But one was all that Conte needed.

Milos Sarcev was a two-time Mr. Yugoslavia and had won the Mr. Universe title in 1989. With his classic physique, Sarcev had been a fixture on the scene for more than a decade. He claimed he was schooled in fitness, and he said he had attended many impressive-sounding academic institutions: Giovane Medical Services Inc., the American Academy of Anti-Aging Medicine, the University of NoviSad-Nutritional

Technology in Yugoslavia, the International Sports Science Association, and L'Accademia del Body Building e Fitness in Italy. Perhaps this education earned Sarcev his nickname, "The Mind."

Sarcev was the only bodybuilder who wanted free blood and urine tests from BALCO. Sarcev was told he was deficient in zinc and magnesium, and Conte gave him ZMA. In May 1998, San Francisco hosted its first professional bodybuilding event, and some 34 competitors representing 12 countries competed. Even for San Francisco, it was a bizarre scene: Grotesquely muscled, scantily clad men parading about, smothered in oil and resembling nothing of this earth; among them, men who had given their bodies over to science, willingly cocktailing steroids and diuretics and growth hormone and insulin in a quest for physical supremacy.

With the help of Sarcev, Conte gained entry into the pre-event competitors' meeting, where The Mind stood up and told his colleagues, "There's a guy here I think you guys should all meet." Conte then reeled off his pitch. He knew virtually nothing about bodybuilding at that point, but with his fast-talking abilities, he didn't need to. He invited the bodybuilders to come to a hotel suite nearby for free testing and analysis the day after the competition, and he promised they would see results.

Two days later, 20 muscle-bound men, most of them longtime steroid users, showed up at the hotel. A phlebotomist drew the blood. Conte was like a bee buzzing about the room. He wore a white lab coat, as did Goodman, who used one that had been given to him by his late father, a doctor. "I think we were trying to, I guess, pick our costume appropriately," Goodman recalled.

Before they tested the bodybuilders, Conte asked them what kinds of steroids they were taking. Many said they were using trenbolone and primobolan. After Conte got the results of their blood and urine analyses back, he said most of the bodybuilders were being duped, that whoever was selling them their stuff was passing off cheap imitations.

He told the bodybuilders he could do a lot better for them.

By this point, Conte had become increasingly educated about steroids. Just as he was a self-taught trace-mineral expert, so, too, had he schooled himself in performance-enhancing drugs. Through his association with Romanowski, Conte was becoming a steroid dealer. And with that came the sincere belief that he was providing a basic and essential service to the elite athlete. He had come to believe as Charlie Francis believed: Cheat or lose.

Chapter 6

Unlike Victor Conte, Patrick Arnold had a scientific background. The cocky, bright son of two high school principals, he had graduated from the University of New Haven in 1990 with a bachelor's degree in chemistry. After college, he gravitated toward the intersecting worlds of bodybuilding and steroids. He became friends with Dan "The Guru" Duchaine, a legendary figure on the bodybuilding scene who was coauthor of *The Underground Steroid Handbook*, a how-to guide for steroid users.

Duchaine was a theater arts major at Boston University who had begun to educate himself about steroids during a failed career as a bodybuilder. He moved from New England to Los Angeles and worked as a writer, chemist, and trainer for athletes and Hollywood stars. He had been jailed twice, first for steroid trafficking and then for dealing the date-rape drug GHB.

Perhaps in part because of his criminal record, Duchaine was revered in the outlaw world that connected supplements, steroids, and bodybuilding. When he died of kidney disease at 48 in 2000, a friend would eulogize him as "a mixture of Andy Kaufman and Albert Einstein, with some Bart Simpson thrown in."

If Duchaine thought well of you, doors opened; so it was for Patrick Arnold when he went into the business of distributing nutritional supplements. With an introduction from Duchaine, Arnold found work in the supplement industry, then opened his own laboratory near the University of Illinois's sprawling downstate campus in Urbana. He became known as one of only a handful of U.S. supplement manufacturers who synthesized his own compounds rather than importing them from Europe or China. He prospected in the scientific literature for new substances to market. Eventually, Arnold became known as "the father of prohormones."

Prohormones were anabolic supplements that were no more than legal steroids, though not nearly as potent. They were steroid precursors, substances that supposedly caused a spike in testosterone levels when ingested. Though their efficacy was debated, the drugs became a financial windfall for Arnold after he popularized one called androstenedione. Andro, as it became known, was first synthesized in the 1930s, and was widely used by the infamous East German doping machine in the 1970s and 1980s, administered to Olympic athletes in a nasal spray to boost testosterone levels. Arnold said he learned of it in the early 1990s while studying German patent documents. He began selling Andro in the U.S. in 1996, and by 1998 the substance already was banned in the Olympics and the NFL, but not in baseball.

Mark McGwire gave a tremendous boost to Patrick Arnold and Andro. In 1998, after the AP's Steve Wilstein reported that the St. Louis Cardinals slugger was using Andro during his assault on the single-season home run record, the story caused a flurry of attention for Andro, and sales of the supplement spiked. Even McGwire's pledge to stop using the substance did nothing to stem interest in Andro. In the days before Congress finally banned the drug in 2005, local nutrition stores scrambled to acquire last-minute batches to keep up with soaring demand.

Like his mentor Duchaine, Arnold became a cult figure in the industry. Because of Andro, he found himself on the *Sporting News*'s list of the top 100 most influential figures in sports. His and other Web sites revealed him in various incarnations: Arnold the bodybuilder, posing shirtless and in mid-flex, with ripped biceps and a rippled stomach; Arnold the chemist, in white lab coat, with thin, round glasses, a receding hairline, and a tiny, triangular soul patch just below his lower lip. He offered personalized advice for $60 an hour: "Live, one-on-one telephone consultation with your favorite steroid/supplement/chemistry Guru Patrick Arnold."

Arnold had a more secretive business on the side: discovering and creating designer steroids—or "supplements," as Arnold called them.

Word spread that he was the man to turn to for the newest, most cutting-edge drugs. He was holed up in his lab, scouring a 1969 pharmacology textbook titled *Androgens and Anabolic Agents, Chemistry and Pharmacology*. As Arnold once explained, the book detailed virtually every anabolic ever tested, including many substances that were "very promising that never made it to the market."

Among the "shining stars" Arnold uncovered in his research was norbolethone, also known as Genabol, a steroid developed in the 1960s by Wyeth Pharmaceuticals in Philadelphia to treat children with growth problems. The drug was never marketed, perhaps because testing on animals indicated it might be toxic. It was forgotten for nearly three decades, until Arnold rediscovered it while perusing his book. "On paper it looks like a real winner, high anabolic with very little androgenic," Arnold wrote of the drug on an Internet message board in 1995. That was the steroid user's dream. "High anabolic" meant more muscle growth, while "less androgenic" meant fewer "manly" side effects like hair growth on the face or chest.

Among Arnold's designer steroid clients was Sarcev. E-mails exchanged by Arnold and Sarcev in February 2000 gave a glimpse into the chemist's clandestine work, along with the bodybuilder's willingness to turn himself into a human lab rat. Sarcev wrote that he would be competing in the Night of Champions bodybuilding event in New York City and needed help. "Is it possible for you to make something for me?" he asked Arnold.

Arnold replied that he had a couple of potential drugs that had not yet been tested extensively. One was norbolethone. "It makes my pee kind of dark yellow, so it may be harsh on the liver somewhat," he wrote. Arnold said he would sell Sarcev four grams of the stuff for $400. The chemist also offered Sarcev oral trenbolone, a bovine steroid used to enhance lean meat in beef cattle, though he cautioned it was "still an unknown because no one else has really tried it in a controlled manner." The oral trenbolone went for $200 a gram, and Arnold had a batch ready. The drugs were potent, he warned. "I trust you have a good liver and would take care of it while using the aforementioned compounds," he wrote.

Sarcev wrote that he would send an overnight payment. In a joking reference to the organ damage that steroids were thought to cause, he asked where he should send "money, gold . . . or kidneys." The bodybuilder also volunteered for future experiments. "As I've tried everything, I could be [a] good guinea pig," he wrote. "But I also work with so many other monkeys (that would like to become gorillas) I can really test the stuff."

Arnold and Victor Conte had first established a relationship on an Internet message board hosted by Google called misc.fitness.weights, which was devoted to bodybuilding and nutritional supplements. The board was a meeting place for both established supplement dealers and wannabes, men who hoped someday to create a breakthrough product that would make them as rich and famous as Patrick Arnold or Bill Phillips, the EAS kingpin. The tone of the interchanges on the board was often rude, the language frequently vulgar, and it offered an unfiltered view of men like Conte.

Conte came under attack on the board soon after he began posting. He was seen as a shameless promoter of ZMA, a "spammer" whose only purpose was to tout his products while criticizing his competitors. Sometimes Conte would relay studies connected to zinc or magnesium or ZMA. At other times he would pop up to extol the virtues of his "Grow As You Sleep" product. On March 24, 1999, Conte created a thread he titled "ZMA Study Results," in which he offered the introduction to the sketchy research paper he coauthored with Lorrie Brilla, the Western Washington professor.

Shortly after Conte's posting, Bill Roberts, a supplement dealer who wrote knowledgeably about steroids and had ties to Dan Duchaine, responded: "DIE, you piece of shit BALCO spammer!"

In other postings, Conte attacked Roberts as a sellout and an opportunist who would turn on anyone. "Let's face it, you are a whore with zero integrity!" Conte wrote. "P.S. How does it feel, now that you have your dick in your own mouth?"

Conte's Internet relationship with Arnold wasn't terribly collegial, either. Conte questioned the usefulness and potential side effects of Arnold's prohormone products. Arnold was not impressed, and he seemed annoyed. "You sell a fucking mineral supplement," he wrote to Conte in April 1999. "You groundbreaker you."

Elsewhere, Conte's ZMA was beginning to get traction through the muscle magazines, though that in itself was a scam. Many magazines existed as publicity arms of the supplement distributors: 200-page, glossy periodicals produced to resemble objective journalism. Often, the magazine publishers and the supplement dealers were one and the same. So, for example, after Biotest AG contracted with Conte to market and distribute ZMA, the supplement company's magazine, *Testosterone Nation* (*T-Nation*), published not one, but two interviews with Conte within five months. The first, in November 1998, was by freelance writer Nelson Montana. He said the interview was set up by the CEO of both Biotest and *T-Nation*.

Montana said he was so openly skeptical about zinc and magnesium that Conte nearly ended the interview several times. "I just thought the whole thing was so smarmy and egregious, based on pseudo-science," Montana says. "It's like selling dirt."

Montana says the story he filed reflected his skepticism, but the CEO rewrote the piece to present a glowing endorsement of Conte. One paragraph read: "Now, this isn't some testosterone pie in the sky, hocus-pocus, typical supplement manufacturer scam either. He's got the studies to back it up, and it's more than likely you could experience the same kind of increases in testosterone and GH production by using his very economically priced supplement."

By 1999, Conte was fully immersed in the culture of bodybuilding. He had a number of bodybuilding clients, and each year he attended the Mr. Olympia contest in Las Vegas and The Arnold Classic in Columbus, Ohio, named for the steroid-using bodybuilder who would become a Hollywood action hero and then, improbably, the governor of California. As always, Conte networked with the people who could help him.

At the same time, Conte's relationship with Patrick Arnold improved. The tone of their exchanges on misc.fitness.weights became more respectful, and Arnold sometimes came to the defense of the oft-attacked Conte. In April 2000, after Arnold stood up for him on the message board, Conte sent a thank-you message, pledging to "evaluate the science on prohormones objectively," and closed on a polite note: "Once again, I appreciate your honesty and value your feedback and comments. VC."

What had happened to the ingrained bitterness? Victor Conte and Patrick Arnold were now doing business together. That business was steroids.

Before he hooked up with Arnold, Conte already was providing drugs to athletes. One major customer was Romanowski, who was receiving human growth hormone. Biotechnology researchers had synthesized the substance to treat dwarfism and other serious medical problems. But by the late 1990s, doctors who endorsed a controversial new medical practice called Anti-Aging had begun touting growth hormone as a Fountain of Youth drug. It became especially popular in Hollywood, where the glitterati fought a constant battle to remain young looking and wrinkle-free. For athletes, the drug provided significant benefits. Growth hormone worked like a steroid to boost muscle mass and hasten recovery, and it was even more effective if used in conjunction with steroids or other performance enhancers. In addition, there was no blood or urine test for growth hormone; athletes who used it would never test dirty.

Conte began providing HGH to Romo in 1998 or 1999, Colorado court records show. Conte made an unsubtle reference to his involvement with the drug during one of his interviews with *Testosterone Nation*. Conte didn't "condone the use of anabolic steroids or growth," he said. "However, I know of a number of athletes who use growth hormone and most are reporting tremendous benefits." Some users were in their mid-30s, he continued (Romo was 32 at the time), and "a few of the older athletes feel that GH supplementation has helped them extend their competitive career."

Conte told *Testosterone Nation* that he knew a 47-year-old bodybuilder named Emeric Delczeg whose use of HGH had raised his growth hormone levels to that of a 20-year-old. Actually, Conte not only *knew* Delczeg, he regularly bought growth hormone from the Hungarian bodybuilder. Delczeg had been suspected of dealing steroids and growth hormone for years—in June 1996, a shipment of steroids sent to Delczeg from abroad was seized by customs agents. Years later, Delczeg told federal agents that an AIDS patient living near Sacramento and an Arizona man with a long criminal record were among his sources for growth hormone. He also told authorities he sold Conte testosterone for $140 per vial and growth hormone for $700 per box.

Conte often badgered the bodybuilder about when he would deliver more drugs, according to a source with knowledge of Conte's business. Conte resold the growth hormone he got from Delczeg to Bill Romanowski, the source said. Conte seemed infatuated with Romo. "Romo used to call, and Victor would hang up the phone and be all glowing," the source said. ". . . Romo calls and Victor thinks *he* sacked the quarterback."

Colorado authorities learned of Conte's drug sales to Romanowski when they investigated the NFL star for prescription drug fraud in the late nineties. During an August 1999 interview with investigators, Julie Romanowski said her husband had obtained growth hormone from BALCO. The Colorado officers didn't pursue the growth hormone issue, and the prescription fraud case against Romanowski was dismissed. Later, when federal agents from the BALCO case obtained Conte's bank records, they found he had received checks totaling $16,700 from Julie and Bill Romanowski between January 2000 and August 2002.

The records also showed that between February 1999 and January 2001, Delczeg, the HGH supplier, received checks totaling $28,882 from Conte's SNAC System Inc. As he began to extend his operation, Conte developed additional sources. Delczeg steered Conte to his Arizona connection, and records from BALCO vice president Jim Valente's American Express account showed purchases from the supplier totaling $7,980 over three and a half weeks in the summer of 2000, before the start of the Sydney Olympics. Conte obtained some norbolethone in the spring of 1999, apparently from Patrick Arnold. It was called "the stuff," but Conte took to calling it "The Clear" because it was undetectable on drug tests.

Conte had funds to buy drugs because his once-failing businesses finally seemed to have turned a corner. His SNAC supplement company was highly profitable, thanks to sales of ZMA. SNAC's gross income in 2000, according to court records, was $1.18 million, up from $42,820 two years earlier.

The publicity machine was gearing up, and Conte had it figured out. He would encourage elite athletes to wear ZMA T-shirts and hats and talk up his supplement to the bodybuilding magazines. In exchange, Conte would provide them with performance-enhancing drugs to help them reach new levels of success. The plan served two purposes for Conte: It would boost sales of ZMA, and it would satiate his desire to be somebody, to demonstrate that he could direct greatness.

Conte set up an elaborate system intended to ensure that his athletes could ingest effective performance-enhancing drugs without fear of getting caught. Olympic athletes faced the toughest steroid policy in sports and were subject to unannounced testing both during competitions and in training. They were required to file a document listing their whereabouts at all times during the year—even when on vacation. A tester seeking a urine sample could show up at an athlete's house, day or night, with no warning. The Olympic testing labs searched for a much larger catalog of performance-enhancing drugs than any other sport. (Baseball, by stark contrast, had no steroid policy in 2000.)

Despite the scrutiny, Conte came to realize that beating the testers was not difficult. He worked to provide a broad menu of drugs that were difficult to detect. Among the drugs he ultimately offered were growth hormone; erythropoietin, or EPO, the oxygen-boosting drug that helped athletes train harder and longer; the diabetes drug insulin, which also was particularly potent when cocktailed with other substances; Patrick Arnold's norbolethone, aka The Clear; a testosterone-based balm Conte called "The Cream"; and the narcolepsy drug modafinil, a powerful stimulant athletes took directly before competing to pump themselves up.

Growth hormone and insulin were completely undetectable. The EPO test couldn't detect all forms of the drug. Testers wouldn't know to check for norbolethone, a drug that had never been marketed, and The Cream was designed to mask the use of other steroids. It was a mixture of synthetic testosterone and epitestosterone. Epi, as it was known in the drug-testing culture, was present in the body but had no known function. But it was important to drug testers, who used it to differentiate between natural testosterone and synthetic testosterone in an athlete's body. Normally, epi and testosterone occurred in about a 1:1 ratio. So, a threshold was set—a loose one at that—in which an athlete whose ratio exceeded 6:1 would be considered to be doping. Conte's Cream helped the athlete maintain a normal ratio, and it concealed what otherwise would be a telltale sign of the use of an undetectable steroid: an abnormally low testosterone level. When a person takes steroids, the body stops producing testosterone to the point that it can bottom out at zero. A zero level would set off red flags for drug testers, but The Cream elevated testosterone enough to avoid suspicion.

Conte created a simple "alphabet" shorthand for his drugs—for example, "E" for EPO, "G" for growth hormone, "I" for insulin—to be used on calendars he and the athletes kept. The calendars would list when athletes were scheduled to take which drugs, and they also indicated the dates of competitions so that the drugs' effects would be peaking at the right time. Conte also kept a ledger that detailed both the types of drugs athletes were using, as well as the results of blood and urine tests conducted on the athletes and their T/E ratios. Conte engaged in this "pretesting" to make sure his athletes would pass drug tests.

It was elaborate and systematic, and to Steven Ungerleider, an Oregon psychologist and doping expert, it was hauntingly familiar. After the Iron Curtain fell, Ungerleider had spent months in formerly Communist East Germany studying the records of the defunct regime's athletic doping program. The result was his 2001 book *Faust's Gold*, the definitive account of the GDR doping machine.

The more Ungerleider learned about Conte's program, the more familiar it sounded. "I'm absolutely convinced he stole many pages from the GDR handbook," says Ungerleider, noting the careful planning to stay under the 6:1 threshold, the calendars, and the pretesting. "Victor obviously took it to another level."

With his system in place and the array of drugs readily available, Conte was certain he could be a major player at the 2000 games in Sydney if only he could insinuate himself into the company of the latest generation of Olympians. He just needed someone to make the introductions.

Chapter 7

He was an unlikely agent for the transformation of Barry Bonds into the greatest hitter who ever lived: a muscular, spike-haired man who was at once unknown, unlucky, and financially strapped. In 1998, Greg Anderson, Bonds's weight guru, was working as a personal trainer at the World Gym in Burlingame, near San Francisco International Airport. The gym was hardcore, intended for serious bodybuilders. It was known as a place where the gym rats sold steroids out of the trunks of their cars. Anderson often spent 12 hours a day in the warehouse-like structure, amidst the clanking of iron, the grunts and yells, and the spray of sweat. At work, Anderson wore a long-sleeved sweatshirt that covered his heavily tattooed arms and concealed just how much muscle he had packed on to his 5-foot, 10-inch, 225-pound frame. With the sweatshirt off, he looked "like a Russian weight lifter," said a trainer who encountered him.

Anderson would train anyone who expressed interest, from high school kids intent on getting their varsity letters to beefy guys who were infatuated, as he was, with power lifting. His clients weren't wealthy. He earned barely enough from them to pay child support for his young son and have money left over for gas and the rent on a shared apartment. Barry Bonds said Anderson was so broke that sometimes he lived in his truck.

Anderson spoke in a surfer-dude patois with a high-pitched voice that seemed incongruous in so imposing a man. He had good manners, and when he chose he could excise the obscenities that peppered his normal conversation and make soft-spoken chitchat. If the situation required, he could be deferential and humble. And he approached life with a calm, expect-the-the-worst attitude. Anderson's life journey had taken several hard turns, the worst of them when he was a little boy.

Like Bonds, Anderson grew up on the San Francisco Peninsula in San Carlos. His mother was a distant poor relation of Joseph L. Alioto, the famed trial lawyer and San Francisco mayor, and his father, Gordon, was a salesman for an ink company.

On the Sunday night before Christmas, 1976, Gordon Anderson was in nearby Redwood City, at the Villa Rosa, a bar on El Camino Real, the six-lane road that ran the length of the Peninsula from San Francisco to San Jose. Through either bad luck or poor judgment, Gordon Anderson was playing dice with an erratic ex-convict named Jim Kerns, who had been imprisoned at San Quentin for trying to run down a policeman after first driving a car through the front wall of a bar.

As the night wore on, another player joined the game: William Stanley Younger, 35, a slender man who had been drinking alone. As policeman Timothy Mellors reconstructed what happened, Younger began losing steadily, perhaps because he was being cheated. Younger wanted to quit, but Kerns and Gordon Anderson insisted that he keep playing. By closing time, Younger was in the hole $1,000; Kerns suggested they all go over to Younger's house a few blocks away to play poker and to get the money that Younger owed them. Younger nervously agreed. He later told police he felt he had no choice.

The poker game ended before 5:00 AM with the sound of gunfire. Officer Mellors would find Younger standing in the shadows outside the house. "I just shot two guys in there," he said, surrendering his .38 pistol. Inside, Anderson's father and Kerns lay dead, cards scattered all around. Younger told police that the men had begun pressing him for money. He got a gun, intending to order them out of his house. But he claimed they rushed him, and he shot both men in the heart. Younger pleaded self-defense, and the district attorney dismissed the charges. Gordon Anderson was 33. In later years, Greg Anderson sometimes described his father as a San Francisco policeman who had been killed in the line of duty.

Gordon Anderson left a wife and a little girl as well as young Greg, a chunky, undersized 10-year-old infatuated with Little League.

The stricken family did what they could to cope. For Greg, it was throwing himself into baseball. At the time of Gordon's death, the family lived a few blocks from San Carlos's Burton Park, where the baseball diamonds were located. Greg often went there to play and hang out with the other young ballplayers. Through them he connected with the family who helped him survive that difficult time, and with whom he was friends ever after.

It wasn't the family of Barry Bonds. Bobby Bonds, then an outfielder for the California Angels, lived in San Carlos, and his boys, Barry, Rick, and Bobby Jr., all played ball at Burton Park. Years later, Bonds would describe Anderson as his "best friend" from boyhood. Barry's real friends from the old days laughed about it. Certainly Greg knew Barry: San Carlos was a small town, and everyone who played ball there knew Barry Bonds. But Barry was two years older than Greg. They never went to the same school and they hadn't been close. They might never have known each other at all but for the McKercher family, who also lived near the park.

Roy McKercher was a husky, athletic San Mateo sheriff's deputy who had been a Giants bat boy when the team first moved out from New York. His wife, Carol, was a cheery woman who encouraged the friends of her sports-crazy sons to hang out at their home. The McKercher boys, Bobby and Tim, were wonderful athletes. Greg had bonded with Tim and was over at their house all the time. There, he also got to know Barry, whose actual best friend was Bobby McKercher.

The relationship with the McKerchers was important to the fatherless boy. Years later, when Anderson returned to the Bay Area after college to figure out what to do with his life, he lived for a time at the McKercher house. In 2003, when Carol was struggling with terminal cancer, Anderson visited often, gave her foot massages, tried to make her more comfortable. Greg "is like my own son," she said before her death.

Sometimes as teammates, sometimes as opponents, Greg, the McKerchers, and the Bonds boys played at Burton Park in a succession of youth baseball leagues. Greg was a decent infielder on teams with an unusual concentration of talented young players. The best of them were bound for Junipero Serra High School in San Mateo, the

Catholic league powerhouse. Bonds went on to star at Serra, as did Bobby McKercher, a shortstop who would play in the College World Series for Oklahoma State. Tim McKercher was another Serra standout who later was starting catcher at UC–Santa Barbara.

But Anderson didn't go to Serra. He enrolled in the public high school in San Carlos and sometimes turned up at Serra games to watch Barry Bonds and Bobby McKercher play. At the end of freshman year, his mother moved the family four hours east to the foothills of the Sierra Nevada to seek a new start. But Greg never forgot Barry Bonds.

He told his baseball coach at Nevada Union High School in Grass Valley that he knew a can't-miss big leaguer, the best, most natural player anyone had ever seen. It was the first time coach Mike Cartan had ever heard of Barry Bonds, and he remembered the name only because he was a Giants fan and had followed Bobby Bonds's career.

By high school, Anderson had come to accept that he had no great gifts as a ballplayer. To continue in the sport, he would have to become a hustle guy, the player who sprints everywhere on the practice field, pitches batting practice, keeps the scorebook, warms up the pitchers, and rakes the mound. He would cheer for his teammates from the bench and high-five them after they scored, but otherwise keep his mouth shut. He would volunteer for all the tasks that a player like Barry Bonds could blow off with impunity.

Teammate Rich Lopp remembered being inspired by Greg's work ethic and the love of the game displayed by his "short, squatty, roly poly" friend. "Here was a guy that was always one hitting streak or a couple of good double-plays or one diving catch from losing his starting position," but he never seemed discouraged, Lopp said.

After graduation, Anderson enrolled in Butte Community College in nearby Oroville, California. He redshirted for a year and then made Butte's baseball team as a utility infielder, a player who "came in when we were way ahead or just smoked out of a ballgame," recalled Lopp, who also played at Butte.

Anderson wanted to continue playing ball, but there seemed few opportunities for a bench player from a community college team. Then an assistant coach from the Midwest made some phone calls, and in 1987 Anderson moved to the dusty plains of western Kansas and enrolled at Fort Hays State University, a school whose baseball program had fallen into disarray. Coach Steve Gillispie, captain of the team only the previous year, was desperate for players—"anyone with a pulse would have been fine," he joked. But he was pleasantly surprised with Anderson: a serious player who sported a flattop haircut and spiked hair before spiked hair had made its way to Kansas.

By the time he got to Fort Hays State, Anderson was infatuated with lifting free weights, then relatively new to baseball. For years the sport had discouraged lifting weights at all, warning hitters they would lose the flexibility that was thought to be essential to get around on a pitch and drive it. The attitude was changing, but weight training in baseball was still far behind other sports. As soon as he showed up, Anderson wanted to check out the weight room. During his time at Fort Hays, he spent as many as four hours a day working out, sometimes persuading a night janitor to unlock the weight room for him after it had closed at 8:00 PM.

As a junior, Anderson played shortstop. In the off season before his senior year, he put on 20 pounds of muscle, almost all of it in his shoulders and upper body—a transformation that would throw up red flags today, but was of little concern at the time. Anderson credited weight training for what was surely his greatest success on the baseball diamond. In 1989 he batted .340, struck out only 14 times, and made the all-conference team.

Center fielder Joe Blandino saw the connection between power lifting and Anderson's terrific year, but he saw a downside to weight training, too. Blandino was from Milwaukee and found it as weird to be in Kansas as Anderson did, and they had become friends. But as Anderson absorbed himself in weight training, he became standoffish, preferring working out to partying with teammates. He'd just tell the guys he didn't drink and would head back to the gym. Blandino also thought Anderson's weight training had cost him something as a player. Although his hitting was better, Blandino thought Anderson had become too muscle-bound to make defensive plays, and that his throwing had deteriorated. Ineffective as the regular shortstop, Anderson was often the designated hitter. He was more of a weight room guy than a baseball player, Blandino concluded.

Anderson had begun using steroids to boost his weight training.

The drugs were legal in those days, and readily available in gyms: At Fort Hays State, a few kids in the dorms were injecting themselves. Years later, in a conversation that was recorded without his knowledge, Anderson would recall that he started using steroids 16 years earlier—that is, in 1987, when he first arrived in Kansas.

Over time, Anderson became a steroids expert, learning the wonderful feeling that could come from using the drugs: rapid recovery after exertion, and the self-confidence that bordered on a feeling of invincibility; so much stamina that the user could work out long past what should have been the point of exhaustion and then come back and do it again the next day. There was also the blessed absence of the deep-down soreness and pain that inevitably accompanied drug-free training. And there was the weight gain, almost all of it muscle, and with that the strength to lift ever greater weights. For a baseball player, it meant the ability to whip the bat with greater force and drive the ball with more authority than ever before. But Anderson also learned the drawbacks. There was the awkwardness associated with shooting oneself in one's own backside, especially on the days it was necessary to switch cheeks and manipulate the syringe left-handed; the acne flare-ups, bloated stomach, testicles seemingly ascending back into one's groin; the libido that raged at first, and then flatlined; and the emotional surges, from flaring anger to crashing depression; the problems with infections and abscesses.

The Fort Hays State Tigers finished under .500. Anderson hoped for a shot at pro ball. But his young coach told Anderson, as gently as he could, that he didn't have the speed or range to take his game any further. Anderson couldn't remember a time in his life when he wasn't playing baseball, but after all those years, he had reached the end of the line. There was more pain and tragedy for him in Kansas: His girlfriend, who had played guard on the women's basketball team, was killed when a drunken driver ran a stop sign and plowed into her pickup truck. Anderson left Kansas without getting his degree. In 1990, at age 24 and at loose ends, he was back in California.

He decided to live on the Peninsula rather than up in Grass Valley. He helped coach a junior varsity baseball team and took other odd jobs. He began reconnecting with baseball friends he hadn't seen much of since middle school. Meanwhile, he spent even more time in the gym than he had in college.

Mike Roza, a friend since youth baseball, thought Anderson was obsessed with working out. In Roza's opinion, Greg wanted to "get big and chase chicks." He became a workout partner and then the roommate of a weight lifter named Rich Custer, who competed in body-building contests. When Custer bought the World Gym franchise on Hinckley Road in Burlingame—on the airport flight path and, it turned out, around the corner from BALCO—Anderson began working out there. Roza called it "an extreme, heavy, intense, body-lifting type of gym."

Anderson loved it. He soon became a trainer himself. It was a way to stay active in sports and make his way past that difficult life challenge, leaving baseball. It seemed like everybody was going through it. By 1990, most of those marvelous players he had known as a kid in San Carlos were at the end of the line, too, looking for a way to make a living and a life outside baseball—everyone except for Barry Bonds, of course. In 1990, while Anderson was scuffling, Bonds was having his breakout year with the Pittsburgh Pirates. He was the National League MVP, with an $850,000 contract.

Anderson set up a business, Get Big Productions, and obtained letterhead and vanity license plates identifying himself as "W8 GURU." He supervised workouts for whatever clients he could find. Often he worked with groups of athletes, primarily baseball players, from Serra High: He charged the kids $5 each for group weight-training sessions. He also worked with power lifters. With them, workouts were intense and grueling: "16 sets of chest, more biceps, to really maximize and expand your muscle," as Bonds later described an Anderson session.

When Anderson didn't have a client, he would work out on his own. When he was paid by check, he reported it on his taxes, but if a client paid in cash, he ignored the IRS. He never came close to making a good living. He lived in small apartments, moving every year or two. For a time, he dated a woman, and they had a son together in 1999 before breaking up.

There were also minor brushes with the law. Just before Christmas,

1990, while moonlighting as a clerk at the Macy's at Hillsdale Mall, Anderson was caught swiping a $37 bottle of Calvin Klein perfume. He got fired, paid a $117 fine, and was put on 18 months' probation.

In 1995, a motorist told police that Anderson, at the wheel of a Mazda sports car, had chased him at high speed on Highway 380, honking and trying to cut him off. When the motorist exited, Anderson continued the chase, yelling and cursing, finally forcing him to a stop in a supermarket parking lot. There, Anderson grabbed him and hit him three times in the head before driving off, the motorist alleged. Anderson told police the other driver had cut him off on the freeway and then accosted him. Nobody was arrested. Two years later, in 1997, San Bruno police questioned Anderson about another reported road rage incident. Again, no one was arrested.

Anderson was not arrested for steroid dealing, either, but law enforcement officials heard about him from time to time. Using steroids without a valid prescription became a federal crime in 1991, and a state offense shortly afterward. Police almost never arrested anyone for simple possession, however, and the narcotics officers would far prefer to bust a cocaine dealer than a juice peddler. Still, the San Mateo County Narcotics Task Force was told that local gym rats were smuggling steroids into the country in bulk from Mexico and Eastern Europe. In 2000, drug agents got a tip that Anderson was dealing steroids out of World Gym.

In truth, he had become extraordinarily knowledgeable about performance-enhancing drugs, as a secret recording made years later would prove. A person who knew Anderson approached him and asked for help: A friend had been shooting steroids into his thigh, and a problem had developed at the injection site. What could be wrong?

While a concealed device picked up the conversation, Anderson began to reminisce about his life with steroids, recalling the reckless behavior of gym rats and bodybuilders he had known who sought to get bigger and faster through chemistry. He helpfully shared Rule Number One for self-administering anabolic steroids: Move the needle around. Rookies don't know any better, and it always gets them into trouble.

"What happens is, they put too much in one area, and what it does, it will actually ball up and puddle and what happens is, it will eat away and make an indentation, and it's a cyst," Anderson said. "It makes a big fucking cyst, and you have to drain it. Oh, no, it's gnarly."

He began to describe the gym rats he had known who had suffered miserably after shooting massive amounts of Winstrol or Dianabol into their butts or quadriceps muscles over and over again.

"No, dude, you'd be amazed at how many bodybuilders—'cause bodybuilders do like fucking sometimes 20 cc's of shit and it's just ugly," he said. ". . . It gets infected, I mean, they got to drain—I've had a guy had two gallons of shit drained out of his ass. It was so gross, you can't even believe it." Anderson paused.

"People don't know what the fuck they're doing, that's the problem," he continued. "No, I've seen all kinds of ugly shit, it's just unbelievable. . . .

"I learned that when I first started doing that shit 16 years ago, 'cause guys were getting some gnarly infections. And it was gross, I mean to the point where you have to have surgery just to get that fucking thing taken out, or it'd be a knot and you can't do anything.

"That's why you never do your quad. Dude, I never, never. I tell you, I knew a guy that went in their quad and they went too deep and they couldn't walk for a week, could not even bend their leg. It was some ugly shit."

Bobby McKercher hooked Anderson up with Bonds. After Oklahoma State, McKercher had been drafted by the Texas Rangers. But he wasn't a first-round pick, and nobody in the organization seemed to believe in him. His minor-league career ended in disappointment. He came home to San Carlos, where he drove a recycling truck and gave baseball clinics for kids. When Bonds became a Giant, McKercher reconnected with his old friend, and briefly they were in business together, running a short-lived bagel shop near Bonds's condo by the Bay in Redwood Shores.

At first, Anderson simply worked out alongside Bonds at the gym. Bonds told of his dissatisfaction with his current trainer, Ray Farris, and Anderson offered to put together a baseball-oriented strength program for him. He would tend to Bonds's weight training and nutritional needs. Bonds agreed, and before the 1999 season began, Anderson was hired to supervise Bonds's strength conditioning. Bonds kept Farris on as his running coach. As he bulked up, he hired Harvey Shields, another trainer who had worked with Jerry Rice, as stretching coach.

Anderson felt he had stumbled into an awesome job. Just when Anderson's connection to baseball had withered down to doing group workouts with high school kids, he suddenly found himself near the center of the game at its highest level. Every year Anderson got a trip to spring training. When the Giants moved into their new ballpark in 2000, Bonds gave him the run of the clubhouse. He met many Giants players and got to see up close how they prepared for the game, how they played it, how they interacted with their teammates, the club, the media. Not only did he get to know the Giants, but eventually, he would form special relationships with two of the game's greatest stars: Yankee Jason Giambi, the American League Most Valuable Player for his 2000 season with the A's; and Gary Sheffield, who had won a batting championship with the Padres and a World Series ring with the Marlins before joining the Yankees. When the Giants finally made it into the World Series, Anderson came along, and to commemorate it, he got a ring. He even went on a baseball barnstorming trip to Japan.

But the most amazing part of it was his association with Bonds, and his opportunity to play an important role in molding him into the greatest player who ever lived—in a way, to fulfill the prediction he had made about Barry when he was a boy. Bonds was dedicated to the program. He was eager to push the workouts, demanding more weight, more repetitions, more sets, and he also showed interest in the nutritional aspects of the training. Anderson kept track of the workouts. He paid attention to Bonds's performance on the baseball diamond, tracking his power stats, analyzing his at-bats, his home run frequency, even his morale.

It was an absorbing job for Anderson, but there were downsides. People believed that anyone doing important work for a multimillionaire ballplayer was well paid, but that just wasn't the case. Bonds had his people give Anderson $10,000 in cash from time to time, but the payments were erratic, and Greg didn't earn nearly enough to give up his other clients, let alone buy a condominium in the Peninsula's overheated housing market. In 1999, Bonds gave him a terrific price on a new truck, but the circumstances only emphasized how wealthy Bonds was and how little of it trickled down. During a three-month period, Bonds had bought three expensive SUVs, getting rid of the first two after a few days because he decided he didn't like them. Anderson bought one of them.

He didn't like to talk about another downside. Anyone who worked for Bonds had to take a great deal of abuse. If Bonds told you to do something, you had to drop everything and do it—no matter what else was going on, no matter whether it was a reasonable request or something off the wall. If you were slow to comply, or if you tried to explain why it wasn't such a good idea, Bonds would get right up in your face, snarling, calling you a "punk bitch," repeating what he wanted and saying, "Did I fucking stutter?" You had to suck it up and take the abuse and the humiliation—everyone did.

In the clubhouse at Pac Bell, Anderson was careful not to talk to anybody while Bonds was present, for fear he would get angry. Anderson would sit in the stall next to Bonds's lockers and try not to move. Once, before a game in 2001, Bonds was napping, and stretching coach Harvey Shields was standing around with nothing to do. Willie Mays was in the clubhouse, as he often was, and Shields started showing the 70-year-old Hall of Famer some stretches. Bonds awoke, couldn't find Shields, and went ballistic. "What the fuck are you doing?" he yelled at him. Shields was Bonds's stretching guy, and he couldn't stretch with anyone else, not even Willie Mays, without prior approval. You really couldn't relax with Barry Bonds. Away from his boss, Anderson sometimes called Bonds "His Highness."

Of course Anderson's primary job was to provide Bonds with performance-enhancing drugs and to track his regimen. Anderson obtained the drugs and administered them. In file folders, and on his computer, he kept calendars of Bonds's use of the substances, recording the drugs, dosages, and cycles.

But Anderson didn't think of himself as Bonds's drug dealer. When Bonds paid him, he liked to think it was for weight training. As far as supplying drugs, Anderson thought of his role as "middleman." In San Francisco, he knew AIDS patients who had prescriptions for

testosterone and human growth hormone. The medicine was supposed to counter the terrible condition called "AIDS wasting," in
which the patient, racked by fever, infection, and HIV-related cancer,
loses weight so rapidly that he is in danger of starvation. But some
AIDS patients were willing to sell their drugs for cash. Anderson
bought the drugs and resold them virtually at cost to clients who
wanted them for their anabolic effects. Likewise, Anderson knew
many sources of conventional bodybuilders' steroids like Deca and
Winstrol. He resold those at almost no markup as well. Bonds was
keenly interested in performance-enhancing drugs. He asked their
pharmaceutical names, and then sought, through third parties, medical
advice about the drugs. The medical advice was negative. You shouldn't
take the drugs, he was told, because we have no idea about their long-
term effects. But Anderson said those concerns were overblown, and
Bonds ignored the advice he had sought.

Certainly the program Anderson devised worked. In the years after he linked up with Anderson, Bonds completely remade his body,
and the results of Anderson's drug regime are now reflected in the
record books. At an age when his father's baseball skills had begun to
erode badly, Bonds's drug use would make him a better hitter than he
had been at any time in his career—and, perhaps, the best hitter of
all time.

Chapter 8

Greg Anderson started Barry Bonds on Winstrol after the 1998 season. It was also known as stanozolol, the old favorite of bodybuilders, infamous as the drug that brought down Ben Johnson. Anderson provided the steroids and syringes and injected Bonds's backside, although Bonds eventually learned how to inject himself. Anderson began keeping calendars to track Bonds's drug cycle: If a user didn't come off steroids periodically, his body would lose the ability to produce testosterone naturally. Anderson held the unused drugs. There was to be no stash at Bonds's home or in his locker.

Aside from such side effects as acne, baldness, shrinking of the testes, mood swings, surges of anger, reduction of libido, and the risk of liver damage and prostate cancer, Winstrol's drawback was that it took months to clear the user's system. No athlete subject to drug testing dared use Winstrol because the likelihood of getting caught was so great. But of course that wasn't an issue for Bonds and baseball as the 1999 season approached. Although Commissioner Selig had promised a medical study after McGwire's Andro controversy, the sport was still years away from confronting its steroid problem.

Bonds worked harder in the gym during the 1998 off season than he had in years. Wearing black gloves, pants, and a sleeveless T, he showed up at World Gym day after day, Anderson at his side. The trainer talked quietly to his famous client or just sat and stared as Bonds went through the monotonous routine of pumping iron. Marvelously, the Winstrol eliminated the pain and fatigue of training. And the results were equally marvelous to behold.

For the first time in his life, Bonds was buff. He often stood in front of a mirror, laughing, saying, "How do I look?" By spring training, his weight had increased from perhaps 210 to 225, and almost all of the gain was rock-hard muscle. When he was with the Pirates, Bonds's body had been long and lean, a muscular version of a marathon runner's build. Now he had been transformed into an NFL linebacker, with broad shoulders, a wide chest, and huge biceps.

When he showed up a day late at the Giants' spring training camp in Scottsdale in 1999, angry at the club for refusing to renegotiate his contract, the change in Bonds's physique was startling. Third baseman Charlie Hayes called it to the attention of the *San Francisco Chronicle*'s beat reporter, Henry Schulman. "Did you see my man?" Hayes asked. "He was huge!" Around the Giants, they took to referring to Bonds as "The Incredible Hulk," joking about the "gamma radiation" that had transformed comic book character Dr. Bruce Banner into the great green superhero. When Bonds took batting practice, he was driving the ball farther than ever in his life. To teammates, writers, and fans in Scottsdale that spring, and especially to Giants management, Bonds's appearance and performance raised a fundamental question: What in hell had he been doing in the off season?

Sportswriters didn't press the question. Most attributed the changes in Bonds's body to a heavy workout regimen, as though a 34-year-old man could gain 15 pounds of muscle in 100 days without drugs. Sleuthing out Bonds's drug use would have been a difficult reporting task, requiring hard work and luck. Also, the example of Wilstein, the AP writer who had broken the story of McGwire's use of Andro, showed sportswriters that if they succeeded in getting the scoop, they would likely be subjected to intense criticism from the most powerful people in the game. It was little wonder that the media wasn't more inquisitive.

The Giants, from Peter Magowan to Dusty Baker, had no interest in learning whether Bonds was using steroids, either. Although it was illegal to use the drugs without a prescription, baseball had never banned steroids—and besides, the Giants were Bonds's team. By pursuing the issue, the Giants ran the risk of poisoning their relationship with their touchy superstar—or, worse, of precipitating a drug scandal the year before the opening of the new ballpark, where Bonds was supposed to be the main gate attraction.

Bonds and Anderson could see the difference the steroids made as soon as the season got underway. Bonds had often started slowly, but in 12 games, he batted .366 with four home runs, six doubles, and 12 runs batted in.

But then, because of his drug use, he blew out his left elbow and nearly ruined his career.

An MRI indicated a bone chip. But there was worse news when the elbow was examined by Bonds's personal physician, Dr. Arthur Ting, an orthopedic surgeon who treated many sports stars. Ting diagnosed a torn triceps tendon, requiring immediate surgery. If the injury hadn't been caught in time, if Bonds had continued playing through the pain, he might have shredded the tendon entirely and ended his career right then. Anderson and Bonds figured out what had gone wrong. The steroids had allowed Bonds to put on muscle too quickly. The elbow had become stressed, and the drugs masked the pain Bonds should have felt as the tendon was torn by continued use. He hadn't felt a thing and continued to pump iron, exacerbating the injury until he blew the elbow out.

Later, while visiting her apartment in Mountain View, Bonds told his Bay Area girlfriend, Kim Bell, about his steroid use. Bonds told her that most ballplayers now were using steroids, and he had begun using the drugs so he could recover more quickly from minor injuries. But steroids also were to blame for the elbow injury because they had made his arm muscles so large that the elbow tendon could not support them. "It makes me grow faster, but if you're not careful, you can blow it out," he told her. Bonds said he would be more cautious in the future. Bonds also implied he was only using oral steroids, saying he wasn't "like those bodybuilders who are injecting themselves . . . it's not like I'm doing it the way other people do."

Fans were told Bonds's injury was the result of wear and tear from a lifetime of baseball. He spent seven weeks on the disabled list. He returned in June, but soon he pulled a groin muscle and was sidelined again. In 1999, Bonds played in only 102 games. He batted just .262 and hit 34 home runs—that was one for every 10.4 at bats, the highest frequency of his career. But it was nothing compared with what McGwire was doing in St. Louis. McGwire had another monster year in 1999, hitting 65 home runs with 147 RBI, leading the league in both categories.

Bonds's frustrations boiled over when the Cardinals came to town. Just as in 1998, everybody wanted to see McGwire take batting practice. When the Cardinals visited, some clubs had begun roping off the area around the batting cage to control the crowd of players, coaches, and club officials who gathered to watch McGwire hit. The Giants set up ropes when the Cardinals arrived at Candlestick for three games in July.

Bonds had never seen the ropes on the field before. "What the fuck is this?" he demanded of the security guards. They told him the ropes were for McGwire. Furious, Bonds began knocking the ropes down. "Not in my house!" Bonds told them.

With Winstrol, Bonds was so muscular, he could hit the ball as far as McGwire. But even after the elbow healed, Bonds wasn't right in 1999. He felt muscle-bound and inflexible and had trouble turning on inside pitches. He also complained of back and knee problems, and about his eyesight, saying he couldn't pick up the rotation on the ball. Bonds' vision always had been incredible—on the freeway he could read the words on the exits when a normal person could barely make out that there was a sign. Perhaps the complaints about his eyes were psychosomatic, a reflection of the worry he felt about his elbow injury, the pressure he felt to perform at the highest level. But Bonds's complaints about knee and back pain and feeling too tight led Anderson to rethink Bonds's workout regimen, and to seek out other drugs for his star client.

If Bonds had any doubts about continuing to use performance-enhancing drugs, they were eliminated just before the start of spring training in 2000. Bonds went to Cashman Field in Las Vegas to compete in the Big League Challenge, a charity home run derby broadcast on ESPN. Jose Canseco, who was then playing for the Tampa Bay Devil Rays, dominated the event. He hit 28 bombs in the final round, while Bonds didn't even make the finals. At one point Bonds saw Canseco take off his shirt, and the big Cuban looked as though he had just won the Mr. Universe contest: 255 pounds, seemingly not an ounce of fat, just gleaming, chiseled power.

"Dude," Bonds said. "Where did you get all that muscle?"

In the new park, there would be new drugs. Anderson put Bonds on Deca, the gym rats' name for the injectable drug Deca-Durabolin. Like Winstrol, it was a bodybuilder's steroid, used in medicine to treat anemia associated with kidney failure. Eventually, Anderson started Bonds on human growth hormone, the synthetic drug being touted by cosmetic surgeons as an anti-aging miracle. Injecting Growth was tricky and painful: Rather than plunging the syringe into a big muscle, the user pinched a bit of skin on the belly with thumb and forefinger and carefully put the needle into the flap. Like a steroid, Growth had a strong anabolic effect, and it could help the user increase muscle mass. But it was also thought to strengthen joints and connective tissue and thus was often cocktailed with Deca or other steroids.

Bonds especially liked growth hormone. It allowed him to maintain his impressive musculature—the "sledgehammer biceps and thick, contoured delts," as *Muscle & Fitness* magazine later described his build—without intensive training. That was important, because he had found it difficult to keep up with weight lifting while playing ball. An NFL player can pump iron because he has six days off between games. But during a 162-game baseball season, workout opportunities were limited. Anderson usually didn't travel with the Giants, so Bonds's supervised workouts could occur only when the team was at home. At home or away, a baseball player is always either getting ready for the upcoming game or unwinding from the one just played. Bonds was doing well to manage 15 or 20 minutes of pumping iron each day during the season, and that wasn't nearly enough to keep one's body looking like a locomotive. But with HGH, Bonds remained buff and more energized to train, and touching his bicep was like touching an oak table. And yet, he felt more flexible. There was an added benefit to the new drug regimen: Bonds stopped complaining about his eyes. Although medical experts say there's no scientific basis to the claim, some growth hormone users have reported improved vision. At age 35, Bonds felt better than he had in years.

The ballpark in China Basin turned out to be all that Magowan had promised. It was an architectural gem that evoked the best of the great old parks of the past: the brickwork of Wrigley Field and Philadelphia's long-gone Shibe Park, an angled outfield fence somewhat like the Green Monster in Fenway. But it had modern amenities and amusements and 40,000 seats with unobstructed views. A unique feature was McCovey Cove, the stretch of bay front beyond the right field fence named after Willie McCovey, the Hall of Fame first baseman of the 1960s. A home run that left the park in right field would land in the water and become a "splash hit." The Giants correctly presumed this would be Bonds's signature spot, and whenever Bonds was approaching a milestone home run, the fans paddled rafts and kayaks into the cove and waited, hoping to retrieve a ball. A cottage industry of kayak rentals soon developed because of Bonds.

For Giants fans, the best amenity was the summer weather, which was as pleasant as could be had in foggy San Francisco. Unlike Candlestick, the park hadn't been built in a wind tunnel, and even when temperatures dropped into the 50s for night games, the skies were usually clear. Tickets were pricey, and the fans didn't look anything like the bedraggled faithful who had huddled in the cold of Candlestick. They were younger and wealthier, thanks to the dot.com boom that had transformed San Francisco's economy. Many were so handsome and well turned out, they looked as though they had stepped out of a J.Crew catalog. Often, they didn't seem particularly interested in the game, as they called one another on cell phones, arranging to meet at one of the bars or concession stands while the baseball went on as a backdrop to their socializing. Nevertheless, the new fans turned out en masse. To the Giants' delight, Pac Bell Park sold out the first year. The club drew 3.3 million, the greatest attendance in the Giants' 115-year history.

The park had better amenities for players, too. Pac Bell had a 2,700-square-foot clubhouse, double the size of the cramped quarters at Candlestick, and Bonds had the run of the place. Bonds felt he had built the new ballpark, and he insisted on bringing Anderson, Shields, and Farris there with him, one trainer for weights, one for stretching, and another if he wanted to run. Bonds had never tried to bring his people into the clubhouse at Candlestick; there was no room, and Mark Letendre, the longtime trainer, wouldn't have permitted it, anyway. But now Letendre was gone.

Bonds had a rationale for bringing his trainers to Pac Bell: An athlete's body was like a "well-oiled machine," and he wanted his crew with him to keep the machinery running at the highest performance levels. The Giants' new training staff didn't want anything to do with Bonds's three trainers. If Bonds's personal trainers had him do something stupid and the big man got hurt, it would be a disaster for the Giants. New head trainer Stan Conte (no relation to the BALCO president) went to team executives and urged them to ban Anderson and the others from the clubhouse, according to a source familiar with the conversation. The Giants had unofficial background checks done on Bonds's trainers. The club learned that World Gym, where Anderson was a trainer, was known as a place to score steroids, and that Anderson himself was rumored to be a dealer. That only confirmed what Anderson's appearance suggested. "All you gotta do is look at Greg Anderson" to know he was a juicer, a Giants employee said. "He's just this big, tattooed, huge weightlifting dude." But the club decided it didn't want to alienate Bonds on this issue, either. The trainers stayed.

Along with the trainers, Bonds brought a 27-inch television and a $3,000 vibrating lounge chair to Pac Bell Park. The leather lounge chair became the centerpiece of Bonds's wing of the clubhouse, which expanded to include four lockers. For his critics, the chair became a symbol of Bonds's arrogance and isolation from the rest of the team. But Bonds believed the chair was good for both himself and the Giants. He had a disc problem, and his back had bothered him ever since he had begun lifting weights with Ray Farris. Elevating his feet in the lounge chair helped. Bonds needed to sleep before games, or at least catnap. Lying quietly with his eyes closed, relaxed and calm, had become part of his preparation for games. At Candlestick, he used to sleep on a training table, but that annoyed Letendre. Letendre had only two tables for the team, and if Barry racked out on one of them, there wasn't room for players who truly needed the trainer's attention. But with the lounge chair, Bonds no longer had to sleep in the trainer's room—although he still did it sometimes. To Bonds, the lounge chair was a way of accommodating the Giants.

He was trying to be more accommodating in 2000, to become fan friendly and media friendly. In recent years, Bonds's behavior had been so unpleasant that his advisers feared it was going to cost him millions of dollars when he became a free agent after the 2001 season. Although Bonds's skill as a player was undisputed, the buzz about him was all bad, and it was made worse by his problems with his manager. The Giants had fired Bonds's father as part of a purge of coaches after the disappointing 1996 season. Bonds was upset with Dusty Baker for not protecting his dad. Bonds told associates his father knew more about the game than Baker, but Dusty wasn't man enough to accept it.

Everyone in baseball knew how much Baker had come to dislike dealing with his star player. Baker disliked having to coddle Bonds to get him to play. Nor did he appreciate having to alibi for him when he behaved like a spoiled teenager, as when he refused to run out a routine ground ball, or blew off the team picture two years in a row. There were constant struggles over control. If Baker took Bonds out of the lineup to rest him, Bonds would throw a tantrum. Baker was disrespecting a three-time MVP, he would say. Of course Bonds wanted a day off from time to time, but he wanted to dictate when he played. Occasionally, Bonds would ask for a day off and Baker would put him in the lineup anyway to assert control. To retaliate, Bonds would counter by declaring he had tweaked a hamstring and couldn't play. Bonds wanted everyone to know it was his team, not Baker's.

The worsening problem with Baker worried Bonds's advisers, especially because his rudeness to fans and writers was already so well known. They feared some clubs might refuse to pursue Bonds when he became a free agent because they didn't think they would be able to deal with him. Only a handful of clubs could afford the mega-contract Bonds wanted, and it was crazy to drive any of them away.

His advisers talked Bonds into being more of a human being. So, as the 2000 season began he would sign some autographs for the fans, a practice he had tried to avoid unless he was getting paid. He also would do more interviews. They weren't great interviews, because even on a good day, reporters found it difficult to extract a story from Bonds unless he got off on one of his rants. But Bonds suppressed the worst of his rudeness and made himself more available. He even made weekly appearances on a sports talk-radio program. In the excitement after the Giants beat the Diamondbacks to clinch the Western Division pennant, he gave an exuberant television interview that was broadcast live on Pac Bell's video screen. "You're beautiful!" he told the fans.

Meanwhile he had an outstanding year, batting .306, with 49 home runs—a career high, and second in the league to Sammy Sosa—and 106 RBI. He hit the first home run in the new ballpark. And, reflecting his ability to crush the ball with his new musculature, he knocked six "splash hits" into the waters of McCovey Cove. Pac Bell, it turned out, was not really a hitter's ballpark. It looked like a short porch in right field, but real power was required to hit the ball out of the park.

Bonds felt strong all season, and he recovered quickly from minor injuries. In May, he threw out his back after swinging at a pitch in Denver and collapsed facedown in the dirt a few steps from home plate. The Giants feared he would need surgery, but he returned after only four games. The Giants won 97 games but lost in the playoffs, this time to the Mets in four games. Bonds, struggling in the clutch as always, hit .176 with no homers.

Bonds had high hopes for a fourth MVP award. Instead, the trophy went to his hated teammate, Jeff Kent, who batted .334 with 33 home runs and 125 RBI. Bonds had ragged on Kent since he arrived from Cleveland in 1997. Bonds reacted to him in the way he had reacted to Van Slyke in Pittsburgh. Part of it was the "Great White Hope" dynamic: Kent was a big white cowboy, brash and loud.

But Bonds also clashed with Kent because the infielder's personality was similar to that of Sun, Bonds's first wife. Like Sun, Kent would challenge Bonds. Everybody else on the club, from the batboy to the owner, kissed up to Barry. When Kent saw it going on, he would look at them with an incredulous expression, as if to say, "Who the fuck is he?" There was constant friction, and the thought of losing the award to Kent was infuriating. A week before the MVP announcement, Bonds had one of his PR people call Commissioner Selig's office to see if he had won. If not, Bonds wanted to be out of town. Selig's people said they didn't know, and then the award went to Kent. Bonds irately told his people that they could forget about him being media friendly anymore—look at all the interviews he had done, and he still didn't win the MVP. That wasn't the problem, they told him: You lost because your own manager told everybody in baseball that Kent should be the MVP.

Despite the disappointment, it had been a breakthrough year, one in which Bonds had completed the transformation of his body and his game—and, it seemed, had discovered the Fountain of Youth. By age 35, most major-league baseball players are gone from the game; those who remain are generally in decline. At 35, Bonds's father had batted .215 for the Cubs and retired. But at the same age, Bonds had just enjoyed what he considered his best season. There were more to come, as he transformed himself into the game's most feared slugger.

No one was in a better position to note Bonds's transformation and its side effects than Kimberly Bell. Bell was a graphic artist in the Bay Area's Silicon Valley, five years younger than Bonds. She was pretty and intuitive, with brown eyes, clear olive skin, and bad luck with men. Barry was her "Giant mistake," she now says, punning on the name of the only baseball team she ever paid attention to. She should never have gotten involved.

Bell met Bonds in 1994, when she was 24 and a new friend invited her to see the Giants play the Montreal Expos at Candlestick Park. The friend knew some ballplayers, and before the game she drove into the players' parking lot to see who was around. Bonds came up to the car. He was 30 then, lean, mustached, and handsome, with short cropped hair and a dazzling smile, in his second year on the Giants and the team's biggest star. He looked at Bell and told her friend, "I want to know that girl—she's gonna be mine." The next day, her friend invited Bell to a July Fourth barbecue in San Carlos, and Bonds showed up after the Giants game. He had made sure Bell was invited to the party.

As they chatted, Bell saw that Bonds was a narcissist. His whole manner cried out, "Look at me!" If someone didn't have something to offer him or couldn't do something for him, he would ignore them. But Bonds was charming and magnetic, for all that—he could attract people as easily as he could repel them.

He invited her to go for a ride in his new Porsche. Rather than a spin around the block, as she had expected, they wound up blasting down the Bayshore Freeway at 100 miles per hour. They spent the night at his condo in Redwood Shores, and he vowed he would make her fall in love with him. "You're with the Killer B now," he said, using the nickname given to him in Pittsburgh.

At the time, Bonds was separated from his wife, Sun, and locked in the bitter divorce proceedings centered on the validity of the couple's prenuptial agreement. He was determined to keep his estranged wife from getting his money. Obsessed with the litigation, he told Bell there was no way he would ever get married again. Bell told him she didn't want to get married, either.

They began dating. Except when the Giants were on the road, they spent two or three evenings per week together, either at his condo or at her little apartment. Often they went out to dinner or to parties, and sometimes traveled together. She met his agents from the Beverly Hills Sports Council; his divorce lawyer; his parents; and his two little kids. Bonds introduced her to friends as "my girl," telling people how smart she was, that she worked in the computer industry.

When they were apart, Bonds took to calling her at work every morning around 8:00 AM, just to check in. It was a new kind of relationship for him, he told her. He said he usually dated strippers. Bell gave him a key to her apartment, and he would let himself in and leave her notes with idiosyncratic spellings and punctuation. "I stoped by to say Hi," one of them read. Another read, "If you love me! Where are you. And who are you with. I have called you all night on your cell and home."

Bonds also began giving her money: $5,000 to $10,000 in cash in an envelope, on an irregular basis. He said the money came from baseball card shows, where he was paid in cash to sign autographs, or from the sale of autographed balls, bats, and other memorabilia. Often Bonds would tell her how she should spend the money: a new big-screen TV or bed for her apartment, for example. When her car started breaking down he bought her a new Toyota 4Runner. In 1996, he decided she should have breast augmentation surgery, and a check arrived from the Beverly Hills Sports Council to pay for it.

Bell went to many of his games. Candlestick was too windy and cold to be fun, but the road trips were exciting. Over the years, on many occasions she followed Bonds and the Giants to Los Angeles, San Diego, Denver, Phoenix, Cincinnati, Houston, St. Louis, Chicago, and Miami. She would stay in the team's hotel, in a room adjoining Bonds. Sometimes, at his request, the Giants booked her room for her.

Bonds told her they had the perfect relationship. Bell had her own career, she didn't pressure him about money or getting married, she rarely complained, and she did what she was told. It came as a rude shock when Bonds announced one day in 1997 that Liz Watson, a girl he had met in Montreal, had arrived in the Bay Area and was staying at his condo. Bell didn't like it, but she didn't make an issue of it, and soon the relationship seemed back on an even keel.

Then, in January 1998, Bonds came to her apartment and announced that he and Liz were getting married. Bell burst into tears, but Bonds told her that nothing would change between them. He simply needed to get married or his ex-wife would get sole custody of his kids. Bell had her career and had always said she didn't want to get married, he reminded her, while Liz was willing to stay home and raise his children. Besides, Bonds said, Liz was black, and it was important for him to marry an African-American woman. He said he had gotten "too much shit" from the media for marrying a white woman last time.

Bonds dropped by Bell's apartment after he returned from the honeymoon. Against her better judgment, they resumed their affair, but nothing was the same. The way they related to each other, the way Bonds treated her, even the way Bonds looked, underwent radical changes. They couldn't go out together in the Bay Area anymore for fear of being seen. The only time they could have anything like a normal life was during spring training in Scottsdale and when she followed the team on the road. But there were new restrictions on that, too. Because he was married, Barry explained, she could no longer travel with the Giants on "family trips," ones on which the players often took their wives and children. San Diego was a "family city," so it was now off-limits. Bell was welcome to come to Miami, on the other hand: Girlfriends were permitted in "party cities," fun towns where wives weren't invited. Bell also was not allowed to go to New York. Later, she found out why. In New York, Bonds had begun dating a centerfold model from Eastern Europe whom he had met at a club there.

Meanwhile Bell saw less of the sweet, engaging side of Bonds's personality. He became irritable, controlling, and verbally abusive.

And after beginning his training with Anderson, his very appearance had changed: Bonds had bulked up so much that he seemed like a different man.

Bell blamed steroids for the ugly changes. He would reveal his use of drugs to her early in 2000, in what had started as a discussion of his elbow injury. Although Bonds didn't tell her where he got the drugs, she assumed they were administered by Anderson, whom she called his "paid friend." Bell had gotten to know Anderson during spring training. Every year Bonds rented a big house in a gated community in Scottsdale and Bell would come down for a week before Bonds's family arrived. Anderson stayed at the house, too. Bonds had become so rude that the only people willing to hang out with him were his employees, Bell says.

On most mornings in Scottsdale, before leaving to work out, Bonds would grab what Bell called his "man bag," a valise full of what seemed to be medications, and summon Anderson. "I've got to go talk to him for a minute," Bonds would say, and then the two men would go into the master bedroom and close the door.

Bonds's physical changes during this time were consistent with steroid use. His hair fell out, and he began shaving his head. Perhaps it was her imagination, but the head itself seemed to be getting larger, and the plates of his skull bones stood out in bold relief. Bonds's back broke out in acne, and he would stand in front of the bathroom mirror and say, "Oh my God, I don't know where this is coming from." Bonds also suffered sexual dysfunction, another common side effect of steroid use.

Bonds became more quick-tempered. When his anger flared now, he would grab her, stand close to her face, and whisper intimidating, hurtful things. He insisted on knowing where she was at every hour of the day or night. If he couldn't find her, he would become enraged, and he told her he would kill her if he found she was seeing someone else.

Her social life evaporated. He called her so many times at work that her boss began to complain. And his rages became increasingly violent. One evening at her apartment, Kim's crabby neighbor began tapping on the ceiling, complaining about noise. Barry became angry. He stormed out into the hall, shouted, "Bitch, quit fuckin' banging on the ceiling!" and kicked in her door, causing the neighbor to cry out in fright.

Bell used a telephone answering machine with a tape cassette; when one tape filled up, she'd toss it in a drawer and put in a new one. She began saving the messages after a few bleak occasions on which Bonds threatened to kill her, remarking that if she disappeared, no one would be able to prove he even knew her. The messages showed the trajectory of their nine years together.

Some reflected Bonds's gentle side.

"Hey honey bunny, what's going on?" he said in one. "I haven't called you in a couple of days because I've been stuck with one car and I've been getting dropped off at the ballpark, and once I get to work, I don't think about calling nobody."

On other messages, Bonds could be heard amusing himself, bizarrely.

"Hey girl, what's up?" he said in one voice mail of this type. "Kim, hey—who is trying to get in on my shit? No niggah's trying to get into my shit. Don't have me kill a niggah. Ha ha ha ha—later, girl. I'm on my way to San Diego, but I'm still getting the pussy, ha ha! Welcome to the penthouse!"

In some, Bonds sounded disturbingly like a stalker.

"Kim, I just paged you, now I'm pissed," he said in one message. "Fuck it, I don't give a fuck what, you better just find me. Well, why don't you just page me, however, I'll find you. But if I page you, your ass better drop every fucking thing and call me back!"

Once, Bonds left a flurry of messages over a 10-minute period.

"I'll find you," he said. "Now my blood temperature is rising."

Minutes after that, he called again: "Kim, it's 6:36. Now I done called three times. You, I mean you can't even explain it, mother. I'm pissed, 'cause I already called you at work, so you're not at fucking work, either!"

And on yet another occasion, Bonds said, "If I don't know where you are, then a niggah's going to kill somebody, good-bye."

Despite it all, there still were moments when Bonds was attentive and kind, as he had been in the old days. One night during spring training in 2001, they went to dinner at Morton's, and afterward the

Arizona sky was lit up with a spectacular desert sunset. "I would love to live here," Bell said, and Bonds replied, "Is that all you want?" Over the next few days he came up with a plan to buy her a house in Scottsdale. Bonds would accumulate the cash from card shows and give it to her in installments until she had enough to make a down payment. Then he would continue to give her money until the house was paid off. She could get a job in Phoenix—or, if that didn't work out, he would pay to send her back to college so she could finish her degree. Bell was dubious: She was making $80,000 per year in Silicon Valley and had no idea how Arizona would work out. But Bonds became insistent, and she agreed to go along. It was a move they both would come to regret.

Chapter 9

Victor Conte's work as a steroid dealer and star-maker began in earnest in the months leading up to the 2000 Summer Olympics. An introduction came through a former Soviet track coach, Remi Korchemny.

As he would later recount it to many newspapers and magazines, Korchemny was the product of a grim childhood. He was born in 1932 in the Ukranian seaport of Odessa to parents who were dedicated Communists. When the boy was five, his father was among a crew of dockworkers accused of counterrevolutionary activities for purposely delaying the unloading of a ship. The men, including Korchemny's father, were executed by a Stalinist firing squad. His mother, a Jew, was imprisoned in a labor camp for refusing to denounce her husband, and the boy went to live with his grandparents. He grew up poor and on the streets, running races against other kids, with bread and sandwiches the winner's prize. That hungry child became an excellent competitive sprinter—his best time was 10.4 seconds in the 100 meters—and an even better coach. At 20, Korchemny was hired at the Soviet Union's Military Sports Institute, where he coached for more than a decade. He trained a teenager named Valery Borzov, who would become the U.S.S.R.'s greatest sprinter.

At the 1972 Olympics in Munich, with Korchemny on hand as a support coach, Borzov became the first European sprinter to win gold medals in both the 100- and 200-meter races. He shared credit for his remarkable double with Korchemny, though the coach downplayed his role.

Three years later, Korchemny was permitted to emigrate to the

United States. He first coached track at Pratt Institute in Brooklyn, then landed a job as a sprint trainer for the NFL's San Francisco 49ers. Two years later, in 1984, he was hired as an assistant track coach at Stanford University. Eventually, he settled in Castro Valley, a suburb in the east San Francisco Bay Area. There he established himself as one of the premier sprint coaches in the U.S., known for his attention to detail and awareness of mechanics, honed through hours of watching video of athletes. Since 1988, at least one of Korchemny's runners had always competed at the Olympics.

"When you find a diamond, you don't know yet if it's a diamond," he told the *San Jose Mercury News* in late 2003. "You have to clean it, polish it, then it looks like a diamond. It's the same in coaching. You have to find someone who has talent to achieve maximum velocity, and then you can develop it."

In 2002, when the aging track coach celebrated his 70th birthday at a restaurant in South San Francisco, a "who's who of elite runners" were among the 150 guests who gathered to help him celebrate, according to an account in *American Track & Field* magazine. Korchemny was presented with a plaque that read: THE GREATEST TRACK COACH OF ALL TIME.

In 1994, Korchemny began training Bill Romanowski, then 28. After six seasons with the 49ers, he had been traded to the Philadelphia Eagles and feared he had lost a step. Korchemny would later say Romo introduced him to Conte in 1997 or 1998. The idea of steroids hardly could have been a new concept to Korchemny, the product of a Soviet athletic system in which steroid use was common. Conte and Korchemny came to work closely together, as the coach embraced the BALCO program of trace-mineral testing, ZMA, steroids, and growth hormone as a route to athletic glory.

The relationship with Korchemny became Conte's entrée into the world of top-level sprinting, which marked a significant step beyond his connections to beefy shot-putters and discus throwers. The sprinters were the showcase athletes of the Olympics, the stars who garnered the bulk of the airtime during the hours upon hours of television coverage.

Apparently through Korchemny, Conte met Chryste Gaines, the

former Stanford sprinter who won a gold medal in the 4 x 100 relay at the 1996 Atlanta games. Later, Korchemny also is thought to have introduced Conte to the Harrison twins, Alvin and Calvin. The 400-meter runners from Salinas, California, had their own tale of tormented youth. The identical twins had been abandoned by their father when they were in high school and later lived for a time in their black Ford Mustang, 6-foot-two Calvin sleeping in the front seat, 6-foot-two Alvin in the back. At the Atlanta games, Alvin Harrison had won a gold medal as part of the U.S. 4 x 400 relay team.

For the 2000 Games in Sydney, Conte said he provided The Clear to both the Harrisons and to Gaines. Doping calendars kept by Conte indicated the Harrisons also were given human growth hormone and the endurance drug EPO.

After Alvin Harrison began receiving drugs from Conte, he told Tim Montgomery about BALCO. Montgomery was already an elite sprinter, a diminutive, confident 25-year-old runner from South Carolina known in track circles as "Tiny Tim." He was a successful relay man but was struggling to break through in the 100 meters. He had failed to qualify for the 2000 Olympics in the 100 and had been unable to break the 10-second barrier during the year. Although he had boasted that he someday would become the fastest man in the world, his career seemed to be spiraling downward.

Montgomery and Harrison had been talking one day in the summer of 2000 about "using people to help them perform better, as far as taking nutrition supplements, to taking steroids, to taking anything." During the conversation, Montgomery said Harrison mentioned "this guy out in California that was doing nutrition supplements."

At the time, Montgomery recently had begun training with Sprint Capitol USA, an elite track club in Raleigh, North Carolina, coached by Trevor Graham. Graham was a former Jamaican runner who had won a silver medal in the 4 x 400 relay at Seoul. He was known as a skilled, fiercely competitive coach, but several athletes he trained had been banned for using steroids, and Graham's explanations were less than convincing. Once, Graham suggested that an athlete had tested positive for steroids because he had taken a hard fall. The jolt had caused excess levels of testosterone to be secreted, Graham said. It was the doping equivalent of catching VD from a toilet seat.

After talking to Harrison, Montgomery decided to call Conte. But in an indication of the paranoia and secretiveness that pervades track and field, he asked Graham to eavesdrop on the conversation. During the call, Conte made his usual sales pitch, suggesting Montgomery should come to California and learn how BALCO could help him reach elite status.

Not long after, Conte phoned Montgomery back. "Your coach is a snake," Conte told the sprinter.

Conte told Montgomery that as soon as their conversation ended, he received a call from Graham, who admitted eavesdropping. Graham introduced himself to Conte as the coach for Marion Jones, the American superstar who would be vying for five gold medals at the Sydney Games, which were then just two months away. Graham told Conte that Montgomery "wasn't a big fish at the moment." The coach wanted Conte to forget about helping Montgomery and aid Jones instead.

Conte had just one problem: He already was supplying steroids and other performance enhancers to Gaines, one of Jones's rivals in the 100 meters. Montgomery would later say that Conte made a side deal to address the problem: Gaines gave Conte permission to work with Jones in exchange for money. "Whatever you charge her, if you give me a cut of it, then I don't mind," Montgomery quoted Gaines as telling Conte.

On September 8, 2000—one week before the opening ceremonies in Sydney—Victor Conte deposited a check for $7,350 from Mjones & Associates.

Marion Jones embodied the Olympic fairy tale.

When she was eight years old, the 1984 Summer Games came to her hometown of Los Angeles. She attended the opening ceremonies at the Coliseum and watched the games on television, and by the end was hooked on track. "My plans for the future are to be in the 1992 Olympics," she wrote the following year in an essay for school. "I've been training a lot, and the boys at my school are good practice." Four years later, when the flamboyant American superstar sprinter Florence Griffith Joyner set two world records and won three gold medals at the Seoul Olympics, Jones went to the chalkboard in her bedroom and wrote, "I want to be an Olympic champion."

By 1992, Jones had established herself as the fastest high school girl in the country. Then just 16, she had finished fifth in the 100 meters at the Olympic Trials. But she passed up a chance to be FloJo's teammate at the Barcelona Games, declining an invitation to be a part of the Americans' 4 x 100 relay team, which went on to win the gold medal. Jones probably would have only run in the qualifying rounds. "I want to have some sweat on my medal when I get one," she said later.

Two months after the Olympic Trials, Jones, then a junior at Thousand Oaks High School, had her first brush with doping controversy when she failed to show up for an out-of-competition drug test and was threatened with a four-year ban from competition. She and her coach argued that they had never been notified of the test, although someone at her coach's workplace had signed for a letter from USA Track & Field. High-powered Los Angeles lawyer Johnnie Cochran got her reinstated.

Sprinting was not Jones's only sport in high school. She was a top-flight basketball player, too, and earned a full scholarship to the University of North Carolina (UNC). There, as a freshman phenomenon, she led the Lady Tar Heels to the 1994 national championship. But when a foot injury from basketball eventually kept her from competing in the 1996 Olympics, she quit the sport to focus on becoming "the fastest woman on the planet," as *Sports Illustrated* later called her.

In 1996, she became engaged to 330-pound shot-put champion C. J. Hunter, a burly, gruff assistant track coach at UNC. When they began dating, Hunter was 26, married with two children, while Jones was a 19-year-old undergraduate. They were an odd couple, called "Beauty and the Beast" by the European media. But Hunter was important to her career. He traveled with her to track meets, found her an agent, and helped her negotiate an endorsement deal with Nike. Hunter also steered Jones to a coach, Trevor Graham, of Sprint Capitol USA. Graham had been an All-American runner at St. Augustine's College in Raleigh, where Hunter had worked as a strength coach.

In public and in a statement given under oath to federal authorities, Graham has insisted that he never gave anybody steroids. But according to Hunter and Montgomery, Graham often gave his athletes banned drugs. Hunter would tell federal investigators that Graham wanted to be viewed as a "drug chemist." Montgomery said that Graham's drug connection was a "heavy-set Mexican guy" in Laredo whose father was a "horse doctor at a university" in Mexico.

With Graham as her coach, Jones had a spectacular year in 1998. She became the fastest woman in the world in the 100 and 200 meters and the first woman in half a century to win the 100, the 200, and the long jump in the same U.S. Championships. Jones won every race she ran in 1998. *Sports Illustrated* estimated she earned $7 million that year in winnings and endorsements. She began to talk about winning five gold medals at the Sydney Games—one each for the 100 meters, the 200 meters, the long jump, and two U.S. relay teams.

In many public statements and under oath, Jones would insist that she has never used banned drugs. But Hunter and Conte have portrayed her as an experienced drug cheat who used an array of undetectable performance-enhancing substances.

Even before he began his association with Conte, Graham had been providing Jones with EPO, according to Hunter. Graham had added the endurance drug to Jones's training regimen to prepare her to compete in five events at the Sydney Games.

After Graham's initial conversation with Conte, the two men quickly established a business relationship and set out to prepare Jones for the Sydney Games. Graham began receiving packages for Jones from Conte containing The Clear, EPO, and human growth hormone, Hunter said. Before the Olympics, Conte said he started providing Jones with steroids and other exotic substances: insulin, growth hormone, EPO, and The Clear, as well as his SNAC nutritional supplements. The drugs were for Jones, Hunter said, and when Conte grew concerned Graham was stockpiling the drugs and giving them to other athletes, Conte sent the drugs directly to Hunter and Jones's home.

Conte used a fake name, Vince Reed, when shipping the illicit drugs, his real name when sending legal ones. Within a four-day period in early September, Hunter received three shipments from "Vince Reed," including one that had "E+G+O" written on the top. Hunter later said that he didn't know what the "O" stood for, but "E" represented EPO, and "G" was for growth hormone. Hunter also said Jones received insulin from Conte.

Hunter said Jones ingested The Clear by using a syringe to place a couple of drops under her tongue. Growth hormone and EPO were administered via injection. Hunter said at first he injected his wife with EPO because she was squeamish about doing it herself. He also said they brought drugs to Sydney but were careful not to have Jones carry them herself. Instead, Hunter gave the growth hormone and The Clear to Graham, who carried the drugs through customs in his bags. The Clear, per Conte's instructions, was hidden inside a container for flaxseed oil, a legal supplement.

Hunter said he watched Jones inject herself with drugs at the residence they shared in Australia. After an injection, Jones would flush the syringe down the toilet. The steroids caused Jones to break out in acne, Hunter said. To hide it, she began wearing makeup, something she had never done before.

Conte also appeared to be pre-testing Jones to ensure she wouldn't fail a drug test at the Games. According to BALCO documents, a urine sample from Jones was sent by overnight mail to Quest Laboratories in San Diego two days before the Opening Ceremonies.

Jones did not get her five gold medals in Sydney, but she won the prestigious 100–200 double. The races were not even close—she won the 100 by five meters and .37 seconds, the widest margin since the Olympics began using electronic timing in 1968. She also won a gold medal in the 4 x 400 relay and bronze medals in the 4 x 100 relay and the long jump. It was the greatest performance by a woman track athlete in Olympic history, and she emerged as the darling of the Games.

But there was trouble. Unbeknownst to Jones, her husband had repeatedly tested positive for steroids before the Olympics. Hunter had qualified for the Summer Games with a personal-best mark of 71 feet, 9 inches in the shot put. But in August, he was confronted by two officials from the International Association of Athletics Federations, track and field's international governing body, who informed him of the drug test results. As Hunter later said, the track officials offered to cover up his positive tests if he would agree to fake an injury. They wanted to avoid a scandal on the eve of the Olympics, Hunter said.

Hunter insisted he had not used steroids, and Graham suggested he call Conte for guidance. Conte in turn consulted Patrick Arnold, the Illinois chemist who had invented The Clear. "I need your help and this MUST be kept very confidential," Conte e-mailed Arnold on August 23. "A certain shot putter (yes, the husband of the world's fastest female runner) just tested positive for a metabolite of nandrolone called norandrosterone." Conte explained that if Hunter didn't come up with a valid explanation quickly, he would be banned. If that happened, Conte wrote, "This is going to be a huge story!"

In e-mails, Conte and Arnold speculated that Hunter had been sabotaged. But on September 11, four days before the Opening Ceremonies, Hunter announced he was withdrawing from the Games, citing a knee injury. He said he did not tell Jones about the positive test, reasoning that the last thing she needed was to be distracted as she prepared to compete.

But two days after Jones won her first medal, the 100-meter gold, Hunter's positive drug test was revealed in a page-one story in the *Sydney Daily Telegraph*. Later reports said he had tested positive not just once but four separate times in 1999. On September 26, the day after the story broke, Hunter held a press conference in a hotel ballroom to defend himself. Jones, composed as always, was there to support Hunter. "Aside from him being an athlete," she told reporters, "he is my husband."

Then she gave Hunter a kiss and left. Hunter blamed a tainted supplement for the test results, then started crying. "I might not be the most agreeable guy, some might say I'm downright mean," he said. "But no one can say I don't love my wife and kids. I would never do anything to jeopardize their opinion of me." Lawyer Johnnie Cochran, who eight years earlier had helped Jones with her missed-test problem, and who now was famous for winning the O. J. Simpson murder case, stood on the side during the press conference. As Hunter began to cry, Cochran nodded, and a mustached man with wire-rim glasses who was sitting next to the shot putter began to speak. It was Conte. At first he was identified as a doctor, then as a nutritionist working with some Olympians competing in Sydney.

Conte challenged the test results. The International Olympic Committee's chief medical officer had stated that Hunter's urine sample contained 1,000 times the permitted level of nandrolone, but

Conte insisted his own examination showed only "trace" amounts of the steroid. Hunter had innocently taken an iron supplement tainted with steroids, Conte claimed. Poor quality control by the manufacturer could have caused the positive result.

"We have a lot of data that strongly indicates C. J. was not using the anabolic steroid nandrolone," Conte said.

To buttress his case, Conte dialed in R. C. (Craig) Kammerer, a former assistant director at the UCLA Olympic Analytical Laboratory, on a speaker phone. Kammerer initially said Conte's claim of a tainted supplement seemed valid. But when he learned during the press conference there were *four* positive tests, Kammerer admitted he hadn't actually seen all the data. "Without all the information, this is guesswork," he said, and the line went dead.

When confronted by federal agents four years later, Hunter would maintain his innocence. He said the only time he used steroids was in 2001, after he retired. He said he used them to lose weight and he got them from Conte.

Jones wasn't distracted by her husband's problems. She won four medals after Hunter's crisis, and she left Sydney as the world's most famous female athlete. She cruised the talk-show circuit, from David Letterman to Rosie O'Donnell, and entertained a stream of endorsement offers. And she continued to receive banned drugs from Victor Conte, according to Conte and Hunter.

Meanwhile, during his time in Sydney, Conte had gotten to know Montgomery. Conte brought The Clear with him to Sydney, and Montgomery had helped Conte gain access to the heavily guarded athletes' village to see two clients, sprinters Chryste Gaines and Alvin Harrison. Montgomery even gave Conte tickets to events. Conte later claimed he gave The Clear to Montgomery in Sydney, while the sprinter maintained they only talked about it. Either way, Conte worked on Montgomery, telling him, "Watch the 100 meters. Watch what Chryste [is] gonna do. Watch what Alvin [is] going to do in the 400. And watch what Marion [is] going to do. You will see how powerful it is."

Harrison took the silver in the 400 meters, and he and his twin, Calvin, also won gold in the 4 x 400–meter relay. Gaines won a bronze medal on the 4 x 100 relay team with Jones. Montgomery left Sydney knowing that he had a new man in his corner, providing new hope for his career.

"Okay, I'm going to help you out," Conte told him. They planned to get together back in the States.

Six weeks after the Closing Ceremonies in Sydney, Victor Conte convened a steroid summit at BALCO. Emboldened by Jones's rise to stardom and his other successes at Sydney, Conte now had new ambitions. As usual, they were not modest: He wanted to alter the course of sports history. By deploying the world's most advanced training regimens—and the world's most effective drugs—Conte believed he could transform a promising American sprinter into the world's fastest man.

The subject of the experiment was 5-foot-9 "Tiny Tim" Montgomery. He was highly motivated. Conte quoted the sprinter as saying that if he won the gold medal in the 100 meters, "it would not matter if I died on the other side of the finish line."

Conte invited three men with reputations as anabolic experts to the meeting. From Canada came Charlie Francis, the renegade coach who had administered the steroids that made Ben Johnson the fastest man in the world at Seoul and then wrecked his career. From Southern California there was Milos "The Mind" Sarcev, the weight trainer who was unafraid to experiment with untested drugs and who had almost killed himself with the synthol injection. And in from North Carolina, arriving a day after Montgomery, was Sprint Capitol USA's Trevor Graham, coach of both Montgomery and Jones. The men gathered in the lobby of a hotel near the airport and got a ride to BALCO in Conte's Mercedes. They went to work in a conference room, at a table where caps and T-shirts with the ZMA logo lay scattered about.

A poster on the wall quoted Albert Einstein: "Great spirits have always encountered violent opposition from mediocre minds." Conte gave each man a black T-shirt that read PROJECT WORLD RECORD.

It was a brainstorming session, Graham later said. Francis outlined his ideas concerning the biomechanics of sprinting, his theories of stride and motion. He passed out data sheets and wrote notes on a whiteboard. Graham was unimpressed: He whispered to Montgomery that he already knew this stuff. Francis asked Graham to detail Montgomery's present training regimen. Conte and Montgomery seemed bored and ducked in and out. When Conte was in the room, he pressed Francis about the importance of weight training. Graham thought the repeated queries about pumping iron got on Charlie the Chemist's nerves. Finally, everyone went to the BALCO weight room because Sarcev wanted to see how much Montgomery could bench-press.

Graham would be guarded in his statement later to federal agents, portraying himself as a curious outsider, present at the summit to protect his relationship with Montgomery. Nobody talked about drugs, he said.

Conte would describe a far more structured meeting at which drugs were the unifying theme. He said they reviewed videotape and photos of Montgomery in action, dissecting his stride and routine. Francis was assigned to design a new track workout program for Montgomery. Graham would make sure it was followed. Sarcev would supervise the sprinter's weight training. Conte would manage Montgomery's "pharmacology and nutrition program"—a euphemism for steroids and supplements. Montgomery especially needed help in that area, Conte said.

BALCO's tests revealed that Montgomery was an out-of-control juicer. "You're oversaturated with performance-enhancing drugs," Conte told him. Project World Record would take care of that. After the summit, Conte put Montgomery on a cycle of performance enhancers, including The Clear and human growth hormone, Montgomery would later admit. He insisted he was told that The Clear was not a steroid but a legal alternative.

He claimed he declined to use EPO because he had heard it could cause a heart attack and he had a small heart murmur. He and Conte quarreled over using insulin. Montgomery feared it would bring on diabetes.

"You know what, you going to kill a lot of people," Montgomery said he told Conte. "I don't give a fuck," Conte allegedly replied.

Montgomery claimed he didn't like The Clear, either, saying it caused muscular tightness and water retention, and that his results using it were "horrible." That part of Montgomery's story seemed improbable, given that he used The Clear continuously for eight months and he ran faster than ever before while using the substance.

Conte sent Montgomery the drugs using the fake name "Vince Reed," the one Conte employed with Marion Jones and others. Montgomery also said Conte sent The Clear in flaxseed oil to conceal what it was. The sprinter referred to the substance as "the magic potion." Conte said he had Montgomery cocktailing The Clear, growth hormone, insulin, EPO, and adrenaline, and doping calendars supported Conte's account. Although he denied taking other drugs, Montgomery admitted to knowing the alphabetized code Conte used on the calendars.

After the summit at BALCO, Montgomery underwent a startling transformation. By Conte's account, he gained 28 pounds of muscle in only eight weeks. "Tiny Tim" was no more. He was replaced by a compact, ripped, fire hydrant of a man. On March 24, Montgomery signed a contract to run with the ZMA Track Club, a Conte creation to promote his line of nutritional supplements. According to a 2001 filing with USA Track & Field, the ZMA Track Club consisted of Montgomery, Gaines, Calvin Harrison, and the shot putter Kevin Toth. The deal was straightforward: The athletes would wear gear with the ZMA logo and give interviews about the benefits of the supplement. What was unstated in the agreement was that Conte would provide them with performance-enhancing drugs.

On June 22, 2001, wearing ZMA Track Club uniforms, Montgomery and Gaines won the men's and women's 100-meter titles at the U.S. Championships in Eugene, Oregon. Montgomery's winning time was 9.95 seconds, one of six races during the year in which he broke the 10-second barrier. Not only had Montgomery won the American title using Conte's arsenal of banned substances, he also received a letter from the U.S. Anti-Doping Agency congratulating him on providing a clean test sample after his race. The letter reinforced Conte's belief that beating the testers was like "taking candy from a baby." And it strengthened his conviction that in the cat-and-mouse game of the testers versus the cheaters, there was no more elusive mouse than Victor Conte.

A month later, Montgomery won again at the Bislett Games in Oslo, Norway; his 9.84-second dash was the third fastest 100 meters in history. He won that race with shoes borrowed from Marion Jones, his training partner. By the end of the track season, Montgomery was ranked second in the world in the 100 meters. The year before, he hadn't even been in the top five in the United States.

"Now I have started taking sports seriously," Montgomery told reporters after his victory at the Bislett Games. "This is the kind of result you get when you put in work and hit the weight room."

Montgomery returned to BALCO in 2001 to see Conte, and Francis came down from Canada to supervise a workout at least once. While at BALCO, Montgomery testified he would sit around and pretend to read a magazine while listening to Conte make business calls. He found Conte talkative and boastful, not discreet about the illicit side of his business. Montgomery said Conte showed him a locker in his weight room where he stored such traditional steroids as Winstrol.

"He said that he's ready for anyone," Montgomery would say later. "He can take on any client that he pleases. [He's] got everything. There's nothing he can't get."

Montgomery learned, too, about the role of former BALCO medical director Dr. Brian Goldman, the psychiatrist who had become a BALCO "consultant." Montgomery began laughing when asked whether Goldman had actually consulted with any athletes. He said Conte simply phoned Goldman when he needed to get a prescription drug for an athlete, and Goldman would take care of it. Once, Montgomery said he overheard Conte tell Goldman he needed Clomid, a female fertility drug used to help mask steroid use. The drug was for Montgomery, but Conte had Goldman write the prescription in a fake woman's name so as not to raise suspicions.

In guarded terms, Conte also discussed the inventor of the "magic potion." Conte wouldn't use Patrick Arnold's name with Montgomery, instead calling him "The Clear Guy." Conte suggested that Montgomery would be wise to stick with him so he could continue getting The Clear. Conte said The Clear Guy was making the drug for several Greek athletes, and no other "100-meter sprinter would be able to get it except for the athletes in Greece." In 2004, Athens would host the Games, and everyone believed the Greeks were drug cheats.

Conte, naturally, had made it a point to keep connected with Patrick Arnold. Early in the year, Arnold apparently provided Conte a new version of The Clear. "What I am sending you today is a small sample, about 5 ccs, of the supplement," Arnold e-mailed to Conte on February 9. He wrote he had "made" very little of the drug, but there "should be enough for experimental testing. 2.5–7.5 milligram (whatever that comes out to in cc's or drops), under the tongue should be a decent dosing range."

Like Montgomery, Marion Jones continued to use banned drugs in 2001, according to accounts by Conte and Hunter, and BALCO documents with her name on them. On April 21, 2001, Conte said he met with Jones at an Embassy Suites hotel in Covina in Southern California. Jones came to his room so he could show her how to inject growth hormone with a new instrument, a $1,000 NovoPen injector. Conte said he watched Jones inject 4.5 units of Growth into her quadriceps.

Jones was careless about her drug kit, Conte claimed. In May, she forgot an injector at a hotel in Canada and had to go back and get it. A few days later, he said she left the same injector in another room, this time with a "thousand dollars' worth of growth hormone in it!"

The doping calendars laid out, via Conte's alphabetical code, Jones's use of The Clear, EPO, Growth, and insulin. For example, calendars from March and April indicated a plan to start regular use of EPO, The Clear, and growth hormone in the buildup to the April 22 Mt. SAC Relays, where Jones was scheduled to open her outdoor season. She intended to break the 17-year-old record in the 300 meters at Mt. SAC, but her winning time fell .22 seconds short.

In May, the month of Jones's photo shoot for *FLEX* in Raleigh, the calendars reflected continued use of EPO, The Clear, and growth hormone. In June, during the ramp-up to the U.S. Championships in Eugene, the schedule added daily doses of "I," code for insulin. On June 24, the day she won the 200 meters in Eugene, the calendar directed Jones to take insulin, growth hormone, and The Clear.

Jones finished the track season ranked No. 1 in the world in both the 100 and 200 meters. By then, Jones's marriage to Hunter was ending. They had separated—they would divorce in 2002—though, as evidenced by the May photo shoot for *FLEX*, they still worked together sometimes. The relationship had been stressed by Hunter's failed drug test, and stressed further because Jones suspected Hunter was having an affair with another Sprint Capitol USA runner, Michelle Collins. Hunter said he only wrote poetry for Collins and kissed her. Graham said he kicked Collins out of his camp to ease the friction after Jones complained about the (suspected) affair.

Jones turned to Montgomery during this time. She and Montgomery were training partners, and soon sportswriters were already referring to them as "The World's Fastest Couple." Their relationship with Conte was disintegrating, too, partly over money. Conte claimed Montgomery owed him $25,000; Montgomery said Conte had agreed to forgive the debt if the sprinter would wear his ZMA uniform during the U.S. Championships.

There was another issue. Nobody involved in doping wanted attention drawn to what was going on behind the scenes in elite track and field. Conte, the athletes had realized, talked too much and craved too much attention. By the fall, Montgomery and Jones no longer were doing business with Conte. The breakup was bitter—and would come back to haunt all involved.

Chapter 10

Victor Conte's version of the Tim Montgomery breakup went like this: Montgomery was "a punk," an ungrateful nobody who wouldn't even pay his bills after Conte made him into a great runner. Conte decided that he would have the last word—he would create a sprinter even better than Montgomery.

He settled on Dwain Chambers, 23, a British runner whom he met in January 2002 in Miami.

Chambers told reporters he came to America to train under Remi Korchemny, hoping the legendary coach could help boost his sagging career. Actually, Chambers came to the U.S. to get on Victor Conte's program, according to a track-and-field source with intimate knowledge of the BALCO operation.

Like Montgomery when he first met Conte, Chambers was struggling. Chambers was from North London, and he had been European Junior Champion in the 100 meters in 1995, when he was 17. He won bronze at the 1999 World Championships and placed fourth at the Olympics in Sydney. But he fell back to fifth at the Worlds in 2001 and after that was regularly beaten, particularly by the American runner Maurice Greene, the world record holder, and the fast-rising Montgomery. Chambers decided to come to the U.S. to take one last shot before quitting track entirely.

He moved to the San Francisco Peninsula town of Millbrae, about two miles down the road from BALCO. He began working out with Korchemny and soon was listed as a member of Conte's ZMA Track Club. By April 2002, Chambers was taking more than 50 supplements per day, including ZMA, and he said each pill had a specific role to enhance his training.

"I didn't realize what was going on with the guys in the U.S., what was making them run fast," he told the *Oakland Tribune*. ". . . Based on sheer talent, that can only take you so far. My eyes have been opened to what you need to do."

The British runner had become convinced that he needed banned drugs. Conte said that he put Chambers on "the full enchilada": The Clear, insulin, EPO, growth hormone, and, later, The Cream and a new stimulant, modafinil. At least once, Chambers appeared to pay Conte for drugs. On August 22, 2002, Conte's personal bank account received a $1,980 deposit via international wire from Chambers.

Chambers's transformation was soon underway. Initially, Chambers gave credit to Conte.

"Victor Conte trained Marion Jones to be world and Olympic champion and I'm in better shape now than ever," he told the London tabloid *News of the World* on June 16, 2002. ". . . I could be on top of the world by the end of the year. A lot of the credit has to go to Victor. I'm ready to take on the best. There's nobody I fear."

Two weeks later, at the Bislett Games in Oslo, Chambers beat the Americans' one-two punch of Greene and Montgomery. Greene finished second and said of Chambers, "He was just better than me." Montgomery was never in the race and took third. For Conte, it was a vindicating moment; it showed Montgomery precisely who was boss. Chambers, in the glow of his victory, credited Korchemny. "I've found extra horsepower under Remi," he told reporters.

Two days later, Chambers blew Greene away again at a meet in England. Then, on August 7, Britain's fastest man blazed to the European Championship in a record time of 9.96 seconds. The event was held at the Munich Olympiastadion, where another of Remi Korchemny's protégés, the great Soviet sprinter Valery Borzov, had stood atop the Olympic medal stand in 1972. Borzov attended the race and presented Chambers with his gold medal.

"Now go out there and try to bring back the Olympic gold to Europe," Borzov told Chambers.

By September, Chambers had defeated Greene five times in six races, and his fiercest rival became Montgomery. It was Victor Conte's old creation versus his new one.

The showdown came on September 14, 2002 at the Grand Prix Final in Paris. Greene watched from the stands, sidelined by fatigue, but Chambers was ready. He ran an outstanding race, clocking the fastest time of his life, 9.87, matching the European record set nine years before by his boyhood hero, British sprinter Linford Christie.

But Montgomery was even better. Taking advantage of a superb start and propelled by a brisk tailwind, Montgomery flew down the track in 9.78 seconds, faster than any man before him—including the drug cheat Ben Johnson, whose time in the infamous race in Seoul had been 9.79. Project World Record had been completed, but in a way that was bitterly disappointing to Conte. A year after leaving BALCO, Montgomery was the World's Fastest Man. The victory earned him $250,000—$100,000 for the record, $100,000 for the Grand Prix overall title, and $50,000 for the Grand Prix 100-meter season title.

The aftermath of the race was dramatic as well. Montgomery's coach, Trevor Graham, ran onto the track and hoisted Montgomery in his arms in celebration. But Montgomery believed Graham had disrespected him for years, and the resentment spilled out. Montgomery told his coach that he had nothing to do with the world record, that the credit belonged to Charlie Francis, the renegade Canadian doping expert. Graham retorted sarcastically that he hoped Montgomery would pass the drug test, and the sprinter said he would pass with "flying colors." According to the account of Marion Jones, Montgomery's girlfriend, Graham let go of the new World champion and he landed heavily, twisting his ankle.

By then, Jones was on the track, and the couple embraced and kissed. After the victory lap, they walked hand-in-hand to the press area. Montgomery was euphoric, but he seemed more caught up in his rivalry with the British sprinter than in his record.

"My goal today was to show everyone by how far I could beat Dwain," he said. ". . . I had no time objective, I just wanted to beat Chambers."

But the press wanted to talk about the record, and soon the shining moment was hit with a dose of reality. A reporter asked Montgomery if he had been watching on TV when Ben Johnson broke the world record in 1988.

Seemingly oblivious to the subtext of the question, Montgomery responded, "No, the first track meet I ever watched was in 1993."

Jones, though, defended her boyfriend against implications he had come by the record through drug use. "It's unfortunate that you have such an incredible performance and someone will immediately suspect something," she said. "We're all quite aware that we are proponents of a drug-free sport, so let's keep it at that."

For a while, Montgomery was the most celebrated man in track. A month later, after appearing on David Letterman and the *Today* show, Montgomery returned to Norfolk, Virginia. He had landed there in 1994, when he was still "Tiny Tim" and Norfolk State was the only college to offer him a track scholarship. Eight years later, the city was holding a ceremony to honor him. In his speech that day, Montgomery said he was still grasping his accomplishment. When he looked in the mirror, he said he found it difficult to believe that "of all the bodies made by God, this is the fastest in history."

Chambers was devastated by his loss in Paris. "I am traumatized by what Tim did, completely traumatized," he said. But three months later, he had steadied himself and resolved that Montgomery's record would be short-lived. He vowed to break it himself in 2003. Not long after that, he e-mailed Conte.

"i thank you for Giving me knowledge about life in Track and Field," he wrote. "And for what its worth i thank you for taking me under your wings and supporting me."

By then, Conte had had another promising sprinter as a doping client. She was Zhanna Block, a Ukranian 100-meter runner who had handed the great Marion Jones her only defeat in 2001, ending a four-year winning streak that spanned 71 races. Block lived in Johnson City, Tennessee, where she was managed by her husband, Mark Block, a former coach at East Tennessee State University.

Via e-mail, Mark Block gave Conte feedback about his wife's reaction to the drug regimen. In February 2002, he wrote that she would get "tight" if she used The Cream and The Clear just before a race, and she felt "bloated for a day or two" after using the drugs. While Conte supplied Zhanna Block with The Clear and The Cream, Mark Block provided Conte with a substance called ATP that he had obtained in Russia. Adenosine triphosphate is a molecule involved in providing energy in the body. Conte discovered that taking synthetic ATP could increase speed and stamina, but the drug wasn't readily available in the U.S.

Conte still had his hand in the power Olympic events, too. He was providing growth hormone, The Clear, and The Cream to Kevin Toth, the 35-year-old shot-putter from Ohio. Toth was a mountain of a man, 6 feet 4 inches, 295 pounds and, like many athletes who showed up at Conte's door, his career was in decline. Toth hadn't cracked the top 10 since 1999. The Victor Conte program reversed his fortunes.

Before the June 2002 U.S. Championships, Toth described his doping plan to Conte in a handwritten note:

> Vic How does this look up to the Nationals
> 40 c is clear
> 25 g is growth
> 2 cases of cream
> 3 week on 1 week off
> 3 weeks on 2 weeks off before Nationals

Bank records show Conte deposited four checks from Toth worth $1,230 in the first five months of the year. The shot-putter also wrote Conte a check for $2,100 in June 2000.

Toth placed third at the 2002 nationals and continued to improve. By the end of the year, Toth, once seemingly at the tail end of his career, was ranked second in the world, and his success had emboldened him. He talked as though his career resurgence had been achieved without drugs, and he even criticized shot-put champion C. J. Hunter for using steroids, saying his failed drug test had hurt the image of their sport: "That killed us. That deflated the balloon, the excitement. Nobody wants to have throwers in their meet that could possibly test positive."

Conte was also providing at least The Clear and the stimulant modafinil to Regina Jacobs, America's top middle-distance runner. Many in track and field had long suspected that the former Stanford

University star was a drug cheat, but she had eluded detection. In 2000, she had withdrawn suddenly from the Sydney Games three weeks before the Opening Ceremonies, shortly *after* the International Olympic Committee announced it had approved a new test to detect EPO, the endurance drug. The withdrawal deepened suspicions about Jacobs, but the suspicions didn't slow her down.

At the U.S. Championships at Stanford in June 2002, she beat her longtime rival Suzy Favor Hamilton in the 1,500 meters to win her eighth national title in nine years. In February, 2003, at age 39, she set the indoor world record in the 1,500 meters at the Boston Indoor Games, becoming the first woman to break four minutes indoors in the event and winning a $25,000 bonus prize.

After setting the mark, Jacobs sent a handwritten note to Conte in which she alluded to providing him with a little something extra for his assistance:

> *Victor,*
> *Thank you for the help at nationals!*
> *Regina*
> *P.S. A bonus from "Team Jacobs" to "Team Balco."*

Like Kevin Toth, Jacobs was emboldened by her late-career success. Asked how a runner who was nearly 40 could set world records, she didn't mention drugs. Instead, she said, "This isn't old. [If] you have heart, age doesn't matter."

Jacobs was coached by her husband, Tom Craig. Like Zhanna Block's husband, Craig often e-mailed Conte about performance-enhancing drugs. Some e-mails from 2002 reflect Conte's experiments with modafinil—"vitamin S," he called it—as he considered adding it to his regimen. The drug was a central nervous system stimulant used to treat sleep disorders, including narcolepsy and sleep apnea. Conte believed Olympic doping authorities didn't test for it, and he had begun giving it to runners to see if it would enhance their performance.

Conte had anecdotal proof the drug worked. On June 11, 2002, Remi Korchemny took Alvin Harrison to the track at Stanford and gave the sprinter a dose of modafinil before his workout. Conte had advised Korchemny that Harrison should wait an hour after taking the little white pill before beginning to warm up, but Harrison was champing at the bit within 45 minutes. Korchemny cut him loose to do a test 400 meters, and the coach reported to Conte that Harrison ran like "crazy." Korchemny had expected Harrison to run the distance in 45.70 seconds, but instead he was timed in 44.78.

Conte sent an e-mail to Craig and Jacobs recounting Harrison's test run on modafinil that same day. Then he sent a follow-up a few hours later saying he had shipped them the "S" supplement and it would arrive the next day. "We finally got the green light from the testing lab today," Conte wrote. "All six subjects got a clean bill of health. It is time to 'rock and roll.' Best Regards, Victor."

"Wow," Craig replied. "Can't wait to try it at Saturday workout." And the next day, when the shipment arrived, Craig sent a confirmation: "The Eagle has landed."

Once he knew modafinil worked, Conte sought a reliable connection for the drug. A contact came through Patrick Arnold, the Illinois chemist who had given him The Clear. On June 19, Conte began to exchange e-mails with Miles Werre, an associate of Arnold's who worked at a pharmacy in Houston. Conte sent Werre e-mail queries about Provigil, the brand name for modafinil, as well as EPO, growth hormone, and Viagra. (Erectile dysfunction is a side effect of steroid use.) Werre also played a role in the creation of The Cream: Conte shipped testosterone cream and epitestosterone cream to Werre, who mixed the substances to create the undetectable steroid.

Conte also used Korchemny to prospect for new drugs. The coach was with Chambers and others on the European circuit, and Conte wanted him to track down a new form of EPO called Dynepo. "It is undetectable at the moment because it contains only human cells and not animal cells, which are detectable," Conte wrote. ". . . Please keep this information confidential. Looking forward to your response. Best wishes, Victor."

Conte sent a similar query about Dynepo to Andreas Linardatos, a Greek track coach he knew through Korchemny. "Do not be too specific in your response," Conte wrote. "Just say either available or not."

Korchemny had urged Conte to help Linardatos start a business in Greece selling ZMA and other SNAC products. Linardatos was well connected and could prove useful when Conte visited Greece in 2004 for the Olympics. Eventually, Linardatos registered three Web sites to distribute ZMA. In exchange, Linardatos began receiving performance-enhancing drugs for the athletes he coached.

Conte was in action constantly, sending e-mails to coaches, trainers, athletes, and drug connections, seeking and selling drugs and advising on their use. In July, at the same time he was working to get his hands on the new version of EPO, Conte had to advise an alarmed Korchemny, who believed Alvin Harrison was overdosing on EPO. Conte knew this was a problem with Harrison, and he warned Korchemny to monitor the sprinter's drug use, writing on July 13, 2002, that "Alvin has a tendency to want to over do the E. This does make me concerned."

Korchemny reported that Harrison had taken more than twice the maximum dosage recommended for a week, three injections over a five-day span. But, he noted, "Today feels great. Eats lots of food, and also sleeps well. What can we do?"

Conte told Korchemny to make sure Harrison was well hydrated because the danger in EPO was that it thickened the blood. "The way to prevent any type of blood clot is to dilute the blood with water," wrote Conte. "There is no reason to be alarmed. Alvin will be ok."

The next day, Harrison won the 400 meters at the DN Galan Grand Prix meet in Stockholm, setting a stadium record with his time of 44.57 seconds.

In August, Conte had a much more significant issue to deal with: He became convinced that The Clear had been discovered by drug testers. By then, Patrick Arnold's norbolethone had been abandoned as The Clear of choice, replaced by a new substance that Arnold was providing to Conte and others.

But a tip persuaded Conte that the new Clear had been identified. By e-mail, he warned his clients to cease using it immediately. Conte knew track and field was a backstabbing, cutthroat world, and he feared that his enemies—like Tim Montgomery and Trevor Graham—had reported him to Olympic authorities. Dwain Chambers and

Zhanna Block—Conte's athletes—were on their way to becoming the best sprinters in the world, and this was the only way his enemies could stop them.

He laid out his theory to Linardatos in an August 20 e-mail with the subject line, "headsup." Montgomery, Graham, and John Smith, the coach of Maurice Greene, had sent a sample of The Clear to the testers anonymously, Conte claimed. The sample would enable authorities to test for The Clear. "Apparently, Trevor and company saw the performances of Zhana [sic] and Dwain and realized that money was getting ready to be taken from Marion, Tim and Maurice and they became desperate," Conte wrote. "This is why it is so important to work only with athletes that can be trusted."

Conte suggested Linardatos forward the warning to Christos Tzekos, the coach of Kostas Kenteris and Katerina Thanou, the two best sprinters Greece had ever produced. Conte knew that Tzekos was getting The Clear directly from Patrick Arnold, and Conte wanted to make sure Tzekos's athletes didn't test positive.

Tzekos had long been the subject of doping rumors, suspected of hiding his athletes from drug testers and holding them out of meets to avoid being caught. He had once been suspended from track for two years for manhandling a drug tester who had come to his training camp in Germany to collect samples from three athletes. While Tzekos kept the tester at bay, the athletes escaped, not even bothering to check out of their hotel rooms. At Sydney, the stunning success of Kenteris, who won gold in the 200 meters, and Thanou, who won silver in the 100 behind Marion Jones, increased the suspicions about Tzekos and drugs. If Kenteris or Thanou were to test positive, Arnold might be implicated, Conte thought.

"The good news is that we got the headsup in time to prevent any positive tests," he wrote to Linardatos.

Within 10 days, the storm had passed. It was a false alarm. On August 30, Conte sent word via e-mail to many of his clients. The subject line read: "Good news." The coast was clear, but the relief would be short-lived.

Chapter 11

I f the pitch were three inches outside the strike zone, Barry Bonds
would ignore it and work another base on balls. He would draw
177 walks in the summer of 2001, enough to break the mark of
170 set by Babe Ruth in 1923. But if the pitch were located where he
could drive it—and in 2001, that seemed to be anywhere in the strike
zone—he would take a rip. Sometimes it was a sudden vicious upper-
cut, in which he appeared to throw every ounce of the 230 pounds of
muscle he now carried on his frame into pulverizing the ball. On
other occasions, he looked as though he were merely flicking the end
of the bat at the pitch, like a fisherman making a cast.

If he hit the ball squarely, and that season it seemed he almost always hit it squarely, Bonds would toss his maple bat aside and saunter
two or three steps down the first-base line while he watched the ball
sail out of sight—over the fence, out of the park, into San Francisco
Bay. Only then would he begin the slow jog around the bases, often
with a blank look on his face, occasionally with a slight smile.

If he hit a milestone home run—and that season he hit many of
them—he might throw his arms up like a football official signaling a
touchdown before he started his home run trot. Often when he
crossed home plate, he pointed both hands skyward and raised his
eyes, in what he described to interviewers as a tribute to God. If the
home run was special enough, he might come out of the dugout, doff
his cap, and take a curtain call. There were many curtain calls that
summer, as Barry Bonds—systematically, methodically, and with little
suspense—obliterated baseball's single-season home run record, which
had seemed so enduring just three years before.

The fans turned out for Bonds. They took his snapshot with their point-and-shoot cameras, so that when he came to bat in a night game the stands rippled with the tiny explosions of flashbulbs. They gave him standing ovations at the right times. In the bleachers and in kayaks on the Bay, they would race to recover his home run balls. But there was a muted feel to baseball's reaction to Bonds's home run march, a sense of anticlimax. It simply wasn't as big a deal as it had been in 1998 when McGwire was breaking a 37-year-old record and saving the sport besides.

There were many possible explanations for the tepid response to a ballplayer having the greatest offensive season in the history of the game. The explanations began with the image of Bonds himself. After some initial reluctance, Bonds had agreed to continue trying to be fan-friendly in 2001, but his reputation for surly self-absorption was still proving hard to overcome. Although the press coverage was usually positive, he just wasn't popular with fans outside San Francisco. Perhaps, as Bonds himself would say, the reaction to his achievement was muted because he was a black man in a white man's game, and the fans always would be happier when a McGwire or some other Great White Hope was at center stage.

Bonds's appearance—and the way it had morphed over the years—also proved unsettling to some fans. Although McGwire had bulked up, he already was a big man when he hit 49 home runs as an A's rookie in 1987. Mac was still recognizable 11 years later on the Cardinals. But the Barry Bonds of 2001 didn't look anything like the lithe, young Pirate who used to knock the ball into the gap, accelerate as he took the turn at first base, and fly into second for a double. Actually, with his massive, pumped-up musculature, his shaven head, his fierce game face, and the diamond earring dangling from his left ear, the Bonds of 2001 didn't look like any baseball player you had ever seen. Bonds looked like a WWE wrestler, or a toy superhuman action figure, but not a ballplayer. Even the sound of the ball coming off his bat was different—harsher, almost metallic. People around the team would say they knew without looking when Bonds was taking batting practice.

But perhaps what gave the most pause about Bonds's march was that it was occurring so soon after McGwire's. Baseball records were supposed to last, particularly ones as momentous and defining as the single-season home run mark. Now something different and unsettling seemed to be going on with baseball—or with the men who played it. Rather than evoking the history of the game and its limitless future, Bonds's relentless home run march suggested that the game being played on the modern diamond wasn't baseball at all, at least in the way it had long been known.

The numbers suggested that as well. Roger Maris broke Babe Ruth's mark and set the modern record for home runs with 61 in 1961. From then through 1988—the year that Jose Canseco, baseball's self-proclaimed steroids pioneer, was American League MVP—only four players would hit 50 homers in a season, about one every four years. But from 1989 through 2001, when Bonds hit 73 to break the record, players hit 50 or more home runs in a season on 15 occasions. That was an average of one per year. And on six of those 15 occasions, players not only broke the 50-home run barrier, they had also surpassed Maris's mark by hitting more than 61. The Cubs' Sammy Sosa hit more than 61 three times but never won a home run title. McGwire did it twice, and now Bonds was doing it as well.

The milestones fell away. On April 17, Bonds hit his 500th career home run, a splash hit that gave the Giants a win over the Dodgers, his fifth home run in five days. The fans gave Bonds a standing ovation, but there was awkwardness at home plate. Only a batgirl and shortstop Rich Aurilia, who had scored ahead of him, were waiting to greet him. The rest of the team stayed in the dugout as the club brought out Willie Mays, Willie McCovey, and Bonds's parents for a nine-minute ceremony at home plate. Bonds was on a tear. He hit six home runs in six games in April, and did it again in May. By June 1, he had 29 home runs.

On June 22, the Giants traveled to St. Louis for a three-game series that underscored the changed fortunes of Bonds and McGwire. The Cardinals took two of the three games, and McGwire hit a two-run shot in game one, but it was a far cry from 1998. McGwire's body had begun breaking down from weight training and steroids. The home run was only his seventh of the season, and he would finish

2001 with a freak-show batting line: an average of .187 with 29 home runs. Of his 56 hits, more than half were home runs.

Bonds was now the focus of baseball's attention, trailed by a growing media entourage. He arrived in St. Louis with 38 home runs. In the second game of the series he hit number 39, a shot that bounced off a pillar underpinning the right-field stands at Busch Stadium. As they had since the barrage had begun, the press pack wanted Bonds to discuss his incredible power, to explain how he was managing to hit the ball so hard this year. As usual, he wouldn't be drawn out. He had come closest to offering an explanation after hitting six home runs in three games against the Braves in May.

"There are some things I don't understand right now," he said. "The balls I used to line off the walls are lining out [of the park]. I can't tell you why.

"Call God. Ask him. It's like, wow. I can't understand it, either."

But the source of Barry Bonds's newfound power wasn't God at all. It was growth hormone, and Greg Anderson. And now Victor Conte's The Cream and The Clear, too.

After the 2000 season ended, Anderson had wanted somebody to introduce him to Conte. BALCO was around the corner from World Gym in Burlingame, where Anderson spent virtually every waking hour, and where he trained Bonds. Anderson had learned of Conte's reputation as an innovator of performance-enhancing drugs. He approached Ken Lockwood, a son-in-law of the American judo master Willy Cahill, who was still friendly with Conte. Lockwood worked out at World Gym, and one day in the locker room Anderson asked for his help in meeting Conte so Bonds could benefit from the BALCO program.

"My understanding was that he knew Victor was into those trace minerals, and he was looking for an edge because they were going for the record, the home run record," Lockwood recalled.

Conte was very pleased to do business with Bonds's trainer. It meant he could add the greatest baseball player of the modern era to the BALCO stable of athletes. At minimum, it was another big name Conte could drop on the Internet chat boards, another celebrity whose name and photo could be exploited to promote his business and himself.

"Barry takes ZMA every night without fail," he would write on one board in September. "Barry is a big fan of ZMA."

Anderson, meanwhile, sold Bonds on Conte by dropping the names of the Olympians and NFL stars already using BALCO. Of course the real BALCO program had little to do with ZMA—instead, it gave Bonds access to state-of-the-art performance-enhancing drugs like The Clear, which other elite athletes had begun calling "Rocket Fuel" and "the magic potion." A BALCO connection had additional value because it provided Bonds with a cover story for his radically transformed appearance.

Now Bonds could insist that he built his muscular body with intense weight training and the modern science of nutritional supplementation. In baseball, a sport that didn't even test for drugs, the cover story seemed good enough to protect the reputations of Bonds, the Giants, and the game itself. Like all good cover stories, it contained some truth.

There was no question Bonds had worked brutally hard in the gym in the off season. Later, Conte and Anderson would persuade Bonds to plug BALCO and ZMA in a feature story and photo spread in *Muscle & Fitness*, the Weiders' bodybuilding magazine. The story described Bonds's torturous five-day workout rotation: as many as 14 sets per day, 10 reps per set, from a selection of such rugged exercises as Hammer-machine presses, barbell squats, cable tricep pressdowns, stiff-legged dead-lifts, low-back extensions. Each exercise was meant to isolate a specific muscle group; as Bonds preferred, each one was done at maximum bearable weight.

Conte also put Bonds through a battery of blood and urine panels. According to BALCO's pseudoscience, to obtain maximum athletic performance it was important to remedy minute deficiencies of zinc and magnesium with supplements, starting with ZMA. Bonds's own doctor drew his blood, which Anderson transported for testing. In July, Bonds allowed a writer for *The New York Times Magazine* to observe his weight training. That story portrayed Anderson as more of a nutritional technician than a tattooed gym rat. "Every month we take his blood and test his mineral levels to make sure they're in line," Anderson said of Bonds, "so that if he's ten milligrams off in zinc or six

off in magnesium or five milligrams off in copper, that's what we'll replace. . . . That's how he stays in such good condition."

In the BALCO years, Bonds also choked down an exotic health-
food diet. The *Times* piece reported he ate six 350-calorie meals per
day—fish, chicken, vegetables, rarely beef. It described a solicitous
Anderson ordering Bonds a plate of scrambled egg whites, while remarking that the slugger's body fat was 6.2 percent, an astonishingly
low level. The *Muscle & Fitness* piece was accompanied by a list of
more than two dozen nutritional supplements that Bonds was said to
be taking five times per day: pills including chromium, copper, sele-
nium, folic acid, vitamins A, B, C, D, and E, omega-6 fatty acids, and
New Zealand colostrum.

In secret, Conte had offered Bonds a new array of performance-
enhancing drugs, along with more expertise than the gym rat Anderson could provide. Anderson knew steroids, but his knowledge was
from the inject-and-grow school. Conte's drug cocktails were designed
not only to be undetectable, but to enhance an athlete's specific needs.
Conte's real blood and urine-testing program—not the trace-element
workup that Anderson had so solemnly described to *The New York
Times Magazine*—was designed to ensure that the drugs were working
as intended, and to ensure that they would not be detected on a
steroid test. Bonds underwent one such screening on November 18,
2000, according to BALCO documents. Quest Laboratories, the medical concern that was later hired to do Major League Baseball's drug
tests, ran an anabolic steroid panel on Bonds. Like an Olympic drug
test, it measured his T/E ratio. After the 2001 season, on November
12, Lab*One*, another drug-testing lab, did another workup on Bonds's
testosterone levels. (Lab*One* reported a level of 11.2, which the government believed was abnormally high for a man of Bonds's age.)
There was no reason to perform the tests unless Bonds was using
steroids.

In addition to growth hormone and testosterone, doping calendars showed that Bonds used insulin, the diabetes drug, along with
steroids. He had to be mindful of a sudden drop in blood sugar in-
ducing the potentially fatal "diabetic coma," but the drug's anabolic effect was significant, especially when used in conjunction with growth

hormone. He also popped Mexican beans, fast-acting steroids thought to clear the user's systems within a few days. The label of the container read, "Andriol. Undecanoato de testosterone"—in English: testosterone decanoate. Early in the 2001 season, the calendars indicated Bonds tried trenbolone, a steroid created to improve the muscle quality of beef cattle. Within the year, it would be the chemical foundation for a new formulation of The Clear, the undetectable steroid Conte obtained from Patrick Arnold.

Bonds carried around a little bag of pills—what Kim Bell called his "man bag"—and with Anderson's guidance he would take as many as 20 of them at a time. Meanwhile, Bonds began asserting more control over the drug regimen. He could feel the drop of energy that came when he was cycling off the performance enhancers, and he could see it, too, in the distance the ball traveled. He was mindful of the distance of his home runs and his splash hits, and when his power started to decline he would tell Anderson to start him on another drug cycle, according to a source familiar with Bonds. Anderson kept the calendar that tracked his cycles. If he told Bonds he didn't need a cycle, Bonds would just tell him, "Fuck off, I'll do it myself."

Of course the fans weren't aware this was going on, and in 2001, few baseball writers explored the possibility that performance-enhancing drugs might be behind Bonds's power surge. Many writers just accepted that Bonds had achieved his muscular physique "by purifying his diet, supplementing with over-the-counter muscle builders . . . and lifting until he cried," as columnist Skip Bayless put it in the *San Jose Mercury News*. Perhaps Bonds's charm offensive was working.

As PR campaigns go, the media effort wasn't particularly sophisticated: Bonds simply gave press conferences after games and did additional one-on-ones with selected interviewers. Meanwhile, friends of Bonds were available with positive, upbeat commentary for the avalanche of profiles that were being ordered up as he approached McGwire's record. The friends' talking points addressed Bonds's reputation for boorish behavior. Some contended that Bonds was misunderstood and had never been a jerk in the first place. Others acknowledged prior problems but said he had become a better person.

"I think he has changed and I think, frankly, that his marriage has a lot to do with it," Magowan, the Giants' owner, told the *Oakland*

Tribune's Josh Suchon. ". . . He's got a lovely wife and lovely kids. He's a very good father." Bobby McKercher also vouched for his high school teammate and best friend: "He's a human being, a very loving father," McKercher told the *Los Angeles Times*. "A family man. He's really good with kids and very dedicated to his job. He's not as surly as everyone says, but sometimes when you're backed into a corner, you're going to be defensive."

Of course it was impossible for Bonds to maintain the charm 24/7. Back in spring training, sulking again over coverage of his stalled contract talks with the Giants, Bonds had told the *Chronicle's* Henry Schulman that if he held grudges, "I would have punched you a long time ago," according to Suchon's book on Bonds's 2001 season. In the same press conference, Bonds also said, "I don't hold grudges, I'm not a vindictive person. There would be a lot of dead people if I was," writer Steven Travers reported.

In June, Bonds compared his media entourage to a swarm of ants. In August, when a radio reporter in Cincinnati persisted in asking him about home runs after he declared the subject closed, Bonds snapped, "Did you go to deaf school?"

Also in August, *Sports Illustrated* columnist Rick Reilly flew to San Francisco to interview Bonds. He hung around for several days and finally was told that Bonds didn't want to talk about home runs to him, either. The visit produced the toughest piece written about Bonds during the home run chase. Based on an interview with Jeff Kent, Reilly's column portrayed Bonds as selfish, spoiled, hated by his teammates, and coddled by an indulgent management. "In the San Francisco Giants' clubhouse, everybody knows the score: 24–1," Reilly wrote. "There are 24 teammates, and then there's Barry Bonds . . . sequestered in the far corner of the clubhouse with his p.r. man, masseur, flex guy, weight trainer, three lockers, a reclining massage chair and a big-screen television that only he can see. . . . He should be the MVP. But that doesn't mean you have to root for him."

The Reilly column was a big exception to the coverage. Bonds's people believed the media-friendly campaign simply proved how easygoing the baseball press really was, despite Bonds's bitter complaints about their deliberate lies and defamation. The writers cut Bonds slack. Most writers didn't try to provide a nuanced portrayal of the moody, arrogant, self-absorbed athlete they were following around. Instead, they filed upbeat articles about the achievements of the new Home Run King, relying on whatever material he would give them.

Bonds hit his 40th home run in Seattle the day after the All-Star break, and on August 11 he hit his 50th, breaking his personal best of 49, set the previous year. He passed Maris on September 9 in Denver when he pounded Rockies pitchers for numbers 61, 62, and 63. There were still 18 games left in the season.

The Giants were in Houston when the September 11, 2001, terrorist attacks occurred. The crisis put the baseball season on hold and Bonds's home run chase with it. Kimberly Bell, Bonds's Bay Area girlfriend, was flying to Houston as the attacks were underway. She found Bonds sitting on the bed at the hotel, watching the news. On September 12, with the season suspended and commercial airlines grounded, the Giants chartered a plane to get the team back to San Francisco. Bell wanted to come home on the charter. She promised she wouldn't talk to a soul, and she and Barry wouldn't have to sit together. There was no telling how long the airlines would be out of service, and it wasn't even certain that the hotel was going to stay open.

Bonds simply handed her $1,000 cash and said, "You can find your own way home, you're a big girl." He left with the team. She rented a car and drove home to California, 33 hours on the road.

The season was put on hold for a week as America recovered. When the Giants finally returned to Houston, Bonds was on the verge of catching McGwire. On October 4, Bonds hit his 70th homer, an absurd shot that landed in the second deck in right-center field, 454 feet from home plate. It was the hardest-hit ball one member of the Giants organization had ever seen. He would recall it later when he was coming to grips with the reality that Bonds was using steroids: "I've never seen anybody hit a ball like that."

McGwire's record fell the following night at Pac Bell Park. The game reflected the crosscurrents in Bonds's career. The Giants needed to beat the Dodgers to stay alive in the race for the Western Division pennant. Bonds connected twice. In the first inning, he hit a fastball thrown by Chan Ho Park. It went over the fence in right center, 421 feet away, for number 71 and the record. In the third inning, Park threw a breaking ball, and Bonds hit that one out to center for number 72. The home runs thrilled the sellout crowd. But by the time of Bonds's second homer, the Dodgers already had scored eight runs. The Giants lost, 11–10, and were eliminated from the race. After the game, as the clock approached midnight, the club set up risers in center field for a ceremony to celebrate the record. With his family and Willie Mays looking on, Bonds gave a rambling address and at one point he acknowledged how he had gotten there: "Greg Anderson, my strength coach, thank you very much." Later he gave Anderson a ring to commemorate the achievement and a bonus of $20,000.

On the last day of the season, Bonds hit his 73rd home run. After the game, he said he wanted his trainers written into his new contract. Of Anderson and the others, Bonds told the *San Jose Mercury News*, "Those guys are with me for life."

When it came to his new contract, Bonds's grand achievement didn't prompt a bidding war. Bonds's age, his reputation, and his price tag—he was already making $11 million per year—scared off many clubs. So did his new agent, Scott Boras. Boras was the best in baseball at extracting maximum money for his clients. He had just wrested $252 million from the Texas Rangers for shortstop Alex Rodriguez, and some clubs were afraid of him.

Bonds wanted to stay in San Francisco. Boras told him that the Giants would probably come to the table with the most money. Bonds had 567 homers, and was within reach of many career records. Most immediately, he stood an excellent chance of becoming the fourth player in history to hit more than 600 homers, after Hank Aaron, Ruth, and Mays. Beyond that, Mays's lifetime mark of 660 was within striking distance. The Giants could build their marketing around Bonds's pursuit of the records. Boras wanted to get some other clubs interested to drive up the Giants' offer.

The Mets flirted briefly with Bonds, then signed the Angels' Mo Vaughn instead. The Yankees seemed serious, but Bonds misplayed the situation. Owner George Steinbrenner wanted free agents to acknowledge that it was a privilege to be a Yankee. But Bonds put off scheduling a trip to New York, saying that if the Yankees wanted to meet him so badly, they should fly out to San Francisco. He also declared that if he signed with the Yankees, "all my people are coming with me to New York," a reference to Anderson and the other trainers. Steinbrenner's people ruled out Bonds and pursued American League MVP Jason Giambi instead.

With nobody interested, Boras had to bluff—perhaps his greatest talent as an agent. He kept suggesting Bonds would sign with the Yankees long after that possibility had died.

Bonds was a difficult client for Boras. He insisted on accompanying the agent to a meeting at Magowan's house and, while there, ran his mouth. "Without me, you don't make no money," he said to the Giants owner. After that, Boras suggested it would be better to leave the negotiating to him. Later, when nothing seemed to be happening, Bonds phoned Magowan. The call undercut Boras, costing Bonds leverage and money. Finally, Bonds signed for five years and $90 million. Immediately he was disappointed in the contract and wanted Boras to discount his commission.

As soon as the contract was signed, his media-friendly program and fan-friendly program ended, once and for all.

Chapter 12

Barry Bonds was 38 years old in 2002 when he won his first batting title. He batted .370, hit 46 home runs, and drew a ridiculous 198 walks. Once again, Bonds's offensive surge was powered by performance-enhancing drugs, again from the weight guru Greg Anderson, who got them from BALCO and Victor Conte. Conte and Anderson had sent Bonds's blood for testosterone screening at the end of the 2001 season, and they would order another round of tests before spring training, 2002. Then baseball's new Home Run King began another drug cycle, as described in the doping calendars kept by Anderson.

During a three-week cycle, Bonds was injected with human growth hormone every other day. Between injections, he alternately used Conte's two undetectable steroids, The Clear and The Cream. At cycle's end, Bonds took the prescription drug Clomid; doctors prescribe it to women for infertility, but Conte thought it helped his clients recover their natural ability to produce testosterone, which was suppressed by steroid use. Conte recommended a week off between cycles. Usually the drugs were administered at Bonds's home, with Anderson dropping by to inject him with Growth or to squirt The Clear under his tongue, using a syringe with no needle.

Bonds's gaudy numbers would make him an MVP once again. Even better, for a player who had won so much individual recognition but never earned a champion's ring, the Giants made it to the World Series. And, for the first time, Bonds produced in the post-season: Against the Anaheim Angels, he hit .471 with four home runs and a garish on-base percentage of .700.

As late as the seventh inning of Game 6, it seemed likely the Giants would win their first championship since 1954, when they still played in New York. Ahead in the series three games to two, and holding a 5–0 lead, they needed only five more outs. But the Giants' bullpen collapsed in shocking fashion, Bonds fumbled a batted ball along the left-field foul line, and the Angels scored six times to win 6–5. The following night the Angels won again, 4–1, to take the World Series.

Perhaps, Bonds told friends, he was fated only to set individual records but never to play on a championship team. Actually, as a team, the 2002 Giants had achieved great success despite serious internal tension, much of it centering around their moody, indulged superstar.

Baker, of course, was sick of coddling Bonds. Thanks to Reilly's *Sports Illustrated* column, it was well known that Bonds and Jeff Kent, the club's dominant players, hated each other. Owner Peter Magowan remained infatuated with Bonds and was tired of both Baker and Kent, especially after a public blowup during a game in San Diego in June.

With one out and a Padres runner on first, Giants third baseman David Bell had fielded a slow chopper and decided to try to get the lead runner. Kent, the second baseman, yelled to Bell to get the sure out at first. But Bell threw to second anyway, Kent couldn't make the play, and the Padres went on to score four runs.

When he reached the dugout, Kent upbraided Bell: The play was at first, you would have had two outs with their pitcher coming to bat, what were you thinking? Bonds butted in, saying Bell did the right thing, and Kent turned to Bonds and said, "Fuck you." Years of mutual contempt boiled over, and the two MVPs went at it, shouting, cursing, and shoving each other in the dugout before the television cameras. Baker and trainer Stan Conte finally pulled them apart. Then Baker got in Kent's face, screaming, after Kent yelled that he wanted to be traded because it was Bonds's team, anyway.

Afterward, Baker shrugged off the fight, suggesting it might fire up the team, which had been struggling. Kent, too, said it was no big deal, he and Bonds fought all the time. The next day in the clubhouse he dropped his pants and mooned the writers because a local columnist had urged the Giants to trade him. Bonds racked out on his recliner and wouldn't talk. But he complained that his diamond earring had been torn off during the fight and someone had stolen it.

Magowan had blamed Kent for the incident, and Baker, not Bonds, for the toxic clubhouse environment. After the Giants lost the World Series, Magowan refused to offer a new contract to the manager who had won him his only pennant. Baker complained that after firing him, the Giants had slimed him by giving ESPN a story about the IRS attaching his wages to recover millions of dollars in back taxes. Kent said the Giants wouldn't offer him a contract, either, and he signed with Houston. In the end, Bonds wound up with more control over the club than ever.

Soon after the World Series, Bonds joined a team of Big League All-Stars for a baseball tour of Japan. He brought Anderson along. Also on the tour was a new Bonds friend, Jason Giambi, the former Oakland Athletic who had just finished his first season as the Yankees first baseman. The trio had a lot to talk about: Like Bonds, Giambi was an experienced juicer. And baseball had recently announced it would begin steroids testing in 2003.

Bonds had befriended the younger slugger in 2000, when Giambi hit .333 with 43 home runs and won the American League MVP award. With the A's, Giambi was tough and swaggering, the Kid Rock of baseball. He lived with Ron Simms, a custom motorcycle builder, and he rode a scary custom bike with a mammoth 131 cubic-inch engine. When he wasn't on the bike, Giambi drove a Ferrari. He grew his hair long, shaved only occasionally, and had the emblem of a skull's head inside a sun tattooed on his bicep. He brought remote-control racing cars and other electronic toys into the A's clubhouse for pregame fun. He loved to chase women and have fun after games, especially on the road: His life goal, expressed in a slogan on a T-shirt he wore, was to party like a rock star, hammer like a porn star, rake like an All-Star. A famous *Sports Illustrated* cover perfectly caught his Animal Man persona: hatless, clutching a bat, greasy locks dangling into his glassy eyes; a goatee and several days' stubble on his face; big biceps protruding from a ragged sleeveless T-shirt. "The New Face of Baseball," the headline read. "How the Home Run Has Changed the Game."

But Giambi was more sensitive, well mannered, and needy than the wild persona he had adopted in Oakland. He wanted people to like him—his teammates, the fans, his manager, the writers, the grounds crew. He would make sincere efforts to ingratiate himself with all of them. Although he was the leader of the A's, he didn't demand the role; when confronted with a bigger ego and a bigger talent, he would be deferential. Giambi also was a baseball fan, and he could seem starstruck around great players. In 1995, when Giambi was called up to Oakland, Mark McGwire was still on the club, and Giambi came down with a serious case of hero worship. It was obvious that the budget-conscious A's were grooming Giambi to replace their expensive slugger, but he tagged after McGwire, becoming his best friend and his acolyte. He dropped Mac's name in conversation— Mark says this, Mark thinks that—and when McGwire was traded to the Cardinals in 1997, Giambi was crushed.

Giambi was just as deferential to Bonds. Bonds was the Big Dog of San Francisco, and Giambi had the same status in Oakland, but Giambi never presumed theirs was a relationship of equals. He appeared to idolize the Giants star, telling writers Bonds was "the best player who ever played the game." Bonds agreed to accept Giambi's hero worship as the basis of their friendship.

Giambi also was an intensely ambitious player: driven by his own inner needs to succeed at the game, and by the urgings of his father, a baseball-crazy Southern Californian who had built a batting cage in the backyard of the family home so his boys could get more practice. Wanting more than anything to become a star, seeking every edge to take his game to the next level, Giambi personified all the ballplayers who turned to steroids in the 1990s.

Giambi used a slew of banned drugs, including growth hormone, injectable testosterone, and Deca-Durabolin. When he later confessed that he had used steroids, he mentioned nothing before 2001, when he said he scored Deca from a gym rat in a Gold's Gym near his home in Las Vegas. In his memoir, *Juiced*, Jose Canseco would claim that when he met Giambi in 1997, the younger player was already an out-of-control juicer. The A's had a bad team, and they obtained Canseco from the Red Sox in hopes of boosting attendance. Canseco said the friendship between McGwire and Giambi had seemed based on drugs. "I was amazed to see how open and casual those two were about steroids," he wrote. "Sometimes, the three of us would go into the bathroom stalls together to shoot up steroids or growth hormone. I would inject myself, and Giambi and McGwire would be one stall over, injecting each other."

Bonds, Giambi, and Anderson got along well in Japan. The Americans beat a team of Japanese stars in an exhibition series, four games to three. Bonds also beat Hideki "Godzilla" Matsui, the future Yankee outfielder who was then Japan's top slugger, in a home run derby. At one point, Bonds halted the event to give Godzilla a brief back massage and some whispered batting tips. The American stars were treated like gods by the baseball-crazy Japanese fans and media, and Bonds loved it there. Anderson was excited by the trip, too. He met the owner of a chain of Tokyo health clubs, a Japanese business executive who had lived in L.A. and who wanted to expand his business into California. They made a plan: The executive would line up Japanese investors, while Anderson would persuade Bonds to put his famous name on their gyms. Anderson would be the chain's U.S. agent, or perhaps he would own or manage the gym they would open on the Peninsula. Nothing was decided, but Anderson was optimistic.

In Japan, Anderson also talked to Giambi about performance enhancement. Bonds had already broached the subject with Giambi, according to a Bonds friend, telling him, "My shit is better than your shit." Still, the initial conversation between the Yankees star and Bonds's trainer was guarded. Giambi knew Bonds's age. What was Anderson doing to keep Bonds playing at so high a level? Could Anderson help Giambi, too?

Just as he had with Bonds, Anderson first discussed training issues and nutrition. He suggested a sophisticated approach to weight lifting, along with a program of blood and urine testing to catch and correct trace mineral deficiencies. Giambi ignored the weight-training advice. Their discussions would become more specific when they returned to the States. For baseball players after the 2002 season, and for their steroid dealers, the discussion of steroids was more complicated than before. In the back of everyone's mind was drug testing.

*   *   *

Ken Caminiti was a veteran third baseman of medium build and modest skills who transformed himself into a muscle-bound slugger after he joined the San Diego Padres in 1995. In 1996, Caminiti astounded the league with a monster season. He batted .326, 60 points over his career average, and hit 40 home runs, 14 more than he had ever hit in his life, and won the National League MVP award.

Alcohol and cocaine abuse eventually drove him from the game, and in June 2002, he confessed to *Sports Illustrated* that his MVP season had been steroid-powered. Caminiti had built and maintained his powerful physique with drugs from Mexican pharmacies. He said he didn't regret juicing. Drug use was rampant in the major leagues, he said, and was responsible for the unprecedented surge of power hitting that had marked the 1990s. He said a player had to use drugs if he wanted to compete, and he estimated half the players in the game were on the juice.

In addition to the predictable outpouring of scorn for Caminiti, the story prompted a flurry of drug speculation about baseball's other muscle-bound sluggers, and much of it focused on the new Home Run King. On the road, opposing fans chanted, "Steroids!" or shouted jokes about syringes when Bonds came to bat. Writers who had avoided the topic during the home run march now gingerly asked about performance-enhancing drugs. On the occasions when he responded, Bonds denied using banned drugs. He said he took the supplement creatine but had never used steroids. And he compared the writers who asked him about drugs to vampires: "The more blood you can drain, the more successful you can be," he said.

The flap over the Caminiti story pressured baseball to make steroid testing a part of the new labor agreement that was negotiated in the summer of 2002. To Olympic athletes, baseball's testing policy was a joke: Olympians faced year-round, unannounced drug testing and career-ending penalties if they tested dirty; baseball's policy was so weak, it could barely be called a policy at all. During the 2003 season, most players would be tested only once. The tests were anonymous, so no penalties could be imposed on a player who tested dirty. Only if more than 5 percent of the players tested positive in

2003 would a tougher testing program kick in, and even then, the sanctions for violations were absurdly lenient, just a 10-game ban.

The new policy was toothless by design. As the *Washington Post* reported in a reconstruction of the talks that led to the labor agreement, the owners deliberately proposed a weak plan because they feared the players would go on strike over the issue. Indeed, Gene Orza, chief legal counsel for the players' union, said that a tough testing proposal from the owners would have been regarded as confrontational. Orza thought taking steroids was no more dangerous than smoking cigarettes. Asked if he believed the policy was too weak, Orza replied, "Only if you take a dictatorial stance, an anti-American stance. If you're a dictator, if you believe in authoritarianism, then elections are weak."

Weak or not, players still feared getting caught. Bonds despised the thought of being exposed as a drug cheat. He wanted no part of the humiliation he might endure if his status as the game's premier player were called into question. Bonds didn't believe baseball's test results would be confidential, either. Baseball would leak the results to the owners or the writers, and if a player tested dirty, the information would be used against him, Bonds thought. But Anderson guaranteed that Bonds was protected. Anderson had bought the BALCO sales pitch so completely that he could promote The Clear nearly as well as Conte.

"The whole thing is, everything I've been doing, it's all undetectable," he would say during the spring of 2003, when he described Bonds's drug use to an acquaintance who was secretly wearing a wire. "The stuff I have, we created it. You can't buy it anywhere else, you can't get it anywhere else. You can take [it] the day of [a drug test], pee, and it comes up clear.

"See, like Marion Jones and them—it's the same stuff they went to the Olympics with and they test them every fucking week. So that's why I know it works, so that's why I know we're not in trouble. So that's cool."

Soon after they got back from Japan, Anderson offered the BALCO drugs to Giambi. Giambi flew to the Bay Area and met Anderson at World Gym. They went to a nearby hospital to have Giambi's blood drawn and took the blood and a urine sample to BALCO. The sample was sent to Quest Labs, the testing concern that had been recently retained by baseball for its new testing program. Giambi tested positive for Deca-Durabolin, the bodybuilder's juice he had been scoring in the Las Vegas gym. If it had been baseball's test, Giambi would have tested dirty. Don't take Deca anymore, Anderson told him.

Anderson started him off on injectable testosterone, saying the drug would clear his system long before testing began, and then they wouldn't go back to it until after testing. Giambi already knew how to inject testosterone into his backside; Anderson provided the needles. Then he put Giambi on the undetectables. The calendars seized by the government indicate Giambi and Bonds were on similar BALCO cycles: growth hormone, The Cream, The Clear, ending with Clomid, which came in a white pill. Giambi knew how to inject Growth subcutaneously, pinching a fold of skin on the stomach. Giambi also took the yellow and orange pills he received from Anderson, but he never bothered to find out what they were.

Giambi had little personal contact with the weight guru. He sent Anderson money—about $10,000 in all—and in return he received drugs every month via Federal Express. Packages went to Giambi's home in Vegas, to his parents' home in L.A., and to his apartment in New York, where the doorman accepted the package. (The doorman signed his name, A. Rodriguez, the same name as A-Rod, the Texas Rangers star with the $252 million contract. Perhaps Anderson thought it was funny that the doorman shared his name with the shortstop. On another shipment to Giambi, Anderson signed the sender's name as "John Bench," a reference to the Reds' Hall of Fame catcher.)

Giambi asked Anderson to sell drugs to his brother, Jeremy, a journeyman outfielder who had never lived down his base-running blunder in the 2001 American League playoff between the A's and the Yankees. (When he tried to score the go-ahead run without sliding, Derek Jeter made a highlight-reel play to cut him down at the plate, and New York won the pennant.) Dumped by the A's and now on the Red Sox roster, Jeremy Giambi also tested positive for Deca, which he was getting at a gym near his parents' home. Jeremy paid Anderson about $2,000 for drugs and syringes that were mailed to him overnight in Arizona. Anderson promised that if Jeremy Giambi followed the schedule—growth hormone, The Cream, The Clear, and then a bunch of pills—he would pass baseball's test. Jeremy took the drugs without a great deal of thought. Anderson was Bonds's trainer, and that was good enough for Jeremy. ("I didn't think the guy would send me something that was, you know, Drano or something," he would say. Besides, his brother had taken the drugs and "Jason didn't die.") The drugs didn't help his flagging career. He batted .197 for the Red Sox and ended the season on the minor-league Las Vegas Stars.

Jason Giambi hit 41 home runs for the Yankees, but his left knee began bothering him, and he batted only .250. After the All-Star break, Giambi didn't buy any more drugs from Anderson. The knee wasn't coming around, and he worried the drugs were making it worse.

After Bonds had returned from Japan, he decided to supervise the rehabilitation of Gary Sheffield's bad knees. Bonds had met Sheffield, the muscular, contrary slugger then with the Atlanta Braves, through Dwight "Doc" Gooden, the former Mets fireballer who was Sheffield's uncle. Although Sheffield didn't come from a privileged background, he had much in common with Bonds: tremendous hitting ability, and a personality that seemed quite naturally to turn off teammates, general managers, and fans. Like the young Bonds, Sheffield was a power hitter who could also hit for high average and had speed on the bases. He won a batting championship with the Padres in 1992, and in 1996 with the Marlins he hit 42 homers with 120 RBI. But he had frequent, ill-tempered disputes with the front office wherever he played and, as a result, Sheffield was playing for his fifth major-league team in 15 seasons.

Bonds had sought Sheffield's friendship, repeatedly inviting him to California to work out during the off season. But he demanded the same deference from Sheffield that he received from Giambi. Sheffield sincerely liked and respected Bonds, but Bonds's condescension was sometimes a problem for him. Barry is good, he told acquaintances, but I'm good, too.

Sheffield had visited Bonds for the first time after the 2001 season, when Bonds had set the home run record. Sheffield had hit 36 home runs that year for the Dodgers, while complaining constantly about his contract and calling the front office a bunch of liars. For two months Sheffield had lived at Bonds's house in Hillsborough. He rose with Bonds at 6:00 AM and followed the same heavy duty training regimen Bonds had then adopted: the Stanford track with Ray Farris for running and cardiovascular work; Pac Bell Park for the batting cage; and World Gym in Burlingame for weight training with Anderson. Anderson put Sheffield on some of the same performance-enhancing drugs that Bonds was then using: injectable testosterone and human growth hormone. Later, Sheffield would insist he never knowingly took banned drugs. But a drug calendar that Anderson kept for him reflected Sheffield's use of Growth and testosterone in January 2002.

The training was grueling, and Bonds was a taskmaster: When agent Scott Boras phoned to tell Sheffield the Dodgers had caved in to his demands and traded him to Atlanta, Bonds intercepted the call. Sheffield later told the *Chronicle's* John Shea that Bonds withheld the news until the workout was over. Before spring training, Bonds and Sheffield flew to Miami and watched the light heavyweight champion Roy Jones Jr. demolish Australian challenger Glen Kelly. O. J. Simpson and his lawyer, Johnnie Cochran, also were at the fight. Bonds and Sheffield parted as friends and stayed in touch during the 2002 season.

Sheffield would also remain in touch with Anderson: In August, the trainer flew to Southern California to meet Sheffield while the Braves were playing the Dodgers and the Padres. Sheffield would claim the rendezvous was not for drugs but for training. Bonds and Sheffield got together again in the 2002 playoffs, when the Braves faced the Giants. Bonds would go to dinner at Sheffield's house in Atlanta before Game 1.

Then in November, after Bonds had returned from Japan, Sheffield again visited him in the Bay Area. He was in no shape to train. He had batted .307 with 25 home runs for the Braves, but he had slumped during the playoffs, getting only one hit in 16 at-bats.

Now his knees were killing him, and he had developed arthritis in his shoulder as well.

Bonds took charge of the situation. At Bonds's urging, and without informing the Braves, Sheffield underwent arthroscopic surgery on both knees. The operations were performed by Dr. Arthur Ting, Bonds's physician. Ting told Sheffield to elevate his knees for a week. Instead, three days later, Bonds had Sheffield running and lifting weights. The pain was too intense to continue.

Anderson began selling BALCO's undetectable steroids, The Cream and The Clear, to Sheffield. Later, Sheffield would claim that he had been duped into taking banned drugs, that Bonds and Anderson had assured him that The Cream and The Clear were innocent substances. But even as he denied his own use of banned substances, Sheffield portrayed Bonds as being in overall command of the drug regimen, with Anderson following Bonds's orders.

"Nothing was between me and Greg," Sheffield would explain. "Barry pretty much controlled everything."

For some who were familiar with Bonds and Anderson, the account rang true. They found it inconceivable that the gym rat would dare sell drugs to any major-league player without getting at least tacit permission from Bonds.

Anderson also brought Sheffield to BALCO to meet Conte and get briefed on the drugs, although Sheffield would later claim ignorance. Nobody ever told him The Cream and The Clear were steroids, he said. The Cream was supposed to be a balm to rub on his surgically repaired knees and his arthritic shoulder. The Clear, which Anderson administered orally with a needle-less syringe, wasn't supposed to be a steroid, either: It was medicine to clear up a liver problem that had been detected on Sheffield's blood test. Sheffield also admitted taking the Mexican beans, quick-acting steroid pills. Sheffield said he thought they were liver pills, too. Sheffield paid Anderson $10,000 for the products, but he claimed he had no idea they were drugs. Sheffield said he saw Bonds rubbing on The Cream, and he saw Anderson give Bonds The Clear. Bonds had told him, "Don't ask any questions," so he didn't.

But the drugs would speed his recovery from surgery, to be sure, and allow him to maintain the physical strength that made him one of the game's premier hitters.

For his part, Bonds didn't believe that Sheffield's knees hurt too much to work out. He treated Sheffield like a slacker, complaining that Sheffield and his wife, who had accompanied him to California, were mooching off him by living in his guest house and not paying rent.

The friendship began to unravel over the 6:00 AM wakeups. Sheffield's knees hurt, and he resented having to train according to Barry's early-morning schedule when they had all day and night to work out. Sheffield wanted to train at his own pace. Bonds was sick of waking Sheffield up every morning, sick of having him eat his oatmeal in the car on the way to the workout. One morning in January, Bonds didn't bother waking Sheffield, and by the time Sheffield arose, Bonds already had left for Pac Bell Park for a workout with Ray Farris. Sheffield had no car—Bonds had insisted he didn't need to rent one. So he called a cab and waited while it drove around trying to find Bonds's home in the hills. When Sheffield arrived at the park, Bonds was there with Farris and Mark Cohen, who was writing a piece about Bonds's workout program for *Men's Journal* magazine. Cohen wrote that Bonds mocked Sheffield for being slow to wake up in the morning, saying, "I bet he's pissed."

Sheffield's knees bothered him too much to run that day. Later, with his wife he discussed what had happened. Sheffield's wife was a born-again Christian, and she thought Sheffield could bring Barry closer to Jesus. She said to go ahead and rent a car, that he wouldn't get angry. But when Sheffield pulled up to Bonds's house in a rental car, Bonds became enraged. He locked the doors and wouldn't let Sheffield in. Sheffield was tired of Bonds's mind games. His visit had devolved into "a personal kind of beef," as he later put it, and he was done. He and his wife flew back to their off-season home in Tampa.

But Sheffield still wanted The Cream and The Clear, according to a source familiar with Bonds. He had always obtained it from Anderson, and now that he and Bonds were crossways, Anderson wasn't allowed to speak to Sheffield.

Bonds was still angry. He told his people that he had called BALCO and offered Conte $100,000 if he would refuse to give

Sheffield any more of "the shit." Shortly before spring training, Bonds called Sheffield and accused him of not paying Anderson. Sheffield said he asked his wife to write a final check to Anderson for the amount Bonds claimed that he still owed: $430. The cost to his reputuation would be much greater.

Chapter 13

The 400-meter runner Michelle Collins was a portrait in unfulfilled promise. An elite competitor for 14 years, since her days as a prep track star at Lakeview Central High in Dallas, Collins had reached No. 1 in the United States in her event during the 2001 season. But she was unable to break through on the international circuit, where the real money was. She had trained for a time with Trevor Graham, but then was kicked out of the Sprint Capitol USA camp in North Carolina when the superstar Marion Jones suspected she was having an affair with Jones's husband, shot-put champion C. J. Hunter.

By 2002, Victor Conte's connections had gained him access to areas typically limited to athletes and coaches at track meets. He would walk around carrying a little black bag containing ZMA samples and God knew what else, chatting up athletes. He soon began talking to Collins, telling her he could provide what she was missing as an athlete. "You look fast, but you can run a lot faster," he told her. "If you're interested in being a champion, I work with champions."

Collins had few illusions about performance-enhancing drugs. She believed they were pervasive in the sport. Everybody was on drugs, she believed.

BALCO doping calendars indicate that beginning in July 2002, Conte put Collins on The Cream, The Clear, EPO, and modafinil. At the same time he was dealing with his fears that The Clear had been discovered and the concerns stemming from Alvin Harrison's overuse of EPO, Conte had to discourage Collins from experimenting with other drugs. In August, she e-mailed him: "Victor—I have access to a testosterone gel . . . I'm wondering if I can use the cream that I already have? Let me know?"

Conte shot back an urgent reply: Don't do it. The testosterone gel would "cause a positive test result by elevating the T/E ratio," Conte explained. "Whoever told you that it is ok is a complete idiot. You are already getting what you need from the cream, which will not elevate the ratio, and you know why. . . . Have you gone cuckoo! . . . Please understand that too much is just as bad as not enough."

In 2003, at age 32, Collins decided to concentrate on the 200-meter run. Soon, she had a career breakthrough, in part because the landscape of elite track and field had been reshaped that year. Jones, the world's fastest woman and the reigning 200-meter champion, was taking the year off from competition to have a child with her boyfriend, sprinter Tim Montgomery.

On March 2, in Boston, Collins won the U.S. Indoor title in the 200 meters. The victory qualified her to run at the World Indoors two weeks later in Birmingham, England. In England, Collins not only won the World Indoor title, she also broke the American indoor record. Twice. She set it on March 14 by running 22.31, and she broke her own mark the next day, with a time of 22.18, despite a hamstring injury.

She earned $50,000 at the World Indoors, and she gave $10,000 to Conte, according to a source close to Collins. A contract Collins signed with Conte apparently required her to make the payment, according to an e-mail she sent to BALCO that mentioned a "10,000 bonus for the indoor Gold."

Collins felt that Conte had earned his money. "She believed that she won because he gave her all that stuff," said the source. "She had never run so fast, and she was getting older, thirty-one, thirty-two, and running faster than she was when she was twenty-eight."

That had not escaped the notice of one of Collins's chief rivals.

Kelli White grew up in the East Bay suburb of Union City, an April Fool's baby born to be great. Her father, Willie White, was California champion in the 100-yard dash in 1955, and her mother, Debra Byfield, ran the 400 meters for her native Jamaica at the 1972 Olympics. Willie White became a track coach, and his daughter often ran alongside the athletes he trained on the track at nearby California State University–Hayward. Remi Korchemny, the Ukranian émigré coach, also was training his runners at Cal State–Hayward in those days, and when he set his eyes on Kelli in 1987, he concluded the 10-year-old girl had great potential. Korchemny wanted to become her coach, but her father didn't think she was ready.

Three years later, Willie White relented and Kelli began working out with Korchemny. From then until she left for college in 1995, Korchemny was an integral part of Kelli's life. She spent hours with him every day, running with her high school team at school, then undergoing another, more intensive workout with Korchemny at night.

Korchemny helped guide her through perhaps the most traumatic moment in her life. White was 17, walking with some friends to the Bay Area Rapid Transit station in Union City, when they were approached by a girl with a knife. The girl attacked one of White's friends, and in the chaos, White was slashed. The wound went from the middle of her forehead past her left eye—nearly blinding her—and across her cheek. It required more than 300 stitches. She was back on the track in two weeks.

After an All-American career at the University of Tennessee, White returned to the Bay Area to train with Korchemny. In 2000, not long after the Sydney Olympics, Korchemny brought White to BALCO to meet Conte. She and Korchemny discussed nutritional supplements with Conte. Soon, Conte was providing her with what he said were legal supplements.

Among the items was a liquid with a slight yellow tinge that was taken with a needle-less syringe. Two drops under the tongue would do the trick, Conte told her. White said Conte told her the liquid was flaxseed oil, and she took it for a couple weeks. It tasted like a rubber band, she thought.

But soon, Conte admitted he had lied to her, White said later. Actually, he was giving her The Clear, an undetectable steroid.

"I'm not sure if Victor felt guilty for lying to me," White said, when asked why he had decided to tell her the truth. She said she told Conte she didn't want drugs, that she could succeed on her own talents. White said she had no doubt Korchemny was part of the duplicity, but she never confronted him. "I did trust him very much," she said years later. If she complained about being lied to, Korchemny and Conte might worry she would inform on them about the drugs, she said.

So she kept quiet. She continued working with Korchemny and said she used only Conte's legal supplements, such as ZMA. White remained wary of Conte, and not just because he'd lied to her. It troubled her that Conte talked about "everyone's business," as she put it. He would mention other athletes who were clients and describe the illegal drugs they used.

White won a bronze medal in the 200 meters at the 2001 World Championships and finished the year ranked No. 3 in the world. But she injured her foot in 2002 and stopped racing altogether for the rest of the year.

In 2002, before the injury, White again began receiving The Clear from Conte and Korchemny. On July 13, White finished fourth in the 100 meters at the Golden Gala meet in Rome. That day, Korchemny e-mailed Conte. "I want to put Kelli on one week cycle," he wrote. "What is your opinion?"

Although Korchemny and Conte pressed her to take The Clear, White later claimed she did not use any banned drugs in 2002. Instead, she said she accepted the drugs to get the men off her back, and then put them aside. "She was just yessing them," said a source with knowledge of White's involvement in BALCO.

Ultimately, though, White began using the drugs that her trusted coach pressed on her. She suggested that she made the decision at the U.S. Indoor Championships in Boston on March 2, 2003. Collins—the former 400-meter runner and current Victor Conte creation—ran away from White and the rest of the field to win the U.S. Indoor 200-meter title. White finished third, not even qualifying for the World Indoors.

White had noticed dramatic changes in Collins's appearance in 2002. She had become leaner and more muscular. White knew what was going on. White did not name Collins when she talked later about the reasons she started using, but it seemed obvious to whom she was referring.

"In Indoors of 2003, I saw someone doing very well under Victor's program, and I decided that this person was not going to be beating me," White later said. "So I decided to call Victor and we started working together again."

White said she and Conte had an airing-out session, where she let him know she didn't want anybody else hearing about her business, nor did she want to hear about anybody else's. Then, they plotted her regimen.

"There was a full array of things on the menu to choose from," she said. "EPO, The Clear, The Cream, growth hormone, there were lots of things. Insulin."

White said she chose The Clear, The Cream, EPO, and modafinil. Conte later claimed that White also benefited from a new drug, too. Thyroid hormone, called T3, was a drug that "makes all the other drugs work more effectively," he wrote.

White paid attention to her drug program. In her training log, she used a color-coded system of smiley-faced stickers to remind her when to take what. She used an orange smiley face for The Clear, a yellow smiley face for The Cream, a red one for EPO.

White couldn't believe how much the drugs helped her training. She could work out twice a day if she wanted to and get up the next morning and be ready for more. She gained probably 15 pounds of muscle. White assumed everybody noticed the changes in her body, just as she had noticed Collins's transformation. But in the world of track and field, where doping was the unspoken norm, nobody said a word.

The results were incredible, too. She had never had much success in the 100 meters. But on May 24, White ran a personal-best 10.96 to win the Prefontaine Classic in Eugene, Oregon. A week later, at the Home Depot Track & Field Invitational in Los Angeles, with a tailwind just over the maximum to make her time official, she was even better, running the race in 10.79 seconds. Three weeks after that, at the U.S. Championships at Stanford, she ran 10.93—into a headwind—to win the American title. Two days later, she doubled her success, handily winning the 200 meters in 22.21 seconds.

"I wanted this so badly and I worked so hard," she told reporters afterward.

But there were side effects from the drugs. Until Conte cut the dosage of The Clear, she had a menstrual cycle every other week. She broke out in acne, and her voice became so deep and husky, her family always asked if she was sick.

"No, I'm fine, I just have allergy problems," White would say.

Privately, White said she was angst-ridden, weighed down by the burden of having decided to cheat like everybody else.

After Stanford, White went to Europe. On August 24, at the World Championships in Paris, Korchemny handed White a 100-milligram tablet of modafinil shortly before the 100-meter final. She asked if he was certain the drug wouldn't make her test positive. Korchemny said Conte was "100-percent sure" that the authorities were not testing for modafinil at the meet.

White felt the drug take effect, speeding up her heartbeat, getting her so revved up that she almost couldn't breathe. The modafinil also enabled her to clear out all the thoughts flying around in her head, to focus entirely on the race, to see herself winning. And she did, grabbing the 100-meter title in 10.85 seconds, taking an amazing 1/10 of a second off the personal best she had run three months earlier in Oregon. And on August 28, in the last of what would be eight rounds of sprints over six days, she won the 200 in a personal-best 22.06 seconds. The victory made her the first American woman ever to double in the 100 and 200 at the World Championships. She was paid $120,000 for winning the two races.

White, though, had a sense it was all about to come crashing down. She felt no joy when she finished the 200, and it showed in her lack of reaction when she crossed the finish line. She blamed exhaustion, but White later said she had been worn down by her guilt. She had come to loathe looking at pictures of herself, all chiseled and beefed up, no longer a smooth-skinned, radiant, and innocent young woman.

On August 30, several hours before she was scheduled to run for the U.S. 4 x 100 relay team, White and Korchemny went shopping at a Nike store on the Champs-Elysées. In the store, a man asked White to sign his copy of the French sports newspaper L'Equipe, which carried a big story about White. She asked him to translate. The story said she had tested positive for modafinil and faced a doping ban.

White was in shock. She and Korchemny immediately called Conte in California. Over the next several hours they concocted a cover story with the help of Dr. Brian Goldman, BALCO's former medical director. Conte asked Goldman to say White suffered from narcolepsy and he had prescribed modafinil. "This is going to cost you, big-time," Goldman replied. Conte offered $2,500, but Goldman wanted $5,000 to produce documents for the IAAF describing his purported treatment of White and the drugs he supposedly had prescribed.

After speaking to Conte, Goldman called White. It was the first time she'd ever spoken to the psychiatrist. He told her what to say. She would say she had been taking the modafinil for several months, and Goldman had prescribed it because she sometimes couldn't help falling asleep during the day.

At a press conference that night, White told reporters she was taking modafinil because she wanted to feel normal. "The mere fact of this allegation is personally harmful and hurtful," she said. "I have never taken any substance to enhance my performance."

Kelli White didn't know it, but she and Victor Conte's other clients had more to worry about than a positive test for modafinil.

As the 2003 track season had played out in stadiums across the world, the competition behind the scenes had grown unusually bitter and cutthroat. Those who knew Conte and track coach Trevor Graham recognized how much the two former collaborators had come to hate each other. Their venom spilled out on an Internet message board devoted to track and field as the two men fired accusations back and forth across cyberspace.

But they did not stop there, and both ratcheted up the conflict on the very same day. On June 5, at BALCO's office in California, Conte wrote letters to the international governing body for track, the IAAF, and to the U.S. Anti-Doping Agency (USADA), the organization charged with overseeing the drug testing of Olympic athletes. In the letter, Conte accused Graham of systematically doping his athletes.

ATTENTION
IAAF and USADA testing personnel
June 5, 2003

Trevor Graham, former coach of Marion Jones, is giving his IAAF and USATF athletes oral testosterone undeconate from

> Mexico. Trevor is having a friend . . . purchase this substance
> from his group in Mexico . . . he routinely goes over the border
> to Mexico to make the purchases. Oral testosterone undecon-
> tate will clear the body and be undetectable in urine in less than
> a week after discontinuing use. Trevor has his athletes compete
> not more than every two weeks. Trevor's protocol is to "hide" for
> at least 10 days (5 days to use and 5 days to clear) directly af-
> ter a competition and then be available for testing for a few
> days before the next competition. If a urine sample was col-
> lected from any of Trevor's athletes within two days after a com-
> petition, they would likely test positive for T/E ratio. Trevor and
> his group are in the Bahamas at this time taking oral testos-
> terone deconate in preparation for the US national trials. IF
> USADA or IAAF would be willing to collect a urine sample
> from any of the athletes listed below, a positive test result would
> be likely.

Conte's letter then accused four elite athletes of using banned drugs. Only one of them, Calvin Harrison, has ever faced discipline for doping.

But Conte never sent the letters. The only known copies were later found in BALCO's trash. At the same time Conte was composing his letters, Graham was across the country in Raleigh, North Carolina, sending an overnight package to the USADA offices in Colorado. Graham had done more than write a letter; he had placed a call to USADA and told an official there that Victor Conte, whom he described as "the man with the little black bag" at track meets, was giving undetectable steroids to his athletes, including Kelli White and Dwain Chambers.

Worse for Conte, Graham had proof: a needle-less syringe that still contained traces of the "magic potion" Conte had been distributing.

On June 5, Graham sent the syringe overnight via Federal Express. It was in USADA's hands the next day. Soon, the biggest doping scandal in sports history would begin to reveal itself.

Chapter 14

By 2003, Anderson was selling drugs to other Big Leaguers—"the Li'l Guys," the gym rat called them. Most of these customers had been bench players on the Giants at one time or another, men who had their lockers near Bonds's wing of the clubhouse and who, unlike their teammates, could tolerate being around the moody star. The only current starter in the lot was catcher Benito Santiago, who had batted .278 with 16 home runs on the pennant-winning team of 2001. He was a former National League Rookie of the Year who had broken his pelvis and nearly destroyed his knee in a car wreck in 1998, three years before signing with the Giants. Santiago sometimes chatted with Anderson in the clubhouse when Bonds wasn't around, and Anderson sold him Winstrol. Later, Santiago got The Clear, The Cream, injectable testosterone, and growth hormone from Bonds's trainer. Payment records would show that Santiago had paid Anderson $4,000 for drugs in early 2003.

Another customer was former Giants backup catcher Bobby Estalella, who shared Anderson's love of tattoos. Estalella had a green iguana on his right leg, a skull motif on his left arm, and the figure of St. Lazarus behind his right shoulder. Estalella befriended Anderson in the clubhouse in San Francisco. He had played there in 2000 and part of 2001, before the Giants traded him to the Yankees, who soon sent him to Colorado. Estalella had listened to Anderson's pitch about nutritional supplements and agreed to tests of his blood and urine. He was under the impression that Anderson owned his own laboratory. After he was traded, he kept Anderson's phone number. Estalella telephoned after the 2002 season, when he was recovering from shoulder surgery, and Anderson sent him a workout program and drug schedule.

Every Monday, Wednesday, and Friday, Estalella would inject himself with growth hormone. On Monday and Wednesday, he also squirted some of The Clear under his tongue. On Tuesdays and Thursdays he rubbed The Cream into his elbow. The cycle ended with Clomid. It was essentially the same cycle detailed on the calendars Anderson kept for Bonds and Giambi.

Anderson also sent Estalella some nutritional supplements and a diet to follow. He was one of the few players who asked about the health consequences of the drugs. The Cream and The Clear were a derivative of a steroid, Anderson explained. "He said [if] you abuse basically any kind of substance or you started abusing this one, of course, then you were into a risk factor," Estalella would later say. But the gym rat promised there were no health risks "if you're doing it at a low dosage." The drugs certainly seemed to work. "I felt better in my rehab, I can tell you that," he would say. "Yeah, I felt like I had a lot more energy." The Rockies had expected Estalella to be out six months after the surgery, but he was ready to play by spring training, three months early.

Another long-distance customer was outfielder Armando Rios, whom Anderson had befriended at Pac Bell before Rios was traded to the Pirates midway through the 2001 season. Anderson sent him packages of injectable testosterone and Growth. "One you use in your stomach, and one you use in your butt," Rios would later explain. He also received The Cream and The Clear. Two other players received the undetectable drugs: Giants reserve outfielder Marvin Benard, and Oakland A's utility man Randy Velarde, who had retired after the 2002 season.

Anderson was certain that the players would never be caught using the drugs, because of Conte's success doping Olympic athletes. The steroid test employed by Major League Baseball was not capable of detecting The Clear and The Cream, and no test existed for Growth.

Still, Anderson learned what he could about baseball's testing program so he could get a handle on what Bonds would face. He summed up his knowledge in the secret recording, which was made early in the 2003 season.

In spring training, baseball had tested a small number of players. Bonds had not been among that group. Sometime before the All-Star break, a significant number of players would be tested. It was supposed to be random and computerized, and perhaps Bonds would not even get tested, but Anderson assumed he would be. Anderson was confident in the BALCO drugs, but in the meantime, Anderson was being careful not to give Bonds anything that might elevate his testosterone levels and cause him to test positive. But he said he had an additional reason for confidence: an insider who would tip him when the test was to be administered.

"We know when they're going to do it," he would say. "See, the lab that does this stuff is the lab that does . . ." His voice trailed off for a moment. "I'll know like a week in advance or two weeks in advance before they're going to do it," Anderson continued. "But it's going to be either at the end of May or beginning of June, right before the All-Star break definitely. So . . . after the All-Star break, we're like fucking clear."

Testing that year would be uneventful for Bonds. But Santiago had a moment of panic when the testers came to him in the clubhouse to collect his urine sample. "No way," the catcher said, his eyes darting nervously. Santiago was told that he was required to give the urine sample, but there was nothing to worry about: It would be anonymous and there would be no penalties. Santiago would hear none of it, though, and he fled. He returned 20 minutes later, relaxed and ready to cooperate. He had discussed the test with Bonds, he explained. Everything was fine, he was taking the same stuff as Barry.

Armando Rios began the season with the Chicago White Sox and underwent steroid testing with the team. But in July, the White Sox farmed Rios to the Triple-A Charlotte Knights in North Carolina. There, Rios was required to undergo steroid testing again. The minor leaguers had no union protection, so Major League Baseball had been free to impose a more stringent steroid program, which included more frequent testing. On the minor-league test, Rios tested dirty. The club told him that he should immediately stop doing whatever he was doing, and that would be the end of it. Rios complied. It was a case of bad timing, he later said: If he hadn't been sent to the minors, he would never have been retested, and thus would never have tested positive.

Bonds started 2003 more slowly than Anderson would have liked.

In May, he was hitting about .280 and was only fifth in the league in home runs. Anderson blamed a rare loss of self-confidence and intensity.

"He thinks the magic's gone, [that] he doesn't have it any more," Anderson said on the tape. "It's generated by his mind. He's afraid he's like losing it, but like I told him, he's way too nice. Talking to reporters, being way too nice—be an asshole again! Every time he's an asshole, it just fucking works. He fucking plays good because he's being himself."

But after the All-Star game, Bonds broke out, as Anderson had predicted. For the year he hit .341 with 45 home runs and won his third straight Most Valuable Player award. The Giants won 100 games, only to lose in the first round of the playoffs to Florida.

Bonds was now 39, far older than the league's other premier hitters. The runner-up for MVP was the Cardinals' new star Albert Pujols, who batted .359 with 43 homers. Pujols was 23 years old. It was as though Bonds were ageless—at age 39, he put up better numbers than he had when in his prime with the Pirates; they were better numbers, in fact, than at any time before he hooked up with Anderson. Powered by performance-enhancing drugs, he was enjoying the most productive period of his baseball career, and he would continue to hit for higher average and with more power than ever before.

Over the first 13 seasons of his career, from 1986–1998, Bonds hit .290 and averaged 32 home runs and 93 RBI. He hit one home run every 16 at-bats. But in the six seasons after he began using performance-enhancing drugs—that is, from 1999 to 2004, between the ages of 34 and 40—Bonds's batting line averaged .328, 49, and 105. That represented 17 additional home runs and 12 additional RBI per year. He would hit a home run every 8.4 at-bats.

Through 1998, Bonds had never won a batting championship nor led the league in home runs. But in the years to come he would win two batting titles, break McGwire's single-season home run record, and approach the career marks of Babe Ruth and Hank Aaron. He also would be named MVP four years in a row. It was an otherworldly performance. Bonds truly had transformed himself.

But people close to Bonds were concerned about the drugs he was taking. His father, who was terminally ill with the cancer that would kill him before season's end, was told that Bonds was using steroids, according to a source familiar with Bonds. Bobby Bonds asked his son about steroids, the source said. Bonds was risking injury to his joints and damage to his heart, according to the medical advice. He had his big contract. He had the record. He should think about his life. But Bonds wouldn't hear it, the source said. He had hit 73 home runs, he was the best hitter in the game, and no one was going to tell him what to do. Bonds planned to continue playing indefinitely.

In the spring of 2003, Anderson had persuaded Bonds to sit for a photo shoot and interview with *Muscle & Fitness*. The writer was Jim Schmaltz, who had done the story on Marion Jones after the Sydney Olympics, and the thrust was similar. It was an advertorial for BALCO and Victor Conte, who had organized the whole thing. Bonds probably never read the article, but it would later prove an embarrassment.

The story suggested Bonds broke the home run record because of BALCO. The Home Run King was "calibrating his athletic performance at the cellular level" by having Conte run his blood and "prescribe specific supplemental regimens to correct imbalances," as the story put it. Much as champions of the past had eaten their Wheaties, Bonds took his three ZMA capsules every night. Of Conte and Anderson, Bonds said, "I'm just shocked by what they've been able to do for me. . . . Before, I didn't understand how important these nutrient levels were, because I was just listening to old standard nutritionists."

At another point, he said, "People don't understand how important this is. . . . I visit BALCO every three to six months. They check my blood to make sure my levels are where they should be. Maybe I need to eat more broccoli than I normally do. Maybe my zinc and magnesium intakes need to increase, and I need more ZMA. Nobody ever showed it to me in a scientific way before."

For the photos, Bonds wore a black turtleneck, skintight and sleeveless, to accentuate his massive biceps. He also wore a black watch cap, which, like the turtleneck, featured the ZMA logo. Smiling, he posed for a photo with Victor and Greg, his indispensable friends. "Victor will call me to make sure I'm taking my supplements," the story quoted Bonds, "and my trainer Greg will sit near my locker and stare at me if I don't begin working out right away."

Once when Bonds visited BALCO, Conte persuaded him to autograph a poster. It contained a photo of Bonds at bat, with the BALCO logo embossed on one black border. Bonds was photographed as he signed the poster. Later, when Conte needed money for his legal bills, the autographed poster—and the photo of Bonds signing it—turned up for sale on an Internet auction.

Now that he had the new contract, Bonds was more difficult than ever with the press. Bonds deployed Anderson and Shields, his stretching coach, to keep the writers away from his wing of the clubhouse when he didn't want to see them, as was often the case. After games, the media scrum would edge toward Bonds's locker, trying to penetrate the cordon and put a question to the Home Run King that would prompt a response other than a fusillade of obscenities that would be unusable in a paper.

"Uh Barry—they really seem to be pitching around you. Are you frustrated by all the walks?" a writer would venture.

"Can we talk about something else besides my fucking walks?" Bonds would reply.

Fans also were treated rudely. In Scottsdale during spring training, when a mob of autograph-seeking kids approached, Bonds shooed them away, saying, "What the fuck are you doing here? You're supposed to be in school."

Early in the 2003 season, Bonds decided it was time for girlfriend Kimberly Bell to disappear. His promise to buy her a house in Scottsdale, made so casually that night in spring training 2001, had created financial headaches for the multimillionaire athlete. By any conventional measure, Bonds was wealthy. But his pay from the Giants and his investment income went to his accountants, who paid his income taxes and child support, kept him on a strict allowance, and wrote financial reports that his wife could see. If Bonds had used that money to buy a house in Scottsdale, the accountants would ask questions and Liz would find out. So Bonds had planned to use his income from memorabilia sales and autograph sessions, where he received income in cash and didn't report it to the IRS. The accountants knew nothing about it. In those days, a ball autographed by Bonds sold for perhaps $100. During the 2001 season, he would sit in a hotel for hours, signing balls as fast as he could to raise cash for Bell's house.

Getting her the money was tricky. Federal money-laundering laws barred cash transactions of more than $10,000. Bell said Bonds told her to set up several bank accounts to receive the money and deposit no more than $9,000 cash at a time. Even with those precautions, one bank froze Bell's account because of all the cash moving through it. She slowed down her deposits after that. By the end of the season, Bonds had given her $80,000. She made a down payment on a house in Scottsdale, then quit her job and moved to the desert.

There were nothing but problems after that. Bell had been making $40 per hour as a graphic artist in Silicon Valley. In Phoenix, she said she couldn't find anything for more than $10. For a while she worked as a bartender, but when the house payments came due each month, she had to borrow on her credit card. Meanwhile, Bonds told her he was temporarily tapped out. Actually, he was still signing balls for cash, and had begun selling signed bats, as well. But in 2001, in a club in New York, he had met a centerfold model from Eastern Europe, according to a source familiar with Bonds. The model gave Bonds some photos of her and he showed them around the Giants' clubhouse, unaware anyone could download them from the Internet. Bonds began flying the model instead of Kimberly Bell to road games. Once, through some confusion over the tickets, she sat next to Magowan, the owner. Bonds was spending too much money on the model to afford house payments in Arizona for Bell. Bell became frantic as she went deeper in debt to keep up the house payments.

The relationship unraveled on May 2, 2003, the start of a series against the Reds at Pac Bell. Bell said her flight from Arizona was late, and as soon as she got off the plane, he called her cell, saying, "Where the fuck are you?" When she arrived at the room in the Westin Airport Hilton, Bonds was livid. She had blown his whole schedule for the day. She tried to apologize, but by her account, he put his hand around her throat, pressed her against the wall, and whispered, "If you ever fuckin' pull some shit like that again I'll kill you, do you understand me?"

Bell was frightened. He left, and she went back to Arizona two days later without seeing him. She said that when she got home, she called the Scottsdale police and told an officer that a "super famous athlete" had threatened to kill her. But when pressed for details, she hung up.

They saw each other once more, when the Giants were in Phoenix to play the Diamondbacks at the end of May. Bonds stayed at the Phoenician resort in Scottsdale rather than the Ritz-Carlton with the team. Again they discussed her financial problems. By Bell's account, Bonds said he wanted her to move to Los Angeles, where he was building a home. But on his way out of town, he called her from the airport.

"You have to do something for me," Bonds said. "You need to disappear."

"What do you mean?" Bell said. "For how long?"

"Did I fuckin' stutter?" Bonds replied. "Maybe forever."

Bell became angry. "Are you going to make your girlfriend in New York disappear, too?" she asked.

Bonds didn't reply, and his cell phone cut out.

A few days later, she said Greg Anderson called her. He said Barry really loved her and there were no other women. Bell said she knew all about the girl in New York, and Anderson apologized for Bonds. He asked what he should tell Bonds about their conversation. Bell assumed Barry was listening on the line, anyway. She said she didn't care and hung up. In September, a former policeman who worked for Bonds left several messages for her, and then she received a letter from a lawyer who said he represented Bonds, asking for her to call.

By then, Bonds would have other, bigger problems.

Part II

The Investigation

Chapter 15

I t was after midnight on a mild evening in the spring of 2003. In the flood-lit parking lot of a deserted office building on the San Francisco Peninsula, a thin, very tall man with a shaved head was wrapping up another night of digging through garbage.

As these expeditions went, this one wasn't so uncomfortable. It was 50 degrees, with the air still; not like some of the nights he had endured in the past six months, when temperatures were in the low 40s, the wind howled, and rain fell. Mondays had become trash nights for the man, reserved not for relaxing with his wife after putting the kids to bed, but rather for rooting through a week's worth of a stranger's rubbish, looking for evidence of crimes.

Jeff Novitzky was a Special Agent with the Internal Revenue Service's Criminal Investigations unit, known as IRS CI. He was a cross between an IRS auditor and a federal narcotics officer. Like a cop, the 35-year-old Novitzky carried a gun and apprehended criminals, often working on cases that involved financial aspects of the drug trade. But he was trained as an accountant, and like any tax man he preferred to prove his cases with a paper trail. That was where "trash recon" came in. The U.S. Supreme Court had ruled that police could legally seize evidence from a suspect's trash without bothering to get a search warrant. And in his 10 years at IRS CI, Novitzky had found that his target's dumpster often was full of incriminating documents.

That was proving true in his present case, a drug and money-laundering investigation unlike anything he had ever worked. Since August 2002, Novitzky had been probing a little-known lab in Burlingame, the Bay Area Laboratory Co-Operative, and its owner, Victor

Conte. The agent had come to believe that Conte was the mastermind of an international steroid distribution ring, but what distinguished BALCO from an ordinary drug case was its celebrity clientele. Novitzky had discovered that BALCO's client list was a who's who of sports superstars: Marion Jones, Tim Montgomery, Bill Romanowski, Gary Sheffield and, the biggest name of all, Barry Bonds, who had just completed the greatest single season of home run hitting in baseball history.

The agent was working a lot of angles to make his case. Mondays were the best nights for trash recon, and Novitzky's routine was to drive the two miles from his home to BALCO, arriving usually around 9 or 10 at night. He would put the contents of two plastic trash cans and a recycling bin into his car and sometimes drive to a commercial district across the Bayshore Freeway. In the parking lot of an office building not far from where he had attended high school, Novitzky went to work.

It usually took an hour to sort through BALCO's garbage, and the evidence mounted with each visit. He found empty boxes that had contained vials of human growth hormone, testosterone, and EPO; dozens of wrappers for 100-count packages of syringes; a container for Oxandrin, an oral steroid; pill sheets for an unknown drug, with what looked like Russian writing on the paper; other sheets that contained Carsil, a Bulgarian supplement used to treat liver damage. One night he found a torn e-mail that looked like a price sheet for specially made substances, along with descriptions of how to administer the drugs and their efficacy:

> Invisible "BT"—injectable . . . the more genetically gifted
> the athlete the more BT works.
> Invisible "NP"—injectable . . . works best on a high
> protein diet.
> Invisible "HD"—cream . . . works best taken 3 times
> per day.

Trash recon also yielded evidence about the athletes who obtained the drugs. There was a handwritten note to Conte from Kevin Toth, the U.S. shot-put champion. "Vic, you are the man," he wrote.

Another note in the trash was written by Regina Jacobs, a distance runner who, at age 39, had set the world record in the 1,500 meters. The note, to Conte and his right-hand man, Jim Valente, read: ". . . All that I have accomplished this season would not have been possible without your support."

In BALCO's trash, Novitzky also found many Federal Express receipts from professional baseball players. They were addressed to Greg Anderson, whom Novitzky knew as a suspected steroids dealer, as Barry Bonds's personal trainer and as an associate of Conte. The agent discovered paperwork from current and former San Francisco Giants Benito Santiago, Marvin Benard, and Armando Rios, from Jeremy Giambi, and from Gary Sheffield. In January 2003, BALCO investigators had seen Sheffield working out several times with Bonds and Anderson at the World Gym 100 yards from BALCO.

Novitzky's two-hour trash recon on the mild, windless night of Monday, March 3, 2003, was particularly productive. He found more of the usual evidence: a pill jar for a diet drug called hydrochloride diethylpropion; a half-full bottle labeled "Ecdysten, Russian Anabolic Compound, Dietary Supplement"; and four empty pill sheets of omifin, a women's fertility drug also known as Clomid, which was thought to mask steroid use in men.

And, for the first time, Novitzky found documents pertaining to Bonds.

He knew Bonds was a BALCO client because Conte had bragged on the Internet about his association with the outfielder. Still, the agent hadn't found any direct evidence tying Bonds to the steroids ring. Now, one Bonds item in the trash seemed curious: a fax from Conte to Jim Schmaltz at *Muscle & Fitness* magazine, describing the slugger's weight and nutrition program as designed by BALCO. (Novitzky didn't know it, but *Muscle & Fitness*'s splashy article about Bonds was scheduled to be published in June.)

The other Bonds-related documents in the BALCO garbage that night seemed more unusual and incriminating.

The first document showed that a sample of Bonds's blood had been sent to a laboratory for steroid testing. Novitzky had seen this type of document many times in the trash, but never one with Bonds's name on it. A second document heightened Novitzky's interest: It showed that BALCO had tried to conceal that the sample was actually from Bonds.

During his investigation, Novitzky had come to believe Conte was pre-testing his athletes—sending their samples to independent labs for analysis to make sure the performance-enhancing drugs they were taking would go undetected by drug testers. Now the agent had evidence Bonds was among those being pre-tested. Bonds's sample had been sent to Lab*One*, a huge testing laboratory headquartered in Kansas. But the next day, BALCO vice president Valente had sent an affidavit to Lab*One*, swearing the sample was mislabeled. The name on the sample should be changed to "Greg Anderson," Valente wrote. Novitzky knew the affidavit was bogus. In six months, he had seen no evidence that Anderson got his blood or urine tested by BALCO.

In many ways, the BALCO case was tailor-made for Jeff Novitzky. He had grown up on the Peninsula, and for 34 years his father, Don, had coached high school basketball there.

Novtizky excelled in track and basketball at Mills High in Millbrae. He cleared seven feet as a high jumper and in 1986 was named to the *San Jose Mercury News*'s All-Central Coast Section boys' basketball team. He had earned a partial track scholarship to the University of Arizona, but his passion was basketball. He left Tucson and returned to the Bay Area to play at Skyline College, a junior college that was near home and usually had a strong team.

Novitzky, though, was often hurt, and a knee injury limited him to just one game during his second season at Skyline. Still, he was 6 feet 7 inches tall, and Novitzky was given a basketball scholarship by San Jose State University, where he played two years for the Spartans. But he soon developed chronic knee problems, and his career totals were forgettable: two games, four points, two rebounds. Back surgery finally shut down Novitzky for good.

But Stan Morrison, Novitzky's coach for two seasons at San Jose State, saw Novitzky as a positive force on his team, somebody highly intelligent and driven.

"He was so self-directed, so responsible," Morrison says. "He always dressed like—and I use this term in the best meaning—like a

Boy Scout. He was clean-cut, buttoned-down collar, nothing wild in terms of appearance. He was a really mature guy and he knew where he was going in life."

After graduating from San Jose State with an accounting degree in 1992, Novitzky went to work for IRS CI. IRS criminal agents often were assigned to task forces made up of state and federal law-enforcement agents, including undercover operatives. The veteran drug agents dressed casually, like the dope dealers they were investigating. But at first, Novitzky insisted on going to work wearing a standard IRS white shirt and tie. Later, he loosened up, but only a little: He switched to a polo shirt and chinos. Federal records show he worked tax angles on several drug cases and assisted drug agents in other investigative tasks, including trash recon.

Not all his cases involved drugs. In 1999, Novitzky investigated a former sheriff's deputy suspected of extorting more than $1.3 million from the owners of a martial arts studio in San Jose. The former deputy claimed ties to the mob, called himself "The Immortal Tiger," and threatened to cut off a victim's finger with a samurai sword if he didn't get his money. He also told victims, "I kill people for a living." He was indicted for extortion.

In February 2002, as the country was still reeling from the 9/11 terrorist attacks, Novitzky worked security at the heavily fortified Winter Olympics in Salt Lake City. He never dreamed that within six months, he would be thrust into the world of Olympic and professional sports in a far more dramatic way.

Long before the BALCO investigation, police on the Peninsula knew there was a problem with steroid dealing in the local gyms, especially at World Gym. An officer on the SWAT team had earlier described the scene at the gym to San Mateo County Sheriff Don Horsley, and in 2000, when an informant reported that a trainer named Greg Anderson was dealing steroids at World, the sheriff told his officers to try to make a case. But efforts to infiltrate the gym and make a steroids buy from Anderson failed.

Two years later, Novitzky and IRS CI would begin investigating Anderson and BALCO. The government has never revealed how they came to be targeted—in an affidavit, Novitzky blandly wrote that the probe began in August 2002, after "the development of information" that world-class athletes were receiving performance-enhancing drugs from BALCO. Novitzky didn't say where the information came from. But in an account the government denied, a state drug agent named Iran White said the BALCO probe had been initiated not by a tip but by Novitzky himself. Novitzky had become convinced the Giants star was using steroids and sought to prove it, White later told *Playboy* magazine.

At any rate, by September 2002, as the Giants were making a run at the World Series, a team of agents was assigned to BALCO, and Novitzky began digging through the trash. Both the U.S. Drug Enforcement Agency's San Jose office and the San Mateo County Narcotics Task Force relayed near-identical informants' tips to Novitzky: Anderson was dealing steroids to major-league baseball players.

Agents also began to stake out BALCO. On September 11, 2002, the surveillance team saw Anderson stop briefly at BALCO and then drive off. The agents tailed him to Pac Bell Park, where the Giants were playing the Dodgers. Anderson was waved through the guarded entrance to the players' parking lot and entered the stadium, presumably headed for the Giants' clubhouse—where the agents would later learn he had unlimited access. Two hours later, the agents saw Anderson's truck back at BALCO.

Twelve days later, the agents watched as Anderson arrived at BALCO in a truck with Texas plates that was driven by an unidentified man. Conte and Jim Valente came outside, Anderson introduced everyone, and the group went inside. Seven minutes later, Anderson and the man drove off. When the agents ran the truck's plates, they identified another BALCO client: Randy Velarde, the Oakland A's 40-year-old second baseman, who was struggling to finish what would be the last of his 15 seasons in the major leagues. Velarde stopped by BALCO on a rare off day for the A's, before the team headed to Seattle for three games.

In November, on the same day Major League Baseball announced Bonds had won his fifth Most Valuable Player Award, agents saw bodybuilder Emeric Delczeg, a suspected dealer of human growth hormone, arrive at BALCO carrying several boxes. Novitzky had already found two syringes and a medical needle in the bodybuilder's trash.

A few months later, the surveillance team watched the British sprinter Dwain Chambers enter BALCO and leave after just eight minutes inside. When he came out, Chambers's right pants leg was rolled up to his kneecap. From there, he went to World Gym, where Anderson was waiting.

Agents were also tailing Conte. On one occasion, a female agent followed Conte into a branch of Wells Fargo Bank. "Hundreds?" the teller asked Conte, before counting out $2,000 in cash. Conte took the money, said, "See you tomorrow," and then left. Novitzky believed he knew what was going on. Drug dealers work in cash, so there's no paper trail and, thus, no income to report to the IRS.

During this period, Novitzky obtained subpoenas for Conte's bank records. Between January 2000 and September 2002, Conte had withdrawn more than $480,000 in cash. In Novitzky's experience, there was absolutely no reason for a legitimate businessman to be dealing in so much cash.

The records showed that several athletes wrote checks to Conte's personal bank account, and not to his business accounts, as one would expect if they were paying for legal products or services from BALCO. Romanowski, the NFL linebacker, had written checks totaling more than $15,000 over two years, including one for $6,200. Novitzky knew that was far more than what BALCO would charge an athlete for analyzing his blood and urine and selling him legal supplements.

There also was a $7,350 check from Mjones & Associates, from the world's top female track star. In August 2002, Chambers, the British track champion, had wired $1,980 from overseas. Novitzky also found that Conte had written nearly 100 checks to Quest Labs, a third of which had the notation "steroids" on them.

Novitzky also obtained a subpoena to search BALCO's medical waste. Beginning in December and continuing once a month, he drove to a disgusting-smelling industrial plant a few miles south of Oakland Airport. There, he picked up a drum of medical waste and took it to a secure location. The findings were a testament to the tricks of the doping trade: empty vials of EPO; 67 used syringes, some with traces of steroids; vials with a small amount of clear liquid left in them; empty vials of growth hormone; a vial of bacteriostatic water, which was used to dilute growth hormone. Sometimes, the findings spoke to the mad scientist in Conte, as when Novitzky found an unlabeled vial inside a small plastic bag. The front of the bag read: "Analysis, What's in this?"

Particularly with the trash recon and the medical waste, Novitzky needed help to understand what he had found. He knew about sports and money and drug dealers, but the arcane vocabulary of performance-enhancing drugs was like a foreign language. He sought a tutor, somebody to explain what the drugs were and how the elite athletes used them. Somebody to decipher the documents he was finding and educate him about the cat-and-mouse game played by the drug testers and the drug cheats. Fortunately for Novitzky, he would soon have the best in the business at his disposal.

On a side street in West Los Angeles, not far from the UCLA campus and across the street from Bed Bath & Beyond, sits a nondescript, beige building with no address on the outside. The doors and windows are mirrored so no one can see in. Beside the front door is a color-coded, numbered sign, the only indication something serious is going on inside. A passerby would have no way of knowing it, but the sign is posted to warn any firefighters who might be summoned there: The building contains hazardous materials.

Behind the mirrored doors is the UCLA Olympic Analytical Laboratory, the world's foremost sports drug-testing lab. Inside the 10,000-square-foot building is a maze of rooms housing medical instruments the size of copy machines, each used to detect performance-enhancing drugs. One room is dedicated to the study of the blood-boosting agent erthyropoietin, known in the sports world as EPO. Refrigerators are filled with urine and blood samples, some of the 30,000 samples tested there each year. Scientists and technicians in white lab coats walk the halls.

There are scant hints that the facility has anything to do with sports: A couple of UCLA pennants are displayed, as well as a poster from the 2002 Salt Lake City Olympics. But near the visitors' entrance, two framed articles describe the lab's purpose and its proprietor: a *Los Angeles Times* article headlined "Breaking the Code," and a *Time* magazine piece called "The Steroid Detective." The stories tell of Dr. Don H. Catlin, the pre-eminent scientist of the anti-doping movement.

In 2002, Catlin was a sturdy, 64-year-old man who stood 6-foot-2 and looked as if he might have been a football player. In other ways, though, he exuded scientist: the slow, methodical speech, with its scholarly tone; the round, clear-framed glasses that covered a significant part of his face; the confident, precise language.

Sports and drugs were not intended to be Don Catlin's area of expertise. After medical school at UCLA, Catlin worked at Walter Reed Hospital in Washington, where he researched the problems of Vietnam Vets who had become addicted to heroin and morphine. He returned to UCLA in 1972 to create a clinical pharmacology department. A decade later, with the 1984 Olympics coming to Los Angeles, Catlin was asked to set up a lab to test Olympians for drugs. Catlin agreed, figuring he would return to the study of heroin and morphine addiction after the Summer Games.

But the Olympics set him off on a new career path. Twenty years later, his lab would be providing drug analysis not just for the International Olympic movement, but also the National Football League, the National Collegiate Athletic Association, Major League Baseball's minor leaguers, and the Department of Defense. Still, for those two decades, Catlin did his work in virtual anonymity. That would change in 2002, when the UCLA lab discovered an athlete trying to cheat by using a steroid that had never even been put on the market.

The unusual case began when the scientists noticed anomalies in results of a steroid test that otherwise showed an athlete's urine sample was free of banned drugs. A second scan revealed the presence of metabolites somewhat like those produced by a steroid, norethandrolone. Catlin researched steroids with similar molecular structures and focused on a forgotten drug called norbolethone, which Philadelphia-based Wyeth Pharmaceuticals had synthesized in the 1960s but never distributed. Wyeth provided a sample, and tests on a mass spectrometer proved that the athlete had, indeed, been using the 40-year-old steroid.

To Catlin, the norbolethone discovery supported a claim he had been making for years: Doping had become far more sophisticated than anyone thought. At the time, he had only vague knowledge of Patrick Arnold, the Illinois supplements guru later implicated in the distribution of norbolethone. But Catlin realized that drug cheats had now connected with rogue chemists, and catching them would be difficult. The norbolethone case won fame for Catlin and his lab, but in some ways he preferred the old days of anonymity.

The athlete caught using the steroid was the elite cyclist Tammy Thomas, who a year earlier had won a silver medal at the World Track Cycling Championships in Belgium. Thomas looked like a steroid user. She was 5 feet 7 inches tall, weighed 157 pounds, and seemed to be all muscle. She had a deep voice and even some facial hair. Thomas later told a reporter that she was mistaken for a man several times a week. In 2000, she had tested positive for elevated testosterone levels and negotiated a one-year ban. After she tested positive for norbolethone, the U.S. Anti-Doping Agency (USADA) sought a lifetime ban. Thomas denied using drugs, blaming her use of an emergency contraceptive containing a synthetic female hormone for the test results. But the sanction was upheld on August 30, 2002.

Thomas had a reputation for erratic behavior, and some within the Olympic movement feared how she would react. When her appeal was denied, the Colorado Springs offices of USA Cycling were closed for the day. Employees at USADA's Colorado Springs facility and at Catlin's UCLA lab also girded for a violent reaction. Surveillance cameras were installed at Catlin's home and at the lab, and Thomas's picture was posted on the front door of the lab, with a warning: This woman tested positive for steroids, and campus police should be contacted immediately if she was spotted around the building.

Catlin even shopped for a bulletproof vest, but decided he didn't need it.

"We didn't think he was careful enough," said Dr. Caroline Hatton, former associate director at the lab.

Thomas insisted she would never harm anyone. "They probably think I'm a psychopath and that I'm going to blow up the building or something," she told *The New York Times*. "I'm not an ax murderer, I'm an athlete. There's a big difference."

Catlin's life had changed forever. He was now a player in the high-stakes, big-money world of elite sports. Anonymity was a thing of the past. And it was about to get worse.

On the afternoon of October 1, one month after Thomas's lifetime ban was upheld, a receptionist at the UCLA lab answered a call for Catlin. But when the receptionist told the scientist who was on the other end of the line, Catlin became suspicious and had her take a message.

> *Time: 4 p.m.*
> *Phone call for: Dr. Catlin*
> *From: Special Agent Jeff Novitzky*
> *Of: Treasury Dept.*

When Don Catlin returned the call, he spoke to Jeff Novitzky for the first time. Catlin found the conversation fascinating. Novitzky said he was investigating a Northern California laboratory suspected of distributing steroids to athletes. Novitzky did not name the lab, nor did he name the athletes, but he suggested that if Catlin knew who was involved, he would be taken aback.

It was probably better that Catlin did not know. The irony of his work was that the UCLA lab did not deal in names. To the scientists, the athletes were identified only by numbers, and if one tested positive, that was for the policing agencies to deal with. It had to be that way. There could be no room for claims of vendettas or cover-ups. Nevertheless, Novitzky's call was a revelation for the scientist: The government was investigating sports doping as a crime.

Novitzky said he had been digging through the lab's garbage and needed help deciphering what he was finding. Over the phone, Catlin was sworn to secrecy, and Novitzky began describing the stuff he was unearthing.

The agent struggled with the pronunciations. "He started reading things to me—E-rit-ro-potin," Catlin recalled, mimicking Novitzky's efforts. "He couldn't pronounce it. He had all kinds of stuff."

Catlin felt certain that if he tried, he could figure out the name of the lab Novitzky was investigating. But he decided he didn't want to know more than the agent wanted him to know. Instead, for a time, Catlin imagined the clandestine lab high up in a tree house in the redwood forest, far removed from the bustle of everyday life.

The scientist was impressed with the dedicated young agent, so determined to make his case that he worked far into the night digging through trash and medical waste. Later, Catlin would call Novitzky "my hero." They spoke by phone about once a month, and each time, Catlin became more certain Novitzky's probe was important.

"You've got a hold of something," the scientist told the agent. "Something big."

Chapter 16

E arly in 2003, the BALCO task force assigned an undercover agent to befriend trainer Greg Anderson and infiltrate the BALCO steroid conspiracy. Surveillance teams had been watching the former World Gym near BALCO, which had been renamed Bay Area Fitness, and Novitzky himself had purchased a gym membership on New Year's Eve. Agents had seen Barry Bonds and Gary Sheffield working out at the gym under Anderson's supervision. Twice, they had also seen Sheffield at BALCO.

In hindsight, it was a startling thing to consider: Bonds, the greatest player of his era, secretly watched by federal lawmen who suspected him of using drugs to cheat his way into the record books.

The agent chosen for the undercover job was Iran White, a tough, muscular officer with the California Bureau of Narcotics Enforcement, the state drug police. In an unauthorized account that he later provided to *Playboy*, White claimed the task force's real target was not BALCO, but Bonds. Agents were assigned to "find out if Bonds is taking steroids and, if he is, discover how he's beating the system," as *Playboy* put it.

White, 46, specialized in sting operations that targeted drug gangs. He was chosen for BALCO by Novitzky, whom he had known for six years. According to law-enforcement records, the two agents had worked together in 1997 on a task force that investigated a cocaine-distribution network involving a Silicon Valley nightclub owner. White and Novitzky had worked trash recon together, consulted on search warrants, and shared a confidential informant. White also claimed the men worked together in 1997 on a task force that broke up a ring of computer hijackers with ties to Los Angeles's rap music industry, although Novitzky later denied that in court. They became friendly because they shared a common interest in sports, according to White.

By the time he began working on BALCO, White said Novitzky already suspected Bonds was juicing, and wanted to prove it. The IRS agent wasn't a Bonds fan, White said. "He's such an asshole to the press," White claimed Novitzky said.

Wearing a concealed recording device and carrying his .45 Glock handgun, White began pumping iron at Bay Area Fitness. Soon, Anderson was his workout partner. White said the trainer boasted of his relationship to Bonds and said he worked out several other big-league players. White said he saw the British sprinter Dwain Chambers visiting the gym several times to speak to Anderson—but never to work out.

In late May 2003, White thought he was on the verge of a breakthrough; he asked Novitzky if he would have a problem if he went to Pac Bell with Anderson.

"To see Bonds?" White recalled Novitzky asking.

"Yeah," replied White.

"Hell, no," Novitzky said.

But the breakthrough visit never happened. White said Anderson put him though a ferocious daily round of pumping iron, with each lift executed at an excruciatingly slow pace. In June, at home after a particularly tough session, White suffered a debilitating stroke and wound up in a rehabilitation hospital. That was the end of his involvement in BALCO—and, as it turned out, the end of the federal effort to put an informant next to Anderson.

White would later describe the BALCO probe as problematic in several respects. He said the IRS inexplicably declined to obtain a wiretap warrant for Anderson's cell phone or for the phones at BALCO, which could have provided hard evidence of steroid dealing. He claimed he overheard Novitzky talking excitedly about a book deal. He also said the trash recons were botched and as a result the targets learned they were under investigation.

In court, the government would call White's account "self-aggrandizing" and "rife with inaccuracies." White was lying about the book deal, the government maintained; Novitzky never had such a discussion.

There was no dispute about problems with the trash recon, though. To avoid tipping off their targets, investigators on a trash run are taught to return everything without evidentiary value to the dumpster from which it was removed. But at least twice, Novitzky instead shoved BALCO's trash into the dumpsters at the parking lot of the Burlingame office building where he sometimes sorted through the garbage. One morning in 2002, Kent Pearse, owner of the office building, noticed a dumpster stuffed with Federal Express boxes and other trash, including envelopes marked "Caution—Hazardous Medical Waste." Alarmed, Pearse phoned the company whose name was on the boxes: BALCO.

"You don't have to worry—there was nothing dangerous in those envelopes," Conte told him. Conte swore he had no idea how his company's trash had ended up in Pearse's dumpster. But eight months later, it happened again.

This time, Pearse brought some of the trash to BALCO so they could figure out what was going on. Pearse spent a few minutes at the lab, admiring the photos of Barry Bonds and other athletes on the walls. Conte reported the incident to the police; soon, he realized his business was under investigation. By then, though, it was too late to do anything about it.

In early June 2003, reporter Gene Cherry received a tantalizing tip. Cherry had covered Olympic track and field for 25 years, attending every Summer Olympics since 1976, except the 1980 U.S.–boycotted Games in Russia. He was a freelance reporter for Reuters, the international news agency, and a copy editor for the *Raleigh News & Observer*. Cherry was well versed in the history of Olympic doping, and he had covered the Ben Johnson scandal in Seoul in 1988. There, Cherry landed a scoop when he quoted American sprinter Carl Lewis's reaction to the stunning news: "It confirms what we thought all along."

Fifteen years later, Cherry was onto an even bigger story. Because he was based in Raleigh, Cherry knew track coach Trevor Graham, whose Sprint Capitol USA group trained there on the North Carolina

State campus. One afternoon, Graham called Cherry with startling news: Some elite runners on the West Coast were using performance-enhancing drugs and getting away with it.

"Are we going to talk on the record?" Cherry asked. "Are you going to tell me who you're talking about?"

"No, no, I'm not going to do that," Graham replied.

Cherry said he couldn't write a story based on anonymous accusations. A short while later, Graham phoned back and insisted he wanted to stop the cheaters out West. Was there somebody he could trust in the anti-doping movement?

Cherry pressed Graham to go public, but the coach said he wasn't ready. Cherry said he would call the U.S. Anti-Doping Agency in Colorado on Graham's behalf.

On June 4, Cherry phoned USADA spokesman Rich Wanninger, whom he had known for 20 years. Cherry told Wanninger that a well-known coach had information about the use of steroids by athletes and wanted to know what to do. Call me, Wanninger advised. Cherry relayed the message, and Graham assured the reporter he would get his scoop eventually.

The next day, Wanninger received a call from a man who described himself only as a high-profile track coach. Given the heavy Jamaican accent, Wanninger figured it was Graham. The caller named several high-profile track athletes he knew were using drugs. The athletes' drug connection was Victor Conte of BALCO Labs, "the guy who walks around track meets with the little black bag," the coach said. In a later call that same day, the coach said he had proof: a syringe containing steroids that he said he pulled out of the trash at a track meet. (Later, to federal investigators, Graham would claim he got the syringe from C. J. Hunter, the ex-husband of Marion Jones. In that version of the story, Graham claimed Hunter was trying to sell the undetectable steroid to him. Hunter would tell investigators he did no such thing.)

Wanninger had the next day off, so he told the coach to overnight the syringe to his house.

On June 6, a Friday, the package arrived. Wanninger opened it carefully and pulled out a rolled-up paper towel. Wrapped inside was the syringe that would set off sports' biggest doping scandal. Wanninger saw some residue in the syringe. He placed it in a fireproof lockbox for safekeeping.

On June 9, back in California and unaware that a parallel investigation was just beginning in Colorado, Novitzky went on one of his weekly "trash runs." In the garbage, he found copies of Conte's unsent letter to USADA, the one in which he alleged Graham was systematically doping his runners.

The case was bubbling to the surface.

In some ways, Terry Madden was the last guy you expected to find running the United States Anti-Doping Agency. A 1976 graduate of Notre Dame law school, Madden worked briefly as a prosecutor in Texas, then quit the law and moved to Chicago, drawn by the exciting world of the market. He went to work at the Board of Trade and positioned himself to buy a coveted seat on the Board. He finally succeeded, paying $100,000, which he financed with a high-interest loan and the help of his mother.

Madden loved the action of the Board of Trade, and he spent 16 years there, doing well for himself. But in 1995, with a wife and three young kids, Madden moved his family to the quieter pace of Colorado Springs, where he hoped to buy a bank.

Instead, Madden ended up working for the U.S. Olympic movement, which is based there. By March 2000, the former broker was recruited to become the chief executive officer of a new, quasi-independent agency charged with enforcing Olympic anti-doping rules. The agency would be named USADA, and Madden reluctantly took the job.

At the time USADA was formed, the United States had a reputation within the international Olympic community as the ultimate hypocrite. During the Cold War, U.S. officials had branded the U.S.S.R. and East Germany as systematic drug cheats, which was true. But the Americans were loath to admit widespread use of drugs by their own Olympians. To critics, the proof of U.S. hypocrisy came at the 1984 L.A. Games, where positive drug tests from several American athletes had been covered up.

In November 2001—a little more than a year after Marion Jones won her five medals in Sydney—Madden spoke at a Ministers of Sport conference in Strasbourg, France. It was a rude awakening for America's new Olympic drug czar.

"I was shocked to find out that our athletes were held in the same esteem as the East Germans and the Chinese swimmers," Madden recalled of the greeting he received.

In his speech, Madden promised a new day had dawned.

"If any of the accusations are true—of covered up tests, mishandled positives—that is not going to be happening while I am running USADA," Madden vowed.

Two years later, when Rich Wanninger described the high-profile track coach and his mystery syringe, Madden was hopeful. USADA had received tips before, but never an actual substance. Of course, it could still be just a hoax. To find out whether USADA was really onto something, Madden sent the syringe to Don Catlin.

As soon as Catlin received the syringe, Madden began badgering him. Catlin told the USADA chief to leave him alone, that the substance probably was nothing. The UCLA lab had received unknown materials before, and most of the time they turned out to be harmless.

Madden, though, wanted answers immediately.

"There's a sense of priority we get when USADA is calling every day, every hour, which they don't normally do," said Caroline Hatton, Catlin's former associate lab director. "You're like, 'OK, well I guess this is important.' "

Within days, preliminary tests suggested the liquid was, indeed, something. It was a molecular relative of the male hormone testosterone. It was a steroid, but not one the scientists could identify.

Catlin assembled a team of eight chemists and 40 support staff for the crash effort to identify the liquid in the syringe. It was "a once in a lifetime project made perfectly for this lab," he later said.

For the time being, they named it Compound X. When Madden got the news, he stepped up the pressure: It was urgent that Catlin's group identify the drug and develop a bulletproof test for it. The U.S. Track & Field Championships were just days away, to be held at Stanford University, practically in Victor Conte's backyard. If anybody used the drug at the Nationals, Madden wanted them exposed.

He also insisted the project remain a secret. USADA couldn't afford a leak, so only a few people in the office were made aware of the situation. The same was true at the UCLA lab, and Madden and Catlin agreed they would avoid specifics in e-mail exchanges.

Catlin's team tested Compound X on UCLA's mass spectrometer, which identified the patterns unique to each chemical entity. It produced a printout reflecting a substance's chemical fingerprint, with a spike for each chemical that had been detected. Compound X's printout contained multiple spikes, indicating a complex substance. Using the data from the spectrometer, Catlin's scientists began the process of reverse-engineering Compound X. They sketched the structure of a theoretical molecule that they hoped would produce the same readout on the spectrometer.

"You keep working away until you get to the point where you can draw the molecular structure on a piece of paper," Catlin said in 2003. "And we did that. We had pencil and paper fragmentation patterns as to how the molecule would break down in mass spectrometry, and everything fit."

Next, the scientists would attempt to synthesize the theoretical chemical they had sketched. If they succeeded, they could test it on the spectrometer and see if it indeed had the same chemical fingerprint as Compound X. On July 3, Catlin's dream team identified the molecular structure of Compound X. It was related to the banned steroids gestrinone and trenbolone, but it had been altered slightly and thus would not register as a banned drug on a standard steroid test.

The group was impressed. The compound was a specifically designed steroid, concocted by somebody who knew precisely what they were doing.

This was one step beyond the lab's norbolethone discovery: It was a brand-new steroid. Michael Sekera, the lab's scientific director and unofficial naming expert, called it tetrahydrogestrinone, or THG for short.

A test was developed just in time.

In June, the UCLA lab had received 350 urine samples from athletes who had competed in the Nationals at Stanford. The day after the meet had ended, Graham had called USADA again; he said Conte had been at Stanford with his little black bag, distributing steroids. Madden had ordered Catlin to hold the samples until they could be tested for Compound X. Now, USA Track & Field officials, unaware of the secret investigation into their sport, were pressing USADA for the test results from the Nationals.

Two weeks after THG was identified, at 11:45 AM on July 18, Catlin sent a blank e-mail to Madden, USADA medical director Larry Bowers, and the agency's general counsel, Travis Tygart. There was one word in the subject line:

Bingo!

The UCLA lab had found four positives for THG, and it would turn out that all the athletes were national champions: shot-putter Kevin Toth, Hammer throwers John McEwen and Melissa Price, and Regina Jacobs, whose 1,500-meter victory marked her 12th American title. By this time, USADA already had created a BALCO family tree to identify athletes with connections to Victor Conte. None of the athletes accused by the anonymous coach who sent the syringe had tested positive, but the BALCO chart showed Toth, McEwen, and Jacobs each connected to Conte. They didn't know how Price came upon the THG.

USADA now had a name for the investigation: Project Bingo.

One week later, Madden flew to New York and met with Huw Roberts, the chief lawyer for track's international governing body, the IAAF. Madden informed Roberts what was happening, asked him to keep it quiet, and suggested the IAAF collect out-of-competition samples from several international athletes.

Roberts seemed stunned by what he was hearing. He had lots of questions: What lab is this? How do you know this? Madden told Roberts as much as he could, then urged the IAAF to act.

"Huw, you really need to get out and test these guys," Madden prodded.

On August 1, IAAF drug testers showed up at a three-star hotel in scenic Saarbrucken, Germany, looking for Dwain Chambers. The British sprint champion was training there under coach Remi Korchemny, along with the new U.S. champion, Kelli White. They were preparing for the World Championships at the end of the month in Paris. Chambers was having breakfast in the hotel restaurant with British track

Barry Bonds (*left*): As an outfielder on the Alaska Goldpanners in 1983 after his freshman year at Arizona State, and as a young Pittsburgh Pirate (*below right*), he was long and lean, with a build like a marathoner.

Left: (Alaska Goldpanners photo)
Below: (Courtesy of the author)

After BALCO, Bonds, shown here at SBC Park in September 2005, resembled an NFL linebacker.

(Darryl Bush,
San Francisco Chronicle)

Before the 1999 seas[...] Bonds began workin[...] out with weight guru[...] Greg Anderson, show[...] here at World Gym, Burlingame, Septemb[...] 2002.

(Deanne Fitzmaurice, San Francisco Chronicle)

Victor Conte, the genius of BALCO, clowning outside San Francisco federal court in 2004. He hoped to engineer the perfect athlete.

(Kurt Rogers, San Francisco Chronicle)

BALCO, a storefront in a strip mall—and[...] flashpoint of the wo[...] doping scandal in sports history.

(Chris Hardy, San Francisco Chronicle)

"Beauty and the Beast": Marion Jones, star of the 2000 Olympics, with then-husband C. J. Hunter, the shot-put champion, at the Sydney Games. Hunter's positive steroid test had just been revealed.

(Associated Press)

Jones's boyfriend, Tim Montgomery, became the world's fastest man with BALCO's help. But under the stress of the scandal, he failed to make the 2004 U.S. Olympic team.

(Paul Chinn, San Francisco Chronicle)

Jones also faltered at the 2004 Olympic trials in Sacramento, finishing fifth in the 100 meters, her signature event.

(Paul Chinn, San Francisco Chronicle)

Jim Valente, BALCO's vice president— soft-spoken, loyal, and nothing like Conte— outside federal court, 2004.

(Kurt Rogers, San Francisco Chronicle)

Remi Korchemny on the track in 2003 before BALCO enveloped him. The Ukranian émigré coach provided "extra horsepower"—and a BALCO connection— to track stars.

(Kurt Rogers, San Francisco Chronicle)

Sprint champion Kelli White, Korchemny protégé and—through him—a BALCO client. "I just know Marion Jones is going to get off," she told investigators.

(Darryl Bush, San Francisco Chronicle)

The young Jason Giambi, shown here with Oakland in 1996. He began juicing before BALCO.

(Brad Mangin)

By 2001, Giambi was buff, tough, and swaggering, the A's Animal Man: On his bicep was tattooed the emblem of a skull's head inside the sun.

(David Marasco)

With the Yankees, 2005. Giambi solemnly told the New York writers he had never taken steroids, but he confessed his drug use to the grand jury.

(Brad Mangin)

USADA chief Terry Madden: He told the world about Victor Conte and The Clear, then targeted the BALCO Olympians.

(Courtesy of USADA)

Don Catlin of the UCLA Olympic Analytical Laboratory, with a mass spectrometer, the instrument used to identify "Compound X." The discovery proved sports doping had entered a dangerous new phase.

(Courtesy of UCLA)

Kevin Ryan, U.S. Attorney for San Francisco, in 2004. Ryan led the government's efforts to shield BALCO's sports stars from public scrutiny.

(Chris Hardy, San Francisco Chronicle)

Gary Sheffield in 2003 with the Atlanta Braves, fifth of his six teams. Bonds told him, "Don't ask any questions," Sheffield testified.

(Brad Mangin)

Bobby Estalella of the Colorado Rockies in November 2003, the day he testified before the BALCO grand jury. The scene outside court resembled an old-style Mob trial, with witnesses snarling and running for cover.

(Frederic Larson, San Francisco Chronicle)

IRS agent Jeff Novitzky, escorting Barry Bonds to the grand jury in December 2003. BALCO's point man carried a gun, but he preferred to prove his cases with a paper trail.

(Paul Chinn, San Francisco Chronicle)

Kimberly Bell, Bonds's girlfriend. She told the grand jury Bonds admitted using steroids and gave her $80,000 cash.

(Mark Constantini, San Francisco Chronicle)

Rattled by Bell's accusations, Bonds gave a self-pitying press conference in Scottsdale in March 2005. He told ESPN to make sure his son, Nikolai, was in the picture.

(Associated Press)

Bonds, back with the Giants in September 2005, after missing five months of the season with a knee injury. On the road, fans chanted, "steroids" and "BALCO."

(Brad Mangin)

writer Rob Draper when the testers found him and asked for a urine sample. The sprinter seemed unworried by their visit, Draper later recalled.

Chambers tested dirty, and his career was wrecked.

Now there were four THG positives with ties to Victor Conte and his BALCO lab.

By August 2003, it had been one year since Catlin first heard from IRS agent Jeff Novitzky about the unnamed lab in Northern California. As USADA's probe swirled into its second month, Catlin had come to believe the two cases were connected. He didn't know the names of any of the athletes, but he was aware the USADA case involved Victor Conte of BALCO labs.

On August 5, Catlin wrote a note to himself: "I am now convinced that the federal investigation of the Northern California laboratory and the U.S.A.D.A investigation are one in the same."

Three days later, Madden was in Washington, D.C., seeking help on Project Bingo from officials with the Narcotics and Dangerous Drug Section of the Justice Department. Not long before the meeting, Madden received a call on his cell phone. It was Catlin.

Though he wasn't sure whether he should be telling Madden this, he said, "I think you should know there's a federal investigation going on of a laboratory in the Bay Area."

Madden's first thought was, *Oh shit, are there two rogue labs out there?*

That was on a Friday. Madden shared his concerns with the Justice Department, and by Monday, Agent Novitzky was on the phone to USADA. There was just one rogue lab, and it was BALCO.

On August 19, Novitzky and Agent Ed Barberini of the San Mateo County Narcotics Task Force flew to Colorado Springs. There, in a spacious office with a view of the Rocky Mountains, the agents met with Madden, outside counsel Rich Young, and USADA medical director Bowers. Catlin was patched in via conference call, as was Tygart, the agency's lawyer.

Madden found the agents more forthcoming than he had expected. They described in general terms their case against BALCO, offering some detail about the trash runs and other information Novitzky had discussed with Catlin. They said they expected USADA to cooperate fully. The agents also served a subpoena on USADA. They wanted documents related to the Olympic athletes connected to BALCO, as well as a sample of THG. Naturally, USADA complied.

For Madden and company, the government's involvement was a fantastic development. This government probe corroborated some of what they already suspected, and it would produce much more evidence about the BALCO athletes than USADA could hope to develop on its own.

Soon, Madden explained, USADA would have to begin notifying athletes of the positive tests for THG. That was a concern for the federal agents. At some point, perhaps at the end of the year, they intended to raid BALCO, but now that timetable would have to be pushed up.

As the meeting wrapped up, Tygart, a 32-year-old lawyer with the looks of a fraternity boy and a Southern accent, spoke about the importance of the case. He had spent the past few years in USADA's cloistered world. Often, the only time anybody mentioned USADA was to complain. Many athletes and coaches thought the agency was just a bunch of anti-doping zealots out to nail athletes for using nasal spray.

"This is what it's all about," Tygart said to his colleagues and the federal agents. "We get accused for the cold medicines and all that stuff, but this is what we should be doing."

At the time he met with USADA, Novitzky had developed another avenue to gather evidence against Conte: A search warrant was allowing him to read the BALCO chief's e-mails. Conte spent hours on his computer, and though he was aware he might be under surveillance, he was not shy about his steroids business.

"Remember that all emails are saved for a very long time so be careful about how you say what you say," he once wrote to Greek track coach Andreas Linardatos, who was receiving steroids from Conte for his athletes. "Searches for keywords like 'anabolic' and many others are going on at all times by big brother."

And yet Conte freely wrote in e-mails about raised hematocrit levels and EPO and human growth hormone and elevated T/E ratios. Conte couldn't help himself, as sprinter Kelli White had discovered when she first started doing business with the man. He had to be the center of attention, and he had to talk about what he was doing and with whom.

Novitzky could have obtained considerable evidence against Conte without a warrant. All he had to do was cruise the Internet and stumble upon the Google message board misc.fitness.weights. There, Conte bragged about his many sports superstar clients:

"elite athletes like Marion Jones and Barry Bonds routinely pay me for my services with cashier's checks."

It was nearly time for the drug agents to move against BALCO. Even after Conte had discovered his garbage was being picked through and realized he was under scrutiny, he refused to lower his profile. At the end of August, Conte flew to Paris for the World Track & Field Championships, and he was not traveling incognito. Somehow, he gained access to the infield—the area off-limits to all but athletes, coaches, and officials.

Brooks Johnson, a veteran U.S. sprint coach and a fixture on the Olympic scene, was in Paris for the World Championships, and one day during the first week of the meet he saw someone who clearly didn't belong in the warm-up area. He thought to himself, *Who the hell is this character, and what's he doing here?* The man was carrying a little black bag, wore his hair slicked back with gel, and, as Johnson would say later, "looked like a used car salesman. He looked totally out of place in that environment."

Johnson approached another U.S. coach, whom he later declined to identify.

"Who is that guy?" Johnson asked.

"That's Victor Conte," replied the coach. "He's going to get busted for selling steroids within a week."

Chapter 17

After sprinter Kelli White tested positive for the stimulant modafinil at the World Championships in Paris, the BALCO investigators' plans changed fast. USADA was about to send letters notifying Kevin Toth, John McEwen, Regina Jacobs, and Melissa Price they had tested positive for the designer steroid now known as THG. The feds figured they better move quickly on Conte.

A raid on BALCO was scheduled for Thursday, September 4, eight days after White was exposed in Paris and four days before the USADA letters were to go out. A government document explained the urgency: The USADA action likely would subject Conte to "pressure" from his athletes and possibly the media, and that might lead him to destroy evidence.

A large operation was planned, with more than two dozen agents and officials representing five different agencies. Novitzky enlisted Dr. Larry Bowers from USADA to provide technical assistance. There would be a simultaneous raid on Conte's San Mateo home. At the last minute, perhaps fearful that Conte was about to be tipped off, the raid was pushed up a day. Bowers left his house in Colorado Springs early on the morning of September 3 figuring he would have a day to get his bearings in San Francisco. Instead, within three hours of landing, the scientist had joined the raiding party at Bayside Park, one mile east of BALCO.

There, Novitzky handed out copies of a briefing document to the two dozen agents and went over it to make sure they understood why they were there, what they expected to find, and who was in charge. Conte was distributing steroids and other performance-enhancing drugs to well-known professional and Olympic athletes, he said. Novitzky specifically told the officers that Barry Bonds and Marion Jones were receiving the drugs.

Novitzky briefed the group about Conte and BALCO vice president James Valente. Neither man owned registered firearms nor was known to be violent. The agents were told to seize all "controlled substances and other athletic performance-enhancing drugs and paraphernalia," along with documents dating back to 1994. Novitzky was to be informed immediately if the name "Greg Anderson" was found on any documents, or if anyone came across information about a public storage site.

At 12:20, a caravan of unmarked Buicks, some with lights flashing, roared down Mahler Road toward the warehouse-like BALCO building. Bowers, the USADA medical director, was in the final car, and he couldn't help thinking how strange it was to be there. He was dressed in a sports coat while many of the agents wore flak jackets and carried 9 mm handguns. There had been much anticipation within USADA about the raid—how much evidence would be found, who would be implicated, where this would lead.

Half the raid team went in first to secure the premises. Novitzky led the way through an unlocked front door. He walked into a reception area where signed photographs of famous athletes hung on the walls. Novitzky and his team would find similar photos throughout the building, including one particularly striking picture. It showed Conte, hair slicked back, wire-rim glasses, cheesy mustache, wearing a tropical-style shirt. On his left sat the trainer Greg Anderson, wearing a ZMA baseball cap and a ZMA shirt and smiling faintly. On Conte's right sat Barry Bonds, sporting a ZMA black knit beanie and a ZMA tank-top muscle shirt. Bonds wore a big smile. Conte rested a hand on each man's shoulder. Conte "looked like he was trying to be the Godfather," said one person who participated in the raids.

As Novitzky entered BALCO, he called out, "Federal agents, we have a search warrant."

The agents encountered Conte, Valente, and Valente's wife, Joyce, who was BALCO's office manager. Novitzky said no one was under arrest and everyone was free to leave, but the agents did want to speak with each of them.

Joyce Valente was frightened by the sudden intrusion. Later, she claimed the agents were pointing guns. They shouted at her to "show me your hands," she said, and forced her to sit down. Outside, she could hear the noise of what she believed was a police helicopter. In the middle of the chaotic scene, Willy Cahill, the old judo master and Conte's friend, tried to enter BALCO and was turned away.

Novitzky asked Conte if he would be willing to talk, and the BALCO chief agreed. After patting him down for weapons, Novitzky and John Columbet, a local drug agent, escorted Conte to a conference room. It was the same room where Conte had hatched Project World Record, his scheme to turn Tim Montgomery into the world's fastest man.

Novitzky told Conte he already had proof of his guilt, but he said Conte's cooperation might be viewed favorably by prosecutors. The agent wanted Conte to cooperate and lay out his entire operation. Amazingly, Conte did. It was vintage Victor Conte: He couldn't help himself. Over the next three hours, he talked and talked. Although he sometimes dissembled or lied, Conte nevertheless gave the government a remarkable account of the steroid conspiracy he had directed.

According to the government, Conte detailed his distribution of The Clear and The Cream to elite athletes. He explained that The Clear was a liquid with "anabolic effects" obtained from Patrick Arnold, the Illinois chemist. The Cream was a testosterone-epitestosterone mix that was rubbed on the body and designed to keep an athlete's T/E ratio from spiking. He gave undetectable drugs to athletes so they could perform better without fear of being exposed.

The shining moment for the agents came when Columbet pulled out a list of BALCO athletes and asked Conte to identify which ones had received the performance-enhancing drugs.

According to the government, Conte implicated 27 athletes—15 from track and field, seven from the National Football League, and five from the major leagues. The headliners included Marion Jones, Bill Romanowski and, yes, Barry Bonds. Prior to the start of the 2003 season—baseball's first year of testing for steroids—Greg Anderson had brought in several players, including Bonds, to get The Cream and The Clear. Bonds used the substances "on a regular basis," Conte said, which meant taking each drug twice a week, with cycles of three weeks on, one week off. Bonds didn't pay for the drugs; instead, he received them in exchange for promoting Conte's legal supplement, ZMA. Conte told the agents that Anderson had last been in the office to refill his supply of The Cream and The Clear three or four weeks earlier.

If that wasn't enough, Conte also said he kept the drugs in a storage locker on the other side of Highway 101, and he agreed to take the agents there and let them search it.

About an hour into the interview at BALCO, Novitzky emerged from the conference room with a smile on his face. "Conte just gave up everything, he just cashed in everybody," Novitzky told his colleagues. Novitzky specifically mentioned Barry Bonds and Marion Jones.

There was no tape made of the interview. Later, Conte accused Novitzky of misrepresenting his remarks, and claimed he had not implicated any athletes. By Conte's account, much of the interview had involved Novitzky pressuring him to "wear a wire" and gather evidence against Patrick Arnold.

While Novitzky and Columbet talked with Conte, other agents interviewed Joyce Valente. Unlike Conte, she claimed she knew nothing about steroids at BALCO. "I'm totally shocked," she said, when told steroids had been found in the company's medical waste. She did, however, offer a few interesting tidbits. She had seen several athletes at BALCO, including Oakland Raiders Lincoln Kennedy and Chris Cooper, track stars Kelli White, Chryste Gaines, Tim Montgomery, and Alvin and Calvin Harrison, and Giants star Barry Bonds. Bonds occasionally came to BALCO to talk with Conte or have his blood drawn, she said. Bonds's personal physician, Dr. Arthur Ting, recently had been at BALCO to draw blood from the Giants slugger. She also said athletes often met privately with Conte.

At the end of the interview, the agents again asked about steroids and told Joyce Valente it was a felony to lie to federal agents.

"I'm totally shocked," she repeated.

The media learned of the raid while it was still underway. About 45 minutes after the agents had arrived at BALCO, reporters began showing up at the building and telephoning the company. The helicopter that added to Joyce Valente's fears belonged to a television station, not to the agents. Television news vans with satellite booms also rolled up to BALCO. Conte was convinced the press had been tipped to the raid. But the IRS refused to give the press even basic information of what was occurring. A spokesman acknowledged only that an "enforcement action" had taken place.

Some of Conte's clients also learned something was happening. BALCO's phone rang throughout the day. Among the repeat callers were Bill Romanowski and Mark Block, husband of Ukrainian sprinter Zhanna Block, who "must have called like 30 times," as one source put it.

In their search for evidence, the agents found the ledger in Conte's office—listing the names of athletes, the specific drugs they were using, their blood and urine test results, and their T/E ratios. They also found documents detailing lab work performed for various athletes, apparently as part of Conte's trace mineral testing program. One surprising name was on the list: Bobby Bonds, the father of Barry Bonds, who had died just 10 days earlier. Also discovered at the lab were prescriptions written for Romanowski for the diet drug phentermine— the same stimulant he allegedly provided players with prior to games, and the one that was the focus of the the prescription drug fraud investigation in Colorado.

At 2:16, Novitzky grabbed Larry Bowers. He wanted the USADA expert to join him, Conte, Columbet, and an IRS CI photographer for the search of the storage locker. As they arrived, Bowers was slightly nervous. BALCO had been secured by armed agents before he was called in, but here, they were all walking in blind.

Conte signed a form consenting to the search, and then the agents opened locker A-26, which was the size of a large closet. There, they hit the mother lode. Conte helped the agents pull out several boxes of drugs, including his supplies of The Cream and The Clear. Bowers spotted a large plastic bottle that contained a pale, oily-looking fluid. That had to be the THG. The scientist reflected back on his days running an Olympic drug-testing lab in Indianapolis, when he and other scientists mused about whether somebody could be out there creating designer drugs that would go undetected. *This is it,* he thought.

The Cream was in plastic containers with red tops. Some of the other vials and jars were clearly labeled as containing testosterone or human growth hormone, but many others were unmarked. Bowers was struck by the scope of Conte's operation, the array of different drugs. In the end, 13 evidence bags were collected from the storage facility and shipped to the Food and Drug Administration's Forensic Chemistry Center in Cincinnati for analysis. In the locker, they had found testosterone, human growth hormone, THG, testosterone cypionate, and norbolethone—the long-lost steroid that had been unearthed by Patrick Arnold.

Conte also directed the agents to two banker's boxes filled with files on his athlete clients. The files contained calendars, and testing and payment records—essentially diaries detailing the extent of the cheating, down to the day and the dose.

For Larry Bowers, finding all this evidence was perhaps the high point of an exhilarating experience, "the most interesting day of my life," as he told his USADA colleagues when he briefed them. In a conference call the next day, Bowers described all the drugs found in the locker, and the files. Conte had kept files documenting drug use by the athletes who had been expected to be key members of America's 2004 Olympic team—Marion Jones, Tim Montgomery, Kelli White, on and on.

Oh my gosh, what the hell have we gotten ourselves into, thought USADA counsel Tygart as he listened to the briefing. There was much work to do. The Olympics were 11 months away, and USADA had to find a way to get its hands on all that evidence so it could bring doping charges against the athletes. USADA had to move quickly: Nobody wanted the cheaters to win gold medals in Athens, only to be exposed later. It was Madden's worst nightmare: America, still the ultimate doping hypocrite.

At 3:24, while the search of the locker was wrapping up, Novitzky and Columbet took Conte back to BALCO. Conte kept talking. He admitted sending his athletes' urine samples to Quest Diagnostics for steroid testing to ensure they wouldn't be caught. He usually charged $350 each for cycles of The Cream and The Clear. Bill Romanowski was the "first guy" he provided with performance-enhancing drugs. He also provided an incomplete outline of the alphabet used on calendars: "L" stood for The Clear, "C" for The Cream,

"T" for thyroid hormone, "S" for modafinil, and "E" for vitamin E, which he said was used to enhance the effectiveness of The Clear. (He didn't say that on many calendars "E" represented EPO, "G" was for growth hormone, and "I" denoted insulin.) And he also acknowledged distributing diet drugs to some sports figures, particularly ones he described as "fat athletes." They included football players Barrett Robbins and Dana Stubblefield of the Oakland Raiders.

At 3:59, Novitzky and Columbet brought Conte back to the reception area. Now it was Jim Valente's turn. Valente gave the agents a statement that mirrored Conte's but without the hyperbole or slipperiness. The 48-year-old Valente was nothing like Conte: He was soft-spoken and loyal to a fault.

Valente verified that The Clear came from Patrick Arnold, The Cream was designed to keep an athlete's T/E ratio from spiking, and BALCO performed pre-testing to make sure the athletes would test clean. He offered additional insights. Valente explained he was the contact for Greg Anderson, who had become the BALCO connection for baseball players. Valente delivered BALCO drugs and invoices to Anderson.

In addition to The Cream and The Clear, Anderson supplied his ballplayers with human growth hormone and testosterone cypionate, Valente told the agents. Valente said Bonds had received The Cream and The Clear directly from BALCO on "a couple of occasions," but the Giants outfielder didn't like the way The Clear made him feel.

Novitzky asked Valente about the documents from LabOne that he had found in the trash, the papers showing that Bonds's name on a blood sample had been replaced with Anderson's. Valente admitted the sample was Bonds's blood. Anderson had ordered him to change the name on the sample to protect Bonds.

Valente added more names to Conte's list of baseball players: Benito Santiago, Marvin Benard, Randy Velarde, and the Giambi brothers. Also, Valente said Bill Romanowski had been getting steroids and growth hormone from the company dating back to his playing days in Denver.

Finally, at about 5:20, after an hour-and-a-half interrogation, the agents brought Valente from the conference room. At about that time,

Conte's youngest daughter, Keisha, had showed up at BALCO, visibly upset. Keisha had heard her father was in trouble and wanted to see him immediately. Novitzky directed Keisha to Conte. He told her everything was okay, and she left.

Two minutes later, Conte and Valente were on their way, as well. Novitzky brought Conte's Mercedes around the back so that the two men could avoid the remaining TV crews. At 5:25, five hours after the raid began, Conte drove away from his office.

Then the agents turned their attention to Anderson. During the search of BALCO, they had asked the U.S. Attorney's office to get them a search warrant for the trainer's nearby condominium. Agents knew the trainer was around the corner at Bay Area Fitness, so Novitzky and the two San Mateo agents, Columbet and Barberini, drove to the gym. They found Anderson in the back working out some clients. Novitzky took Anderson aside and told him they were about to search his home and car. Did the trainer want to come along, observe the search, and perhaps answer some questions?

Anderson's girlfriend, Nicole Gestas, was at the condo. "She would probably freak out" if the agents burst in, Anderson said, so he agreed to accompany them. Anderson's young son was with him, and he and his boy got in the back of Novitzky's car with Columbet for the short drive to the condo. Barberini drove Anderson's Chevy Tahoe with the "W8 GURU" plates back to the residence. When they searched it, agents found a needle-less syringe containing a trace of fluid that would later be identified as THG, as well as five additional syringes; five empty vials; and pill sheets of diuretics, drugs often taken by steroid users, particularly bodybuilders, to eliminate excess fluids.

Upon arriving at his condo with the agents, the trainer opened the front door and called out, "The BALCO thing has followed me here." As the search began, Anderson pulled out a DVD of the movie *Spider-Man* to occupy his son. He struggled to open the case until an agent handed him a pocketknife that he used to get the movie out.

Anderson agreed to speak with the agents but was more guarded than Conte and Valente.

When he began talking, Anderson would admit only that he gave "a small amount of steroids to people." He thought he was doing nothing wrong by just providing the stuff to a few guys for free. He called himself "the middle man" and reasoned, "If I didn't earn a profit, then I'm not a drug dealer." While Anderson talked, the agents who were searching the residence found more than $60,000 in cash inside a safe above the microwave oven.

Anderson said he had been working with professional athletes since about 1997. His baseball clients included Barry Bonds, Gary Sheffield, Benito Santiago, Bobby Estalella, Marvin Benard, Armando Rios, and Jason Giambi. At first he said he provided steroids only to bodybuilders but then admitted he supplied to other athletes as well. He didn't want to name names.

As the interview continued, Anderson admitted he gave the ballplayers testosterone and human growth hormone, often sending the drugs via Federal Express. He didn't put his own name on the packages because that's "not such a good idea." Asked why, the trainer declined to answer. He acknowledged that after baseball began testing for steroids, he gave players The Cream and The Clear obtained from BALCO. He paid for the drugs with cash. Anderson said he was told the drugs needed to be used concurrently to be most effective.

When pressed to name names, Anderson said only "my little guys" were getting steroids. "Drugs are a very minute part of my little guys," he added. Finally, Anderson gave up some names: Benard, Estalella, Rios, and Santiago were some of his "little guys" who were taking performance-enhancing drugs. He admitted giving Santiago, Estalella, and Rios human growth hormone, too. He told them he obtained the growth hormone, as well as testosterone, from AIDS patients in San Francisco.

Anderson said the cash in the safe represented "several years" of savings for a down payment on a house. He claimed he sometimes was paid in cash by his personal training clients and admitted he did not report those earnings to the IRS. The agents asked whether when they looked at the money they would find older serial numbers to reflect that the cash had been collected over time. Improbably, the trainer claimed he rotated the bills, so most of them were new.

He didn't want to talk about Bonds. When pressed, he claimed the Home Run King never took The Clear or The Cream. But by then the other agents had discovered file folders with the names of baseball players on their covers. Just like the ones at Conte's storage locker, the folders contained calendars detailing the players' drug use—amounts, quantities, intervals. There was a folder for Bonds, and the agents asked Anderson about it. That was the end of the interview. Anderson said he didn't think he should be talking anymore because he didn't want to go to jail.

In addition to the files and cash, the search of Anderson's condo yielded what appeared to be invoices for drugs. One document listed the prices for certain steroids, human growth hormone, and syringes. At the bottom was Anderson's name, above the logo "W8 GURU." Other documents showed Anderson had sent urine samples from some of his baseball clients to Quest Diagnostics for steroids testing. "He was trying to make sure the guys were cycled off" the drugs, said a lawyer familiar with the documents.

And, like Conte's storage facility, Anderson's condo yielded an array of performance-enhancing drugs and paraphernalia: 32 vials, some labeled to indicate they contained steroids or growth hormone; 12 plastic containers holding various cream and liquid substances; 130 syringes; 6 needles; 178 pills; and 68 alcohol pads. His lawyers would later claim it was all for his personal use.

The FDA's lab determined the substances included growth hormone, testosterone, insulin, and testosterone cypionate.

The warrant did not allow the agents to search computers in the house, and when Anderson wouldn't consent to a search of his computer, they finally left.

While the raid was underway, an athlete who knew that Anderson had computerized his doping calendars was frantically trying to get in touch with Bonds. They're raiding Victor, the athlete said in a phone message that was left on an answering machine. Tell Barry he better get Greg to dump all that stuff off his computer.

Two nights later, the agents were back with another search warrant. The Giants, cruising to the National League West title, were playing a night game at Pac Bell Park against the Arizona Diamondbacks when the agents arrived at 7:25 PM to seize Anderson's computer. The agents thought Anderson was at home: His car was there, and a TV was playing loudly inside. After knocking for 45 seconds and announcing their presence, they rammed the door down, fearful Anderson was inside destroying evidence.

He wasn't home. When Anderson did turn up, Novitzky explained the new warrant. In the earlier raid, the agents had found computer printouts of invoices detailing Anderson's distribution of steroids to pro athletes, Novitzky said. Anderson said he didn't know what Novitkzy was talking about.

A few days later, an acquaintance called Anderson on his cell phone. Anderson said he couldn't talk because he feared the feds were tapping his phone.

"It's a little late for that, isn't it?" the acquaintance asked.

Chapter 18

Victor Conte had no choice. Actually, he told people close to him that *No Choice* would be the title of his autobiography. The premise was simple: Conte had no alternative but to help elite athletes who wanted banned drugs. They were going to cheat, anyway—after all, *they* had no choice, because anyone who competed at the elite level without drugs was certain to fail. So Conte would give them drugs to help them cheat more effectively and with less health risk.

He told this story a few days after BALCO was raided, when he and Jim Valente drove the 90 miles to Sacramento to talk to attorney Troy Ellerman about the case.

Ellerman was a former rodeo cowboy–turned criminal defense lawyer. He had met Conte in 1997, when he had helped Conte's middle daughter, Alicia, out of some legal trouble in Sacramento. Late on the night of the raid, Conte had called Ellerman at home. For an hour, the lawyer stood in his kitchen with the phone to his ear, listening to Conte complain about the agents. Conte said he had been bullied into giving a statement. They kept him locked in a room and forced him to say things. They coaxed him into consenting to the search of his storage locker. They never read him his Miranda rights. Conte was creating his defense right there on phone as he went along. Ellerman told Conte to relax. They could meet in a day or two and go over everything. In the meantime, Conte should not talk to anybody. Conte agreed.

But the next day, Conte called agent Jeff Novitzky's cell phone several times. Conte told the agent he was being hounded by the press. He was staying away from BALCO, keeping a low profile, Conte said.

Novitzky asked about the names Vince Reed and Vince Constantino, which appeared on FedEx receipts. They were fake names, Conte explained: "I was sending things I shouldn't be sending."

Conte said athletes were calling wanting to know what was going on. What should Conte tell them? Tell the truth, Novitzky advised. He warned Conte not to do anything to obstruct justice or interfere with the ongoing investigation. I would never do that, Conte replied.

Conte didn't mention any of this when he got to Ellerman's office a few blocks from the state Capitol and began his monologue. As Valente sat silent, Conte told the lawyer his entire life and times, describing his evolution as a self-made scientist and entrepreneur, how he developed his businesses, the legitimate one as well as the one that had gotten him into trouble. He gave Ellerman a history of doping in sports and a primer on performance enhancers—what they were, how to use them, why they work. He also dropped the names of the big-time athletes he had been supplying with performance-enhancing drugs, from Barry Bonds to Marion Jones, and bragged about his role in their successes.

The guy is brilliant, Ellerman thought, *he knows all the science.* But he also concluded Conte was a bit nuts.

Ellerman recognized Conte would be a high-maintenance client, impossible to control. He didn't want to represent him. Still, because of his friendship with Alicia Conte, Ellerman wanted to help. He called Robert Holley, a lawyer with whom Ellerman often partnered. They made an odd pair: Ellerman, the muscular, conservative cowboy with the shaved head, and Holley, a wizened liberal with a scruffy beard. They decided to go in together on the case. Ellerman would represent Valente, and Holley would take Conte.

"He and Bob initially connected," Ellerman said of Conte and Holley. "They would sit around and talk about how they used to smoke dope and how they were into music and how they did all these wild things back in the day."

Holley soon realized, though, that it would be a big challenge to keep Conte's mouth shut. Throughout the case, Holley battled Conte's desire to go public. As information about the BALCO investigation began to appear in the media, Conte yearned to tell his "No Choice" story on national television. He was convinced that the American people, the prosecutors, and even the president of the United States would understand—the public needed to know the truth about the pervasiveness of drugs in sports. Conte badgered Holley to let him call *60 Minutes* or *20/20* or ESPN.

Conte craved attention, but he also seemed to want to convince the world that he hadn't revealed his clients' drug use to authorities and essentially become an informant. Later, as the extent of his cooperation became known, Conte made sweeping denials: He had never named names, never told Novitzky and the other agents how the business worked, never said anything to anybody.

"He believed he could go on any TV show and they would be convinced that he was a victim and he wasn't a rat," said a source who worked with Conte. "And I think it really stemmed from the fact that now he realized he was a rat."

Whenever Conte became too insistent about going on television, the lawyers would say, "Fine, we'll be '60 Minutes' and we'll interview you.".One such mock program took place in a booth at Max's Restaurant in Burlingame, a deli-style eatery near BALCO.

Holley played Mike Wallace, hammering Conte, leaving him stuttering repeatedly and inconsistent with his responses. His faux TV appearance convinced Holley and Ellerman that Conte would be a disaster on TV or the witness stand. Conte didn't agree. Within three months of hiring Holley, Conte was threatening to fire him. The threats would continue for the next 18 months.

In addition to pestering his attorney, Conte tried to manipulate the athletes targeted in the investigation. Conte reassured the athletes that their drug use would remain secret as long as they did what he told them. Admit nothing, he advised. The government had nothing on him, and if everyone just played dumb, they could all beat the case.

"Everybody—the athletes, the coaches, Victor—everybody was circling the wagons," said one lawyer. Conte concocted cover stories. The alphabet code was recast so that C on the doping calendars stood for vitamin C, not The Cream; E was vitamin E, not EPO; and so on.

If they were asked about The Clear, the athletes were supposed to say they thought they were taking flaxseed oil. Alternatively, they could say they had no idea what they were taking. In any event, they were to say that Conte had never told them the substance was illegal or banned. He tried to leverage reluctant athletes, telling them that all the other athletes had already agreed to go with the cover story. Conte's campaign came close to obstruction of justice, one lawyer said.

"It was all to crank up the pressure so they would fall in line," the lawyer said. "All he was doing was directing responses. . . . He was very offensive in terms of his obstructionist tactics. He tried to pull a lot of levers, he was trying to run the investigation and it was very disheartening. He could have been indicted on that easily."

By the end of September, a federal grand jury had convened to investigate BALCO. Athletes received subpoenas directing them to appear at the federal courthouse near San Francisco's city hall. Eventually, three dozen athletes from Major League Baseball, the National Football League, Olympic track and field, pro boxing, swimming, cycling, and bodybuilding, all with ties to BALCO, were ordered to testify. The subpoenas frightened many athletes. Their fear helped Novitzky extract confessions.

Novitzky visited a supplements company on the Peninsula owned by Emeric Delczeg, the Hungarian bodybuilder whom the surveillance team had seen at BALCO. Delczeg told Novitzky that he had sold testosterone to Conte for $140 per vial and growth hormone for $700 per box. Delczeg also confessed to helping Conte make a drug connection in Arizona so he could obtain a special kind of insulin.

Some athletes phoned Novitzky and confessed. John McEwen, the U.S. champion hammer thrower, called to inquire about his subpoena. In the conversation, McEwen admitted Conte gave him The Cream and The Clear. He said The Clear was a molecularly altered steroid that would not show up on drug tests. He thought The Cream was testosterone, but he wasn't sure how he came to believe that. McEwen told Novitzky that Kevin Toth, the shot-put champion, had hooked him up with Victor Conte.

Novitzky made calls himself. He got a cell number for Armando Rios, the former Giants outfielder, and phoned him at his home in Florida to tell him he would be subpoenaed. In that conversation, Rios confessed to buying growth hormone and testosterone from Bonds's trainer, Greg Anderson.

*   *   *

The BALCO case could not have come at a worse time for Major League Baseball. Earlier that year, after years of stalling, the sport had finally, grudgingly begun testing its players for steroids. To doping experts and athletes in other sports, the baseball program seemed laughably easy to beat: Most players faced only a single test per year. The weakness of the program made the results even more shocking: Seven percent of major leaguers—the equivalent of two full teams—had tested positive for steroids. How many more juiced players had temporarily cleaned up so they could pass the test? How many were using growth hormone, for which no test existed? To doping experts, the results underscored that baseball was awash in steroids, that the big power numbers of the 1990s were drug-fueled. The baseball test results indicated "that so much of what we've come to believe has no legs, that the records we thought were incredible may, in fact, have been incredible," as Dr. Gary Wadler of the World Anti-Doping Agency told the *Washington Post*.

The steroid test results had been a public-relations headache for the game. Now, baseball faced far worse. Three of the game's greatest stars—the Yankees' Jason Giambi and Gary Sheffield, and Barry Bonds, the Home Run King—were among the major leaguers caught up in BALCO, subpoenaed by the grand jury. Grand jury proceedings were secret, but if there ever were a BALCO trial, the game faced the nightmarish prospect that a star player might be compelled to testify in open court and admit he had been using banned drugs. For baseball, another possibility seemed equally grim: A star might fall into a perjury trap. A player could go before the grand jury, claim to be drug free, and get himself indicted for lying. There were precedents for both scenarios.

Looming over BALCO was the specter of the 1985 Pittsburgh drug trials, in which seven ballplayers were forced to testify about buying cocaine in the Pirates' clubhouse and using drugs with their teammates. In all, 25 players, including some of the brightest stars of the era, such as Keith Hernandez and Dave Parker, were caught up in the long-running drug scandal.

More recently, there had been the case of Chris Webber, the

National Basketball Association All-Star who had fallen into a perjury trap in 2002. Webber had been subpoenaed by a federal grand jury investigating a payoff scandal from his days on the University of Michigan basketball team. Webber lied about his involvement and was indicted. He escaped prison perhaps only because a key prosecution witness died from a heart attack. Webber was forced to plead guilty to contempt, pay a huge fine, and publicly admit he had lied under oath.

Even before the stars testified before the grand jury, the BALCO prosecutors ratcheted up the pressure on baseball with another round of subpoenas. This time the target was baseball's steroid-testing program and the labs that had conducted the 2003 tests. Testing had been done anonymously, but the prosecutors sought both the test results data and the players' actual urine samples. With that information, the government could match players' names to their samples.

The move outraged players and owners alike, who viewed the subpoenas as an intrusion on players' privacy. The anger, though, was muted by fear. If a player testified that he was drug-free, the government could check his test results—or even retest his sample to see if he had been using BALCO's designer steroids. If the sample came back dirty, the perjury trap would spring.

Baseball's hierarchy was deeply concerned about a player getting indicted for false testimony in BALCO, as David Cornwell, a well-connected sports attorney from Orange County in Southern California, learned soon after he got into the case. Cornwell represented Benito Santiago, who had been subpoenaed after the agents found drug calendars with his name on them in the BALCO raid. Just days before Santiago was scheduled to testify, Cornwell was driving along the 405 Freeway when his cell phone rang.

The caller was Gene Orza, the No. 2 man at the Major League Baseball Players Association and Cornwell's old friend. The men chatted casually about BALCO and Santiago's impending appearance. Then Orza got to the point. He was calling with a message, not as a friend, but as a top baseball official.

"I want you to know that I, Gene Orza, will hold you, David Cornwell, personally responsible if anybody that you represent commits perjury in this process," he said.

Cornwell got it. Other lawyers in the case were also confronting the issue. For the BALCO lawyers, the task was to prepare their clients so they could give truthful answers, but not volunteer any information. That way, they would avoid perjury charges, but at the same time come off as lousy prospective witnesses in the event the case went to trial.

"You wanted to make your client as non-valuable to the government as you could without having him commit perjury," said one attorney.

The risk of perjury was one of several issues of concern to Michael Rains, Barry Bonds's new lawyer. Rains was a veteran criminal defense lawyer who often represented policemen accused of brutality. BALCO had come to him through one of his law-enforcement connections—a Bonds bodyguard who was a former South San Francisco cop. As soon as he took the case, Rains began trying to learn what evidence the government might have against Bonds. The task wasn't easy. Federal grand juries conduct themselves in great secrecy, and evidence is closely held by the prosecutors. Rains was having trouble developing sources of information.

In his effort to find out what he was up against, Rains invited Bob Holley and Troy Ellerman to come to his office in the East Bay suburbs. Their clients, Conte and Valente, were two of the grand jury's targets. They would have a grasp of the case if anyone did. Also at the meeting was William Rapoport, Anderson's lawyer. Rapoport was Rains's friend. Rains had set him up with Anderson, unaware that Rapoport had a history with Victor Conte: Three years earlier, he had represented BALCO in a lawsuit and then had sued the BALCO owner when he didn't pay his bill.

To the other lawyers at the meeting, Rains appeared to have two goals: keeping his famous client's reputation from being stained by the BALCO scandal, and ensuring that Bonds did not fall into a perjury trap by making a provably false statement under oath. Conte and Valente insisted they had said nothing to the authorities that would implicate Bonds in the use of banned drugs, their lawyers told Rains. Anderson said the same, according to Rapoport. Anderson believed Bonds would be okay because he didn't think there were any documents with the slugger's name on them.

Rains didn't find any of that particularly reassuring. He had the impression that Conte and Anderson had talked too much to the agents. Rains was particularly frustrated with Anderson. The trainer had been sloppy. He hadn't kept copies of his documents or backed up his computer, so he was going by memory when describing what the feds had seized. Rains also suspected that Anderson was sugarcoating the evidence.

"I wonder to this day," Rains said later, "whether or not Greg actually did have some things that maybe he just didn't want to talk about, he was too scared to tell us."

As the case unfolded, the BALCO defense lawyers had other meetings, and they developed a good rapport. Ellerman and Holley came to like Rains, and they sympathized with him for his unenviable job: representing a difficult client who obviously had been juicing. According to Rains, Bonds's position was that he had never taken steroids, although it was remotely possible he had taken them unknowingly.

"Barry knew, Barry is lying when he says he didn't know," Ellerman said later. "We had meetings with his attorney. . . . We met three or four times, and he made it very clear to us that he wanted us to do everything we could to make sure Barry's name was protected. There wasn't any payment involved, there weren't any threats, there wasn't any quid pro quo, but he made it very clear that Barry would appreciate it if we kept him out of it. And we had several discussions about how Mike Rains knew what the score was—and that is that he knew Barry was using."

Rains also sought a meeting with Jeff Nedrow, the Assistant U.S. Attorney who was assigned to BALCO. It went well enough. Nedrow said Bonds could come to his office in San Jose on December 1, three days before his scheduled testimony, to look through BALCO-related documents that pertained to the Giants star. The government was giving witnesses a sneak peek as encouragement to be as truthful and forthcoming as possible. Rains left feeling guardedly optimistic. But as the date approached, Nedrow called and canceled. He said that if Bonds came to the courthouse early on the day of his testimony, he could look at the documents then. Now Rains was getting worried.

In late November, the lawyer floated a trial balloon in the press.

Two days after Bonds collected his latest National League MVP award, the *Los Angeles Times* ran a story that quoted Rains as saying Bonds might have taken steroids "unwittingly, mixed into a supplement or nutritional shake without his knowledge." Bonds, too, had been working to distance himself from BALCO. During a teleconference the day he won the MVP, Bonds told the media that Rains advised him against answering specific questions about the case. But of his trainer, he said, "I can't answer any questions about Greg Anderson because I don't know what a person does after they leave me."

Eventually, Rains realized his biggest problem was that his client was a loose cannon. There was no way to be sure what Bonds would say when confronted by prosecutors. Bonds was impulsive, with a tendency to pop off. As he told a clump of reporters in New York a few months later: "I don't really believe half the shit I'm saying, anyway."

To minimize the chance that an impulsive statement would get him in trouble, Rains put Bonds through several mock cross-examinations. Rains asked tough questions. Bonds got angry, reacting like a bully. "What kind of a stupid question is that?" Bonds responded to some questions. "Go fuck yourself," he replied to others.

That would not play well with the grand jury, Rains reminded Bonds. He warned Bonds about his tendency to drift off into non sequiturs with his responses. Rains worried that that would appear as if Bonds had something to hide.

By then, the BALCO grand jury was already in business.

On Thursday, October 23, Don Catlin had flown up from Los Angeles. Agent Novitzky picked him up at the airport. At last they met in person. For a year, Novitzky and Catlin had developed a bond over the phone—the student and his teacher, or the sleuthing agent and the scientific expert. It was the first day of testimony, and Catlin was the lead-off witness. En route to the courthouse, Novitzky drove past BALCO. There it was, a nondescript storefront in a strip mall, a far cry from the tree house in the redwoods Catlin had mused about.

A few hours later, Dr. Don H. Catlin, director, UCLA Olympic Analytical Laboratory, took the witness stand. His task was to educate the grand jury about performance-enhancing drugs. He sat in the front of the room facing the grand jurors, with prosecutor Nedrow at a podium 20 feet away. Soon after Catlin was sworn in, Nedrow reached into a bag and pulled out items seized from the BALCO raid.

What's this? That's erythropoietin, EPO.

And this? That's a bottle of human growth hormone.

As he testified, Catlin thought about the two decades he had spent researching doping in sports. His work on BALCO seemed the culmination of his efforts, and for a moment he choked up, struggling with his responses.

"In many ways, this was the personification of a lot that I had worked for," Catlin would say later. Still, it wasn't a "very happy moment," he said. All that he had been "whining" about for years—the nightmare of clandestine labs engineering undetectable steroids—had turned out to be true.

The following week the first of the elite athletes turned up at the courthouse, subpoenas in hand, accompanied by lawyers and in some cases bodyguards as well. The athletes were met by a crowd of reporters and photographers. The press had learned that the BALCO grand jury was meeting every Thursday. So the media camped out on the sidewalk in front of the federal building. Their editors hoped they could grab a quote or shoot some video of the world's fastest man and his Olympic gold medalist girlfriend; or the all-pro linebacker with the four Super Bowl rings; or, especially, baseball's Home Run King.

The athletes weren't at all happy to see the media. Thursdays at the federal building began to have the feel of an old-style Mob trial, with reporters and camera crews trying to intercept the famous stars who were being quizzed in secret about their drug intake, and the reluctant witnesses running for cover or snarling in anger as they came and went from the courthouse.

One Thursday, after three hours on the witness stand, world sprint champion Tim Montgomery slunk into the backseat of a waiting car, hiding his face from photographers behind a travel bag. On another Thursday, Tyrone Wheatley, a running back with the Oakland Raiders, ran into a group of photographers on his way into the building. "Take a picture, I'll fucking mess you up," Wheatley snarled. When an Associated Press photographer raised his camera, Wheatley rushed him, laying a karate chop on the photographer's right wrist.

One week later, Bobby Estalella, the former Giants catcher, walked into the courthouse and was asked by reporters what he was doing back in San Francisco. "I'm on vacation," he replied. Asked his name by a writer who didn't recognize him, Estalella said, "John Doe." Later, as he left, the muscular journeyman shoved his way through TV cameras and, to cap off his day, flipped off a bunch of photographers.

The athletes were on far better behavior once they got inside. Before they took the stand, they had to say good-bye to their expensive lawyers and buff, attentive bodyguards, because by law, every witness must go before the grand jury alone. Before the athletes took the stand, Nedrow or one of the other prosecutors would go over the ground rules. The athletes were granted immunity from prosecution if they testified truthfully before the grand jury. Their lawyers had been assured that the prosecutors had no designs on going after athletes for taking illegal drugs. But if the athletes lied on the witness stand, there would there be trouble; then, the federal government would come down hard, and they'd face the same fate as Chris Webber.

So with few exceptions, the more than three dozen athletes who appeared before the grand jury admitted taking steroids—through injections in their bellies, by droplets squirted beneath their tongues, with creams rubbed into their bodies. They weren't asked why. Perhaps the answers were too obvious: It was all to run faster, jump higher, hit the ball farther, and, ultimately, make more money. Some of the confessions were grudging and evasive. Others were extremely forthcoming. It came down to the same thing: Competitive sports, it turned out, was part mirage, a game of shadows.

Montgomery, for instance, admitted he regularly took steroids and the banned drug human growth hormone before breaking the world record in the 100 meters. And Estalella, only minutes before he got tough with the camera crews, acknowledged to the grand jury that he had been injecting himself with testosterone.

If the confessions had been made in public, careers would have been ruined and entire sports tainted. But because they confessed in a secret proceeding, the athletes seemed confident their secrets would never be revealed. Afterward, Montgomery and many of the rest resumed their lies, insisting to the fans who paid their enormous salaries or appearance fees that they had never used steroids, never taken anything more powerful than a protein shake or a supplement pill you could buy legally down at the local GNC.

Barry Bonds, too, had publicly insisted he had never touched a steroid in his life. But what would he say to the grand jury, under oath and with the feds bearing down on him?

Nobody had a clue what would come out of the mouth of baseball's greatest player after he swore to tell the whole truth and nothing but—not even his own lawyer.

Chapter 19

The morning of December 4, 2003, was chilly and bleak in San Francisco. At 7:00 AM, reporters and photographers were already gathering outside the courthouse to await the Home Run King. The Phillip Burton Federal Building occupied an entire block, but there were only two ways into the steel-and-glass high-rise: a public entrance on Turk Street, and an underground garage that was restricted to judges, lawmen, and other officials. Most of the press pack stood on the sidewalk on Turk Street.

Lawyer Mike Rains had arranged for his superstar client to enter the courthouse as discreetly as possible, avoiding the gauntlet of reporters. At mid-morning, Rains, Barry Bonds, and a retired police captain who was Bonds's bodyguard that day drove up from the Peninsula and met IRS Special Agent Jeff Novitzky about a mile from the courthouse. The agent had been assigned to drive Bonds, his lawyer, and his bodyguard to the federal building in an unmarked car.

Bonds knew who Novitzky was. He felt Novitzky was responsible for forcing him to testify. It was a short ride, but Bonds wasted little time starting in on the agent, grousing that the government had wrongly dragged him into this thing and made him the focus of the probe.

Rains wished Bonds would shut up.

The IRS agent didn't respond.

At about 10:50 AM, the car approached the Larkin Street entrance to the building's underground garage, around the corner from where most of the cameras were waiting. The agent had to stop for another car, and a few photographers rushed forward and captured the image of a startled Bonds arriving for his day in court. The slugger grumbled that Novitzky had set him up; the feds, Bonds was sure, wanted to make him look as bad as possible, wanted to make certain they got their photo op of baseball's greatest player under subpoena.

Again, Novitzky did not bite.

Novitzky and the group rode an employee elevator to the lobby, where they had to change elevators for the ride up to the 17th floor. As word spread that Bonds had arrived, the photographers at the front entrance pointed cameras through the plate glass and into the building—some photographing the lanky, bald Novitzky ushering the muscle-bound baseball superstar, dressed in a shimmering gray suit and matching tie. A sign in the background directed employees to the "Federal Fitness Center."

At 10:56, Bonds arrived on 17, breezed past another group of reporters, and went inside for his date with the grand jury.

Bonds wasn't scheduled to begin testifying until 1:00, but Rains had arranged with the government to look through the BALCO documents that allegedly pertained to Bonds. It would be their only chance to examine the evidence before Bonds testified, and Rains desperately wanted to see what they were up against. Rains had a bad feeling about the day. Despite the prosecutors' assurances about immunity from prosecution, the lawyer was fearful that, in the end, BALCO would become the U.S. versus Barry Bonds. He became more concerned soon after arriving on 17.

Rains met with the prosecutors without Bonds present. They cut to the chase: The deal was off. Bonds would not be permitted to look at any documents. The prosecutors offered no reason, and Rains was furious, believing the government was out to get Bonds. When Rains relayed the news, Bonds was livid, too. With nothing else to do but wait, the men spent the next two hours seething and cursing, Rains mother-fucking the prosecutors, Bonds mother-fucking Novitzky. Even so, Rains worked to compose himself and, more importantly, Bonds, hoping his client would be focused when he had to walk into the grand jury room all alone. A witness can prepare extensively, but when he takes the stand in front of a federal grand jury, the options narrow dramatically: He can take the Fifth Amendment, tell the truth, or lie and risk a perjury indictment. And if the government offers an immunity deal, as they had in the BALCO case, taking the Fifth is not an option.

At 1:05 PM, Bonds stuck his head out into the public waiting area and asked reporters, "Is my mother here yet?" Assured by reporters that Pat Bonds and Barry's wife, Liz, were in the building, he ducked back out of sight. Shortly after, the Home Run King entered the grand jury room. Rains remained back in an anteroom, waiting nervously.

After Bonds was sworn in, prosecutor Jeff Nedrow tried to explain the ground rules. Bonds mocked him.

"You are confusing—I'm telling you," Bonds said. The immaculately dressed slugger looked at the 16 grand jurors, most of whom were dressed casually, as though they had just stepped out of the house to run to 7-Eleven for a quart of milk.

"Is he confusing to you guys?" Bonds asked. "I'm glad it's not [just] me."

Nedrow persisted. He described Bonds's immunity agreement, which had already been discussed in the meeting with Rains: Nothing Bonds said before the grand jury could be used to prosecute him for any crime, as long as he told the truth. But the immunity didn't extend to perjury, Nedrow emphasized.

The session began innocently enough, with Bonds describing his long association with Greg Anderson, the boyhood friend who now was his weight trainer. Briefly, he told how Anderson had introduced him to BALCO.

Soon, though, Nedrow and his veteran boss, Ross Nadel, began to show Bonds page after page of documents that implicated him in the use of steroids and other performance-enhancing drugs. There were doping calendars that detailed specific drugs to take on specific days. Ledger pages that logged testosterone levels in his body at various points. Documents from steroid tests completed on samples of his blood and urine. The prosecutors peppered him with questions, beginning first with The Cream and The Clear, the undetectable steroids distributed by Conte specifically to evade drug testers. Bonds's answers meandered, but he admitted nothing, yielding virtually no ground on his long-standing claim that his tremendous sports achievements had been all natural, the product of hard work and God-given talent.

"At the end of 2002, 2003 season, when I was going through my dad died of cancer . . . I was fatigued, just needed recovery you know, and this guy says, 'Try this cream, try this cream,' he said. And Greg came to the ballpark and said, you know, 'This will help you recover.' And he rubbed some cream on my arm . . . gave me some flaxseed oil, man. It's like, 'Whatever, dude.'

"And I was at the ballpark, whatever. I don't care. What's lotion going to do to me? How many times have I heard that 'This is going to rub into you and work'? Let him be happy, we're friends, you know?"

Bonds was shown a vial the government believed had contained The Clear. Bonds insisted it was for flaxseed oil. He said he had ingested the substance by placing a couple of drops under his tongue—the prescribed method for taking the BALCO steroid, but hardly the common way to down flaxseed oil, a product sold at health-food stores.

"And I was like, to me, it didn't even work," he told the grand jury. "You know me, I'm thirty-nine years old. I'm dealing with pain. All I want is the pain relief, you know? And you know, to recover, you know, night games to day games. That's it. And I didn't think the stuff worked. I was like, 'Dude, whatever,' but he's my friend. . . .

"I never asked Greg. When he said it was flaxseed oil, I just said, 'Whatever.' It was in the ballpark . . . in front of everybody. I mean, all the reporters, my teammates. I mean, they all saw it. I didn't hide it. I didn't hide it. . . . You know, trainers come up to me and say, 'Hey Barry, try this.'"

Bonds's approach was obvious: He didn't know what he put in his body, he simply ingested whatever substance his trainer gave him. If his trainer told him it was flaxseed oil and arthritis cream, then that's what it was. To people who knew Bonds's meticulous and controlling nature, the claim was absurd, but the prosecutors didn't pursue the point.

Instead, they began quizzing Bonds about doping calendars and documents showing the results of blood and urine tests, all pulled from folders marked with Bonds's name or initials.

Did the notations for "Growth" and "G" mean Bonds had been taking the anabolic substance human growth hormone?

"I don't know what G is," he replied. He had never injected himself with drugs, he declared. He knew nothing about paperwork showing the results of steroid screens run on his blood. Questions about a document reflecting the purchase of growth hormone—"!G! one box off season and two box season $1,500," the note read—prompted a nonresponsive answer.

"Greg and I are friends," Bonds said. "I never paid Greg for anything. I gave Greg money for his training me. . . . You're going to bring up documents and more documents. I have never seen anything written by Greg Anderson on a piece of paper."

Nadel showed Bonds a bottle and asked about a calendar notation that referred to the steroid depotestosterone.

"I have never ever seen this bottle or any bottle pertaining that says depotestosterone," Bonds said.

"It's an injectable steroid, right?"

Bonds denied using it, then began rambling again: "Greg is a good guy, you know this kid is a great kid. He has a child."

What about Clomiphene, an anti-estrogen drug employed by steroid users when coming off a cycle?

"I've never heard of it."

Erythropoietin, aka EPO, an endurance-boosting drug?

"I couldn't even pronounce it."

Modafinil, a stimulant?

"I've never heard of it."

Of the substances Anderson provided, Bonds said, "If it's a steroid, it's not working."

While Bonds was parrying the prosecutors' questions, about 25 reporters had gathered outside the entrance to the grand jury room, waiting for the slugger. At one point, T. J. Quinn of the New York *Daily News* slipped away from the pack, made his way down a back hallway, and put his ear to the wall. He overheard an exchange about trenbolone, a steroid sold to improve the muscle quality of beef cattle.

"I never heard of it," Quinn heard Bonds say.

Meanwhile, former Giants catcher Benito Santiago arrived with David Cornwell, the sports attorney from Orange County, and another lawyer. The men were directed to a room near the one where Rains was waiting. Santiago and his lawyers spent an hour with Agent Novitzky looking through a pile of documents that related to BALCO and Anderson.

After they were done, Cornwell went to introduce himself to Rains. Cornwell sensed that Rains was agitated. When Rains learned that Santiago had been allowed to get an advance look at documents, he fumed about how the government had reneged on his deal.

Why? asked Cornwell.

"Because they're trying to set my guy up," Rains said.

Cornwell stated the obvious: No problem if his guy testified truthfully.

Rains agreed. But he continued to worry.

Inside the grand jury room, the prosecutors were quizzing Bonds about a calendar entry that said, "Barry 12-2-02 T, 1CC G—pee." Did that reflect events on December 2, 2002, when Bonds used testosterone and growth hormone, and then gave a urine sample to Anderson for a private drug test?

"T could mean anything," Bonds replied. "G could mean anything. And pee could probably mean anything."

He couldn't explain a medical report describing his testosterone levels—"I wouldn't even understand it anyway, so they wouldn't talk to me about that," he said—nor calendar entries kept by Anderson that reflected his use of steroids and the anti-estrogen drug Clomid.

"I've never had a calendar with him, never had anything," Bonds said.

"Did Greg ever give you insulin?"

"Insulin? I'm not a diabetic."

A mention of the Giants prompted a Bonds discourse on his deep suspicions about his sport: "We don't trust the ball team. We don't trust baseball. . . . Believe me, it's a business. The last time I played baseball was in college. Believe me, it's a business. . . . I don't trust their doctors or nothing."

As for Anderson, Bonds said he had paid his boyhood pal $15,000 for supervising his weight training. "I paid him in cash,"

Bonds testified. "I make seventeen million." Bonds later added that he gave Anderson a $20,000 cash bonus after hitting his record 73rd home run, and he bought the trainer a World Series ring after the Giants reached the Fall Classic in 2002.

At the end of the more than three-hour session, the grand jurors were given a chance to question the superstar. "With all the money you make, have you ever considered building a mansion" for Anderson, a grand juror asked.

"One, I'm black," Bonds replied. "And I'm keeping my money. And there's not too many rich black people in this world. There's more wealthy Asian people and Caucasian and white. And I ain't giving my money up."

With that, they were done. Nedrow seemed pleased. It had been a slow process, but the prosecutor understood why it had taken so long: When you know what a witness knows, and they won't tell you what you know they know, it takes more time.

Bonds, too, seemed to think the session had gone well: He left the room confident he had asserted control over the government's inquiry, just as he controlled his baseball team and, for that matter, most of the people in his life. He believed his reputation had been preserved and his well-guarded secret had not been revealed.

When Bonds emerged from the grand jury, Rains met him in the hallway. The lawyer started to discuss their exit with Bonds's bodyguard. Nedrow tapped Rains on the shoulder.

"Mike, would you talk to your client?"

Rains turned to find Bonds chatting up some grand jurors, acting as if he were about to start signing autographs. Rains corralled his client, and at 4:27, some five and a half hours after he had arrived at the courthouse, Bonds emerged and swept past the waiting media.

And then they were gone, down the elevator, out the garage, headed off into a driving rain. There was no say-it-ain't-so moment—no heartbroken tyke confronting Bonds as he left the grand jury in the way a sniffling kid had confronted Shoeless Joe Jackson during the 1919 Black Sox Scandal, imploring his hero to deny that he and his teammates had fixed the World Series. Instead, there was only a truck driver who slowed as he passed the federal building and yelled, "Barry didn't do it!"

The sign on the side of his truck read: "Competition Specialties/ Your one-stop high-performance warehouse."

Bonds might have been less confident that his secret was secure if he had known what other witnesses were telling the grand jury.

Santiago would follow Bonds to the witness stand. The catcher did his best to dodge the prosecutor's questions. Frequently he responded, "I don't know" or "I don't remember." Santiago was Puerto Rican, and he implied he didn't speak English well enough to understand what he was being asked.

He claimed he didn't remember whether he got growth hormone from Greg Anderson. Then he admitted he did get Growth from the trainer and injected it into himself. Then he again became vague about what he had been provided.

"So, I'm sorry, but I have to ask," Nedrow said. "You injected these items into your body, but didn't know exactly what they were?"

Replied Santiago: "Believe it or not."

Santiago also said he had never spoken to Bonds about Anderson and what the trainer was doing for Bonds. Still, by the end of his testimony, Santiago had acknowledged that Bonds's trainer had sold him The Clear, The Cream, liquid testosterone, and the bodybuilders' steroid Winstrol. Two former Giants, Estalella and Rios, already had testified that they, too, had bought steroids from Anderson. All three players knew Bonds's trainer as a steroid dealer. Although the players dodged the topic of Bonds's drug use, the obvious import of their testimony was that they were receiving the same drugs that Anderson was giving to Bonds.

The sprinter Tim Montgomery had addressed Bonds's drug use more directly. Montgomery said that when he visited BALCO in 2000 or 2001, he had discussed Bonds's use of steroids with Victor Conte. Conte had bragged he was providing Winstrol to Bonds, Montgomery said. Winstrol was no problem for a ballplayer in the days before steroid testing, but a track athlete couldn't touch the stuff because it was so easily detected, Montgomery explained to the grand jury. "You could definitely get busted off of them steroids," he said.

A week after Bonds testified, Jason Giambi of the Yankees appeared before the grand jury. Initially nervous, Giambi became relaxed, then confessed to using steroids and many other drugs. He acknowledged that he knew precisely what he was taking.

Giambi said Bonds had introduced him to Anderson. He said he had paid Bonds's trainer more than $10,000 for steroids. At one point, Giambi described how he self-administered growth hormone by "pinching the fat" on his stomach and injecting the substance just below his skin. Testosterone, on the other hand, required an ordinary injection.

"So, you would put it in your arm?" prosecutor Nedrow asked Giambi.

"No, you wouldn't," he said. "You'd put it in your ass."

On January 20, 2004, with more than 130,000 American troops stationed in Iraq and U.S. unemployment rates persistently high, President George W. Bush invoked steroids in his State of the Union Address.

The president spent nearly two hours test-marketing themes to kick off his reelection campaign, but what stood out in that 5,230-word speech was a 98-word passage that seemed to come out of nowhere. After proposing additional funding to test high school students for drugs like cocaine and marijuana, the former owner of the Texas Rangers said, "To help children make right choices, they need good examples: Athletics play such an important role in our society, but unfortunately, some in professional sports are not setting much of an example." Bush then decried the use of performance-enhancing drugs in sports, and he called upon athletes, coaches, owners, and union representatives "to take the lead, to send the right signal, to get tough, and to get rid of steroids now."

On Capitol Hill, the steroid passage came to be known as "the crazy two sentences." At the time, public awareness of the BALCO steroids case was limited to a smattering of news reports of famous athletes testifying at the San Francisco federal courthouse.

The morning after Bush's State of the Union Address, Attorney General John Ashcroft and his staff convened for their daily morning briefing. About 20 members of Ashcroft's team sat around a rectangular conference table, with the 61-year-old A.G. seated so he could look out two big windows at the FBI building, where he sometimes played pickup basketball games in the FBI gym.

The officials began talking about the reference to steroids in the president's speech. "We all looked at each other and giggled, 'Where did that come from?' " Mark Corallo, Ashcroft's director of public affairs, recalled.

Although the War on Terrorism was clearly Ashcroft's top priority, he had begun taking a personal interest in the BALCO case. That interest reflected Ashcroft's rigid views of right and wrong, as well as his love of sports.

The son of a Pentecostal minister, Ashcroft was a solid athlete growing up in Springfield, Missouri, good enough to make the football team at Yale. Even in college, Ashcroft was a staunch social conservative; a member of the Assemblies of God church, he disdained smoking and drinking and premarital sex, and presented himself as a young man with a strong moral compass.

After law school at the University of Chicago, he set off on a career in Republican politics back home. A champion of the death penalty and staunch foe of abortion and gay rights, he was elected to two terms as Missouri's Attorney General, two terms as governor, and one term in the U.S. Senate. In 2000, though, he had been defeated for reelection by a dead man—Democrat Mel Carnahan, killed in a plane crash the month before the vote. Ashcroft's political career seemed at an end until then-President-elect Bush chose Ashcroft as America's new top cop, a selection celebrated by the religious right and condemned by many liberals.

In addition to his religious fervor, Ashcroft was a real sports fanatic, especially partial to the St. Louis Cardinals. His office was adorned with sports memorabilia, including a bat signed by Hall of Famer Stan Musial, who broke in with the Cardinals in 1941 at the age of 20 and played his entire 22-year career in St. Louis. Now *that* was a ballplayer, and ballplayers were Ashcroft's heroes.

Ashcroft was not alone. His office was full of baseball fans, many of whom were fathers passing their passion down to their sons. Corallo, the chief press spokesman, was obsessed with the Yankees. His office was like a shrine: with posters of Lou Gehrig, Babe Ruth, and Roger Maris; a large, signed picture of Mickey Mantle; a framed stamp of Yankee Stadium; a picture of Joe DiMaggio; a yellowed copy of his hometown newspaper, the *Mount Vernon Daily Argus*, from 1978, with a sketch of the entire club, including Corallo's boyhood hero, All-Star catcher Thurman Munson, who died the following year in a plane crash.

Ed McFadden, Ashcroft's chief speechwriter, was a fan of the San Francisco Giants. McFadden had grown up in San Francisco, his family had had Giants season tickets, and his dad had even introduced him once to Willie Mays. In September 2001, McFadden had taken his son to Pac Bell Park, and they were treated to Barry Bonds smacking his 60th home run of the season.

BALCO and baseball became such a regular subject at the morning briefings that the women at the table often rolled their eyes, as if to say, "There go the boys again."

Each time there was a BALCO update, Ashcroft and the others would express contempt for the suspected drug cheats. Kevin Ryan, the United States Attorney in San Francisco, relayed few details of his case, but they all knew what was going on: The players were juicing. Ashcroft's aides insisted that their interest in BALCO had nothing to do with politics. Rather, it was a guy thing. The players were cheating the sport they loved, showing disrespect for the achievements of Stan Musial and Hank Aaron and Mickey Mantle. There was a serious public health issue as well: The drugs were dangerous, and kids were using them, convinced by the example of superstars that steroids were a ticket to the big leagues.

"Stan Musial didn't need steroids," Ashcroft would tell his aides. "Let me tell you something, back before they were allowed to wear body armor, if some guy was known to be taking drugs like that, you can bet Bob Gibson would give him some chin music."

In early February, the BALCO grand jury was ready to hand up indictments. Corallo couldn't wait. As much as anybody in the office, the longtime Yankees fan had railed against the BALCO athletes. The announcement of the indictments would also be poignant for McFadden, the Giants fan. He had coincidentally attended the same San

Francisco high school as Kevin Ryan, Saint Ignatius College Preparatory. McFadden was a few years younger than Ryan, but he recalled the U.S. Attorney as a running back on the school's last outstanding football team. Now, he knew Ryan as a no-nonsense prosecutor who also shared his love of the San Francisco Giants. Months later, McFadden would joke with Ryan: "Whatever you're doing, it better not affect our pennant run."

At the urging of his staff, Ashcroft decided that he would announce the BALCO indictments himself at a press conference in Washington. The announcement was scheduled for February 12—one week before the start of spring training. Ryan would be there to receive his credit, as would IRS CI Special Agent Jeff Novitzky and representatives of the Food and Drug Administration and the San Mateo County Narcotics Task Force. The day before, McFadden was provided general details of the expected indictments so he could begin to put together Ashcroft's statement. It was not a difficult one to write.

"Integrity was a natural thing to work in there," McFadden said. "You can't be a fan of sports, especially baseball, and not understand what integrity means to the game. It was a natural."

On the morning of the 12th, Corallo, McFadden, and Ryan were among about 10 people who convened in Ashcroft's office. Ashcroft, as was his custom, read his statement aloud, and then he asked Ryan to go through the indictments. Four men—Victor Conte Jr., James Valente, Greg Anderson, and Remi Korchemny—were named in the 42-count indictment, charged with conspiracy and money laundering in a scheme to corrupt sports.

Ashcroft congratulated Ryan. "This is really, really important," the A.G. said. "It's so disturbing. This is a good thing we're doing today."

Not long after, Ashcroft began the press conference, which ESPN broadcast live.

"Illegal steroid use calls into question not only the integrity of the athletes who use them but also the integrity of the sports those athletes play," he said. "Steroids are bad for sports, bad for players, bad for the young people who hold athletes up as role models."

Corallo thought his boss was completely on his game that day, seizing a moment and a cause he believed in.

"This really wasn't about BALCO," Corallo said. "In the end, it had nothing to do with Victor Conte and Greg Anderson and their activity. It had to do with the guys who had been cheating Stan Musial and Mickey Mantle and Lou Gehrig and Hank Aaron and Willie Mays, that's what this was about. That's who they're cheating, they're cheating the baseball immortals and they're cheating the fans. And it means something."

When Ryan spoke, he echoed his boss's views. "Like anything in life, true success must be earned," he said. "Nothing can replace hard work and dedication."

But there was a problem with the notion that the Attorney General and the government were cleaning up sports, exposing the drug cheaters in the biggest way possible. In the press conference, they didn't name a single athlete. In fact, in the end, they bent over backward to protect the very men they claimed they wanted to expose. When the indictments, affidavits, and other court papers from the BALCO case were made public, the only names to be found were those of the four indicted men and a pair of other suspected steroid dealers.

Where mentioning athletes was unavoidable, their names either were redacted or replaced by phrases like "a professional baseball player" or "an elite track and field athlete and Olympic gold medal winner," or "a current NFL player." The secrecy continued when the case went to court.

Instead of exposing Barry Bonds, Marion Jones, and Bill Romanowski for the cheats the Justice Department believed them to be, Ashcroft and Company had left the public guessing.

The public wouldn't be guessing for long.

Part III

The Most Wanted Man in America

Chapter 20

From the time the raids were first reported in the fall of 2003, the media had been scrambling to unravel BALCO. The probe was shrouded in secrecy, with no arrests made and the government remaining quiet about why agents had descended on the unknown laboratory and what they had found there. As much as anything, it was Victor Conte's genius for self-promotion, as reflected in his online advertising, that helped propel the BALCO case into a national news story.

Names make news, and Conte's SNAC Internet site was a who's who of elite athletes who were somehow involved with an enterprise that had been targeted by federal law enforcement. The site named 65 individual sports stars and the entire rosters of several professional teams—all said to be using BALCO's "nutritional consultation and supplements." As proof of Conte's sports connections, the site was decorated with bold color photos of the stars. There was Conte with Marion Jones; there he was again, with Tim Montgomery; and there was he was, grinning, standing over Barry Bonds and Greg Anderson, the trainer whose door had been kicked in by federal agents.

In the months following the raids, reporting teams from as far away as England decamped in San Francisco and began roaming the Peninsula. They knocked on doors, sought interviews, and looked for leads in an attempt to break the BALCO story and be the first to report what they had begun to suspect: that those star athletes had been going to BALCO to get banned drugs. Every news organization wanted to be the first to name the names.

But the big BALCO story proved tough to get. And so began a cycle that repeated itself throughout the case. A reporter would pry loose a piece of new information and break it as a BALCO exclusive. Then the hundreds of media outlets that were interested in BALCO—and they ranged from the television networks and the nation's biggest newspapers down to local sports talk-radio programs and little community weeklies—would report and comment on the scoop. Eventually, the media barrage would grow to such a level of intensity that it would force an official reaction or even a promise for reform. And then the story would quiet down for a while, until the cycle cranked up all over again.

In mid-October, the *San Francisco Chronicle* reeled off three BALCO scoops in six days, reporting facts that others assumed but that no one else could pin down: A grand jury was investigating BALCO, Bonds had been subpoenaed, and investigators had seized steroids in the raid. After the media learned the grand jury was hearing testimony, reporters and camera crews regularly staked out the federal building.

The U.S. Anti-Doping Agency also added to the public focus on Conte and BALCO. Some reporters with sources inside track and field had obtained pieces of the story of USADA's role in investigating BALCO. Worried that his agency's actions would be incorrectly reported, CEO Terry Madden decided to go public and tell the world about the drug they called THG.

On October 16, USADA issued a press release outlining the story of the undetectable steroid: the anonymous track coach, the mysterious syringe, the unnamed athletes testing positive for THG. Then Madden, his lawyers guiding him, presided over a teleconference with the national media. It was not USADA's finest hour.

The U.S. Attorney's office in San Francisco had urged Madden not to reveal anything at all. As a result, he felt constrained in what he could say. And so he was vague and unspecific, unable to tell the reporters why he was "fairly certain" that Conte was responsible for distributing THG. The teleconference turned into an inquisition, with the reporters demanding that USADA substantiate its claim that a massive sports doping conspiracy had been uncovered and that Conte was behind it. Madden, feeling constrained by the government, couldn't comply. At one point, he was asked if his comments had been approved by his attorneys. "Every statement is vetted by lawyers," the USADA chief snapped.

"It was very awkward," Madden admitted later.

He couldn't tell the reporters that his own man, Larry Bowers, had been on the BALCO raiding party and had seen the athletes' files and the drugs that had been seized. Nor could Madden reveal that he, too, had seen documents that implicated some of America's greatest athletes in systematic cheating. After the raids, the government had faxed some of the seized evidence to USADA, seeking help deciphering them.

Madden was troubled by the material—lists of BALCO athletes and the diverse inventory of drugs they had been using. It was staggering. One night he went home and threw up, overwhelmed by the task that lay ahead. He had less than a year to clean up the U.S. Olympic team.

On November 13, one week after Tim Montgomery testified before the grand jury, Madden and Rich Young flew to the Bay Area to meet with the BALCO prosecutors. USADA needed help. America would be humiliated if these track stars were allowed to compete in the Olympics and the world later learned that the U.S. government knew all along they were drug cheats. USADA wanted evidence to bring doping charges against the BALCO athletes.

The discussion was cordial, but prosecutors were noncommittal. Madden and Young left hoping the government would eventually help.

That same day, a letter addressed to Madden arrived at USADA's offices. It was postmarked Los Angeles, with the return address of Don Catlin, the UCLA anti-doping scientist. When Madden returned to Colorado and found the envelope on his desk, it didn't look right to him.

Inside, he found a single typewritten sheet, with these words, some in red ink:

> *It is better to risk saving*
> *a guilty person than to condemn*
> *an innocent one. . . .*
> —Voltaire

Terrance Mad-Man,
Sorry you did not get the pony you so dearly
wanted as a child. Get over it, and grow up!
Enjoy your time on earth because your time
In Hell won't be short or sweet!!!!!!
DC

Madden called Catlin, thinking it was maybe a twisted joke. But Catlin didn't know anything about the letter. Then Madden contacted the BALCO prosecutors, who called in the FBI.

Madden was shaken. He told his wife they needed to be more cautious when their kids were playing outside. He told his staff about the letter, added a security camera to the outside of USADA's building, and made sure the alarms were working. When he got to work in the morning, Madden made a point of checking around the building. The FBI never identified who wrote the letter.

Two days before Christmas, Madden and lawyer Rich Young flew back to the Bay Area, this time to meet Victor Conte. USADA wanted Conte and Jim Valente to testify when they brought doping cases against BALCO athletes. In the meantime, USADA wanted them to translate the coded documents obtained from Novitzky.

They met in the lobby of a hotel near the San Francisco airport, with defense lawyers Bob Holley and Troy Ellerman present. USADA intended to clean up track and field, Madden and Young said. If Conte helped, USADA would intercede for him with the U.S. Attorney. Conte, naturally, was itching to talk. Here was a chance to tell his "No Choice" tale to a powerful audience, and it was all his lawyers could do to rein him in, to keep his mouth shut and listen to USADA's pitch.

Every now and then, his face turning red, Conte would say, "I want to say something here." But Holley and Ellerman managed to keep Conte muzzled.

As the meeting was breaking up, Conte said to Madden, "I think you're the type of guy who really wants to clean up this mess."

"Yes, I am," said Madden. "And we need to start now with you."

Media interest in BALCO spiked again in February, with Attorney General Ashcroft's announcement of the indictments. But the story the news organizations really wanted—the names of the athletes, and details of their role in the scandal—proved as elusive as ever. The BALCO affidavits left no doubt that Conte and Anderson were drug dealers. By any reasonable inference, the affidavits implicated Bonds as well: Anderson, after all, was Bonds's friend and personal trainer, and Conte claimed to be his nutritionist. But the government had decided to redact athletes' names from the documents, and that left the media with suspicions but no proof that Bonds had used steroids. For himself, Bonds denied using drugs.

Still, the indictment of Bonds's trainer emboldened some in the game to openly discuss the Giants superstar and juicing. Among the most outspoken was Colorado Rockies pitcher Turk Wendell. "If my personal trainer . . . got indicted for that, there's no one in the world who wouldn't think that I wasn't taking steroids," he told the *Denver Post*. "I mean, what, because he's Barry Bonds, no one's going to say that? I mean obviously he did it."

Jason Giambi also found himself under scrutiny. His teammates did double takes when the former MVP walked into the Yankees' spring-training clubhouse in Tampa: He was downright skinny, a shadow of his muscular former self. Giambi said he had lost four pounds in the off season. The sportswriters and the club guessed it was closer to 40, and they speculated that Giambi had dropped the weight by going off steroids after he was hauled before the grand jury. Believing that his grand jury testimony would never become public, Giambi solemnly told the writers he hadn't taken steroids.

Nearly a month passed before government secrecy was penetrated. On March 2, quoting information that had been provided to the BALCO investigators, the *Chronicle* reported that Bonds had received The Clear and The Cream from Anderson, who had obtained the drugs from BALCO. The newspaper named six other athletes who received BALCO drugs: baseball players Jason Giambi, Gary Sheffield, Marvin Benard, Benito Santiago, and Randy Velarde, along with Bill Romanowski of the NFL. Citing a source close to Anderson, the story said the trainer had obtained human growth hormone and steroids for Bonds dating back to 2001, when he broke the home run record. The press pack renewed its pursuit of BALCO. More than 200 broadcast outlets from around the country reported on the *Chronicle's* scoop the day it broke; more than 100 newspapers followed up the next morning.

Anti-doping advocates seized on the *Chronicle* report. By coincidence, on the day the story broke, Major League Baseball had scheduled a press conference in New York City to announce support for federal legislation to toughen penalties for steroid trafficking. Commissioner Selig opted not to attend the event, and instead released a statement supporting the legislation.

Representative John Sweeney, the New York Republican who wrote the bill, used the press conference to skewer Bonds. Sweeney declared that asterisks should be placed next to the records of any athletes "involved in illegal substances." He also called on the players' union to "stop obstructing and stop walking away from their responsibilities" on the issue of banned drugs. Baseball executive Bob DuPuy said the game's officials were "distressed" by the report about Bonds. That same day, Selig issued a gag order to all 30 major-league clubs. Nobody in baseball was permitted to comment on BALCO or steroids. Among the first violators: Hall-of-Fame slugger Reggie Jackson, who worked in the Yankees' front office.

"Somebody definitely is guilty of taking steroids," Jackson told the *Atlanta Journal-Constitution*. Through the newspaper, he addressed Bonds directly.

"Henry Aaron never hit 50 home runs in a season, so you're going to tell me that you're a greater hitter than Henry Aaron?" Jackson said. "Bonds hit 73 and he would have hit 100 if they would have pitched to him. I mean, come on, now. There is no way you can outperform Aaron and Ruth and Mays at that level."

The day the interview was published, Jackson was called on the carpet for violating Selig's edict.

Meanwhile, reporters descended on the Giants' spring training camp in Scottsdale. Owner Peter Magowan and General Manager Brian Sabean dropped from sight, while Giants Public Relations Director Blake Rhodes patrolled the clubhouse to shut down attempted interviews about Bonds and drugs. He interceded when a reporter approached Bonds's locker and opened his mouth.

"Dude, don't even try," Rhodes said.

"Do you agree with that, Barry?" the reporter asked.

"Get out of my locker," Bonds said.

Later, Bonds made one defiant statement. As he headed for the showers after his workout, he spoke loud enough for the reporters to hear.

"The most wanted man in America," he said. Then he clenched his fist and raised it in the air. "Black Power!" Bonds cried.

Within days, a picture of Bonds's massive head adorned the cover of *Sports Illustrated*, along with an asterisk and the question: "Is Baseball in the Asterisk Era?" A week later, baseball was on trial in Washington. The Senate Commerce Committee had convened a hearing to examine the steroid policies in various sports, and the *Chronicle's* story ratcheted up the pressure on baseball. Doping in sports was a serious matter to committee chairman John McCain. The Arizona Republican was a major sports fan who, like John Ashcroft, couldn't abide cheating.

USADA's Madden was called to testify, along with Gene Upshaw, head of the NFL players' union, and NFL Commissioner Paul Tagliabue. But they essentially were spectators, as the lawmakers teed off on Selig and union chief Donald Fehr for baseball's failure to address its steroid problem.

Baseball was on the verge of "becoming a fraud," McCain told Selig and Fehr. Jay Rockefeller, a Democrat from West Virginia, said modern baseball records were meaningless because of the players' drug use. "Roger Maris still holds the home run record," he said. "I've been a baseball fan since I was six years old and there's no question in my mind about that."

George Allen, a Republican from Virginia, also addressed the question of tainted records. "You talked about an asterisk next to certain records," he said. "You know, maybe [there should be] a question mark or maybe an 'RX' next to some of these records."

Fehr took the most heat during the two-and-a-half-hour session. The lawmakers blamed the union for standing in the way of a tougher policy. Their threat was explicit: If baseball's leaders didn't enact a tougher steroid program, Congress would do it for them.

Days later, Selig seized the public-relations momentum and fired off a letter to Fehr. He called on the union to agree to take the unheard-of step of reopening the Basic Agreement to beef up the steroid policy. The commissioner's office also floated the idea that Selig might act in the "best interests of baseball" and unilaterally change the policy. The players' union was unimpressed: Selig had allowed baseball's problem with performance-enhancing drugs to get out of control, they contended, and now the commissioner was posturing for the politicians in Washington.

Privately, one high-ranking Major League Baseball official insisted Selig was serious about ridding the game of steroids. The commissioner hoped to use the outrage over BALCO to leverage the union and put a tougher policy in place. But Selig thought the case presented only a brief window of opportunity to clean up the game: Unless he was able to move quickly, he feared nothing would ever get done.

"I think the union is just hoping this story goes away on Opening Day," the official said. "I think they're waiting to see what happens. If the furor over steroids died down on Opening Day and the only thing that gets written about is the glory of the game, they'll believe, 'We weathered the storm.'"

The Giants cited Selig's gag order and refused to comment on the *Chronicle*'s story. Privately, though, club officials clung to the notion that there was still no proof their marquee player was using banned drugs. The BALCO defense lawyers publicly defended the slugger.

At a hastily called press conference in Sacramento, Bob Holley and Troy Ellerman insisted that Victor Conte and Jim Valente had not implicated Bonds in drug use. "There's no evidence that Bonds did anything, other than rumor and innuendo," Ellerman said.

The lawyers also accused Bush and Ashcroft of politicizing the case. The government had put their clients' chances of getting a fair trial at risk by leaking the story to the *Chronicle*, they claimed.

Holley also noted that Conte was not intimidated by the government. The BALCO judge had granted Conte permission to attend the 16th Annual Arnold Fitness Expo in Columbus, Ohio, beginning the next day. There, as he had done in years past, Conte would work the rooms and hawk his legal supplements. The event's namesake,

California Governor Arnold Schwarzenegger, was scheduled to attend as well.

Asked whether Schwarzenegger, the former bodybuilding legend and admitted steroid user, had ever taken any of Conte's supplements, Holley said, "I don't know, but I'm sure that we'd be happy to send him a free sample of ZMA."

That weekend in Columbus, DEA agents descended on the convention center, serving subpoenas on several bodybuilders as part of a new steroids probe. Among the targets: Milos "The Mind" Sarcev, the self-proclaimed anabolic expert who was Conte's friend and had provided training to some of the BALCO owner's athletes, including Tim Montgomery. Sarcev would later be indicted on charges of importing and distributing steroids; he would ultimately cut a deal, pleading guilty to a misdemeanor possession charge and being hit with a $10,000 fine.

A few weeks after Holley and Ellerman held their press conference, Greg Anderson's new lawyer, J. Tony Serra, picked up where the other defense lawyers had left off: He attacked the BALCO prosecutors. Serra had taken Anderson's case after the trainer was unable to pay lawyer Bill Rapoport, Mike Rains's friend. Serra was among the last of the Bay Area's old counterculture defense bar, a flamboyant attorney whose high-profile clients had included Black Panther Huey Newton. At 67, he wore his long, gray hair tied back in a ponytail.

Outside court in San Francisco after a minor hearing, Serra complained to the press that the government was trying to "destroy baseball" with the BALCO indictments. The case was no more than a "head-hunting expedition," he declared.

Playboy had recently broken its own BALCO exclusive, an insider's account of the probe from the perspective of Iran White, the undercover agent who had suffered a stroke after lifting weights with Anderson. Serra said the *Playboy* story demonstrated that IRS Special Agent Jeff Novitzky's probe was "not a genuine investigation," but rather was driven by a glory-seeking agent who was out to bag "the trophy." He called Novitzky a "failed athlete" who was "jealous of all the attention Bonds received."

The legal maneuvering and posturing seemed to work with the

public, or at least with Giants fans. Though the *Chronicle* thought its big story had exposed Bonds as a drug cheat and demonstrated that he had produced his amazing numbers by using steroids, the response from the newspaper's readers suggested that most Giants fans didn't believe the story, didn't care, or didn't want to know. As the season opened and Bonds began what would be another MVP year, as always he was booed on the road—though even opposing fans cheered when he homered.

He hit his 659th career home run in Houston to move within one of tying his godfather, Willie Mays, for third on the all-time list. He hit number 660 in the Giants' home opener, launching a ball into McCovey Cove. Mays greeted him outside the dugout and handed him a diamond-encrusted torch for a symbolic photo op. Only Ruth and Aaron were ahead of him now. Bonds, naturally, received a prolonged standing ovation from the crowd, which chanted, "Barry, Barry . . ."

In a post-game press conference, the subject of steroids was barely broached. One reporter started to ask about the government's attempt to seize urine samples from the 2003 tests. Rhodes, the PR chief, cut in and said, "Sorry, next question."

As Bonds addressed the media, Mays sat by his side. They wore caps inscribed with the number 660. They also wore matching T-shirts that celebrated their joint place in history—with sepia-toned pictures of themselves on the front and a list of home runs on the back. Both cap and T were for sale on Bonds's web site, barrybonds.com.

As the season continued, the furor over steroids in baseball seemed to die down, just as the baseball official had suggested it might. Baseball had deflected and denied its steroid problem, and now the fans were showing up at ballparks in record numbers. The storm seemed to have passed.

In reality, it merely shifted directions. Perhaps baseball's greatest fortune during a season that could have been consumed by steroid talk was that 2004 was an Olympic year. Within weeks of the baseball season beginning, the focus of the BALCO steroid case turned to track and field.

Chapter 21

In many ways, Terry Madden was in the same boat as the reporters chasing the BALCO story. The USADA chief was hunting for documents and names.

When he learned that the prosecutors were refusing to disclose the identities of the athletes caught up in the scandal, Madden was dismayed. Some of America's greatest track stars, including Marion Jones, Tim Montgomery, and Kelli White, appeared to have used BALCO drugs, but they had never tested positive for THG or conventional steroids. If the anti-doping agency hoped to charge any of them with cheating, it needed more evidence.

To prosecute the athletes, USADA would be forced to employ a concept in the World Anti-Doping Code called the "non-analytical positive." Even an athlete who had passed all his tests could be banned if there were other convincing evidence that he had used drugs, according to the code. But in practice, no athlete had ever been disciplined in the absence of a positive drug test. Without a drug test as proof, USADA would need powerful evidence to persuade an arbitration panel to ban the BALCO athletes. Madden didn't believe that the documents the government had provided to USADA, and Larry Bowers's observations from the raid, would be persuasive enough.

If the government had simply left the athletes' names in the BALCO affidavits rather than redacting them, USADA's task would have been far simpler. Madden knew the BALCO prosecutors had thousands of pages of documents—calendars, test results, e-mails—that pertained to track athletes. USADA desperately needed them.

The problem grew in urgency with each passing day. The American Olympic team would be chosen in July, at the U.S. Track & Field

Trials in Sacramento. It was important to try to purge the drug cheats before the meet began. USADA was sitting on "The Golden Time Bomb," as Rich Young, Madden's top outside counsel, put it.

"We have all this great information," said lawyer Bill Bock, Young's USADA colleague. "But at some point it can blow up in our faces because if we don't get enough to do something about it, we've known some athletes are potentially guilty and done nothing."

In meetings, phone calls, and letters, USADA pressed the BALCO prosecutors for the evidence. But by early March, Madden realized the Justice Department was simply unwilling to provide USADA with evidence from an ongoing criminal investigation.

At that point, John McCain, chairman of the Senate Commerce Committee, interceded. The Arizona Republican cared deeply about the integrity of the Olympic Games, and his Commerce Committee had jurisdiction over the Olympic movement. If anybody would go to bat for USADA, it was McCain.

In early March, McCain and ranking Democrat Senator Ernest Hollings of South Carolina wrote to Attorney General John Ashcroft, urging him to provide the BALCO evidence to their committee. The letter expressed USADA's fear that American drug cheats would win medals in Athens, only to be exposed later. If that happened, "our Olympic team will be tarnished and mired in scandal for years to come," the senators warned. They requested the documents be turned over within five days.

The Justice Department was silent for four weeks. Then, on March 31, McCain got the response: The documents are part of an ongoing investigation. Sorry, we're not giving you anything.

Undeterred, McCain's committee took the unusual step of issuing a subpoena for the Justice Department files. On April 14, 9,408 pages of evidence from the BALCO case were delivered to the committee. The names of all athletes not connected to track and field were redacted. The evidence should be treated with "appropriate sensitivity," Justice said in a letter. The committee staff began reviewing the documents, to decide what if anything could be provided to USADA.

While USADA waited anxiously, Madden and Young returned to California. They met again with Conte, pressing for cooperation.

Conte could help considerably if he testified against the BALCO athletes at disciplinary hearings. But lawyer Bob Holley wasn't about to allow his client to incriminate himself at a doping hearing unless he got a break on his criminal case; and USADA, of course, couldn't guarantee anything.

The next day, the USADA officials again met with the BALCO prosecutors. In the name of the Olympic movement, they urged the prosecutors to cut a plea deal that would require Conte to help USADA. The "Golden Time Bomb" was ticking. But the prosecutors wouldn't help; their investigation was ongoing, they said.

After the meeting, Madden was apoplectic. He couldn't understand why the prosecutors didn't comprehend the urgency; nobody saw the bigger picture.

Marion Jones had taken a break from track in 2003 to have her baby son, and she ended the year testifying before the BALCO grand jury. Despite the long layoff and the scandal, she was determined to star in the Athens Games. To succeed, she would have to avoid being targeted by the government or USADA as a drug cheat. So, as the BALCO case began to mushroom, Jones decided to pursue a legal and public-relations strategy of aggressive denial, no matter how damning the evidence against her. She first employed it at the grand jury, where she denied using banned drugs, politely but emphatically. She sought to defuse the government's tough questions about the doping calendars seized at BALCO by repeatedly addressing Nedrow, the prosecutor, as "Jeff."

Later, as the Olympics drew near and questions about steroids arose, Jones downplayed her association with BALCO. At the Mount SAC Relays near Los Angeles, she brushed off queries about her testimony at the BALCO grand jury, saying, "I'm drug-free, always have been and always will be." She emphasized she had never failed an Olympic drug test—a meaningless point to the authorities, given that The Cream and The Clear were designed to be undetectable. Jones was doing all she could to spin her way out of trouble.

Life in the Fast Lane, her glossy, celebratory autobiography published for the Olympic year, was spin from first page to last. In the book, Jones wrote that she knew nothing about drug use by her ex-husband, the disgraced shot-put champion C. J. Hunter. She complained that Hunter had failed to tell her about his positive drug test until after the press got onto the story in Sydney. Jones referred to BALCO as "infamous," called Conte "C. J.'s pal," and claimed she hadn't seen Conte since Australia, not mentioning the North Carolina interview and photo shoot that resulted in the eight-page spread in *FLEX*. And in a statement printed in red ink with type so large that it filled an entire page, Jones wrote: "I am against performance enhancing drugs. I have never taken them and I never will take them."

At about the time USADA approached McCain, Jones called in expensive help. She already was represented by the savvy lawyer-agent Rich Nichols, who had been an All-American track star at Dartmouth College. Now she hired a former federal prosecutor from San Francisco, Joseph Burton, and an expert in crisis public relations, Chris Lehane. Lehane was a hard-edged Democratic party operative known as "the Master of Disaster," the PR man President Clinton deployed in his efforts to tamp down the Monica Lewinsky scandal. Soon after he was hired, Lehane had his hands full.

The *San Francisco Chronicle* got access to a portion of the secret investigative report written after Conte confessed to Novitzky during the BALCO raid. On Saturday night, April 24, the newspaper posted a story on its Web site headlined "Olympians got steroids, feds told." Conte had provided The Cream and The Clear to Jones and her boyfriend, Tim Montgomery, as part of a ZMA endorsement deal, the newspaper reported. Jones's team frantically tried to knock down the story, which was also headed for page one of the Sunday newspaper. Burton said Conte was lying, and he accused the newspaper of committing "character assassination" by publishing the report. But a few hours later, the *San Jose Mercury News* posted its own story on the Web, also based on the secret Conte statement, also reporting that Jones had gotten banned drugs from BALCO.

There was worldwide coverage of the news that two of the brightest stars that America expected to send to the Athens Olympics were implicated in doping. The stories about Jones and Montgomery made USADA's need for the BALCO documents seem even more urgent.

On May 5, Terry Madden, Rich Young, Dr. Don Catlin, and representatives from the United States Olympic Committee met with McCain in a closed hearing in Washington. The senator wanted assurances the material would not be misused. McCain's committee had held the documents for three weeks, and time was running out. If USADA didn't get them soon, it couldn't stop the drug cheats from going to Athens.

The next day, McCain announced that USADA would get what it needed.

The morning after that, USADA's Travis Tygart flew to Washington to pick up the evidence. Tygart had been on vacation in Florida. He scheduled a tight layover so he could get back to Colorado as quickly as possible: He would land at Reagan National Airport and have three hours to get downtown, collect the documents, and then make it out to Dulles Airport, a 45-minute drive from the Capitol, for the flight home.

In an airport gift shop, Tygart bought a duffel bag for the documents. Then he caught a cab, and the scene in the backseat was comedic: Sweating profusely from the D.C. humidity, Tygart changed from his vacation garb, shorts and a T-shirt, into slacks and a decent shirt. When he arrived at the Russell Senate Office Building, he asked the cab to wait. Committee counsel Ken Nahigian was expecting him.

"Watch your back," Nahigian said, as Tygart stuffed the papers into the large bag. It weighed about 65 pounds. "There are a lot of people who want these documents."

Tygart assured him he would be careful, and they walked together outside. As Tygart got into the cab, Nahigian looked down the street nervously, then back at Tygart with a dead stare.

"I'm serious," he said. "Watch your back."

On the ride to Dulles, again soaked in sweat, Tygart changed back into shorts. As it turned out, his flight sat on the runway for several hours. He hadn't checked the bag, not wanting to risk losing it; with nobody sitting next to him, Tygart took the opportunity to start examining the material.

Holy shit, he thought to himself.

Back in Colorado Springs, Rich Young and Madden waited nervously. Young imagined all sorts of scenarios: the plane would go down or Tygart would get "knocked off." When Tygart arrived safely, he called Madden and jokingly said, "The eagle has landed."

On Saturday morning, May 8, just two months before the start of the Olympic Trials, USADA officials began reading the BALCO files. The evidence, including e-mails and blood and urine test results, was far stronger and more explicit than what Novitzky had faxed to the agency after the raid. The officials were shocked at the extent of the doping conspiracy. But there was more evidence against some athletes than others. Quickly, USADA needed to decide which athletes to pursue. It was a critical decision. Madden and his lawyers were convinced that if the agency prosecuted an athlete and lost the case, USADA's reputation would be ruined. Nobody would take it seriously after that.

At the same time, USADA decided to try to cut deals with some athletes, to offer them shortened bans in exchange for their testimony against other athletes. The agency approached Kelli White, the reigning 100- and 200-meter world champion.

White already faced a sanction because of her positive test for modafinil at the World Championships. On that case, Bill Bock had gotten along well with White's lawyer, Jerrold Colton. Bock was deeply religious, and Colton did not fit the stereotype of a sports agent: he was compassionate and earnest.

Bock phoned Colton and told him White's career was in jeopardy.

"The BALCO documents implicate Kelli in some serious wrongdoing involving steroids and other substances, and she could face a lifetime ban," Bock said. There was no way White would compete in Athens. She would be well-served to get out in front of this thing and cut a deal. A two-year suspension might be possible.

On May 12, Bock and Madden met White and Colton at the Burlingame Marriott, less than a mile from BALCO, the same hotel where Madden had met with Conte months earlier. Bock described the BALCO evidence connected to White: the calendars, the blood tests that indicated her use of EPO, the ledger entries that indicated elevated T/E ratios. White didn't say much; she sat scrunched up in her chair, knees to her chest, sighing occasionally. Madden urged her to accept a deal and agree to testify or face the possibility of a long ban.

Bock said USADA would soon approach several other athletes; the first one to cooperate would get the best deal. USADA wanted an answer now. Colton and White talked privately, and when they returned, Colton said White was inclined to take the deal: a two-year ban, with USADA agreeing to recommend early reinstatement in exchange for her cooperation.

White didn't want to sign anything yet. That afternoon she was flying to the Persian Gulf to compete in the IAAF Super Grand Prix meet in Doha, Qatar. Colton said White had to attend the meet. She was getting paid, she had sponsors to answer to.

"OK," said Bock. "But this is the last meet."

White finished sixth in the 200 meters in Qatar. Meanwhile, Colton called Bock. White was upset, she had been talking to her agent, she wanted to pull out of the deal.

On May 16, Bock and Tygart returned to San Francisco for another meeting with White and Colton. By then, attorneys for other BALCO athletes had heard White was ready to cut a deal. They called Colton, urging him not to go through with it. If you delay long enough, they can't keep White from running in Athens, Colton was told. USADA can't make the case.

But Bock told White and Colton that USADA was confident that it could keep White from competing in the Olympics. White was very emotional at the second meeting. She pressed for reassurance that USADA would play fair, that it would go after the other BALCO athletes.

"I just know Marion Jones is going to get off," she said.

Bock assured her USADA wouldn't play favorites, and again promised to help her win early reinstatement. Once again, White signed off on the deal, and this time she put her name to a contract.

But the next morning, when White met with Bock and Tygart to provide details of the BALCO conspiracy, she was still upset and regretting her decision to cooperate. Bock knew White was consumed with guilt over her doping. He told her that pleading guilty was the right and ethical action to take. White should put aside her doubts. He pulled out his Bible, opened to James, Chapter 1, Verse 8: "The double-minded man is unstable in all his ways."

"If you try to go back on the decision you made, you'll just tear yourself up and feel confused," Bock told her. "You've made a decision to do what is right. Don't have two minds about it. Move forward with your life."

"I've never seen a lawyer with a Bible before," said White.

On May 19, White made her public confession, admitting she had used EPO and undetectable steroids. "In doing this, I have not only cheated myself, but also my family, friends, and sport," she said in a written statement released by Colton. "I am sorry for the poor choices I have made."

It was a breakthrough in the effort to control sports doping: An active athlete—a world champion, no less—had admitted cheating her way to the top.

Four days later, Madden, Young, and Tygart met with Michelle Collins and her lawyer, Brian Getz, at the Dallas/Fort Worth International Airport. We're going to charge you with a doping offense, USADA told Collins. You will lose and face a lifetime ban. Cut a deal. USADA offered Collins a two-year ban with the chance for early reinstatement if she agreed to testify against other athletes.

Of all the BALCO athletes, Collins had perhaps the least hope of beating a doping case. Her e-mail exchanges with Conte were probably enough to convict her. Still, she wanted to fight. She was 33 years old, at the end of her career, anyway.

"I'm not snitching off these people," she said.

Getz knew his client should take the deal, but Collins felt she couldn't admit to her parents that she was a drug cheat. Madden offered to meet with her family and tell them that she had made mistakes but was doing the right thing. Collins refused. Like White, she was certain other athletes were going to get away with it. Both women had told USADA that the use of the drugs was rampant: White suggested that six out of eight sprinters in any given elite 100-meter final were on the juice. Collins said it was more likely all eight. Collins never made the deal.

Two weeks later, USADA charged four athletes with doping, based on the BALCO documents: Collins, Tim Montgomery, Chryste Gaines, and Alvin Harrison.

*   *   *

While the deal making was underway, Marion Jones had been ratcheting up her rhetoric, threatening to sue if USADA came after her. At a media event in New York to tout the Athens Games, Jones once again asserted she had never used banned drugs. And she seemed to be warning USADA to back off.

"I'm not just going to sit down and let someone, or a group of people, or an organization, take away my livelihood because of a hunch, because of a thought, because of somebody who is trying to show their power," she told several hundred journalists. If she were kept from the Olympics, "you can pretty much expect that there will be lawsuits," she said.

Jones's boyfriend, Tim Montgomery, had been scheduled to attend, but he pulled out at the last minute. He was said to have a stomach ailment; Jones said "he just wasn't up for making the flight."

Jones and her lawyers demanded to meet with USADA. On May 24, during a tense, three-hour session in Colorado Springs, they got copies of the BALCO documents related to her.

Hours later, Joe Burton and Rich Nichols held a teleconference with reporters to demand that USADA exonerate Jones. Her PR machine sent out pages of material in her defense. Even Victor Conte stepped up. That evening, Conte sent an e-mail to the *San Francisco Chronicle*. The subject line read: "USADA is the Taliban." In the e-mail, he criticized the anti-doping agency, saying it was pressing Jones even though it lacked evidence to prove beyond a reasonable doubt that she had used drugs. Conte had told confidantes that he hated Jones and all her posturing, and he still had hard feelings from his bitter falling out with Montgomery. Why, then, was Conte defending Jones?

"Sometimes you have to choose between the lesser of two evils and my position and choice could change at any time," Conte wrote.

For her part, Jones called USADA a "secret kangaroo court" and asked the U.S. Senate to hold a hearing on whether she should be allowed to compete in Athens. That move came just one day after Conte's attorney had—at his client's urging, of course—sent a letter asking President Bush to cut him a plea bargain so he could help ensure a clean team went to Athens.

The day after their meeting with USADA, Jones's lawyers had given *The New York Times* and the *San Jose Mercury News* a selection of BALCO documents in an effort to undercut the doping suspicions swirling around her. The lawyers picked out documents that made the case seem flimsy—a negative urine test; drug calendars with notations that suggested they pertained not to Jones but to a male sprinter. Later, Jones also announced she had been exonerated on a private lie-detector test.

By then, Montgomery was also enduring the withering glare of press scrutiny. Like Jones, he defended himself aggressively. In response to the disclosures in the *Chronicle* and the *Mercury News*, his lawyer, Cristina Arguedas, declared there was "no evidence" that Montgomery had used banned drugs. She accused Conte of lying, saying Conte had "incentive to seek to ruin Tim's career and reputation." But then, on June 24, the *Chronicle* published Montgomery's secret grand jury testimony, in which he had confessed to using growth hormone, Clomid, and BALCO's "magic potion," The Clear. The defense that Conte was lying to hurt Montgomery was no longer available: The *Chronicle* story quoted Montgomery's own words as he admitted using enough banned drugs to get him a lifetime Olympic ban.

The BALCO stories guaranteed that when the Olympic track trials got underway in Sacramento, talk of doping would dominate the event. Jones finally seemed to wilt under the scrutiny. She failed to qualify for the Olympics in her best event, the 100 meters, finishing fifth in a field of eight.

After the race, she fled the stadium, accompanied by the same burly bodyguard who had escorted her to the BALCO grand jury. Before bolting in a golf cart, she faced the mob of reporters. "When I talk, you guys have something negative to say," she said. "When I don't talk, you guys have something negative to say. I'd much rather not talk and spend time with my son if you guys have something negative to say. So, have a nice day."

By then, USADA had decided not to charge Jones. She had broken with Conte more than two years earlier, and there were fewer documents related to her than the other athletes. Without Conte's testimony, a case against her was problematic. USADA's lawyers would wait for the BALCO criminal case to play out, hoping it would produce more conclusive evidence.

By the time the trials were over, USADA's fear that BALCO cheats would compete in Athens had faded not in the courtroom but on the track. The other BALCO athletes—Montgomery, Collins, Gaines, the Harrison twins, Regina Jacobs—either withdrew, citing injuries, or ran so poorly that they failed to qualify for the team. Jones, the great star of Sydney, was the only competitor to make the team.

After failing to qualify in the 100, she pulled out of the 200 meters, citing fatigue; finally, she qualified in the long jump. But more trouble was looming. The day before the trials began, Novitzky had visited her ex-husband, C. J. Hunter, in North Carolina. When they divorced, Jones and Hunter had signed a nondisclosure agreement, promising not to speak about each other after they parted. In her new autobiography, Jones had claimed to be an honest athlete, while portraying her ex-husband as a lying drug cheat. Hunter resented how he was depicted, and he thought the book violated their agreement. He gave Novitzky a detailed account of Jones's drug use.

Hunter described his ex-wife as an experienced drug cheat. At Sydney, where she won five medals, Jones had injected herself with human growth hormone and used BALCO's Clear, he said. She continued to use banned drugs after the Games. Four days after the Trials ended, the *Chronicle* published a story based on Hunter's statement to the agent. The newspaper had revealed evidence of systematic cheating by America's most renowned Olympian—three weeks before the Opening Ceremonies in Athens.

Chapter 22

The tone of the Summer Olympics in Athens was set the day before the Opening Ceremonies. Dick Pound, the outspoken head of the World Anti-Doping Agency, publicly chided Marion Jones for her ties to BALCO. If Jones were caught using drugs, "it's going to be a dark and deep hole into which she goes," he told reporters.

Later that evening, the Games erupted with a doping scandal that had BALCO overtones. Sprinter Kostas Kenteris, Greece's most famous athlete, missed a doping test and faced an Olympic ban. Kenteris had come out of nowhere to win gold in the 200 meters in 2000 at Sydney, and the victory turned him into a national icon. A ferry boat, a street, and a stadium were named after him. Fans called him "Son of the Wind." He was to receive the honor of lighting the Olympic cauldron, marking the return of the modern Games to their birthplace. Instead, with the world watching his country, Kenteris was being exposed as a drug cheat. Stranger still, Kenteris and another Greek hero, Katerina Thanou, the 100-meter silver medalist in Sydney, were said to have been injured in a mysterious motorcycle crash, perhaps while fleeing the drug testers.

Greece was in an uproar. One daily newspaper, the *Ethnos*, described the saga as "the equivalent of a multi-megaton bomb exploding at the Olympics' foundations." The paper implored both runners: "Tell us the truth!"

Finally, Kenteris and Thanou withdrew from the Games; at a press conference attended by hundreds of reporters, the spokeswoman for the International Olympic Committee held up the sprinters' identity cards for the eager cameras—as if they were trophy heads.

The coach for the two Greek athletes, Christos Tzekos, was connected to the BALCO scandal. According to BALCO e-mails, Tzekos had received The Clear directly from its creator, Patrick Arnold, and then distributed it to his athletes. Beginning in 2002, Arnold had used a Greek shipping company to send packages containing a clear liquid to Tzekos. In 2002, when Conte became convinced that drug testers had identified The Clear, he had asked another Greek track coach to relay a warning to Tzekos.

Also in the spotlight in Athens was Trevor Graham, the North Carolina track coach who had sent the BALCO syringe to USADA and whom Conte had accused of doping in his unsent letter. Graham's top sprinter, Justin Gatlin, won the 100-meter final, and after the race, for the first time, Graham publicly admitted his role in setting off the BALCO investigation.

"I was just a coach doing the right thing," he told reporters. "No regrets." A few days later, he told an Italian newspaper he turned in the syringe to "save the credibility of American sport." He added that he obtained the syringe from Marion Jones's ex-husband, C. J. Hunter. Hunter had "wanted to construct an athlete capable of beating Marion," Graham claimed.

Jones herself performed poorly at the Games. She placed fifth in the long jump. In the 4 x 100 relay finals, Jones and teammate Lauryn Williams botched a baton handoff, and the heavily favored U.S. team didn't even finish. Back in Colorado, USADA officials breathed a sigh of relief. The one BALCO athlete to make the U.S. team was leaving without a medal.

The Games themselves were consumed with doping rumors. One evening, the Olympic Stadium was abuzz with word that a prominent athlete was about to be busted for doping. Over the next few days, the rumor ran hot. It was a male sprinter, no, it was a woman. It was a medalist, no, not a medalist. It was an American, no, not an American.

The media had no shortage of suspects. Yuliya Nesterenko of Belarus won gold in the 100 meters—just a year after 101 other women had run the 100 faster than she had. Greece's Fani Halkia also came out of nowhere to win her event, the 400-meter hurdles. One year after clocking the 50th best time in the world, Halkia set an Olympic record during her semifinal heat, then went on to win the gold in a time 3 1/2 seconds faster than her best from 2003. Asked what she thought of Halkia's dramatic improvement, American hurdler Brenda Taylor said, "I have to plead the Fifth on that question."

The whole scene became surreal. If the performances didn't elicit suspicion, the sight of the sprinters' bodies was enough to fuel rumors. They seemed severely ripped, with veins bulging from their muscles and nary a sign of body fat. Just looking at them made you think they were drug cheats.

By the end of the Games, a record two dozen cheaters had been caught. Still, the rumored bust of the prominent athlete never occurred. No American, and no high-profile athlete from any country, was caught doping at the games. In reality, the last "name" athlete to be snagged was Ben Johnson, 16 years before. Without questions, the cheaters remained well ahead of the testers.

On December 1, the BALCO case was back in federal court. The defense lawyers complained that their clients' right to a fair trial were being destroyed by a systematic program of government leaks. First the *Chronicle* had published Tim Montgomery's grand jury testimony; then it printed C. J. Hunter's statement to Novitzky. Now there was what defense lawyer Tony Serra called the latest outrage: On October 16, the *Chronicle* had revealed the existence of a secret recording. On it, Greg Anderson admitted giving banned drugs to Bonds. Serra urged Judge Susan Illston to interrogate the newspaper's reporters about their sources. "Poison ink is being disbursed by government agents to the press," he said dramatically. Conte's lawyer, Holley, also attacked the government. "We've been slandered from one side of the world to the other," he said.

Holley wasn't entirely comfortable making the argument. A few weeks before, he had finally lost control of his willful, publicity-hungry client. Over Holley's adamant objections, Conte told his "No Choice" story to ABC's *20/20* program. The interviewer was Martin Bashir, whose specialty is getting his subjects to incriminate themselves on camera: Indeed, Bashir's interview with the pop star Michael Jackson had been so incendiary that Jackson was indicted on child molestation charges. Holley told Conte he was making a terrible mistake. The interview, when aired, would kill any hope they had of getting the BALCO indictment dismissed because of the leaks. Conte couldn't complain he was being victimized by leaks if he, too, was talking to the media, the lawyer pointed out.

And if Conte admitted any crimes in the interview, the prosecutors could use that to bury him at his trial, Holley warned. Nevertheless, Conte was exuberant about his upcoming television exposure, confident it would redeem his reputation and solve his problems.

He even began to flaunt his upcoming appearance in e-mails to reporters.

"Get ready for the truth, the whole truth and nothing but the truth," he wrote to the *Chronicle*. "Everyone in the entire world is finally going to learn that there is no Santa Claus, Easter Bunny or Tooth Fairy in the world of sport. . . . The Olympic Games and, in fact, all sports at the elite level are a fraud and the world is going to find that out in great detail."

In the days before the BALCO hearing, ABC had begun promoting the *20/20* segment. As soon as Holley finished his remarks, prosecutor Jeff Nedrow told the judge about the promos, and Holley found himself in an embarrassing interchange. How could Holley complain about pretrial publicity when his own client was doing a television interview? the judge asked. It was the very point Holley had made to Conte. "I didn't know until it was too late," Holley replied. But the judge wouldn't let it go: You mean you didn't know your client was going on television?

The next morning, the front page of the *Chronicle* was dominated by a bold headline: GIAMBI ADMITTED TAKING STEROIDS. The newspaper had obtained Giambi's grand jury testimony. The story detailed his confession to drug use, complete with his description of how to inject human growth hormone. The uproar that followed exceeded even the reaction to the Bonds story from March. Virtually every broadcast news program in the country reported the *Chronicle's* scoop. Newspapers ran hard after the BALCO story, and on the morning of Friday, December 3, stories were published in every daily in the U.S. The New York tabloids were brutal in their treatment of the Yankees' star: The *Post* headline blared LYIN' KING and offered an editorial headlined: BOOT THE BUM—WHY THE YANKEES MUST FIRE

UGLY DRUG CHEAT JASON GIAMBI TODAY. The rival *Daily News*'s various headlines included, DAMNED YANKEE and A BIG DIRTY LIAR! JASON DID 'ROIDS. The *Daily News*'s package included a report that the Yankees wanted to void Giambi's $82 million contract.

But that same morning, the *Chronicle* broke one more story: WHAT BONDS TOLD BALCO GRAND JURY, the headline read. The newspaper had Bonds's transcript, as well. The story featured an account of the grueling session in which prosecutors had confronted Bonds with evidence of his drug use, and Bonds had retorted that he had only been using flaxseed oil and arthritis cream. The Bonds story blew every bit as high as the one on Giambi, and the combined one-two punch convulsed baseball. ESPN's Peter Gammons said the stories had revealed the sport's "dirty little secret . . . a cesspool of needles, creams, performance-enhancing corporations, illegal (not to mention immoral) leaks and lawyers' fees." Bonds's home run record had been exposed as "a steroid lie," wrote the *Post*'s Thomas Boswell. Without drugs, "there is no reason to believe Bonds could have approached, much less broken, any of the all-time marks for which he lusted so much that he has now ruined his name."

New York Times columnist William Safire summed up the altered landscape baseball faced after the grand jury stories broke. "Fans are dismayed and infuriated," he wrote. "The Senate Commerce chairman, John McCain, threatens legislation unless the 'national pastime' cleans up its act; Major League Baseball's see-no-evil officials belatedly promise to deal with the worst scandal since the Black Sox of a century ago; even the players' union may consent to more than one drug test per season."

Indeed, the Senate Commerce Committee posed the most immediate danger to baseball. McCain, attending the Army-Navy game with President Bush the day after the Bonds story was published, demanded a crackdown on steroids in baseball, saying he would introduce legislation if the sport didn't act. "I don't care about Mr. Bonds or Mr. Sheffield or anybody else," McCain said. "What I care about are high school athletes who are tempted to use steroids because they think that's the only way they can make it in the major leagues."

Senator Joseph Biden said he was ready to move against baseball's anti-trust exemption unless baseball dealt with steroids. "The grand jury made it clear," he said. "There's no more saying it's only a rumor."

In San Francisco, the story was also met with fury—perhaps more at the hometown newspaper than at Bonds. The *Chronicle* received hundreds of e-mails from readers, and the ones from Giants fans were harsh and angry. But the tenor of the negative e-mails had changed. On the earlier stories, angry readers had accused the newspaper of lying about Bonds. Now, the unhappy Giants fans accepted that Bonds had used steroids—but they passionately insisted they didn't care, while pillorying the newspaper for reporting the truth.

The *Chronicle* heard nothing from another reader who was infuriated by the BALCO grand jury stories: U.S. Attorney Kevin Ryan, who was in charge of the investigation.

After the story on Montgomery's grand jury testimony, and again after the reports on Hunter's statement, the *Chronicle* had received stern letters from Ryan. Whoever had given the newspaper the material had broken the law, Ryan contended. The *Chronicle* was breaking the law merely by possessing the documents. The newspaper was instructed to return everything to the government and name whoever leaked them.

The *Chronicle* had refused to comply, but its legal position was tenuous. Under federal law, reporters had no protection against being subpoenaed to identify their confidential sources. Around the country, federal prosecutors were becoming more aggressive in leak investigations, and in one case a reporter had been sentenced to six months' house arrest.

After the Bonds story, Ryan didn't bother to write another threatening letter. Instead, he asked the U.S. Justice Department to track down the newspaper's sources and "take appropriate action."

Somewhat lost in the barrage of coverage of Giambi and Bonds was Conte's *20/20* interview. Still, it made for interesting television. Conte had tossed aside all the promises of confidentiality he had made to the athletes who had bought drugs from him. On television, and in a story under his byline in *ESPN the Magazine*, Conte betrayed 11 elite athletes: Bill Romanowski, Barrett Robbins, Chris Cooper, and Dana Stubblefield of the NFL's Oakland Raiders; American runners Chryste

Gaines, Kelli White, and the twins, Alvin and Calvin Harrison; British sprint star Dwain Chambers; and the world's fastest couple: Tim Montgomery and Marion Jones. Conte also said he had given drugs to Trevor Graham, the track coach who had informed on him.

He saved most of his vitriol for Jones. Conte said he had put the Olympic champion on a regimen of The Clear, EPO, and insulin and described watching her inject growth hormone into her quadriceps muscle before a track meet. He also accused her of lying to the BALCO grand jury. Having trashed Jones, Conte timidly ducked questions about Bonds, except to say that he had provided Greg Anderson with The Cream and The Clear.

As Holley predicted, the interview was ruinous to Conte's legal defense. Bashir had pointedly asked Conte if he had been "breaking the law" and committing "criminal activity" by giving drugs to the athletes; lamely, Conte replied there had been "risks involved." The interview was the end for Holley: After 18 months, he would no longer represent a client who so obviously suffered from "narcissistic personality disorder," as he later put it.

In the USADA offices in Colorado Springs, Terry Madden and his team watched Conte's television performance in stunned silence. One lawyer kept track of the number of crimes to which Conte confessed. And they all paid close attention to specific athletes Conte implicated in doping, especially Jones.

Six weeks later, a team of FBI agents from Los Angeles arrived in the Bay Area with a search warrant. They raided Conte's San Mateo home and took away his computers, fax machine, and cell phone and various documents. They were convinced they had identified the *Chronicle*'s secret source.

Chapter 23

I n March 2005, the steroids scandal returned to Washington. Baseball was on trial again.

One year after Senator McCain warned that the sport was "becoming a fraud," a convergence of events had put baseball under intense pressure: The *Chronicle*'s stories detailing Bonds's and Giambi's grand jury testimony; Jose Canseco's tell-all book in which he exposed Mark McGwire as a juicer; and concerns about escalating steroids use among high school athletes.

Seizing the moment, the House Government Reform Committee invited commissioner Selig and players' union chief Fehr to testify at another hearing. Signaling that this event would be different, the committee also sought testimony from several current ballplayers, even though spring training was in full swing. Giambi, Baltimore Orioles Rafael Palmeiro and Sammy Sosa, Chicago White Sox star Frank Thomas, and Boston Red Sox pitcher Curt Schilling were invited, along with Canseco. And the committee also wanted McGwire, the man who had resurrected baseball in 1998.

At first, baseball acted as if it had been invited to an inconvenient tea party. Selig would send his lieutenants, and the players—sorry, they had other plans. Asked whether he would testify, Palmeiro said, "That's my wife's birthday. That should tell you right there what the answer is." Sosa wasn't sure he would go, and Giambi described himself as in "limbo land." McGwire remained conspicuously quiet. During negotiations with the commissioner's office and the players' association, the committee came to understand the great fear that underlaid baseball's reluctance to participate in the hearings. Nobody in the sport wanted McGwire to have to answer questions under oath about his use of steroids. Nobody wanted the magical 1998 season to be exposed as a fraud.

As the hearing approached, the committee became impatient with baseball's foot dragging. It subpoenaed the players to compel them to appear. Ultimately, Selig and Fehr testified, along with all the players except Giambi. The BALCO prosecutors had asked Congress to excuse him because of their ongoing criminal case.

On the morning of March 17, Room 2154 of the Rayburn House Office Building was packed with reporters, the most since the Clinton impeachment proceedings. So many media credentials were issued that some reporters were forced to watch the hearing on television in a nearby room. One interested party who had a reserved spot was Jeff Novitzky, the IRS agent who had sparked the BALCO case.

Denise and Ray Garibaldi had front-row seats in the gallery. They were from Petaluma, California, a town 40 miles north of San Francisco, across the Golden Gate Bridge and near the fabled wine country. The Garibaldis had been invited to testify, but, unlike the ballplayers, they were eager to speak.

They wanted to tell the story of their son, who once was one of the nation's premier college baseball players. Rob Garibaldi had grown up passionate about baseball, a huge fan of Bonds and McGwire. The sport was his life, and he was very good at it; good enough, in fact, that at age 16 he was recruited to join a traveling all-star team sponsored by the California Angels. Rob, though, was a kid with major-league tools but minor-league size, a rail of boy who ate and ate but couldn't put on weight. His coach on the all-star team was a former power lifter who worked as a salesman for a nutritional supplement company. Rob began using an array of weight- and muscle-gaining substances to bulk up. By the end of his prep career in 1997, Rob was a high school All-American—but he was still a lean 5 feet 11 inches, 150 pounds. That summer, he began taking steroids.

Over the next five years, Rob injected himself with Deca-Durabolin and Sustanon. In the fall of 1998, as McGwire was taking down Maris's record, Rob, now up to 165 pounds, hit .459 with 14 home runs and 77 RBI for Santa Rosa Junior College. He was named the state's Community College Player of the Year and was offered a scholarship to the University of Southern California—McGwire's alma mater and a top Division I program. Rob also was selected by the Yankees in the 41st round of the major league amateur draft. He chose USC and helped lead the Trojans to an appearance in the 2000 College World Series. *Baseball America* magazine heralded him as one of the nation's top 100 college players.

But over the next year and a half, Rob's life fell apart as he struggled to stop using steroids. He became violent, delusional, and despondent in what his parents later concluded was an adverse psychological reaction to the powerful drugs. In 2002, when he finally confessed his steroid use, Rob explained he was just modeling his big-league heroes. First he told his mother, calmly explaining that in order to make it to the majors, a player had to take steroids. Barry Bonds was doing it, Mark McGwire was doing it, so surely he had to do it. When his father confronted him, Rob screamed and physically attacked his dad, pinning him down and choking him.

"I'm on steroids, what do you think?" Rob yelled. "Who do you think I am? I'm a baseball player, baseball players take steroids. How do you think Bonds hits all his home runs? How do you think all these guys do this stuff? You think they do it from just working out normal?"

On October 1, 2002, while sitting in car parked around the corner from his parents' home, 24-year-old Rob Garibaldi shot himself in the head with a .357 Magnum pistol. His suicide occurred five years after he had begun using steroids. His parents blamed the drugs for the crashing depression that led to his death.

After the Garibaldis told Rob's story and urged baseball to get tough on steroids, they took their seats and waited for the ballplayers to testify. The players entered the room, trailed by a swarm of lawyers. Palmeiro, the handsome, mustached first baseman of the Orioles, approached the couple and offered his condolences.

The Garibaldis were optimistic. They hoped McGwire and the others would come clean. Instead, a surreal scene unfolded. Sosa, the Dominican star who had transformed himself from a scrawny shortstop into the Cubs' greatest home run hitter, acted as if he could hardly speak English. It was like watching the old *Saturday Night Live* skit with Garrett Morris as Dominican ballplayer Chico Escuela. Palmeiro, in a moment that seemed scripted, looked up from a prepared statement, pointed his finger at the committee chairman, Representative Tom Davis of Virginia, and said firmly, "Let me start by telling you this: I have never used steroids. Period."

At first, it appeared as if McGwire was going to confess his use of performance-enhancing drugs, ask the nation for forgiveness, and pledge to fight the steroid battle. He nearly cried as he read an opening statement that praised the Garibaldis and others for their courage. "My heart goes out to every parent whose son or daughter were victims of steroid use," he said haltingly. "I hope that these hearings can prevent other families from suffering." Sitting almost close enough to touch him, Denise Garibaldi fought back the maternal urge to reach out and console Big Mac. The urge passed quickly. After a recess, McGwire turned evasive. He had nothing to say about anything. Pressed about whether he had used performance-enhancing drugs, he responded over and over again, "I'm not here to talk about the past." The refrain became so pathetic and predictable that McGwire was mocked by some of the politicians, while the audience chuckled each time he uttered his non-denial denial.

Denise Garibaldi was crestfallen. McGwire's opening statement had raised her hopes.

"I really got the sense they wanted steroids out of baseball. It was like he was listening," she said in a hallway after the players had finished testifying. "But then for him to deny and not participate in the rest of the panel, I was completely disappointed. Maybe I was counting on him because of Rob's love for him."

When Selig and the other baseball officials testified, the session became combative. The politicians pounded away, while the officials scrambled to defend themselves. By the end, Denise and Ray were infuriated. Baseball didn't get it. Its policy was a joke, and the Garibaldis left Washington with little hope that attitudes were changing.

Most infuriating of all, the one player who should have been forced to testify, the player Rob had idolized most, was absent. Where was Barry Bonds, Denise wondered? How did he get off the hook?

In fact, the BALCO prosecutors had made sure Bonds was not subpoenaed. They had asked the House to back off.

Bonds himself was under investigation.

At about the time Denise and Ray Garibaldi completed their testimony, a far more secret hearing on baseball and steroids got underway at the federal courthouse in San Francisco. The BALCO grand jury was back in business, and this time the witness was Kimberly Bell, the former girlfriend whom Bonds had told to disappear. During their relationship, Bell said Bonds had confessed that he was using steroids, and she said he gave her $80,000 cash—the proceeds from the sale of autographed baseballs—for the down payment on a house in Scottsdale. Novitzky had tracked down Bonds's aggrieved former lover and persuaded her to become a government witness.

After Bonds had broken up with Bell by cell phone in May 2003, she heard nothing from him for months. Over the summer, the pain of rejection mingled with her worries about money. Bell's move from California to Arizona hadn't worked out: She never found a job that paid enough to cover the monthly payment on the house Bonds had promised to buy her. While she was trying to decide how to get on with her life, Bonds's people began trying to get in touch with her.

On September 5, 2003, two days after the BALCO raids, Bell received three urgent voice mail messages from the former police officer who worked as Bonds's bodyguard. Bonds wanted to speak to Bell "about some stuff to let you know what happened," the bodyguard said. "In a nutshell, he lost control on that issue," he said cryptically. Bell didn't know what he was talking about, and she didn't call back. Then Bell got a letter from Michael Rains, Bonds's lawyer. Bonds wanted to "convey to you certain information," Rains wrote. There was a "need for confidentiality." Bell didn't call him, either. Instead, she hired her own lawyer. She would try to force Bonds to pay for the house.

Bell's lawyer wrote to Rains, suggesting a financial settlement. Rains's reply was harsh. He dismissed the relationship between the athlete and the graphic artist as "meretricious," one in which Bonds simply paid Bell for sex. He denied Bonds had promised to buy her a house. In the months that followed, the tone of Rains's correspondence became more conciliatory, as Bell's lawyer laid out her evidence: hotel and airline receipts and baseball ticket stubs showing that Bell frequently had traveled with Bonds and the Giants; bank records to support her claim that Bonds had given her large sums of cash; her collection of abusive voicemails; and Bonds's admission that he was using "supplements," as Bell's lawyer delicately put it. Rains' final letter was almost apologetic. He hoped Bonds could avoid inflammatory publicity and unnecessary turmoil. Nevertheless, Bonds would pay Bell only $20,000 to settle her claims; she would also be required to sign a confidentiality agreement.

Bell needed $100,000 to pay off the house; $20,000 would barely cover her legal bills. She rejected the offer, but she had no money to pay for a trial, either. So she sold the house and moved back to California, intent on writing a memoir about Bonds. When Congress began showing interest in steroids and sports, she wrote an e-mail to Senator McCain telling what she knew, but she got no response. She met a freelance writer and started work on a book. In February, the writer wangled an appearance on Geraldo Rivera's program to talk about Bonds and steroids. The writer thought Bell's appearance would create buzz and bring them the book deal they sought.

Instead, three days later, it brought Novitzky to Bell's apartment in San Jose. They talked for a long time. The agent was interested in Bell's account of Bonds's use of steroids, and he immediately understood the legal implications of Bonds's use of cash from autograph shows. Novitzky wanted Bell's bank records to verify her story. Bell was cooperative, but she needed to run it by a lawyer, and the session finally began to wind down.

"Why didn't you come to us instead of going to the media?" Novitzky asked her.

"But I did go to the government," Bell replied, explaining the e-mail to Senator McCain.

"Usually people start a little lower down the chain," Novitzky said.

On March 17, while the nation's attention was riveted on the congressional hearings, Bell drove to San Francisco to testify. Half of her time on the witness stand was spent discussing steroids, the rest on Bonds's use of cash. At times, the prosecutors were confrontational:

You mean Bonds never told you he didn't pay taxes on his income from the autographs? Why didn't you look in Bonds's "man bag" if you thought he kept drugs in it? Bell tried to explain Bonds's controlling, secretive personality.

The grand jurors wanted to know about physical changes that might indicate Bonds was using steroids. Bell described everything from the acne on his back to his outbursts of rage. One grand juror asked whether Bonds's head had gotten larger; use of human growth hormone can cause the extremities to grow. Bell said it was possible. She thought she could see the plates of his skull.

Another grand juror wanted to know about Bonds's testicles. Two weeks before, at spring training, Bonds had impulsively begun discussing steroids with reporters from the *Oakland Tribune* and ESPN. He had insisted he had no physical symptoms of steroid use. "I can tell you my testicles are the same size," Bonds told them. "They haven't shrunk. They're the same and work just the same as they always have." The grand juror recited the quote to Bell. They hadn't disappeared, Bell replied, but they were not as big as they used to be. In all, Bell spent more than two hours on the witness stand. After it was over, Novitzky made her promise to keep in touch.

Three days later, the story of Bell's grand jury testimony led in the Sunday *Chronicle*, with details of her allegations about Bonds. The story attracted a flurry of attention around the country, and it was of particular concern to the San Francisco Giants. To people who knew Bonds, the episode with Bell showed him at his most arrogant and reckless. Bell wanted $100,000, a pittance for a player who earned $17 million per year. Indeed, at the very time Rains was playing tough with Bell, telling her $20,000 was all she would get, Bonds received a $500,000 bonus from the Giants for winning the National League MVP award. Instead of paying Bell and parting as friends, Bonds tried to humiliate her. Bonds hadn't considered what might occur if Bell refused to be intimidated. Now she was helping Novitzky investigate him for perjury and tax fraud. The tax issue was of particular concern: Unlike perjury, the government could make an ironclad tax case with documents alone. Bonds hired tax lawyers in Los Angeles to be ready if the government moved against him.

Bonds had laid low since December, when the *Chronicle* published his grand jury testimony. He knew he would face questions about steroids at spring training. When the baseball writers approached him in Scottsdale, he threw a preemptive tantrum. Refusing to answer any questions about BALCO or steroids, he subjected them to an abusive, semi-coherent monologue.

"All you guys lied," he raged at the writers. "Should you have asterisks beside your name? All of you lied. All of you said something wrong. All of you have dirt, all of you. When your closet is clean, then come clean somebody else's."

One month later, the news about Bell's grand jury testimony rattled Bonds. Two days after the *Chronicle* report, he brought his teenaged son to the Giants' clubhouse at Scottsdale. Bonds was walking with a crutch, hobbled by knee surgery. Approached by a crush of reporters, Bonds agreed to an impromptu press conference.

"Can you get my son in this, too?" he said to an ESPN cameraman. "Not just on me. So you guys can see the pain you're causing my family?" Then Bonds began another monologue, this one self-pitying and accusatory.

"My family is tired," he said. "I'm tired. You guys wanted to hurt me bad enough. You finally got there . . .

"Everybody else has tried to destroy everything that's supposedly been positive or good . . . I'm really tired.

"You wanted me to jump off the bridge. I finally jumped. You wanted to bring me down. You finally have brought me and my family down. You've finally done it, everybody, all of you.

"So now go pick a different person. I'm done."

The boy looked uncomfortable during his father's remarks. He said nothing. A few days later, Bonds and the boy were at a BMW dealership in San Francisco. Bonds's son was 15. Bonds was shopping for a car for the boy.

By the summer of 2005, Terry Madden and his U.S Anti-Doping Agency team had gotten 13 BALCO athletes banned for drug use. Thirty-four year old Michelle Collins, who had transformed herself into a 200-meter world champion through Victor Conte's drug program, accepted a four-year ban that effectively ended her career. Alvin Harrison, another athlete USADA charged based solely on BALCO documents, also accepted a four-year ban.

Dwain Chambers, Conte's follow-up to Project World Record, found his career destroyed as well. Banned from competition for two years and from the Olympics for life, the British sprint champion returned to the Bay Area to try American football. The experiment was short-lived. Korchemny got him a spot on a junior college team in Hayward. Chambers spent the summer of 2004 working out as a wide receiver for the Chabot College Knights, but he never played in a game. His visa didn't come through, and he finally returned to London, where newspapers regularly referred to him as "disgraced sprinter Dwain Chambers."

Though USADA still had not brought charges against Marion Jones, her career seemed dead. She had sued Conte for libel after the *20/20* interview, but the lawsuit was viewed as a public-relations ploy because she sued neither of the media outlets—ABC or ESPN—that allowed Conte to tell his story. By the spring of 2005, the former Olympic superstar was a pariah on the European track circuit. At events where she once was paid $150,000 appearance fees, she was no longer even allowed to compete. Meet directors cited the taint from BALCO. Jones's "Q" rating, a measure of her marketability, plummeted nearly 30 percent. And her negative rating with consumers spiked 35 percent between March 2004 and March 2005, the *Chicago Tribune* reported.

In April, Jones opened her track season at the Mt. SAC Relays in California and finished last in a field of six in the 400 meters. In mid-June, she finished fourth in the 100 meters at a meet in Monterrey, Mexico. Finally, on June 24, at the U.S. Championships in Carson, California, Jones prepared to compete in a 100-meter qualifying heat. She took a practice run and paced up and down her lane. Then, abruptly, she walked past the starting blocks, gathered her warm-up gear from a plastic bucket, and left the track. Jones's agent, Charlie Wells, said the sprinter pulled out because of a "minor" injury.

Only a few hours earlier, Tim Montgomery bailed out of his 100-meter race. "He wasn't able to concentrate enough," Wells told reporters. "He had some business concerns and he was not 100 percent ready to run."

It had been a bad month for Montgomery. Ten days earlier, his world record in the 100 meters had been broken by Jamaica's Asafa

Powell. Meanwhile, Montgomery had been in San Francisco to fight the doping charges that his lawyer had dismissed as a "witch hunt." Before the arbitration hearing, Montgomery told reporters he never "knowingly or unknowingly" used performance-enhancing drugs, despite the *Chronicle* report of his sworn testimony to the BALCO grand jury.

Montgomery did not testify at the doping hearing, which was held in a law office in the city's financial district. USADA presented reams of documents proving the former 100-meter world record holder had used banned substances. The agency's case also benefited from two significant witnesses: Novitzky testified about the evidence he had gathered during the BALCO investigation, and world champion sprinter Kelli White offered details about the BALCO conspiracy, right down to a translation of the calendars.

One witness USADA couldn't get was Conte. The agency repeatedly asked him to testify, but Conte left them guessing; he might show, he might not. Even as the hearing was underway, one of USADA's lawyers kept checking the door, thinking Conte still might make a grand appearance.

One week after the Montgomery hearing, USADA presented its case against Chryste Gaines, the last of the four athletes charged based on BALCO documents. In December, more than two years after the mysterious syringe arrived on its doorstep, USADA finally received some closure: Montgomery and Gaines were given two-year bans by the Court of Arbitration for Sport. They received the same sanction as Kelli White, the sprinter who had confessed and cooperated with the doping agency.

As USADA was wrapping up its cases, so, too, was the U.S. Attorney's office in San Francisco. In July, after months of desultory negotiations, U.S. Attorney Kevin Ryan agreed to drop 40 of the 42 counts in the BALCO indictment that had been announced with such fanfare the previous year. Conte would plead guilty to two felonies and serve four months in prison, followed by four months of house arrest. Anderson, Bonds's trainer, would serve three and three. Valente, Conte's right-hand man, and Korchemny, the aging Ukranian track coach, would not be jailed at all. Significantly, the government's plea deal did not require the defendants to testify against their crime partners—athletes, drug suppliers, or anyone else. Conte would never have to recite his list of celebrity clients in open court—not even the ones he had named on national television. Anderson would not have to admit in public that he created the drug protocol that had made Barry Bonds the Home Run King.

The plea bargain only made sense if BALCO were viewed as an ordinary drug prosecution. Under federal law, penalties for dealing steroids were far lighter than for dealing crack cocaine or heroin. Even if a jury had found Conte guilty on all counts, most of those convictions were irrelevant in determining his sentence. The BALCO defense lawyers believed Conte's maximum exposure was two years in prison. U.S. Attorney Ryan said it was one year. Conte faced relatively little punishment, trial or no trial.

Nevertheless, a tough prosecutor might have refused to negotiate with Conte simply because of his outrageous conduct in the months after he was indicted. Conte had filed an affidavit denying he had named athletes in his confession and accusing Novitzky of "fabricating" evidence. Then Conte had repeated the gist of his confession on television, in essence acknowledging that his legal plea was a lie. In e-mails to reporters, Conte had vilified Novitzky, accusing him of everything from framing the defendants to leaking evidence. At one point, he sent an e-mail to the *Chronicle* with the subject line: "Novitzky masturbates while reading the Chronicle." Conte had pushed his lawyer into writing the grandstanding letter to President Bush complaining about the U.S. Attorney's office. And he had shown no remorse for his crimes. In *ESPN the Magazine* he wrote: "People have asked me: Do you feel guilty about what you did? Are you ashamed? The answer is no." Then there were Conte's attempts to orchestrate the grand jury testimony of the athletes. Indeed, there were many reasons for a prosecutor to play hardball with Conte and force him to go to trial or plead guilty to every count of the indictment.

Besides, BALCO was not an ordinary drug case. It had been touted by the president in the State of the Union Address and announced by the Attorney General. The BALCO evidence, obtained through the McCain subpoena, had helped USADA purge drug cheats from the U.S. Olympic team. News reports about the case—the *Chronicle's* grand jury stories, in particular—impelled Congress to convene the hearings that forced baseball to confront its steroid problem. A BALCO trial in which athletes testified about their drug use had tremendous possibilities for educating the public about the crisis of steroids in sports, anti-doping advocates believed.

But by the summer of 2005, the cast of characters had changed in Washington. John Ashcroft, the hard-line, moralistic fan of Stan Musial, had retired as Attorney General, and the baseball-crazy aides who had tracked BALCO so closely were gone as well. The new A.G. was Alberto Gonzales, Bush's friend from Texas. Perhaps the only president who had ever owned a baseball team had listened to the pleas of baseball's establishment, some close to the case speculated. Throughout the summer, Congress had continued to pound away at the game over its lax steroid policy. Then, in August, Rafael Palmeiro, the Orioles star who had wagged his finger and denied he used drugs, was suspended for using stanozolol, the Ben Johnson steroid, and Congress opened a perjury investigation. With all that as a backdrop, a BALCO trial that focused on drug use by baseball's greatest home run hitter could be devastating to the sport.

Lawyers who knew Kevin Ryan believed the decision to dump BALCO had been made in Washington. Ryan was a former local judge who became United States Attorney through a combination of patronage and political accident: He was one of a handful of conservative officials in the left-liberal enclave of San Francisco, and his father-in-law was a wealthy real estate developer with GOP connections. Ryan hoped Bush would name him a federal judge. He would never make an important decision on his own, his associates believed.

Or perhaps the Justice Department in D.C. had actually left the decision on BALCO to Ryan, knowing what the outcome would be. Anti-doping advocates believed that nobody in San Francisco except Novitzky had grasped the crisis of doping in sports and the opportunity BALCO presented for cleaning it up. From first to last, Ryan seemed to want to limit BALCO's impact. He had decided to keep the names of the BALCO athletes secret. He had spurned USADA's pleas for help and threatened to prosecute the reporters for publishing the leaked files.

Once the plea bargain was struck, Conte indulged in another act of defiant self-promotion. The night before he went to court, he distributed a press release announcing his light sentence and emphasizing that he would not become a government witness. The statement was attributed to Conte's new lawyers.

On July 15, Conte, Anderson, Valente, and Korchemny walked the gauntlet of media cameras at the federal building in San Francisco once again. In court, Conte smiled confidently. While waiting for the case to be called, he edited a handwritten statement that Korchmeny intended to read. In the end, Korchmeny asked for a continuance, but the other three men entered guilty pleas.

A discordant note was struck when Anderson pleaded guilty to steroid dealing and money laundering. Judge Susan Illston quizzed him to make certain he had committed the crimes. "Did you distribute steroids to athletes?" she asked Barry Bonds's trainer. "Yes," he replied. There was a pause. But the judge didn't ask Anderson to name the athletes to whom he had given banned drugs. Then, moments later, the judge insisted that Anderson identify the person who had assisted him in money laundering. Anderson named a 72-year-old suburban grandmother who worked part-time as a bookkeeper. The grandmother had cashed a check for Anderson while doing his bookkeeping. And so the case ended, with the grandmother's name in the public record as Anderson's crime partner, while Bonds and the others remained protected.

Ryan and the Justice Department were sharply criticized for the plea deal. Dr. Gary Wadler, the steroid expert who served on the board of the World Anti-Doping Agency, said the failure to name the BALCO athletes would "fuel international cynicism and sarcasm" about the United States' efforts to clean up drugs in sports.

"For the public, the question is, 'What was the bargain that let you walk away almost scot-free from such egregious behavior?' " he said.

Ryan defended the plea bargains. In an interview with the New York *Daily News*, he denied that the *Chronicle*'s grand jury stories had forced baseball to address its steroid problem. He contended the impetus had come from Ashcroft's press conference. Ryan wouldn't comment on whether there would be more indictments, other than to say he hoped to indict "the individuals identified with the leaks."

On October 18, Conte and Anderson returned to court for sentencing. Judge Illston chastised them for helping the athletes cheat; she told Anderson what he did was "criminally wrong and morally wrong." In the end, though, Illston approved the sentences. The plea agreement prohibited the co-conspirators from contacting one another while they were on parole. Conte's lawyers wanted that amended to allow the men to see each other for "business purposes."

"That business is exactly what?" the judge asked.

Nutritional supplementation and conditioning, she was told. The judge agreed and the prosecutors didn't object. Outside court, Conte read a statement. Once he was out of prison, he intended to help solve the doping problem and work to make "sports more honorable for the athletes and the fans." He would share "what I've learned about the rampant use of drugs at the elite level of sport" and explain "exactly how elite athletes routinely beat the existing anti-doping programs."

In the cat-and-mouse game of sports doping, the self-proclaimed greatest mouse ever now wanted to become a cat. As Conte walked away from the cameras and the microphones, he was asked how he intended to help clean up sports. "We haven't discussed that yet," one of his lawyers replied.

Six weeks later, Victor Conte drove himself to the Taft federal prison near Bakersfield, California. He wore a shirt advertising SNAC, and he invited a television crew along to capture his big day.

Even after the plea bargains had been struck, agent Novitzky pursued the BALCO case. On September 29, he led raids on Patrick Arnold's office and home near the campus of the University of Illinois. On November 2, Arnold was indicted by the BALCO grand jury on steroid conspiracy charges for supplying norbolethone, THG, and another undetectable steroid to Conte. Novitzky continued to investigate Bonds. Still, by January 2006, the government had not acted on Kim Bell's allegations regarding Bonds and tax evasion.

It had been a lost baseball season for Bonds. On January 31, 2005, he underwent arthroscopic surgery for a cartilage tear in his right knee. The Giants believed it was a routine procedure. They promised that Bonds, with his 703 career home runs, would be in the lineup on Opening Day, ready to pursue Babe Ruth's mark of 714 and Hank Aaron's 755. But there may be no such thing as routine surgery on the arthritic knee of a 40-year-old athlete, especially one who has taken up steroids and power-lifting late in his career.

The surgery was performed by Dr. Arthur Ting, the sports orthopedist who had drawn Bonds' blood at BALCO, and who had operated on Gary Sheffield's knees in 2003. Afterward, Bonds ignored the Giants' trainers and pursued his own rehabilitation program. He was aggressive, as he had been when supervising Sheffield's rehab. In the off season, Bonds had moved to a new home in Beverly Hills. He went home and within days he was lifting weights. The arthritic knee became swollen with fluid, and Ting flew to Southern California to drain it.

In February, Bonds reported to spring training. With Anderson not allowed to travel because of his indictment, Bonds had a new weight trainer, Greg "Sweets" Oliver. In fact, after Anderson was indicted a year earlier, the Giants had circumvented Major League Baseball's ban on personal trainers in the clubhouse by putting both Bonds's stretching guru, Harvey Shields, and "Sweets" on the club's payroll. Giants personnel began calling them "the Coneheads," after the old *Saturday Night Live* routine, and joked that Anderson would join the others as soon as he was out of prison.

Bonds continued his aggressive rehab during spring training, and Ting flew to Arizona to drain the knee again. In all, Ting drained the knee at least six times in six weeks.

On March 10, while a cameraman videotaped the performance for Bonds's Web site, the Giants star underwent a monster workout at the ballpark in Scottsdale. He took seven rounds of batting practice, ran stop-and-go sprint exercises, and shagged fly balls. A few days later he and Oliver went to the gym, and the trainer watched as Bonds leg-pressed 400 pounds with the damaged knee. Predictably, the knee couldn't stand up to the pounding, and a week later, Dr. Ting operated again to repair a new cartilage tear. Bonds left Scottsdale for San Francisco after the second operation. The Giants said he needed to use the state-of-the-art equipment at SBC Park to rehabilitate the knee.

Bonds also headed for the gym near BALCO, Bay Area Fitness, and linked up with Anderson. "He's my guy," Bonds explained, when an acquaintance asked why he was still with Anderson. "Look at my upper body." On April 9, the *Chronicle* reported that Bonds was still working out with Anderson, illustrating it with a photo of Bonds entering the gym for a workout. But neither the Giants nor Major League Baseball told Bonds to stop associating with the steroid dealer.

The Giants were forced to begin the 2005 season without their marquee player, but they held out hopes for an early return. However, Bonds's knee problems were an expensive setback for the club. When Peter Magowan had re-signed Bonds in 2001, the club had sought financial protection against this sort of late-career injury. The club had the right to terminate the contract if Bonds failed to make 400 plate appearances in 2005. But in 2004, Bonds had badgered Magowan until he agreed to drop the clause and guarantee his contract for both 2005 and 2006. As a result, the club would pay Bonds $17 million in 2005 and $17 million again in 2006, whether he played or not.

The Giants told the beat writers they were imposing a news blackout regarding Bonds' knee, but in truth the club knew little about the progress of his rehabilitation. Often the club had to rely on postings on Bonds' Web site for information. In the offices at SBC Park, worries about their marquee player's knee mingled with fears that the BALCO grand jury might indict Bonds for tax evasion or perjury. Then, in May, the club was stunned by more bad medical news: Bonds needed yet another knee operation, this time to put down a bacterial infection. The third operation would put Bonds out of action indefinitely.

Another jolt soon followed: ESPN reported that Bonds's orthopedist, Ting, was on probation with the state medical board for unprofessional conduct, accused of prescribing "dangerous drugs and controlled substances" to friends and athletes without keeping proper records. The athletes weren't named. Ting denied wrongdoing.

Without Bonds, the Giants were a losing team. But they hung in the pennant race because the National League West was the weakest division in baseball, with only the San Diego Padres playing .500 ball. Bonds was gone for five months. In June, fed up with Bonds's unwillingness to follow their trainers' instructions, the Giants suggested he go elsewhere to rehab. Bonds went home to L.A., where he worked with physical therapist Clive Brewster, who regularly treated sports stars. Bonds took along Shields and Oliver, even though the trainers were supposed to be working with the entire Giants team. The Giants, of course, continued to pay their salaries.

Before Bonds left, he got into a scuffle with one of his teammates, pitcher Jason Christiansen. Christiansen was in the lunchroom at SBC Park when he overheard Shields offer some batting tips to another player. The pitcher interrupted, telling Shields he was "full of shit" and should mind his own business.

"You're disrespecting me," Shields responded.

The argument flared, and the two men got into a shoving match, during which Shields spilled a Coke on himself. He then fled the room. A few minutes later, Bonds, trailed by his entourage, rushed in and tossed a cup of Coke at the 6-foot-5, 230-pound Christiansen. The two players started going at it, and Bonds landed a blow to the jaw. Christiansen got Bonds in a headlock and took a couple of shots at the outfielder before the two were separated. Later, Christiansen was traded to the Angels; when asked about the fight, he told reporters, "I have a lot of respect for Barry."

Bonds's knee was slow to come around. In August, he told a writer for Major League Baseball's MLB.com Web site he didn't think he would play in 2005. Once again, the Giants were blindsided. Manager Felipe Alou told television reporters he heard the news from his wife, who read it in the newspaper and told him about it at breakfast. "I wanted to go back to bed," Alou said.

But on September 12, Bonds finally returned to the Giants. The club was 14 games under .500 and seven behind the division-leading Padres. Although only 18 games remained in the season, the front office was happy to see him: They had feared ticket sales for the 2006 season would suffer unless Bonds gave fans hope that he could still play.

Bonds's knee was a wreck. He had to take a day off after playing only two games, and in late innings, Alou pulled him for a pinch runner or a defensive replacement. When Bonds sat out a game, Alou was uncertain about the star's status: Before one game, the manager had a coach ask one of the Coneheads whether Bonds was available to pinch hit. (He wasn't).

Nevertheless, when he could play, Bonds remained a powerful

force. He went on a hot streak, hitting a home run in four consecutive games. The first two homers were struck at home, and the Giants fans celebrated with standing ovations.

It was a different story on the road. Bonds's first road trip of 2005 began in Washington, D.C. The fans seemed unusually hostile. In the first game, on September 20, they began booing Bonds when he was introduced, chanting "steroids" and "BALCO," and they kept it up throughout the game. In the fourth inning, Bonds turned on an inside pitch thrown by the Nationals' John Patterson and crushed it, knocking the ball into the upper deck of RFK Stadium, 460 feet away. The astounding shot was his 706th, leaving him only eight behind Ruth, and at first the fans cheered. But as Bonds jogged past second base, the boos began again, along with another chant: "Cheater, cheater." Perhaps it was a glimpse of things to come. If Bonds came back in 2006 and made a run at Ruth and Aaron, the atmosphere would be nothing like McGwire's celebratory traveling circus of 1998. Bonds's involvement in BALCO had soured many fans, convincing them he was a drug cheat, guaranteeing that any record he might set would be met with derision.

The Giants professed not to understand the hostility, nor why anyone thought Bonds had used banned drugs. Unlike Rafael Palmeiro, Bonds had never tested dirty for steroids.

The case against Bonds was mere innuendo, the club claimed.

The argument ignored the mountain of evidence: Bonds's grand jury testimony; the secret recording of Greg Anderson and his guilty plea; Kimberly Bell's story; the confessions of Conte and Valente; C. J. Hunter's statement; the grand jury testimony of Tim Montgomery, Jason Giambi, and the other baseball players; the steroid calendars and other documents; the dramatic changes in the superstar's body and performance.

"They've just got their heads buried so deeply in the sand," explained one person familiar with the front-office mentality. "They're trying to hold their noses and get to 715 and then to 755."

The night Bonds returned to the lineup, Giants executive vice president Larry Baer was interviewed on the team's flagship radio station, KNBR. Baer, Magowan's right-hand man, said he was eager to see "the greatest player of all time take his position in left field." Baer sounded cheery and upbeat, but then he mentioned *USA Today* sports columnist Christine Brennan, and his mood darkened.

Brennan was convinced that Bonds was a drug cheat, and she believed the steroid scandal had hurt the game. She foresaw nothing but trouble for baseball if Bonds came back and broke the records of Ruth and Aaron. In a recent column, she had urged Bonds to simply go away. "How we wish we could just avoid Bonds once and for all, have him and those muscles, however they were made, fade away, never to return," she wrote. "How we wish he would do what was best for his game and leave the records of Babe Ruth and Hank Aaron intact."

Brennan's column was "just completely outrageous," Baer said. "And everybody including Bud Selig said that was outrageous.

"To save the game, don't come back?

"Possibly the greatest player that ever wore a uniform not to play the game, to save the game. Why?"

Epilogue

On October 26, 2005, the Chicago White Sox completed a sweep of the Houston Astros to capture the World Series, the team's first championship since 1917. More than ending an 88-year drought, the team's victory marked the exorcism of baseball's worst demon and darkest hour: The Black Sox Scandal of 1919. At last, baseball could bury the memory of the eight ballplayers—the heart of the best team in White Sox history—who had committed the grievous sin of throwing the World Series and selling out the game to gamblers. No longer would there be cause to conjure up the ghosts of Eddie Cicotte, Buck Weaver, Chick Gandil, and, of course, Shoeless Joe Jackson, the illiterate farm boy and fabulous hitter whose Hall of Fame–caliber career was destroyed by the scandal. Now when baseball thought of the White Sox, it could revel in the memory of manager Ozzie Guillen and his no-name band of overachievers—the gritty South Side Sox of 2005—who had stormed through the postseason against all odds.

But the White Sox's victory also underscored that baseball's great scandal of long ago had been superseded by one that posed an ongoing threat to the game. By the fall of 2005, it was apparent to the general public that a great many players, including some of the game's biggest stars, had been using steroids and other illegal drugs for years, and that the steroid problem had become a continuing embarrassment and distraction. Before Game 3 of the Series in Houston, when the Fall Classic was at the center of the sporting universe and the talk should have been about the glory of the game, Commissioner Bud Selig once again found himself deflecting reporters' questions about the sport's weak policy for controlling its drug problem. Even in the middle of an exciting World Series, baseball was unable to shake the taint of drugs, no matter how hard it tried.

When the BALCO steroid scandal erupted in 2003, baseball had simply tried to ignore it, much in the way the sport had downplayed the initial rumors that the World Series had been fixed in 1919. But by January 2005, baseball finally had been forced to act. The game had been shaken by the drumbeat of BALCO revelations—especially the publication of the grand jury testimony of Jason Giambi and Barry Bonds, which removed any lingering doubt about how prevalent drugs had become in the game. As baseball came under intense pressure from politicians in both parties, Selig and union chief Don Fehr had announced their first new, improved steroid program. Rather than the drug counseling imposed by the old system, a first positive test would now earn a player a modest 10-day suspension. After four positive tests, cheating players would face a one-year ban. But given all the loopholes and limits to the plan, it was unlikely a player would test positive two times, let alone four. Still, Selig and Fehr tried to insist that this new program would solve whatever problem existed.

But the sport's ruinous image problem only seemed to get worse. After the twin disasters of Mark McGwire's congressional testimony and Rafael Palmeiro's failed drug test, it was obvious that the new plan just wouldn't cut it. Baseball faced the real threat that Congress would legislate an Olympic-style steroid testing program, and perhaps assign the U.S. Anti-Doping Agency to run it. And so, three weeks after the White Sox won the World Series, baseball's leaders responded to the continued pressure with yet another new Joint Drug Agreement. Under this latest policy, a player would be suspended 50 games for a first positive test and 100 for a second. And anybody caught three times would be banned for life. In addition to steroids, amphetamines—the drug of choice in baseball for decades—were also added to the banned list.

Selig told reporters it was a "historic" day, and he predicted the new plan would "eradicate steroid use in baseball." Fehr issued a statement trumpeting the agreement as proof major leaguers were "committed to the elimination of performance-enhancing substances."

*   *   *

Unquestionably, baseball had come a long way on the issue of performance-enhancing drugs, and the officials, especially Selig, deserved credit for the reforms. Still, there were problems. Although it was a vast improvement, baseball's new policy was riddled with unanswered questions and potential loopholes. It was still far weaker than the so-called "Gold Standard"—the Olympic program that the world's track stars faced—and too often could be beat by using human growth hormone, insulin, or other undetectable drugs. Baseball had been dragged kicking and screaming into adopting the new program, pressured by Congress and the press coverage of BALCO. When viewed in that context, Selig and Fehr's boasting about baseball's tough new policy seemed disingenuous. Had there been no BALCO investigation, there would have been no new baseball drug policy, it was that simple. If Agent Novitzky had not decided to dig through Victor Conte's trash, or if Don Catlin had not cracked the code of THG, or if the *Chronicle* had not published the secret testimony of the baseball stars and inspired Jose Canseco to recast his autobiography into a memoir of drug abuse, nothing would have been done at all.

To finally put the steroid era behind it, the game also had to confront the issue of tainted records. Baseball needed to get to the bottom of the drug use that lay beneath the magical 1998 season of McGwire and Sosa. It needed to launch a probe into Bonds's 73-homer season, and thus into the legitimacy of his run on Hank Aaron's career mark.

Senator Jim Bunning of Kentucky, the Hall of Fame pitcher on the Tigers and Phillies of the 1960s, said he was disappointed that the new policy failed to address the records and statistics produced by players who had cheated with drugs. "Baseball and all other sports should deal with this," Bunning said. "If they think it's important to put an Rx or an asterisk next to the name of someone convicted, it's up to them."

Representative John Sweeney, whose district included the Baseball Hall of Fame in Cooperstown, New York, urged the game to address the issue of the players whose records were tainted by their association with BALCO. "If anything in life is attained improperly," Sweeney said, "it ought to be scrutinized and possibly taken back."

But neither Selig nor Fehr nor the club owners seemed remotely interested in investigating the steroid era. McGwire, it turned out, had been speaking for all of the baseball establishment when he said he didn't want to talk about the past. No one in a position of authority in the game thought the steroids crisis was so urgent that they were willing to debunk a decade of inflated statistics or sort out the drug cheating that underlay the records. No one, it turned out, wanted to play the role of Kenesaw Mountain Landis.

In *Eight Men Out*, his definitive account of the Black Sox scandal, author Eliot Asinof provides an unsparing portrait of Landis, the federal judge brought in by baseball owners to clean up the gambling mess. As baseball commissioner, Landis was arbitrary and ruthless. He showed no mercy to the impoverished players who had been duped by the gamblers into selling out the Series. Nor was Landis interested in understanding what had led them to their actions—the question, as Asinof puts it, of "the pressures of the baseball world, of America in 1919 itself, that would turn decent, normal talented men to engage in such a betrayal." Instead, Landis had meted out rough justice and lifetime bans to the eight players, with little regard for legal niceties.

There was no question that Landis was deadly serious about dealing decisively with the gambling crisis afflicting the game. Landis would confront the problem head on and punish the crooked players even though they were never convicted of any crimes (the Black Sox eight had been acquitted in a trial). Baseball had to make examples of the corrupt players if the game were to recover from the scandal, Landis believed. And so, in the name of integrity, he banned them all, including Jackson, one of the greatest hitters of his day.

Selig talked about the integrity of the sport, too, but he took a far different approach to the steroid crisis. Hemmed in by the players union, granted far less autonomy by the owners, and facing political and business pressures that Landis never dreamed of, Selig refused to confront the steroid problem head-on. Instead, he tried to finesse it, to deal with it through damage control while hoping it would go away.

If that weren't the case, if Selig really had been interested in coming to grips with the problem, why didn't the commissioner ask the government to present him with the thousands of pages of evidence that linked Bonds and other superstars to drug use? Why, after the

Chronicle published the story, didn't he ask to listen to the recording of Greg Anderson admitting he helped Bonds cheat? Why, after Anderson was indicted as a steroid dealer, didn't Selig order Bonds to stay away from him? Why didn't the commissioner order the San Francisco Giants to enforce baseball's rules that would keep the rest of Bonds's entourage out of their clubhouse?

And why, if steroids were of real concern, would Selig and baseball even contemplate organizing a "celebration" for the day in 2006 when Bonds broke Ruth's home run mark? It was as if Landis had announced a new anti-gambling policy after the Black Sox scandal, and then agreed to personally award Joe Jackson his next batting trophy.

Perhaps baseball believed the steroid problem could be finessed because of the public's complicated reaction to the scandal. In some ways, the nation regarded BALCO as more of a cultural phenomenon than a crisis, fodder for everything from late-night talk shows to Internet entrepreneurs. David Letterman did a Top 10 list of "Signs Your Kid Is on Steroids." No. 3 was, "Instead of girls, he's constantly on the phone with BALCO founder Victor Conte." No. 1 was, "Last year she was the Prom Queen. This year—Prom King." Jay Leno, during a monologue, told his audience, "It turns out Pete Rose has been betting on whether or not Barry Bonds used steroids." At the Academy Awards, comedian Chris Rock told Hollywood's nipped-and-tucked glitterati, "We've given out ten awards so far, and not one of the winners has tested positive for steroids."

Even Conte seemed to enjoy the jokes, and revel in the attention he received from the army of pitchmen who popped up on the Internet hawking BALCO products: T-shirts, hats, baby bibs, bobblehead dolls, boxer shorts. In September 2004, Conte sent the *Chronicle* a series of lighthearted e-mails with links to several Web sites offering BALCO-related goods. Conte said he intended to hold off suing anybody for copyright infringement "until they make some real money." He signed one e-mail: "Victor Conte, the nutritionist for the BALCO Basher, Barry Bonds."

BALCO became such a slice of Americana that Conte ultimately had to take down the sign outside his Burlingame office; too many tourists kept stopping by to get their picture taken.

Baseball fans seemed conflicted about BALCO. In polls, they consistently said they considered baseball's steroid problem serious and by wide margins said they wanted cheaters punished. When Giambi slumped at the beginning of the 2005 season, the Yankees fans treated him roughly, booing and heckling him for his admitted drug use. After Palmeiro tested dirty, the fans booed him so lustily that he began wearing earplugs. And on the road in his brief return at the end of the season, Bonds received similarly rough treatment.

But fans also showed up in record numbers in 2005, despite the scandal. And when Giambi turned his season around, batting .271 with 32 home runs, the same fans who had pilloried him in the spring voted him "Comeback Player of the Year," although he might only have been coming back from self-inflicted problems related to his use of illegal drugs.

Even the great Hank Aaron seemed conflicted. At first, he had said he was withholding judgment until there was proof Bonds had used steroids. Then, after the publication of Bonds's grand jury testimony in December 2004, Aaron said, "Let me say this. Any way you look at it, it's wrong." And nine months later, when he appeared alongside Selig at Senator McCain's hearing, Aaron testified that it was imperative that "we make sure that we clean up baseball."

But a month after that, Aaron seemed to be backtracking. At the World Series, reporters asked him if he thought Bonds would break his record. "I think he will; I hope he does," Aaron replied. "I've had [the record] long enough."

But what about steroids? Aaron was asked. "Barry has been a tremendously gifted player," he said. "We can't sit here and accuse him of anything. He's been found guilty of nothing. We talk about it and talk about it."

Those who were cynical about the game believed the fans would forgive and forget the sport's drug problem. Perhaps BALCO—and baseball's reaction to it—was merely an extension of a society driven to enhance its performance and appearance.

During commercials while watching a ballgame on TV, fans were regularly bombarded with images of products that promised more hair, better sex, magical pain relief, and on and on. Somewhere, there was always a pill that could make every problem go away. Besides, who really cared if baseball was phony or not? Weren't sports just a great escape, a form of entertainment like movies or pop music concerts? In the long run, the only thing that mattered was that the fans weren't disappointed by the spectacle. Wasn't it likely that when fans shelled out the big bucks to go to a Giants game—and in 2005, a family of four had to fork over $191.37 for tickets, parking, hot dogs, scorecards, and two ball caps—all they really wanted was to see Bonds hit a ball into the San Francisco Bay? Some argued that if a ballplayer found it necessary to turn himself into a pharmaceutical guinea pig to attain greatness, so be it, as long he was entertaining. The fans would forgive and forget, and move on.

It was a cynical argument, and no one expressed it more bluntly than Bonds himself. During spring training in 2005, he was with two reporters in the clubhouse in Scottsdale when he suddenly began "running his mouth," as one old friend had characterized his occasional bouts of chattiness. In the monologue that followed, Bonds came as close as he ever came to publicly admitting his drug use.

"All this stuff about supplements, protein shakes, whatever," Bonds said. "Man, it's not like this is the Olympics. We don't train four years for, like, a ten-second [event]. We go 162 games. You've got to come back day after day after day. We're entertainers.

"If I can't go out there [to play], and somebody pays $60 for a ticket, and I'm not in the lineup, who's getting cheated? Not me.

"There are far worse things like cocaine, heroin, and those types of things.

"So we all make mistakes. We all do things. We need to turn the page. We need to forget about the past and let us play the game. We're entertainers. Let us entertain."

What about cheating? Bonds was asked.

"You want to define cheating in America?" he replied. "When they make a shirt in Korea for a dollar fifty and sell it here for 500 bucks? And you ask me what cheating means? I'll tell you how I cheat. I cheat because I'm my daddy's son. He taught me the game. He taught me things nobody else knows. So that's how I cheat. I'm my daddy's son."

As the BALCO probe moved into its fourth year, 41-year-old

Barry Bonds prepared for his 21st season in the Big Leagues. Opening day of the Giants' 2006 season was set for April 3—about the time Victor Conte was scheduled to complete his prison term—and, knee willing, Bonds would come to the plate needing only seven home runs to pass Babe Ruth.

Then, it would be on to Aaron.

In San Francisco, they were preparing to celebrate the Home Run King.

Afterword

B y the time the 2006 season began, Barry Bonds was a pariah in every major league city but his own. The Giants opened on April 3 in San Diego. The Padres fans, usually so laid-back, were in no mood to celebrate Bonds as a future Hall of Famer about to pass the immortal Babe Ruth on the list of all-time home run hitters. Rude signs were everywhere in Petco Park: BARR-ROID; BARRY IS A CHEATER; ASTERISK; CHEATERS NEVER PROSPER; BONDS, 1ST INTO THE HALL OF SHAME.

The fans began booing Bonds even before the first pitch; so loud was the mockery that at one point the public address announcer could not be heard. "BALCO," they chanted, and "steroids" and "cheater." The defining moment came at the end of the eighth inning. As Bonds trotted toward the visitors' dugout, a fan tossed a needle-less toy syringe onto the field in the superstar's direction. Bonds, non-plussed, scooped up the syringe with his glove and flipped it into a camera well near the dugout "so no one would get hurt," as he said afterward. Video of the incident was replayed endlessly on ESPN and local and network newscasts. It was noted in every major newspaper the next morning.

And so Bonds's season began with a series of road trips unlike anything baseball had ever seen. When the Giants came to town, Bonds was treated as though he were a pro wrestling villain, with the fans booing and taunting him, mimicking the act of injecting themselves with steroids, and competing with one another to see who could devise the rudest sign or the noisiest, most abusive chant. At Dodger Stadium, they hung a sign reading, GOT JUICE? and chanted, "Bonds sucks!" and "Just say NO!" In Denver, a fan paraded through the stands wearing a two-foot tall model of a syringe on his head. In Phoenix, a Diamondbacks fan was arrested for throwing a tube of liniment into left field. "To Barry Bonds," the homemade label read. "The CREAM. From Victor Conte." And in Oakland some fans came up with a new chant with which to torment the Giants slugger. "Game of Shadows!" they yelled.

On March 7, just as spring training was kicking into high gear, *Sports Illustrated* had run a 10,000-word excerpt from *Game of Shadows*, with a picture of the Giants star, hatless and pensive, on the cover. *SI* had considered using the headline GUILTY, but instead settled on THE TRUTH. The excerpt provoked an intense reaction, with hundreds of broadcast outlets and newspapers chasing the story of Bonds's long-term use of banned drugs. The furor was just starting to die down when, two weeks later, the book itself was published, setting off another round of intense news coverage and commentary.

In a mournful editorial, *The New York Times* called the story of Bonds and steroids as reflected in *Game of Shadows* "A Baseball Tragedy."

For those who cared about the game it was a difficult time, as Dodgers radio announcer Vin Scully, the dean of baseball broadcasters, told the *Los Angeles Times*. Scully had been at the microphone in 1974 when Atlanta's Hank Aaron hit his 715th home run, against the Dodgers, to break Babe Ruth's record. Scully cherished that memory, but he wanted no part of Bonds making history.

"With Aaron, it was a privilege to be there when he did it," Scully said. "With Bonds, no matter what happens now, it will be an awkward moment. That's the best word I can think of now. If I had my druthers, I would rather have that awkward moment happen to somebody else."

Of course the book also made Bonds and baseball subject to ridicule. The slugger and his sport were mocked and parodied on David Letterman and *Saturday Night Live*, in *The Onion*, in *Mad* magazine, in countless editorial-page cartoons, and even on the cover of *The New Yorker*.

Corporate sponsors shared the fans' disaffection with Bonds. Both Home Depot and Bank of America declined to participate in a proposed advertising campaign that the Giants had hoped to build around Bonds's assault on Ruth's mark. "A company like ours is always going to choose the untainted opportunity," a Bank of America spokesman said. Steering clear of Bonds made good business sense, according to a consumer poll taken by a Dallas marketing agency. Davie-Brown Entertainment found that of 1,500 celebrities who might be hired to endorse products, consumers rated Bonds No. 1,486 in likability and No. 1,488 in trustworthiness.

Nothing about the way the 2006 baseball season got under way was amusing to Commissioner Bud Selig. Selig was said to be so angry at Bonds that he wanted to suspend the Giants star solely on the basis of the revelations in *Game of Shadows*. The commissioner's lieutenants convinced him such a move faced legal challenges. Selig's concern over Bonds's use of performance-enhancing drugs was eclipsed by a sense of personal betrayal: twice the commissioner had confronted the ballplayer in the midst of the BALCO scandal, offering him the chance to come clean. Instead, Bonds had told Selig he had nothing to worry about.

Now Selig faced the prospect of another season of scandal, with Bonds making his run past Ruth and then on to Aaron, who was the commissioner's close personal friend. That would not do. One week after the book hit bookstores, Selig announced he had appointed former Senator George Mitchell to oversee a probe into steroids in baseball.

On the field, Bonds reacted stoically to the harsh treatment from opposing fans. When he tried to counter the barrage of negative publicity set off by the book, his moves backfired. On March 24, Bonds sued both Gotham Books, the book's publisher, and the *San Francisco Chronicle,* where the story was first reported. Bonds didn't sue for libel, and he didn't contend that the reports of his drug use were false. Instead, he claimed that the publication of *Game of Shadows* had been an illegal "unfair business practice" because the authors had used secret grand jury material in writing their book.

Legal experts scoffed at the lawsuit. On his MSNBC show, Keith Olbermann wondered whether Bonds's filing didn't make him look "more guilty." A San Francisco judge refused to issue the restraining order Bonds had sought to confiscate profits from the book, and he warned Bonds that his lawsuit had little chance of success. Facing a countersuit from the *Chronicle*, Bonds dropped the complaint.

In another attempt to revamp his image, Bonds teamed up with ESPN for the quasi-reality show "Bonds on Bonds." It was nearly as short-lived as the lawsuit. The program tried to portray Bonds in sympathetic terms, showing him hanging out with his daughter, visiting his father's grave, and weeping as he discussed unspecified pressures in his life. Steroids were not directly addressed.

The series was another subject of mockery: The *San Jose Mercury News* began publishing a weekly column, "Bonds on Bonds: We Watch . . . So You Don't Have To," that poked fun at the previous night's episode. The reviews were awful, the ratings worse, and ultimately the show faded away with no notice.

The Giants did their best to ignore *Game of Shadows*. In the front office, denial reigned. Asked about the furor over Bonds and drugs, owner Peter Magowan said, "None of it detracts from his performance." Giants fans continued to cheer for Bonds, but their response was muted and attendance fell off. Bonds was closing on the mark of the most famous baseball player ever, and the Giants couldn't even fill their ballpark. Beyond the all-consuming steroids story, Bonds appeared to be fading rapidly as a ballplayer. His arthritic, surgically-repaired knee continued to give him trouble. He ran poorly, had little range in the field, and only occasionally showed flashes of his old offensive power. His season was starting to have the look and feel of Mark McGwire's pathetic final year in the game.

On May 7 in Philadelphia, before another hostile crowd, Bonds hit a trademark home run to give him 713 for his career, a 450-foot shot that left him one shy of The Babe. As the Giants returned home, hundreds of reporters descended on San Francisco to mark the moment Bonds passed Ruth. It was a long wait, as Bonds didn't homer for 13 days, tying Ruth's mark across the bay in Oakland on May 20. That home run was greeted with more disrespect. The fan who caught the ball, Tyler Snyder, 19, was asked whether he would consider giving it to Bonds. "Hell no, I hate the guy," Snyder replied. The next day, *The Oakland Tribune* illustrated its package of stories on Bonds's home run with a cartoon asterisk that took up much of the front page.

After the series against the A's, the Giants went back to San Francisco for six more games. By the final day of the homestand, Bonds still hadn't passed Ruth. With the long delay, the media contingent had dwindled to the point that manager Felipe Alou joked, "I'm gonna be here all by myself" by the time Bonds hit the home run they were waiting for.

Finally, on May 28, just before he and the Giants were set to go back on the road, Bonds hit number 715. In the fourth inning, after walking Giant Steve Finley, Colorado's Byung-Hyun Kim threw a full-count fastball to Bonds, who crushed it. The 445-foot shot sailed into the center field bleachers, ending what *The Washington Post* described as a "tedious and, in many ways, uncomfortable spectacle."

Everything seemed wrong about the moment. As the play had unfolded, Giants announcer Dave Flemming began what he thought would be a historic call in his career. "Three-and-two. Finley runs," Flemming said into his microphone. "The payoff pitch. A swing and a drive to deep cen—" At that instant, Flemming's mike went dead.

When Bonds crossed home plate, he was greeted only by his 16-year-old son, Nikolai. Virtually all of the Giants remained in the dugout.

In the bleachers the scrum of fans never got the chance to wrestle for possession of a ball that under different circumstances might have fetched millions. Instead, the ball bounced out of the bleachers and landed in the hands of a man waiting in line at a concession stand to buy beer and peanuts. He had left his seat completely unaware Bonds was scheduled to come to bat that inning.

If *Game of Shadows* persuaded many in baseball that Bonds was a drug cheat, the book also seemed to energize the federal investigation of the Giants star. A year had passed since Kimberly Bell gave the BALCO grand jury the outlines of a perjury and tax-evasion case against the Home Run King: his admitted use of steroids back in 1999 and the $80,000 cash from memorabilia sales that he gave her to buy the house in Scottsdale. But in the months that followed her testimony, the probe seemed to languish. Then, after the *SI* excerpt, a flurry of grand jury subpoenas went out.

The point man, as usual, was IRS Agent Jeff Novitzky. He began a search for more proof that Bonds had lied under oath in 2003 when he testified that he had never used steroids. The agent sought to reinterview the other baseball players who had been witnesses at the BALCO grand jury, including Yankees Jason Giambi and Gary Sheffield and retired Giants catcher Benito Santiago, who had been assured he would pass baseball's drug test in 2003 because he was using the same stuff as Bonds. This time, the focus was not on the players' own drug use, but on what they knew about Bonds and steroids. Novitzky also reached out to BALCO defendants, Giants personnel, and present and former Bonds confidantes.

In his travels, the agent carried a copy of *Game of Shadows*. "It's the Bible of the steroid shit for him," said a witness he approached. Not everyone was glad to see him. Sheffield referred Novitzky to his lawyers. A nervous Giambi met with him in New York but professed to know little more than what he had already said under oath.

If the government pressed them, of course, witnesses had little choice but to cooperate. One subpoena target was Jim Valente, Victor Conte's right-hand man, who had escaped a prison sentence in the BALCO plea bargains. Novitzky had debriefed Valente during the raid on BALCO back in 2003; BALCO's vice president had described himself as Greg Anderson's "primary contact point" for The Cream and The Clear. Valente knew that Anderson was giving BALCO's undetectable steroids to Bonds so he could beat baseball's steroids tests. Valente also had admitted his role in putting Anderson's name on the sample of Bonds's blood that had been sent to Lab*One* for steroid pretesting. In addition, Valente could interpret the Bonds doping calendars for the grand jury.

Dr. Arthur Ting, Bonds's orthopedist, also got a subpoena. In 1999, Ting had operated to repair the elbow Bonds shredded while using Winstrol. Ting knew Anderson—they talked on the phone about Bonds—and he knew BALCO. In 2003, Ting had gone to the lab with Bonds to draw the slugger's blood for testing. Ting also had seen the tremendous physical changes the steroids had wrought in his star patient: the impressive musculature, the weight gain, and the side effects.

The government subpoenaed the Giants to get the club's medical records on Bonds. Three team employees were ordered to testify: athletic trainer Stan Conte, equipment manager Mike Murphy, and "Conehead" Harvey Shields, Bonds's stretching coach. Like Ting, Conte could describe the changes in Bonds's body, and the Giants' trainer had expressed his own concerns about steroids on the ballclub. In 2000, after the Giants heard rumors that Greg Anderson was a steroid dealer, Conte had wanted him banned from the clubhouse; fearing Bonds's wrath, the team's executives backed down. For his part, Murphy could document Bonds's physical changes via the changes in his uniform size. Since joining the Giants, Bonds had gone from a size 42 to a size 52 jersey; from size 10½ to size 13 cleats; and from a size 7⅛ to size 7¼ cap, even though he had taken to shaving his head. The changes in his foot and head size were of special interest: medical experts said overuse of human growth hormone could cause an adult's extremities to begin growing, aping the symptoms of the glandular disorder acromegaly. Shields, meanwhile, had spent years hanging around the Giants clubhouse with Anderson and Bonds; Novitzky believed Shields knew about Bonds's use of drugs.

Novitzky also scored important new evidence by connecting with new witnesses who had seen Bonds using banned drugs. More than a year after the *Chronicle* had revealed the existence of the secret recording of Greg Anderson, the government obtained its own copy. The investigators could hear Anderson describing the undetectable steroids that he had been giving to Bonds in 2003.

Early in the baseball season, the prosecutors decided to put the squeeze on Anderson. Throughout the BALCO case, he had balked at informing on Bonds, rejecting a proposed plea bargain that would have allowed him to avoid prison by becoming a government witness. To persuade Anderson to plead guilty, the government dropped the demand for his cooperation. But after Anderson had pleaded guilty, he could no longer use his Fifth Amendment right against self-incrimination to deflect the government's questions about Bonds. So Anderson got a subpoena, too. In front of the grand jury, prosecutors would ask him whether he had given banned drugs to Bonds—and play the recording if he hedged. He could either testify truthfully or face a perjury indictment. Anderson protested that he had been double-crossed: He would never have pleaded guilty if he had known the government planned to drag him before the grand jury afterward. News of the subpoena, made public by Anderson's lawyers, attracted nationwide attention. The federal investigators in San Francisco seemed dead serious about indicting Bonds.

Novitzky's next moves suggested he had taken on the additional task of cleaning up performance-enhancing drugs in all of baseball. On April 19, at about the time the subpoena for Anderson was being drafted, Novitzky and a team of drug agents watched a postman deliver a package in suburban Scottsdale, not far from where Kim Bell once lived. The agents knew the package contained two kits of human growth hormone, $3,200 worth. It was addressed to a man who would soon come to symbolize just how pervasive banned drugs had become in major league baseball: Jason Grimsley, a right-handed relief pitcher for the Arizona Diamondbacks.

Soon after Grimsley signed for the package, Novitzky was at the front door. He had a search warrant and a team of agents ready to take the house apart. Or would Grimsley like to come with him and talk? Grimsley had houseguests. He would have to be at the ballpark soon, where the Diamondbacks were playing the Giants. He went with Novitzky, and for two hours they talked about baseball and drugs.

The Diamondbacks were Grimsley's seventh team in a 15-year career in the big leagues. Drugs helped him hang on. He had used steroids, growth hormone, and amphetamines; clenbuterol, an asthma drug that promotes muscle growth much in the way steroids do; and an Andro-like prohormone called 1-AD, which he bought on the Internet. In 2000, when he hurt his shoulder pitching for the Yankees, he used Deca-Durabolin to recover from surgery. In 2003, when baseball conducted what was supposed to be anonymous and confidential steroids testing, Grimsley nevertheless was informed that he had tested positive for steroids. After that, he switched to growth hormone, knowing baseball didn't test for the drug. When he had elbow surgery after the 2004 season, growth hormone helped him recover.

Many players used growth hormone, Grimsley told Novitzky; they connected with drug dealers through personal trainers. He knew four players who got growth hormone from a physician at a "wellness center" in Florida. Grimsley wanted no part of going undercover for Novitzky. Soon after their meeting ended, the pitcher hired a lawyer and broke off contact. And so, on June 6, Novitzky returned to Scottsdale with 12 agents and a search warrant and took Grimsley's house apart. No more drugs were found and Grimsley was never accused of a crime, but within 48 hours he had been released by the Diamondbacks. The Grimsley affair, made public when Novitzky's affidavit was filed in the courthouse in Phoenix, rattled a baseball establishment already uneasy over the investigation of Bonds, and fueled more cynicism about baseball's power hitters. One target was Philadelphia slugger Ryan Howard, who was suspect merely because he was having a great year. "Is Ryan Howard juiced?" columnist Dan Wetzel wrote on the Yahoo! Sports Web site in September. "There is no reason, no whisper, no allegation that suggests Howard is cheating," he wrote. "In fact, there is plenty of talk that he is clean. But how can you blindly trust anyone anymore?"

By the time of the Grimsley raid, baseball's own steroids probe, announced with so much fanfare by Selig in response to *Game of Shadows*, had already stalled. Senator Mitchell's investigators couldn't get anybody to talk to them. Novitzky and the prosecutors were unavailable, of course, and the government also made Kim Bell and other witnesses in the Bonds perjury case off limits. The players wouldn't talk, on advice of the union. In the end, Mitchell's investigators were left interviewing front-office personnel and waiting, along with all of baseball, for the shattering event that was expected to occur shortly after the All-Star break—the indictment of Barry Bonds.

By June, the prosecutors in San Francisco believed they had built an airtight perjury case: the doping calendars, drug price lists, and other documents seized in the raid of Anderson's home; the secret recording; and the testimony of Kim Bell and the new witnesses. Taken together, the evidence proved that Bonds had been using banned drugs for years, had known exactly what he was doing, and had lied about it under oath. Once Anderson told the grand jury how he had provided Bonds with drugs, the case would be so solid that no jury could find Bonds innocent. But long before the case got to trial, the government could offer Bonds a plea bargain not unlike the one prosecutors had made with NBA star Chris Webber in his perjury case in Michigan. Under the plan, Bonds could admit his drug use, pay his taxes, plead guilty to some lesser charge, and escape a prison sentence. Case closed.

But Anderson refused to play along. Through evidentiary hearings and appeals, he stalled his grand jury appearance for almost two months. On June 29, when he finally took the witness stand, Anderson refused to say anything about Bonds. A week later, tough-talking U.S. District Judge William Alsup was fed up. "Mr. Anderson, this is going to be a learning experience, and probably one you won't forget for a long time," the judge said. He sentenced Bonds's trainer to prison for contempt of court.

Michael Rains, Bonds's lawyer, made it clear that his star client didn't intend to play along with the government, either. Like baseball's establishment, Rains presumed Bonds would be indicted in July, when the term of the grand jury expired. If an indictment came, Bonds was going to fight, Rains declared. As the day of the expected indictment approached, Rains contended in a round of media interviews that Bonds was innocent of perjury and tax evasion. No jury would ever convict Bonds, he confidently declared.

Rains also attacked two former Bonds confidantes who he presumed would be important government witnesses: Kim Bell and Steve Hoskins, who was Bonds's former business manager. Bonds had severed ties with Hoskins in 2003 after an angry dispute over the proceeds of sports memorabilia sales. Bonds had accused Hoskins of selling fake jerseys with forged Bonds autographs and keeping the money. But Hoskins had records of Bonds's memorabilia sales and photos of Bonds signing some of the very items that he claimed were forged, and the FBI had exonerated Hoskins after an investigation. The men, friends since boyhood, had become bitter enemies. Bell was a gold-digger, Rains told a local TV station, while Hoskins was a "vengeful ex-employee" with a motive to lie. The government's case amounted to nothing more than "The Kim and Steve show," Rains said on talk radio. He promised to demolish them at trial.

It made for an effective sound bite, but as Rains himself may have recognized, trashing Bonds's former girlfriend and his former business manager didn't actually rebut the most compelling evidence of Bonds's guilt. After all, Bell and the business manager had nothing to do with creating the doping calendars, drug pretest reports, and other documents about Bonds's steroid use—what the government called the "mountain of evidence" seized in the raids at BALCO and at Anderson's home. More to the point, if Bonds actually was innocent of using steroids, as Rains claimed, why in the world didn't Anderson tell that to the grand jury? Instead, the trainer sat silent in prison, like a mobbed-up witness in a racketeering trial.

Nevertheless, Rains's bluster seemed to have a profound effect on Kevin Ryan, the cautious chief federal prosecutor in San Francisco. The grand jury's term was set to expire on July 20, and virtually everybody involved in the case was eager for Bonds to be indicted. In 16 months, the investigators had built a solid case, even without Anderson; the trial prosecutors were ready to roll. But then the prosecution team grew agitated. Suddenly, it became clear that Ryan might refuse to pull the trigger and approve the indictment. As the deadline approached, top officials at the IRS and the FBI began lobbying the Justice Department in Washington, hoping the DOJ would push Ryan to indict.

The urgings didn't work. Two-and-a-half years after Bonds had testified before the first BALCO grand jury, Ryan announced that he wanted more time. He transferred the perjury probe to yet another grand jury, postponing an indictment "in light of some recent developments," he told reporters. At about the time Ryan's office issued a press release regarding the perjury case, two government officials arrived at the federal detention center in Dublin, in the East Bay suburbs of San Francisco. They were there to intercept trainer Greg Anderson, who was scheduled for release because the old grand jury was expiring. The two officials handed Bonds's trainer a new subpoena from the new grand jury. "You guys are pathetic," Anderson said.

Anderson managed to stall for another month, but he had no chance. He was headed back to prison. "Sometimes sitting in the cooler for a long time will have a therapeutic effect," Judge Alsup remarked on August 28, after again finding Anderson in contempt.

"Maybe in 16 months he will change his mind." For the moment at least, baseball had avoided the humiliating spectacle of the reigning Home Run King facing indictment.

As the summer wore on, other American sports heroes were buffeted by steroids scandals. Cyclist Floyd Landis, who competed despite a crippling hip injury, won the grueling Tour de France race after one of the most dramatic come-from-behind rides in the sport's history. Less than a week later, it was revealed that Landis tested positive for high levels of testosterone. Landis protested his innocence, but he faced a suspension that might end his career.

Two days after Landis was exposed, so, too, was American sprinter Justin Gatlin, who had won gold in the 100 meters at Athens and then gone on to tie the world record. Gatlin also tested positive for elevated levels of testosterone. He faced an eight-year ban. The case was especially dismaying because Gatlin had presented himself as the new face of American track, a drug-free competitor who would make fans forget BALCO.

Actually, Gatlin had a BALCO connection: his coach was Trevor Graham, who had ignited the scandal by sending a syringe laced with The Clear to the U.S. Anti-Doping Agency in the summer of 2003. BALCO investigators had interviewed Graham in June 2004, and, though several of his athletes had tested positive for banned drugs, Graham steadfastly denied knowing anything about anybody using steroids. He simply knew nothing. Two years later, with Gatlin's positive test, another of Graham's clients had been exposed.

Graham went to Gatlin's defense; although behind the scenes, Gatlin and his lawyers cringed as the coach tried to explain away the positive test. His account was right out of a spy novel: A masseur with a grudge had pulled a tube with a crooked S on it from his pocket, forced himself on Gatlin, and rubbed a mysterious cream on the sprinter's inner thigh. "I know it was sabotage," Graham told ESPN.com.

(In the end, Graham himself faced a harder fall than Gatlin. In November 2006, Graham was indicted on three counts of lying to federal investigators, crimes punishable by a maximum 15-year prison sentence. The indictment focused on an interview Graham had given to Novitzky and another agent in North Carolina in the summer of

2004. Graham had denied supplying his athletes with banned drugs, and the agents believed he was lying. His lawyers complained it was unfair of the government to target Graham, whom they styled as the key whistle-blower in the BALCO case, while giving a free pass to the elite athletes who had used drugs.)

Three weeks after Gatlin was nabbed, the great Marion Jones—who once had been coached by Graham—was notified that a sample of her urine taken about two months earlier at the U.S. Track and Field Championships had tested positive for EPO. Jones professed to be "shocked," then awaited testing of her backup, or "B," sample. Finally, it seemed that Jones, long dogged by doping allegations that never quite stuck, had been exposed. But weeks later, Jones's "B" sample came back negative, and she was free to keep running. Jones went on *Good Morning America* and proclaimed that she had never used banned drugs. For the anti-doping movement, the turnabout was a major setback.

As all this was playing out, back in San Francisco, Barry Bonds was suddenly rediscovering his youth. In a 15-game stretch starting at the end of August, he morphed from a lifeless .240 hitter to the Bonds of old. He hit .404 with seven home runs in the hot spell, and he had six homers in nine games. Finally, on September 23 in Milwaukee—where Aaron had started and ended his career and where Commissioner Selig lived—Bonds hit career home run No. 734 to break Aaron's National League record. He was booed loudly as he rounded the bases, and the moment was not acknowledged by MLB. Still, the homer was Bonds's 26th of the season; once he seemed certain to end 2006 well short of Aaron's mark, but now he was in position to set a new home run record in 2007. To some around the Giants, it was no surprise that Bonds—his contract expiring at the end of the year—would get hotter and healthier down the stretch.

Bonds had vacillated about his intentions for 2007: He probably would play another year, he probably wouldn't be back, it would be up to his family, it would be up to the Giants. Peter Magowan had said a decision on a new contract for Bonds wouldn't come until after the season. Still, the left fielder had looked so awful it seemed the Giants owner might finally find the strength to cut ties with Bonds.

But then Bonds got hot, and the dynamic changed. The Giants suddenly seemed poised to offer yet another multimillion-dollar contract to their 42-year-old marquee player—despite a perjury probe, tax issues, the Mitchell investigation, old age, and bad knees.

Even as Kevin Ryan's office wavered on Bonds in the summer of 2006, the federal government moved forward with a related investigation focused on the authors of this book. Prosecutors threatened to have us imprisoned unless we revealed the confidential sources who had provided us access to the grand jury testimony of Bonds, Jason Giambi, and other prominent athletes. The testimony was reported in the *San Francisco Chronicle* and in this book.

Since the FBI raided Victor Conte's home in January 2005, we had known the government was trying to identify our sources. Still, we had been optimistic that the Justice Department would abandon its leak investigation. BALCO was about sports and drugs. The government had demonstrated that it thought the case was of little consequence—prosecutors had implicitly condoned the athletes' steroid use and offered lenient plea deals to the drug dealers. The grand jury leak had posed no harm to national security, and there was no threat to anyone's physical safety. The case did not appear to meet the Justice Department's own guidelines for when it was permissible to force reporters to testify about their sources—guidelines designed to address the First Amendment concerns such coercive efforts inevitably raised.

An encounter with President Bush also encouraged us to believe that the government wouldn't press on with the leak probe. We had met the president on April 30, 2005, at a private reception before the White House Correspondents' Dinner at the Hilton Hotel in Washington, D.C. Bush seemed familiar with our work. "You've done a service," the president told us. Then, for a few minutes, we discussed baseball and steroids and the congressional steroid hearings, which had recently concluded. Bush was dismayed by Mark McGwire's embarrassing refusal to answer questions about whether he had used banned drugs, describing Big Mac's testimony as, "Sad, sad, very sad." Rafael Palmeiro's defiant, unequivocal denials had impressed the president: Palmeiro had played on the Texas Rangers when Bush had owned the team, and the president obviously hoped Palmeiro was telling the truth. Bush mentioned the BALCO stories again as the conversation came to an end. "You've done a service," he repeated.

Like the Bonds perjury probe, the investigation into the grand jury leak seemed to languish through the end of 2005. But in the spring of the 2006, after our book was published, we learned that prosecutors still were trying to track down our sources. On May 5, we received subpoenas ordering us to testify before a grand jury. The prosecutors wanted us to identify the sources of the leak, with the threat of prison if we refused to comply. U.S. Attorney General Alberto Gonzales had personally approved the subpoenas. He told his hometown paper, the *Houston Chronicle*, that the grand jury leak was "a terrible crime."

To advocates of a free press, the case was alarming. Gonzales already had approved subpoenas in several other press cases. If the Justice Department could target reporters whose work had been praised by the president himself, the press advocates reasoned, every reporter in the country with a confidential source, and every media outlet that published a story that was of interest to federal law enforcement, was vulnerable.

The leak investigation infuriated Mark Corallo, the former public affairs director for John Ashcroft, Gonzales's predecessor as attorney general. Ashcroft never would have approved going after us, Corallo said: He was shocked Gonzales had disregarded the DOJ's guidelines. "This is the most reckless abuse of power I have seen in years," Corallo told *The New York Times*. Of Gonzales's Justice Department, he said, "They really should be ashamed of themselves." Corallo filed an affidavit in support of our legal efforts to get the subpoenas set aside. Others who joined him included former Major League Baseball Commissioner Fay Vincent, famed Watergate reporter Carl Bernstein, and Denise Garibaldi, whose son committed suicide after taking steroids. But in August, U.S. District Judge Jeffrey White ruled for the Department of Justice and ordered us to testify. And one month later, White sentenced us to up to 18 months in prison for refusing to testify. "The only appropriate sanction is to incarcerate these two individuals to

the full extent permitted," said the judge, who allowed us to stay free on appeal.

We remained determined not to betray the sources who had helped tell the BALCO story. And so, unless an appeals court intervened, it was likely we would be sent to prison. We stood to serve more time behind bars than any of the steroid dealers convicted in the BALCO conspiracy and any of the athletes we reported on, including Barry Bonds.

Appendix One

Bonds and Steroids

When they raided BALCO in September 2003, federal investigators began to accumulate evidence that Barry Bonds was a steroid user. By the summer of 2005, investigators had convincing proof that Bonds had been using performance-enhancing drugs for years and that drugs had been provided to him by his trainer, Greg Anderson, who obtained the drugs from BALCO and other sources. The evidence also showed that Bonds had not been truthful when he told the BALCO grand jury under oath that he hadn't knowingly used steroids.

Bonds continued to insist publicly that he had never used banned drugs, and the San Francisco Giants, who were paying him $17 million per year, made no move to investigate his conduct or restrict his contact with suspected steroid dealers, arguing that there was no proof of wrongdoing.

Nevertheless, proof of Bonds's drug use exists, most of it in the possession of federal agents, much of it in the public domain. The evidence includes the statements of confessed steroid dealers, the account of a Bonds confidante, and considerable documentary and circumstantial evidence as well. It also includes the account of a source familiar with Bonds who has specific knowledge of his use of banned drugs. That evidence forms the foundation of this narrative. Here is the evidence in review.

Statements to Federal Agents

1. When he was questioned during the BALCO raid, Jim Valente told IRS Special Agent Jeff Novitzky that Bonds had received the

undetectable steroids The Cream and The Clear from BALCO. Valente said Anderson had brought Bonds to BALCO before the
2003 season, seeking steroids that would not show up on drug
tests. Valente said he provided drugs to Anderson to give to
Bonds. Valente pleaded guilty to a steroid conspiracy charge.

2. In his own statement during the raid, Victor Conte gave an identical account of Anderson bringing Bonds to BALCO and Bonds's
subsequent use of The Cream and The Clear. Conte said Bonds
used the drugs on a regular basis. Conte later repudiated his statement about Bonds, claiming Novitzky's report contained words he
never said. But it is significant that in 2005, Conte backed out of
an evidentiary hearing where he could have confronted Novitzky
about the supposedly incorrect statements and sought to have
them thrown out of court as inadmissable evidence. Instead,
Conte pleaded guilty to a steroid conspiracy charge.

3. When Anderson was questioned by agents on the day of the raid,
he admitted giving banned drugs to "baseball clients." He said he
gave steroids and growth hormone to Benito Santiago, Bobby Estalella, and Armando Rios, and steroids to Marvin Benard. He said
he gave The Cream and The Clear to his "baseball clients" but denied giving drugs to Bonds. In a search of Anderson's residence,
agents found calendars referring to Bonds that plotted his use of
steroids. When they sought to question Anderson about the calendars, the trainer said he didn't think he should talk any more
because he didn't want to go to jail. He pleaded guilty to steroid
conspiracy, and acknowledged in court that he dealt drugs to pro
baseball players.

4. In the summer of 2004, the former Olympic shot-putter C. J. Hunter
told Agent Novitzky that Conte had confided to him that Bonds
was using The Clear. Hunter said their conversation had taken
place in 2003, dating it by recalling Conte also told him that a
"big article" about Bonds was soon to be published. This was an
apparent reference to the *Muscle & Fitness* story featuring Bonds,
Conte, and Anderson, which was published in June 2003. Hunter's
lawyer later said the federal agent's report was incorrect and that
Conte had had not implicated Bonds to Hunter.

U.S. Grand Jury Testimony

1. In 2005, Kimberly Bell, Bonds's former girlfriend, told the BALCO grand jury that in 2000, Bonds had confided to her that he was using steroids, saying they helped him recover from injuries but also blaming them for the elbow injury that sidelined him in 1999.

2. In 2003, sprinter Tim Montgomery told the grand jury that when he visited BALCO in 2000 or 2001 he saw vials of the steroid Winstrol in BALCO's weight room. Conte said he was giving Winstrol to Bonds, Montgomery testified.

3. In 2003, five baseball players told the grand jury they got steroids, growth hormone, and other drugs from Anderson, whom they had met because he was Bonds's trainer. The obvious import of their testimony was that they were receiving the same drugs that Anderson was giving to Bonds, but the players claimed no direct knowledge of Bonds's steroid use. For example, the Giambi brothers testified that they assumed Bonds was using the same drugs they got from Anderson but claimed they were never specifically told that. A sixth player, Gary Sheffield, testified that Anderson gave him The Cream and The Clear, that he saw Bonds taking it, and that he took it himself at Bonds's direction. But Sheffield claimed he didn't know the products were steroids. On that point, his account was identical to Bonds's testimony before the grand jury.

Documents

At Anderson's apartment, investigators found steroids, growth hormone, and $60,000 cash, along with a folder that contained doping calendars and other documents detailing Bonds's use of steroids. Prosecutors questioned Bonds about the documents at the grand jury. Some document entries reflect payments for drugs for Bonds: $1,500 for two boxes of growth hormone; $450 for a bottle of depotestosterone; $100 for 100 clomiphene pills; $200 for The Cream and The Clear. Other entries reflect Bonds's drug cycle: For February 2002, a calendar showed alternating days of The Cream, The Clear, and growth hormone followed by "Clow," or Clomid. (A similar calendar reflected Jason Giambi's admitted steroid use.)

A document labeled "BLB 2003" listed cities where the Giants played away games in 2003, with notations for the use of growth hormone, The Clear, The Cream, and insulin on specific days. Other documents associated with Bonds referred to the use of trenbolone and "beans," the Mexican steroid. At Anderson's apartment, and in a search of BALCO's trash, the agents also found evidence of Bonds's blood being sent to drug labs for steroid testing.

Recording of Greg Anderson

During the 2003 season, a person familiar with Anderson made a secret recording of a conversation with the trainer. In the recording, Anderson acknowledged that Bonds was using an undetectable performance-enhancing drug to beat baseball's drug tests.

Circumstantial Evidence: Added Muscle

To some experts, the changes in Bonds's body over the course of his career constitute persuasive evidence of steroid use. No one at his age could put on so much muscle without using steroids, these observers reason.

According to team media guides, Bonds has grown one inch in height and gained 43 pounds since his rookie year of 1987. In 2004, the Giants reported his weight as 228, but sources familiar with Bonds say he was heavier. Bonds himself has claimed all the weight gain is muscle, not fat. In 1997, when the Giants reported that he weighed 206, Bonds told *USA Today* that his body fat was an extraordinarily low 8 percent. In 2002, when Bonds's weight was reported to be 228, Greg Anderson told *The New York Times Magazine* that Bonds's body fat was even lower: 6.2 percent.

The belief that the changes in Bonds's body reflect steroid use is supported by the research of Harvard University psychiatrist Harrison Pope, an expert on the mental-health effects of steroid abuse. In 1995, in *The Clinical Journal of Sports Medicine*, Pope and three colleagues published a mathematical formula for use in determining whether a person is using steroids.

The "Fat-Free Mass Index," as the formula is called, predicts steroid use from a series of computations involving the subject's "lean muscle mass," which is determined from height, weight, and percentage of body fat. The higher the index number, the leaner and more muscular the individual is. The average 30-year-old American male scores 20, Pope says, while the former Mr. America Steve Reeves, the most famous muscle man of the pre-steroid era, scored 25 in his prime. A score of more than 25 indicates steroid use.

In 1997, when Bonds reportedly weighed 206 and had 8 percent body fat, he scored 24.8 on the index—near the upper limit of muscularity one can attain without steroids.

In 2002, when Bonds reportedly weighed 228 and had body fat of 6.2 percent, Bonds's score on Pope's index was 28—well over the level of a "presumptive diagnosis" of steroid use.

Appendix Two

Bonds's Numbers

The transformation that Barry Bonds achieved through the use of performance-enhancing drugs is reflected in his batting statistics. Bonds began using steroids before the start of the 1999 season, when he was 34 years old. His numbers, as compiled by the Baseball-Reference.com Web site, show that his performance improved dramatically at a time when otherwise he might have been approaching the end of his career.

Of the five best offensive seasons in Bonds's career, four came after he was 35 years old—and after 1999, the year he began using steroids. The historic 2001 season, when he was 36 years old (his age as of Opening Day), was the best of all: .328 batting average, 73 home runs, an on-base percentage of .515 OBA. But 2002, when he was 37 (.370, 46 HR), and 2004, when he was 39 (.362, 45 HR), were also excellent seasons for Bonds, and 2003, when he was 38, was not far off the mark.

In fact, of Bonds's five best seasons, only one came in what is usually considered a baseball player's prime. That was 1993, pre-steroids, when Bonds was 28 years old and playing his first season for the Giants.

Bonds's Best Seasons

Year	Age	AB	R	H	2B	3B	HR	RBI	BB	SO	BA	OBP	SLG	RC
2001	36	476	129	156	32	2	73	137	177	93	.328	.515	.863	228
2002	37	403	117	149	31	2	46	110	198	47	.370	.582	.799	206
2004	39	373	129	135	27	3	45	101	232	41	.362	.609	.812	204
1993	28	539	129	181	38	4	46	123	126	79	.336	.458	.677	189
2003	38	390	111	133	22	1	45	90	148	58	.341	.529	.749	173

Bonds's home run production also increased after he began using steroids. In his career through 2005, Bonds hit 45 or more home runs in six seasons. Five of those seasons were after 1999—after age 35, and after he had begun using performance-enhancing drugs.

Top HR Seasons

Year	Age	HR
2001	36	73
2000	35	49
2002	37	46
1993	28	46
2004	39	45
2003	38	45

Another measure of Bonds's power surge is home run frequency—the number of at-bats it took him, on average, to hit each home run. Over the first 13 years of his career—that is, before steroids—he hit a home run every 16.2 at-bats. His most productive year during that period was 1994, when he hit a home run every 10.6 at-bats. (Bonds played in 112 of the Giants' 115 games in 1994, the season that ended in the lockout. He hit 37 home runs in 391 at-bats.)

From 1999 through 2004—after steroids—the frequency with which Bonds struck homers nearly doubled, to one every 8.5 at-bats. His best year was 2001, when he hit a home run every 6.5 at-bats.

At-bats-per-HR Ratio

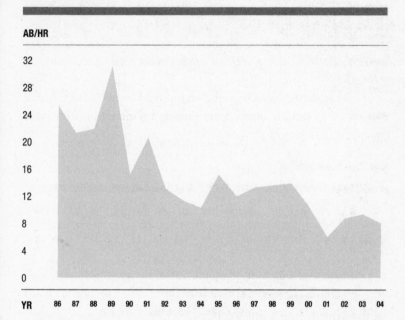

AB/HR

| 32 |
| 28 |
| 24 |
| 20 |
| 16 |
| 12 |
| 8 |
| 4 |
| 0 |

YR   86 87 88 89 90 91 92 93 94 95 96 97 98 99 00 01 02 03 04

Before steroids, Bonds was an outstanding player and a likely Hall of Famer, the numbers affirm. In 6,600 at bats over 13 seasons, he batted .290 and hit 411 homers with 1,216 RBI. He made the All-Star team eight times and was selected the National League's Most Valuable Player in 1990, 1992, and 1993. Had he retired after the 1998 season, he would rank 40th on the all-time home run list, above Duke Snider. His 1,357 walks would rank 28th.

Using a mathematical average to roll those 13 seasons into a single year, we see that Bonds, before steroids, hit for average and power and was an excellent base runner. The composite Bonds year during that period looks like this:

Before Steroids: A Composite

	G	AB	R	H	2B	3B	HR	RBI	SB	CS	BB	SO	BA	OBP
'86–'98	146	509	105	147	31	5	32	93	34	10	104	81	.290	.411

But after age 35—after steroids—Bonds improved his game in every category except stolen bases. From 1999 to 2004, he had far better power and drove in and scored more runs. His batting average increased by an astonishing 38 points, and his on-base percentage soared because of a big increase in his walk total, which already was high.

At what should have been the end of his baseball career, Bonds became a significantly better hitter than at any time in his life, as a composite of those years shows.

After Steroids: A Composite

	G	AB	R	H	2B	3B	HR	RBI	SB	CS	BB	SO	BA	OBP
'99–'04	136	413	118	136	27	2	49	105	10	2	158	63	.328	.517

The post-steroids Bonds also became one of the greatest hitters of all time. Lee Sinins, creator of the *Baseball Sabermetric Encyclopedia*, used statistician Bill James's "runs created" formula, a measure of total batting production, to determine the best offensive performances in baseball history. As Sinins ran the numbers, Bonds's 73-homer year in 2001 was the second best offensive season any player has ever had—second only to Babe Ruth's 1921 season, when the New York Yankees star hit .378 with 171 RBI.

Best Seasons: Ruth and Bonds

	Year	Age	AB	R	H	2B	3B	HR	RBI	BB	SO	BA	OBP	RC
RUTH	1921	26	540	177	204	44	16	59	171	145	81	.378	.512	243
BONDS	2001	36	476	129	156	32	2	73	137	177	93	.328	.515	228

Three of Bonds's post-steroids seasons were among the top 10 in baseball history, according to Sinins's list. Only Ruth had more, with five top-10 seasons.

Sinins's study also underscores the fact that in baseball terms, Bonds was an old man when he emerged as one of the greats of the game.

Top 10 Offensive Seasons

#	Name	Year	Age	Team	BA	HR	RBI	RC
1	RUTH	1921	26	NYY	.378	59	171	243
2	BONDS	2001	36	SFG	.328	73	137	228
3	RUTH	1923	28	NYY	.393	41	131	227
4	RUTH	1920	25	NYY	.376	54	137	216
5	GEHRIG	1927	24	NYY	.373	47	175	215
6	RUTH	1927	32	NYY	.356	60	164	211
6	FOXX	1932	24	PHA	.364	58	169	211
8	RUTH	1924	29	NYY	.378	46	121	209
9	BONDS	2002	37	SFG	.370	46	110	206
10	BONDS	2004	39	SFG	.362	45	101	204
10	GEHRIG	1936	33	NYY	.354	49	152	204
10	HORNSBY	1922	26	STL	.401	42	152	204

Bonds was 36 when he had his 73-home run season, the first of three seasons that rank in the top 10; he was 39 in 2004, which Sinins puts as 10th best of all time, tied with Lou Gehrig's 1936 season for the Yankees and Rogers Hornsby's efforts for the 1922 Cardinals.

No other player was older than 33 when he performed at this high level (Gehrig was 33 in 1936). Ruth was 26 in 1921, which Sinins rates as the best season of all time. The average age of the other players on the top 10 seasons list—along with Ruth, Gehrig, and Hornsby, there is Jimmie Foxx, the old-time Philadelphia Athletic—was 27.

Yet another measure of Bonds's late-in-life power surge: By the end of 2005, he had hit more home runs after age 35 than any of the game's great sluggers.

Home Runs After Age 35

Name	HR 35 & UP	%	TOTAL HR	Name	HR 35 & UP	%	TOTAL HR
BONDS	263	0.37	708	MAYS	118	0.18	660
AARON	245	0.32	755	ROBINSON	111	0.19	586
PALMEIRO	208	0.37	569	BANKS	108	0.21	512
RUTH	198	0.28	714	WILLIAMS	103	0.20	521
JACKSON	153	0.27	563	KILLEBREW	86	0.15	573
McCOVEY	137	0.26	521	SOSA	49	0.08	588
McGWIRE	126	0.22	583	OTT	48	0.09	511
MURRAY	125	0.25	504	MANTLE	40	0.07	536
SCHMIDT	123	0.22	548	MATTHEWS	19	0.04	512
				FOXX	7	0.01	534

Sean Forman, proprietor of Baseball-Reference.com, used a different statistic to track Bonds's power surge post 1999. In a study done in 2004 for the *San Francisco Chronicle*, he applied a measure of offensive performance called OPS, for On-Base Percentage + Slugging Percentage, to compare Bonds to other great hitters.

Forman's conclusion: Starting in 2000, after Bonds had recovered from the 1999 elbow injury, he put together the greatest five consecutive seasons of any hitter in baseball history. During that stretch, when he was age 35 to 39, Bonds batted .339, hit 258 homers, and drove in 544 runs, for an OPS rating of 1.316. His performance was slightly better than what the study showed was the second-best five-year run of all time: Babe Ruth's first five years with the Yankees. From age 25 to 29, Ruth hit .370 with 235 home runs, 659 runs batted in, and an OPS of 1.288. No other players in baseball history came close, the study found.

Source Notes

This narrative is based on documents and interviews. In our reporting on the BALCO story for the *San Francisco Chronicle*, we obtained the secret grand jury testimony of Barry Bonds, Jason and Jeremy Giambi, Benito Santiago, Gary Sheffield, Bobby Estalella, Armando Rios, and Tim Montgomery. We also reviewed confidential memoranda detailing federal agents' interviews with Trevor Graham, C. J. Hunter, John McEwen, Emeric Delczeg, and Rios. Other sealed material we reviewed included unredacted versions of affidavits filed by the BALCO investigators; e-mail between BALCO owner Victor Conte and several track athletes and coaches regarding the use and distribution of drugs; a list of evidence seized from the BALCO storage locker; and a document prepared to brief participants in the raid on BALCO.

Memos detailing the statements of Victor Conte, James Valente, and Greg Anderson to Agent Jeff Novitzky were sealed when we first consulted them, but have since become part of the public file in the BALCO case. The BALCO search warrant affidavits and other court records provided significant information. We also obtained a recording made without Anderson's knowledge in 2003; in it, Bonds's trainer discussed Bonds's use of banned drugs. Kimberly Bell provided legal correspondence, transcripts, audiotapes of voice mail, and many documents regarding her relationship with Bonds.

From September 2003 until the autumn of 2005, we interviewed more than 200 people, some of them repeatedly, about BALCO. Many of their names appear in the text, or in the chapter notes that follow. Some sources requested anonymity to avoid interfering with the

federal BALCO investigation and a related grand jury probe that continued into 2005. Some additional information about sources who requested anonymity appears in the chapter notes.

The baseball reporting of the *Chronicle's* Henry Schulman and
John Shea assisted us in understanding Bonds and the Giants. We
consulted Jose Canseco's memoir, *Juiced,* as well as Bonds biogra-
phies by writer Steven R. Travers and *Oakland Tribune* baseball reporter Josh Suchon. Sean L. Forman's Baseball-Reference.com Web
site was our source of baseball statistics. The Retrosheet.org Web site
was consulted for box scores and accounts of specific games. Baseball-
almanac.com provided attendance data. A key to abbreviations used
in the notes follows:

AP—*Associated Press*

Canseco—*Jose Canseco,* Juiced (*New York: ReganBooks, 2005*)

CT—Chicago Tribune

GJ testimony—*2003 BALCO grand jury testimony*

Jones/Sekules—*Marion Jones* (*with Kate Sekules*), Marion Jones:
    Life in the Fast Lane (*Warner Books, New York: Melcher Media,
    2004*)

LAT—Los Angeles Times

NYT—New York Times

OT—Oakland Tribune

Recording—*secret recording of Anderson, 2003*

SFC—San Francisco Chronicle

SFX—San Francisco Examiner

SI—Sports Illustrated

SJM—San Jose Mercury News

Suchon—*Josh Suchon,* This Gracious Season: Barry Bonds and the
    Greatest Year in Baseball (*Winter Publications, 2002*)

Travers—*Steven R. Travers,* Barry Bonds: Baseball's Superman
    (*Sport Publishing, LLC, 2002*)

TSN—The Sporting News

USAT—USA Today

PROLOGUE:

A source familiar with Bonds provided significant information about Bonds's decision to begin using steroids. **Bonds in St. Louis, remarks about McGwire:** Kim Bell interview, 2004. **Batting practice:** "McGwire's Pregame Fireworks," SFC, 5/23/98. **Attendance data:** baseball-almanac.com; media guide compilations by Kenn Tomasch for his kenn.com Web site. **Post-strike finances:** "A Cash Cow Transforms Itself into a Dead Horse," NYT, 9/15/94; "Ballpark Figures Slide," USAT, 8/11/95. **"Metaphor for the Best":** "News for the Culture: Why Editors Put Strong Men Hitting Baseballs on Page One," by University of Iowa Associate Professor Judy Polumbaum, *Newspaper Research Journal,* 3/22/00. **"Mt. Everest":** Pat Gallagher interview, 1998, SFX. **Andro:** Steve Wilstein interview, 2005; Wilstein's "McGwire Legend Grows in Season-Long Home Run Derby," AP, 8/15/98; " 'Andro' OK in Baseball, Not Olympics," AP, 8/22/98. **Arnold and Andro:** "McGwire's Spiked Swing Raises Health Questions," CT, 8/26/98. **Selig's statement:** "Baseball Tries to Calm Down a Debate on Pills," NYT, 8/27/98. Fehr also signed.

CHAPTER ONE:

Marion Jones and *FLEX*: Jim Schmaltz interviews, 2003 and 2004; "A Jones for Bodybuilding," *FLEX,* 9/01. **ZMA hype:** www.snac.com. **Jones as pitchwoman:** "Marion Jones Timeline," CNNSI Online, 1/03/02. **Jones doing business with Conte:** C. J. Hunter statement to Novitzky, 2004. ***FLEX* part of $1 billion empire**: "How Joe and Ben Weider Became the Founding Fathers of Bodybuilding," *FLEX,* 9/95. **Supplement industry big business:** "Supplements Lure Athletes, Skirt FDA," CT, 8/20/01. **ZMA and deficiencies, promotions:** www.snac.com. **Milos "The Mind" Sarcev:** Milos Sarcev interview, 2003; *FLEX,* 10/00. **Jones and ZMA logo:** Hunter statement to Novitzky, 2004. **Florence Griffith Joyner:** "Kersee to FloJo's Defense," LAT, 9/23/98. **Jones and drug use:** Hunter statement to Novitzky, 2004; Conte interview with Novitzky, 2003; "BALCO Owner Comes Clean," *ESPN the Magazine,* 12/2/04; Conte *20/20* interview, 12/3/04. **Penalties for doping in track:** U.S. Anti-Doping Agency. **Conte growing up:** e-mails from Conte to SFC;

a 2005 interview with cousin Bruce Conte provided significant details about Victor Conte's background, family, and personality. **Conte in high school:** Bob Fries and Ken Dose interviews, 2003. **Surf tunes, budding musician:** E-mails from Conte; interviews with Bruce Conte and a guitarist known as "Dulo." **Eastern philosophy:** Dulo interview and e-mails, 2005. **Bruce with Tower of Power:** Bruce Conte interview, 2005. **TOP history, drugs:** www.bumpcity.com; www.epicrecords.com/towerofpower; Emilio Castillo and Stephen "Doc" Kupka interviews, 2003. **Conte in TOP:** Conte e-mails; Kupka, Castillo, and Bruce Conte interviews, *The Fresno Bee,* 10/28/77. **Conte fired from TOP:** Kupka, Castillo, and Bruce Conte interviews. **Married Audrey:** Conte divorce papers. **Weights and vitamins:** Kupka, Castillo, and Bruce Conte interviews. **Audrey drug problems:** Conte divorce papers, Audrey Conte court records. **Audrey and Victor champion health:** Conte divorce papers. **End of musical career:** Conte e-mails; Dulo and Bruce Conte interviews. **Millbrae Holistic:** Conte divorce papers. **1983 incident:** Audrey Conte interview, 2003; Alicia Conte interviews, 2003; information provided by San Mateo Police Department; a source close to the Contes. **Hours at the Stanford Medical Library:** Dr. Brian Goldman interview, 2003; a source familiar with Conte. **BALCO opened in 1984:** Conte divorce papers.

CHAPTER TWO:

Willy Cahill: Cahill interview, 2005; www.dawave.com. **The ICP:** lqa.com, Web site for Quantum Analytics. **Pseudoscience:** Dr. Gary Wadler and Dr. Candy Tsourounis interviews, 2003. **Mineral deficiencies:** *The Merck Manual of Diagnosis and Therapy,* online edition at merck.com. **Conte as nutritionist/scientist/inventor:** www.balcolab.com (now defunct). **Dr. Brian Goldman and Conte**: Goldman interviews, 2003. **Shares in BALCO:** Conte divorce papers. **Services free to athletes:** Cahill interview, 2005; Randy Huntington interviews, 2003–2005; sources familiar with Conte. **The Reverend Ernest Holmes:** Bruce Conte interview, 2005. **Tafralis as client:** "Olympic Price for Scandal," SFC, 10/19/03. **Tafralis career info:** www.usatf.org. **Tafralis on Conte:** SFC (John Crumpacker) interview, 10/03. **Jim Valente:** BALCO court documents; source familiar with Conte. **Doehring crash:** "Doehring Casts Aside Doubts of His Shotput Capabilities," *Orange County Register,* 6/16/88; "Dream Comes True for Southland Shotputter," LAT, 6/16/88. **Conte and 1988 "BALCO Olympians":** "Getting Athletes in Tune," SFX, 9/16/88. **Tafralis and Doehring at Olympics:** United Press International, 9/23/88. **Timmerman and doping:** "Battle Against Sport's Drug Takers," The Press Association, 7/3/98. **Johnson doping scandal:** "He Was the World's Fastest Human," *The Gazette* (Montreal), 3/18/05. **Charlie Francis and his history of doping:** Report of the Dubin Inquiry, 1989; "Anabolic Athletics—A Brief History of Drugs in Sport," *Testosterone Nation,* 10/01; "Coach's Drug Use Shaped Philosophy," NYT, 3/6/89. **Heidi Krieger:** "East Germans Steroids Toll: 'They Killed Heidi,'" NYT, 1/26/04. **East German success:** "East German Women Excel as Olympic Competition Opens," NYT, 7/21/80. **Doehring admission:** "Olympian Feels Forced to Take Steroids," LAT, 8/6/89. **Doehring tests positive:** "Doehring Suspended for Failing Drug Test," LAT, 2/27/91. **Tafralis tests positive:** "Newswire," LAT, 10/31/95. **Tafralis's steroid knowledge:** "BALCO Owner Comes Clean," *ESPN the Magazine,* 12/2/04. **Conte and athletes:** Richard Goodman interviews, 2003 and 2004; sources familiar with Conte. **Wilkins amazed it's legal:** "Sports Nutrition Guru Trailed by Allegations," LAT, 10/26/03. **Biondi and Karl Mohr:** Karl Mohr interview, 2005. **Biondi and Wilkins statistics:** U.S. Olympic Web site; USATF Web site. **Goodman's hiring:** "The Atomic Level Athletic Frontier," *Health World,* 2/90; Goodman interviews, 2003–2005. **Supporting '92 Olympians:** Former BALCO employee interview, 2005. **Zap Your Zits:** "A Search for Truth in Substance," WP, 1/4/03. **ICP test on breast implants:** "Researchers Focusing on Silicone Breast Implants and Immune Disorders," *Biotechnology Newswatch,* 8/2/93; BALCO court filings, 2005. **1993 investigation:** California State Health Department records. **BALCO's financial woes:** Conte divorce papers; state and federal records. **Failing marriage, aftermath:** Details on the Contes' breakup, the fire, and life after the marriage are culled from divorce papers, interviews with Audrey Conte, Alicia Conte, and a source familiar with the family.

CHAPTER THREE:

A source familiar with Bonds provided significant information about Bonds's youth and relationship with his father. **Bobby Bonds's career:** "Giant on the Field, and in His Hometown, *Riverside Press Enterprise,* 8/24/03. **Jim Crow South:** Bobby Bonds interview, ESPN's 1999 "Sports Century" broadcast, cited by Travers. **Arrests:** "Bobby Bonds Jailed as Drunk Driver," SFC, 8/14/73; "Bobby Bonds Arrested," SFC, 11/30/73. **Youth baseball, relationship with father:** SFX prep sportswriter Merv Harris, interview, 2005. **Complaints about father:** "Barry Bonds, Baseball Player," *Playboy* interview, 7/93. **"Job" and "sitting there":** source familiar with Bonds. **"Celebrity Child":** Bonds GJ testimony. **School parties:** "Bonds Big on Family, Home Fans," OT, 2/13/02. **"Everything was easy":** *Playboy,* 7/93. **Car and suspension at ASU:** "Homer King Bonds Was a Prince, Too" (interview with ASU teammate Todd Brown), *Binghamton Press & Sun Bulletin,* 10/10/01; Travers. **Brock:** "Pittsburgh's Barry Bonds Sees Those Numbers Coming," SI, 6/25/90. **Pittsburgh career:** "Barry Bonds Has Been Rude and Booed," LAT, 10/7/01. **"Get my name":** A source familiar with Bonds. **Epiphany:** *Playboy,* 7/93. **Salary arbitrations:** "Bonds Stock Rising Quickly," TSN, 7/2/90. **Grandmother:** "Baseball without Metaphor," *NYT Magazine,* 9/1/02. **Bradenton incident:** "Bonds Learns Leyland Has a Breaking Point," *Pittsburgh Press,* 3/5/91; "Leyland Gets Attention of Bonds and Pirates," *Baltimore Evening Sun,* 3/5/91; *Playboy* interview, 7/93; ESPN's 1999 "Sports Century," cited by Travers. **Sid Bream scores:** Travers; Suchon.

CHAPTER FOUR:

Safeway: "A Buyout's Bitter Fallout," WSJ, 5/27/90. **Stoneham and Candlestick:** Roger Angell's *Five Seasons: A Baseball Companion* (New York: Simon and Schuster, 1977). **Lurie's frustrations:** "Lurie: Mayor was 'Blowing Smoke,'" SFX, 8/9/92. **"St. Peter," Giants' financial issues:** "Executive of the Year," *San Francisco Business Times,* 1/7/94. **The 1993 contract and Magowan:** A source familiar with Bonds. In November 2005, we sought to interview members of the Giants' front office. At their request, we provided in writing a list of questions pertaining to information detailed in the book. The team declined to comment. **"I got you"**: SJM Sports Editor Bud Geracie, ESPN's "Sports Century" interview cited by Travers. **"Printing lies" and early Giants days:** "Is Bonds a Jerk?" SFX Magazine, 5/16/93. **Interpersonal conflicts:** Kim Bell interview, 2004. **"Ain't gonna sign":** A source familiar with Bonds. **Approach to Glavine:** "Bonds Might OK a Trade," SFC, 12/14/98. **Farris and the card shows:** Bonds GJ testimony. **Anderson's program and Bonds's interest:** recording; source familiar with Bonds.

CHAPTER FIVE:

Michael Conte and Medicare: Federal court records; "Medicare Suit is 2nd Woe for Lab," LAT, 10/20/03; "Ex-Musician at Center of Steroid Accusations," CT, 12/4/03; Goodman interview, 2005. The suit settled in 2004. **Randy Huntington:** Randy Huntington interviews, 2003–2005; **"If you want to push . . .":** "Science of Sports: The Latest Technology Can Engineer Gold-Medal Performances," *Baltimore Sun,* 7/19/92. **Music in Sync:** "Fitness Buff Tunes In to New Set of Melodies," LAT, 8/4/87. **Mike Powell stats and training:** US-ATF Web site; Huntington interviews; "Science of Sports . . ." *Baltimore Sun,* 7/19/92; "Toning the Mind to Visualize," *The Oregonian,* 10/13/91; "Engineering the Perfect Athlete," *Time* magazine, 8/3/92. **Huntington meets Conte:** Huntington interviews. **Bill Romanowski stats, background, rap sheet:** NFL.com; ESPN.com; Oakland Raiders media guide; Williams v. Romanowski lawsuit; "Raiders Suspend Romo," SFC, 8/26/03. **Conte impressed with Romo:** Goodman interview; a source familiar with Conte's business. **Romo training and supplementation:** Huntington interviews; "Denver's Iron Man," *Denver Post,* 10/22/00; "Taking His Medicine," SI, 5/25/98. **Steroids part of Romo regimen:** Huntington interviews; court documents from Colorado prescription drugs case— including statements to agents by Huntington, Martin Harrison, and Debbie Harrison. **Conte and Valente to Denver:** Huntington and Goodman interviews. **Conte gave away ZMA:** Goodman interviews. **Conte and Brilla, ZMA study:** Brilla interviews, 2003 and 2004; "Effects of a Novel Zinc-Magnesium Formulation on Hormones and Strength," Brilla and Conte, 11/98; "Study Finds Nutritional Supplement Called ZMA . . ." *Business Wire,* 11/18/98. **Rebuffed by Biochem:** Will Brink interview, 2005. **Deal with EAS:** Conte divorce; "A Search for Truth in Substance," WP, 12/4/03. **EAS and Bill Phillips:** "EAS Bulks up with Creatine, Broncos," *Rocky Mountain News,* 6/28/98. **Deals with other companies, threaten to sue:** "SNAC System Files Lawsuit Against Next Nutrition, Inc. for ZMA Trademark Infringement and False Advertising of Their Designer Protein Products," *Business Wire,* 8/24/00. **Goodman pitching BALCO, Sarcev only taker:** Goodman interviews, 2003–2005. **Sarcev bio:** www.qfac.com/advice/milos.html. **1998 S.F. bodybuilding event:** "Night Crawler," *SF Weekly,* 5/6/98; Wayne DeMilia interview, 2005. **Pre-event meeting:** A source familiar with Conte and SF competition; DeMilia interview. **Testing at hotel:** Goodman interviews; a source familiar with Conte and competition; "BALCO Owner Comes Clean," *ESPN the Magazine,* 12/2/04.

CHAPTER SIX:

Patrick Arnold bio: www.mesomorphosis.com; www.ergopharm .net; "Shape Shifter," *ESPN the Magazine,* 5/9/05. **Dan Duchaine bio:** "Dan Duchaine Unchained—The 'Guru' Breaks the Silence on Steroids," www.musclezine.com. **Duchaine death/tribute:** www.qfac.com /articles/tribute.html. **Prohormones:** www.bodybuildingforyou.com; www.brinkzone.com. **Andro:** "Andro Hangs in a Quiet Limbo," NYT, 6/11/99; *Faust's Gold,* by Steven Ungerleider (New York: St. Martin's Press/Thomas Dunne Books, 2001). **Andro and Arnold:** "Scientific Studies Don't Address Androstenedione," *Dallas Morning News,* 8/28/98. **Andro and McGwire, baseball:** Steve Wilstein interview, 2005; Wilstein's "McGwire Legend Grows in Season-Long Home Run Derby," AP, 8/15/1998, and " 'Andro' OK in baseball, not Olympics," AP, 8/22/98. **Andro sales spike:** "Supplement Users Stocking Up Before Thursday's Ban," AP, 1/18/05. **Arnold Top 100:** "TSN's Power 100," *The Sporting News,* 12/14/98. **Arnold side business:** BALCO e-mails. **Arnold and steroid hunting:** Patrick Arnold postings on Google Internet message board misc.fitness.weights, 1995. **Genabol history:** *Detection of Norbolethone, an Anabolic Steroid Never Marketed, in an Athlete's Urine,* by Don Catlin, Brian Ahrens, and Yulia Kucherova, UCLA Olympic Analytic Laboratory, 5/14/02. **Sarcev exchanges with Arnold:** BALCO e-mails; Patrick Arnold search warrant affidavit. **Arnold, Conte, and Internet message board:** Postings on misc.fitness.weights, 1999. **Conte, supplement companies, and muscle magazines:** "Testosterone Production . . . An Interview with Victor Conte," *Testosterone Nation,* 11/13/98; "ZMA vs. Andro— An Interview with Victor Conte," *Testosterone Nation,* 4/9/99. **First T-Nation story:** Nelson Montana interview, 2005; "Testosterone Production . . ." *Testosterone Nation,* 11/13/98. **Conte and bodybuilding:** "BALCO Owner Comes Clean," *ESPN the Magazine,* 12/2/04; Goodman interviews; a source familiar with Conte. **Arnold and Conte in steroids business:** BALCO court documents; Arnold indictment; search warrant affidavit. **HGH info:** "Aging Baby Boomers Turn to Hormone," SFC, 11/17/03; "Miracle Worker," CT, 5/7/00; "Anti-Aging Potion or Poison?" NYT, 4/12/98. **Conte HGH to Romo:** Colorado court records from prescription drug case, 1999. **Conte knows athletes using HGH:** "Testosterone Production . . ." *Testosterone Nation,* 11/13/98. **Delczeg suspected dealer:** BALCO court documents. **Delczeg sold HGH to Conte:** Delczeg interview with Novitzky, 2003; source familiar with Delczeg and Conte. **Conte sold HGH to Romo:** Source familiar with Delczeg and Conte. **Julie Romanowski and BALCO:** Julie Romanowski interview with authorities in Colorado case. **Romo money to BALCO, Conte money to Delczeg, Valente uses Delczeg drug source:** BALCO court records, search warrant affidavit. **Conte and norbolethone in '99:** BALCO e-mail from Arnold to Conte; "BALCO Owner Comes Clean," *ESPN the Magazine,* 12/2/04. **SNAC finances:** Conte divorce. **Endorsements in exchange for drugs:** Conte statement to Novitzky; a lawyer for a BALCO athlete, interviewed 2003–2005. **Testing of Olympic-level athletes:** U.S. Anti-Doping Agency. **Beating testers was easy:** Conte e-mails to SFC. **Drugs Conte provided:** BALCO court records, including Conte statement to Novitzky; "BALCO Owner Comes Clean," *ESPN the Magazine,* 12/2/04; Conte *20/20* interview, 12/3/04. **Testing for the drugs:** U.S. Anti-Doping Agency; BALCO court records. **Alphabet, calendars, ledger:** BALCO court records; USADA case against Michelle Collins; USADA case against Alvin

Harrison; Kelli White interview with SFC, USAT, LAT, 12/2/04. **Comparison to East German doping machine:** Ungerleider interviews, 2003–2005.

CHAPTER SEVEN:

Early life, baseball career, and return to the Peninsula: Interviews with former teammates Mike Roza, Rich Lopp, and Joe Blandino, former coaches Mike Cartan and Steve Gillispie, grandmother Darlene Alioto, and the late Carol Armanino, mother of the McKercher boys, all in 2003. **Gordon's death:** Retired officer Tim Mellors, 2005 interview; San Mateo County court records. **Steroid use at Fort Hays State:** 2003 secret recording; a former athlete who asked not to be named. **College batting line:** Fort Hays State sports information office. **Arrests:** Police reports. **Experience with steroids:** Recording. **Business names, license plates, tips received by drug agents:** BALCO affidavits. **McKercher after baseball:** "Bonds as Prep: Signs of a Superstar," SFC, 7/7/93. **McKercher connects Anderson and Bonds, and Bonds's workouts with Anderson:** Bonds GJ testimony. **Anderson as Bonds's best friend:** A source familiar with Bonds. **Anderson's perspective on Bonds:** Two sources familiar with Anderson. **Bonds's abusive interactions with Anderson:** Kim Bell, 2004. **Calendars, Anderson as drug "middleman":** Anderson's statement to Novitzky, 2003. **Stretching incident and medical advice:** A Bonds source. For a first-person account of the positive effects of performance-enhancing drugs, see "Drug Test," *Outside* magazine, 11/03, by Stuart Stevens.

CHAPTER EIGHT:

Winstrol use: A source familiar with Bonds; Montgomery GJ testimony, quoting Conte. **Calendars:** Bonds GJ testimony. **Workout routine and stash:** A source familiar with Bonds. **Steroid side effects:** *The Merck Manual of Diagnosis and Therapy,* at www.merck.com; *Physicians' Desk Reference,* at www.pdrhealth.com; the National Institute on Drug Abuse at www.nida.nih.gov; www.steroid.com. **Hayes sees Bonds:** "Bigger, Stronger Bonds Doesn't Go Unnoticed," SFC, 2/26/99. **"Gamma radiation," and the risks of alienating Bonds:** A

Giants source. **Torn tendon:** "Bonds to Miss 10 Weeks Following Surgery on Arm," SFC, 4/21/99. **His steroid use:** Kim Bell, 2004; two sources familiar with Bell's grand jury testimony, 2005. **Ropes for McGwire's BP, physical complaints, Canseco in Las Vegas:** A source familiar with Bonds. **New drugs:** Bonds's doping calendars, referenced in Bonds GJ testimony; a source familiar with Bonds. **Pac Bell and the inquiries about Anderson:** A Giants employee. **Contract strategy, problems with Baker and Kent:** A source familiar with Bonds. **Back injury:** "Bonds Optimistic of Weekend Return," SFC, 5/15/00. **Giants' fears:** A Giants source. **Call to Selig:** "He Love Himself Barry Much," Rick Reilly column, SI, 8/27/01. **Bonds's relationship with Kim Bell:** Kim Bell, interviews, 2004; ticket stubs, airline and hotel receipts, handwritten notes, transcripts of voice mails and letters provided by Bell, 2004. In 2003 and 2004, Michael Rains, Bonds's lawyer, wrote four letters regarding Bell's claims. Rains denied that Bonds had promised to buy a house in Arizona for Bell or pay for her college education and said Bonds had "absolutely no recollection" of giving Bell money. But Rains's letters verified many aspects of Bell's account of her long-term relationship with Bonds.

CHAPTER NINE:

Korchemny bio and coaching philosophy: "Remi Korchemny: The Art of Coaching," *American Track & Field,* 2002; "Caught in a Tempest," SFC, 11/4/03; "Tragic Past of the Sprint Coach Who Can Make Dwain World Champion," *Sunday Mail,* 8/3/03; "Remi Korchemny, A Legend in Track . . ." SJM, 11/2/03. **Gail Devers medals:** USATF Web site. **Korchemny and Romo and Conte:** Randy Huntington interviews, 2003–2005; "Lab Owner in Drug Probe Forced into Spotlight," LAT, 10/22/03. **Romo feared lost step:** Huntington interviews. **Conte and Korchemny work together:** BALCO court documents; "With a Helping Hand, Chambers Hopes to Go Faster and Faster," OT, 12/24/02. **Korchemny introduces Conte to Gaines, Harrisons:** Sources familiar with Conte, BALCO investigation. **Harrison bios:** "Sprinter's Life Back on Track, WP, 6/21/96. **Conte gave The Clear to Harrisons, Gaines:** "BALCO Owner Comes Clean,"

ESPN the Magazine, 12/2/04. **Harrisons' calendars:** BALCO court records. **Montgomery bio:** USATF Web site; "Nowhere to Run," *ESPN the Magazine,* 6/7/04. **Harrison and Montgomery talk about Conte:** Montgomery GJ testimony. **Trevor Graham and steroids:** "Graham Can't Outrun Questions," USAT, 8/7/05. **Graham falling-down excuse:** Graham statement to Novitkzy, 2004. **Montgomery call to Conte, Graham follow-up call:** Montgomery GJ testimony. **Check for $7,350:** BALCO court records. **Marion Jones bio and missed test:** Jones/Sekules; "Jones Sprints to Two-Sport Success," WP, 7/4/94; "The Summer of Marion Jones," *The Sporting News,* 7/23/00; "Golden Decision for Jones," *Boston Herald,* 6/5/94; "A Tiger's Tale," LAT, 6/25/93. **Jones and Hunter, Hunter background:** "Jones Excels in Her Transition Game," WP, 8/3/97; "The Fast Lane," SI, 6/29/98; Jones/Sekules. **Jones intro to Graham:** "He Guides Them to Gold," Raleigh *News and Observer,* 9/17/00. **Graham steroids denial, Montgomery and Hunter allegations:** Graham statement to Novitzky, 2004; Hunter statement to Novitzky, 2004; Montgomery GJ testimony, 2003. **Jones in 1998:** "Marion Jones Timeline," CNNSI Online, 1/03/02; USATF Web site; "Jones Keeps It Simple: Run Fast. Jump Far. Win," NYT, 8/13/98. **Jones denies steroids:** Jones/Sekules; BALCO GJ testimony; "Jones Far From Super in 200 Loss," NYT, 4/19/04. **Hunter and Conte on Jones's drug use:** Hunter statement to Novitzky, 2004; Conte interview with Novitkzy, 2003; "BALCO Owner Comes Clean," *ESPN the Magazine,* 12/2/04; Conte *20/20* interview, 12/3/04. **Conte pretesting Jones:** BALCO court documents. **Jones results in Sydney:** USATF Web site; "Marion Takes to the Air," *Newsweek,* 10/2/00. **Hunter positive tests, cover-up:** Hunter statement to Novitzky, 2004; "Hunter: Officials Offered to Suppress News of Positive Test," SJM, 12/9/03. **Conte contacts Arnold about Hunter:** BALCO e-mails. **Hunter withdraws:** "Knee Injury KOs Hunter in Shot Put," AP, 9/11/00. **Hunter positive becomes public:** "US Field Star Fails Drug Test," *Sydney Daily Telegraph,* 9/25/00. **Hunter press conference, with Conte:** "Shot Putter Denies Taking Banned Drug," *Philadelphia Inquirer,* 9/26/00; "Hunter Tainting the Show," *Dayton Daily News,* 9/27/00; "Officials: Hunter Failed 4 Tests," WP, 9/26/00. **Jones and talk shows:** "Jones

Can't Go Anywhere Without Being Recognized," LAT, 11/4/00. **Jones continued drug use:** Hunter statement to Novitzky; "BALCO Owner Comes Clean," *ESPN the Magazine,* 12/2/04. **Conte and Montgomery:** Montgomery GJ testimony; "BALCO Owner Comes Clean," *ESPN the Magazine,* 12/2/04. **Harrison's and Gaines's results:** USATF Web site. **Project World Record:** Montgomery's GJ testimony; "How BALCO Built The World's Fastest Man," SJM, 5/26/04; "Nowhere to Run," *ESPN the Magazine,* 6/7/04; Graham statement to Novitzky, 2004. **Montgomery and drugs, quarrel with Conte:** Montgomery GJ testimony. **Montgomery transformation:** "BALCO Owner Comes Clean," *ESPN the Magazine,* 12/2/04. **ZMA Track Club:** 2001 filing with USATF. **Montgomery and Gaines at Nationals:** "U.S. Outdoor Track Championship Results," UPI, 6/22/01. **Letter clearing Montgomery:** Conte interview with *20/20,* 12/3/04. **Montgomery at Bislett:** "Monty and Jones Run Fast at Bislett," AP, 6/13/01. **Monty eavesdropping at BALCO:** Montgomery GJ testimony. **Conte and new version of The Clear:** BALCO e-mails. **Jones HGH at hotel:** "BALCO Owner Comes Clean," *ESPN the Magazine,* 12/2/04. **Doping calendars:** BALCO court records. **Jones and 300 meters at Mt. SAC:** "Jones Breezes to Mt. SAC Win," AP, 4/22/01. **Jones world rankings:** USATF Web site. **Marriage ending:** Jones/Sekules. **Hunter and Michelle Collins:** Hunter statement to Novitzky, 2004; Graham statement to Novitzky, 2004. **Jones and Montgomery:** "Fast Times," Raleigh *News and Observer,* 9/18/02. **Montgomery and Conte breakup:** Montgomery GJ testimony; "BALCO Owner Comes Clean," 12/2/04; sources familiar with Conte. **Conte talked too much:** Kelli White interview, SFC, USAT, LAT, 12/2/04; sources familiar with Conte.

CHAPTER TEN:

Conte's version of Montgomery breakup, Chambers as replacement: Two sources who worked with Conte. **Chambers to America:** Track source with knowledge of BALCO operation. **Chambers bio, one last shot:** www.athletix.org; "Chambers Ruins Greene's Day," *The Guardian,* 6/29/02. **Move to Bay Area, regimen with Korchemny/BALCO:** "With a Helping Hand, Chambers Hopes to Go Faster and

Farther," OT, 4/24/02. **The full enchilada:** "BALCO Owner Comes Clean," *ESPN the Magazine,* 12/2/04. **Wire transfer:** BALCO court records. **Credit to Conte:** "I Wanted to Hit Olympic Champion Greene," (London) *News of the World,* 6/16/02. **Bislett Games:** "Chambers Ruins Greene's Day," *The Guardian,* 6/29/02. **Win in England:** "Chambers beats Greene again in 100 meters," AP, 6/30/02. **European Championships:** "Olympic Gold Now the Goal for Chambers," (London) *Evening Standard,* 8/8/02. **Five of six v. Greene:** "Chambers Confirms His Superiority," (London) *Times,* 9/7/02. **Montgomery world record:** "Montgomery's 9.78 Sets New Standard for the 100 Meters," NYT, 9/15/02; "Montgomery Sets the Standard—Chambers Reeling as American Takes Record," *The Guardian,* 9/16/02; "100-Meter Record Set in a Blur," CT, 9/15/02. **Race aftermath with Graham:** Montgomery GJ testimony; Jones/Sekules. **Jones and Montgomery press conference:** "Love Conquers All for Montgomery," (London) *Times,* 9/16/02. **Montgomery celebrated after record:** "Fastest Human Humble," Norfolk *Daily Press,* 10/19/02. **Chambers devastated, vows revenge:** "Montgomery Sets the Standard," *The Guardian,* 9/16/02; " 'I'll Break the World Record,' Says Chambers," (London) *Daily Telegraph,* 12/21/02. **Chambers e-mail to Conte:** BALCO court documents. **Zhanna Block bio:** "Keeping Ahead of the Jones," (London) *Independent,* 2/17/02. **Block e-mails to Conte:** BALCO court records. **Block buys ATP:** Valente statement to Novitkzy. **Conte and Toth:** BALCO court documents. **Toth bio:** USATF Web site. **Toth, career and steroids:** "An Interview with Kevin Toth, Shot Putter," Track Profile News Service, 2/03. **Conte gave drugs to Jacobs:** BALCO court documents. **Jacobs withdrawal from Sydney:** "Ready, Set, Go," SI.com, 9/21/00. **Jacobs U.S. Championships:** "Jacobs Maintains 1,500 Meter Dominance," OT, 6/24/02. **Jacobs indoor record:** "Jacobs on Top of World," *Boston Herald,* 2/2/03. **Jacobs note to Conte:** BALCO court records. **This isn't old:** "Jacobs, 39, Wins 11th Title," USAT, 6/24/02. **Craig e-mails to Conte:** BALCO court records. **Modafinil as stimulant:** www.provigil.com. **Harrison tests modafinil:** BALCO court documents. **Conte e-mails Werre:** BALCO court documents. **Werre mixed epi and testosterone:** Valente statement to Novitkzy. **Conte** seeking EPO: BALCO court documents. **Korchemny, Conte, and Linardatos:** BALCO court documents. **Linardatos and Web sites:** "Filling in the BALCO Blanks," *Track Profile Report,* 2/23/04; www.networksolutions.com. **Linardatos receiving drugs from Conte:** BALCO court documents. **Alvin Harrison panic over EPO:** BALCO court documents. **Harrison and DN Grand Prix:** "Harrison Sets 400 Mark on Track in Stockholm," *Philadelphia Inquirer,* 7/17/02. **Fears about The Clear** : BALCO e-mails, particularly exchanges between Conte and Linardatos. **Tzekos and manhandling drug tester:** "Greek Coach Has History of Evading Drug Testers," (Queensland) *Courier Mail,* 8/14/04.

CHAPTER ELEVEN:

Fans' cool reception to Bonds in 2001: "The Magic Is Missing as Bonds Approaches 70," NYT, 9/26/01. **Awkwardness at home plate:** "A Baseball Milestone," SJM, 4/18/01. **Bonds's homer in St. Louis:** "Cards Make Giants Pay in Ninth Inning," SFC, 6/24/01. **"Call God":** "Barry Lacks Power to Describe Stretch," SFC, 5/22/01. **Anderson's quest to meet Conte:** Ken Lockwood interview, 2003. **Conte's post:** "Barry Bonds hits #69," 9/29/01, on misc.fitness. weights, a Google message board. **Workout routine and diet:** "The King of Swing: What Fuels Baseball Superhitter Barry Bonds?" *Muscle & Fitness,* 6/1/03. **Doctor drew blood:** Bonds GJ testimony. **Weight training story:** "Baseball Without Metaphor" op cit. **Bonds's testing:** Bonds GJ testimony. **Drug use:** Bonds GJ testimony; prosecutors questioned Bonds about the drug calendars. C. J. Hunter told Novitzky in 2004 that Conte had warned Marion Jones to be careful using insulin lest she suffer a stroke. **Power started to decline:** source familiar with Bonds. **Bayless:** "Dumbbells and Diets Have Replaced Old Vices," SJM, 10/2/01. **Magowan:** Suchon. **McKercher:** "Barry Bonds Has Been Rude and Booed," LAT, 10/7/01. **"Deaf school":** Suchon. **"Dead people":** Travers. **Ants:** Ann Killion column, SJM, 6/27/01. **Reilly:** "He Loves Himself Barry Much," SI, 8/27/01. **Houston, 9/11:** Kim Bell interview, 2004. **The record home run:** Hall of Fame's account at baseballhalloffame.org. **"My strength coach":** "Bonds's Trainer," ESPN's "Outside the Lines," 4/18/04. **Contract negotiations:** A source familiar with Bonds.

CHAPTER TWELVE:

Bonds testosterone screening: Bonds GJ testimony. A prosecutor questioned Bonds about seized BALCO documents reflecting the tests. **Bonds drug cycle:** Bonds GJ testimony. A February 2002 calendar entry reflected Bonds's use of "alternating clear, cream, .25 G and . . . several days of Clow." Conte told Novitzky that in 2003, Bonds regularly used The Cream and The Clear. Conte said the protocol was twice-weekly uses of The Cream and The Clear for three weeks, with a week off at the end. **Anderson dropped by:** a source familiar with Bonds described his use of growth hormone and The Clear. **Tension on Giants:** A source familiar with Bonds; a Giants source. **Fight with Kent:** "Giants Now Battling Each Other," SFC, 6/26/02; Kim Bell interview, 2004. **Magowan's reaction:** "Can This Marriage Be Saved?" SFC, 6/27/02. **Baker slimed:** "Tax Woes for Ex-SF Manager Baker," SFC, 9/9/02. **Japan tour:** Jason Giambi GJ testimony. **Giambi's lifestyle and T-shirt:** "The Cleanup Man: How a Former MVP Became Baseball's Fall Guy," GQ, 4/05. **Giambi and Simms and the tattoo:** "A's Giambi Takes Pleasure in Living Life by the Seat of His Pants," USAT, 8/20/99. **SI cover:** 7/17/00. **"The best ever" and Japan:** "Barry's Sunny Disposition Is Rising," MLB.com, 11/9/02. **Giambi drug use post 2001:** Jason Giambi GJ testimony. **Giambi drug use pre 2001:** Canseco. **Neck massage:** "Bonds vs. Godzilla," *Yomiuri Shimbun*, 11/16/02. **Japanese business connection:** a source familiar with Anderson. **Bonds broached subject:** a source familiar with Bonds. **Giambi's discussions with Anderson:** Jason Giambi GJ testimony. **Caminiti:** "Totally Juiced," SI, 6/3/02. **Vampire:** "To DH or Not to DH?" SFC, 6/8/02. **Toothless policy, Orza:** "Baseball's Steroid Policy Was Made in Fear," WP, 12/21/03. **"It's all undetectable":** Recording. **Jeremy Giambi drug use:** Jeremy Giambi GJ testimony. **Sheffield, Bonds, and Anderson in 2002:** Sheffield GJ testimony. Prosecutors questioned him about calendars reflecting his drug use in 2002. **Bonds the taskmaster:** "Bonds Leaves Big Impression on Braves' Sheffield," SFC, 3/17/02. **Fight in**

Miami: "Jones Doesn't Disappoint," *Palm Beach Post,* 2/3/02. **Playoff meeting:** "Buddies Bonds, Sheffield Will Become Foes Today," SFC, 10/2/02. **Sheffield knee surgery:** "Knee Surgery Benefited Sheffield," *Atlanta Journal-Constitution,* 6/21/03; Sheffield GJ testimony. **Sheffield's use of The Clear and The Cream, claim of being duped, breakup with Bonds, $430 check:** Sheffield GJ testimony. **Pac Bell workout:** *Men's Journal,* 5/03. **$100,000 offer:** A source familiar with Bonds.

CHAPTER THIRTEEN:

Michelle Collins bio: USATF Web site; "400 Standout Collins Withdraws from Trials," *Dallas Morning News,* 7/13/04. **Kicked out of Graham camp:** Hunter statement to Novitzky, 2004; Graham statement to Novitkzy, 2004. **Conte pitch to Collins:** a source close to Collins. **Collins believed steroids pervasive:** two sources with knowledge of Collins's comments to USADA. **Collins calendars, e-mails:** BALCO court documents. **Collins 200 meters:** USATF Web site. **Jones's year off to have baby:** "Marion Jones Gives Birth to Boy Named Tim," Reuters, 6/29/03. **Collins at U.S. Indoors, World Indoors:** "U.S. Indoor Championship Results," Reuters, 2/2/03; "Collins Toughs Out Victory," Reuters, 3/16/03. **Winnings and bonus to Conte:** A source close to Collins; BALCO court documents. **Believed she won because of Conte:** A source close to Collins. **Kelli White bio:** USATF Web site; "Kelli White Out of the Blocks," SFC, 6/18/03; Kelli White interview with SFC, USAT, LAT, 12/2/04. **Training with Korchemny:** Kelli White interview, SFC, USAT, LAT, 12/2/04. **Knife attack:** "Kelli White Out of the Blocks," SFC, 6/18/03. **Tennessee All-American:** "Lady Vols' White Fourth, Fifth in NCAA Sprints," *Knoxville News-Sentinel,* 6/7/98. **White and Conte:** Details of the introduction to Conte, taking the "flax seed oil," Conte admitting he lied to her, and the foot injury are taken from White interview with SFC, USAT, LAT. **White results:** USATF Web site. **White set aside drugs:** White interview; a source familiar with BALCO investigation. **White begins using, notices Collins, menu of drugs:** White interview; a source familiar with White testimony in USADA hearings. **Conte and T3:** "BALCO Owner Comes Clean," *ESPN the Magazine,* 12/2/04. **White doping experience:** White interview. **Results were incredible:** "East Bay's White Runs Fastest 100 in World in 2003," SFC, 5/25/03; "Fast Start for New Track," LAT, 6/2/03; "Explosive White Steals 200," SFC, 6/23/03. **Modafinil from Korchemny, effects:** White interview. **World championship results:** "With Win in 200, White Emerges from Jones' Shadow," WP, 8/29/03. **Winning 200, the modafinil positive, Goldman cover story:** White interview. **Conte and Goldman make a deal:** A source who worked with Conte; investigative documents. **Press conference:** "U.S. Sprinter Tests Positive for Stimulant," NYT, 8/31/03. **Graham and Conte message boards:** A source familiar with message board postings; "Feud Lit Fuse on BALCO Scandal," SJM, 7/4/04. **Conte letters to USADA, IAAF:** BALCO court documents. **Graham calls USADA:** USADA interviews 2004–2005; sources familiar with phone call. **Graham sent syringe:** Graham statement to Novitzky; USADA interviews, 2004 and 2005.

CHAPTER FOURTEEN:

Li'l Guys: Anderson statement to Novitzky. **Santiago's drug use and payments:** Santiago GJ testimony. **Estalella's tattoos:** "Nomad Catcher Has Home for Now," *Arizona Republic,* 3/20/04. **Estalella's drug use and cycle:** Estalella GJ testimony. **Rios drug use:** Rios GJ testimony. **Benard and Velarde received drugs:** Valente statement to Novitzky. **Anderson and MLB drug testing, analysis of Bonds's slow start:** Recording. **Santiago's panic:** A source familiar with Santiago. **Rios's bad timing:** Rios statement to Novitzky. **"Be an asshole:"** Recording. **Bobby Bonds's concerns:** A source familiar with Bonds. *Muscle & Fitness:* "King of Swing," 6/1/03. Even after he was sentenced to prison in 2005, Conte kept the story about Bonds posted on his snac.com Web site. **Poster:** www.greyflannelauctions.com, 6/05. **Kids:** a source familiar with Bonds. **Giving Kim Bell cash from autograph sales, end of relationship with Bell:** Kim Bell interview, 2004; two sources familiar with Bell's grand jury testimony, 2005. **Surveillance of Anderson:** BALCO search warrant affidavit. **Voice mail after raid:** A source familiar with Bonds.

CHAPTER FIFTEEN:

Trash-digging scene: BALCO court documents; www.almanac.com; www.wunderground.com. **Novitzky career background:** BALCO court documents; Don Novitzky interview, 2005. **Novitzky investigation:** BALCO court documents. **Novitzky bio:** Don Novitzky interview, 2005; BALCO court documents; Stan Morrison interview, 2005; "Call IRS' Top BALCO Investigator 'Dirt Novitzky,' " SJM, 2/19/04. **Novitzky attire:** A source with knowledge of the BALCO investigation. **1999 extortion case:** "Kickboxer, Wife Face Extortion Charges," SJM, 6/5/99. **Winter Olympics:** "Novitzky Retiring from Coaching," OT, 2/20/02. **Steroid probes on the Peninsula:** Don Horsley interview, 2005; "Rivals Turn to Tattling in Steroids Case Involving Top Athletes," NYT, 4/11/04. **IRS CI and BALCO:** BALCO court documents. **Iran White account:** "Gunning for the Big Guy," by Jonathan Littman, *Playboy,* 5/04. **Tips from local agencies, surveillance, bank records, medical waste:** BALCO court documents. **UCLA lab description, Catlin's career, views on doping:** Don Catlin interview, 2005; "Catching the Drug-Taking Athlete," *UCLA Today,* 1999. **Lab and its clients:** "Leveling the Playing Field," *UCLA Magazine,* Spring 2004. **Discovery in 2002:** *Detection of Norbolethone, an Anabolic Steroid Never Marketed, in an Athlete's Urine,* by Don Catlin, Brian Ahrens, and Yulia Kucherova, UCLA Olympic Analytical Laboratory, 5/14/02; "Drug Testers Have Designs on New Steroid, WP, 3/8/03. **Tammy Thomas:** "Seeking Her Way Out of Infamy," NYT, 8/10/04. **Thomas denial:** "Cyclist Asks for Appeal on Ban," AP, 7/8/02. **Lifetime ban:** "Arbitration Panel Disqualifies Cyclist for Life After Positive Drug Test," AP, 8/30/02. **Thomas reputation, fears:** Catlin interview, 2005; sources familiar with US-ADA, USA Cycling, and USOC; Caroline Hatton interview, 2005. **Thomas says she'd never hurt anyone:** "Seeking Her Way Out of Infamy," NYT, 8/10/04. **Novitzky call to Catlin:** Catlin interview, 2005.

CHAPTER SIXTEEN:

Iran White: "Gunning for the Big Guy," *Playboy,* 5/04. **Problems with trash recon:** Kent Pearse interview, 2005. **Cherry and Graham:**

sources familiar with conversations. **Wanninger phone call:** Wanninger interviews, 2004 and 2005. **Graham claims Hunter gave him syringe:** Graham statement to Novitkzy. **Wanninger receives syringe:** Wanninger interviews, 2004 and 2005. **Terry Madden bio:** Madden interview, 2005. **Syringe to Catlin, interactions with Madden:** Catlin, Madden, and Hatton interviews, 2005. **Identifying the drug:** Catlin interview, 2005; "Decoding a Steroid," NYT, 11/2/03; "Breaking the Code," LAT, 11/6/03; "How Sleuths Tracked a Mysterious Steroid," SFC, 10/26/03. **Madden pressure, secret project:** Catlin, Madden, Travis Tygart interviews, 2005. **Samples from Nationals:** Madden and Tygart interviews, 2005. **Bingo e-mail:** Tygart interview, 2005. **Four THG positives:** "Jacobs Banned for Four Years," LAT, 7/18/04. **Madden and Huw Roberts:** Madden interview, 2005. **Chambers in Saarbrucken:** Rob Draper interview, 2004; "The Day Dwain's World Began to Fall Apart," (London) Mail, 10/26/03. **Catlin note to himself:** Catlin interview, 2005. **Madden in D.C., one rogue lab:** Madden, Tygart interviews, 2005. **August 19 meeting at USADA:** Madden, Tygart interviews, 2005; a source with knowledge of meeting. **Novitzky and BALCO e-mails:** BALCO court documents. **Conte bragging on Web:** Postings on Google message board, misc.fitness.weights. **Conte at World Championships:** Brooks Johnson interview, 2005.

CHAPTER SEVENTEEN:

Raid pushed up a day: Larry Bowers, Madden, Tygart interviews, 2005. **Pre-raid meeting at Bayside Park:** BALCO Search Warrant Briefing Document; a source with knowledge of the raid. **Bowers participation and reaction:** Bowers interview, 2005. **Account of raid, interviews:** BALCO court documents, including minute-by-minute account from IRS CI; statements to Novitzky by Conte, Valente, and Joyce Valente; defense filings with accounts by Conte and the Valentes. **"Conte just gave up everything":** A source with knowledge of the raid. **BALCO phones ringing:** Two sources with knowledge of the raid. **Bobby Bonds and Romanowski documents:** A source with knowledge of the raid. **Bowers nervous at storage locker:** Bowers interview, 2005. **Findings at storage**

locker: BALCO court documents; Bowers interview, 2005. **USADA briefing:** Madden, Tygart, Bowers interviews, 2005. **More from Conte, rest of the raid:** Novitzky interviews with Conte and Valente, BALCO court documents. **Anderson at gym, drugs in car:** BALCO court documents. **Search of Anderson's home, statement:** BALCO court documents. **Athlete trying to get in touch with Bonds:** A source familiar with Bonds. **Second raid at Anderson's:** BALCO court documents. **". . . a little late":** A source familiar with Anderson.

CHAPTER EIGHTEEN:

No choice: Two sources close to Conte. **Ellerman bio:** Ellerman interview, 2005. **Conte called Novitzky:** BALCO court documents. **Conte's conversations and meetings with Ellerman:** two sources with knowledge of their interactions. **"He and Bob initially connected":** Ellerman interview, 2005. **Conte badgered attorneys, mock 60 Minutes:** Two sources with knowledge of Conte's dealings with his attorneys. **Conte's sweeping denials:** BALCO court documents, Conte e-mails. **Threats to fire Holley:** Three sources with knowledge of Conte's dealings with his attorneys. **Conte tried to manipulate the investigation, concoct stories:** A lawyer for an athlete connected to BALCO; a lawyer involved in the BALCO investigation. **Grand jury:** BALCO court documents. **Athletes frightened:** Lawyers connected to athletes and the case. **Novitzky and Delczeg, calls to Novitzky from athletes:** BALCO court documents. **Baseball and testing policy:** "Doping Experts Say Baseball Faces Tough Job," NYT, 12/9/04. **Wadler on testing:** "A Search for Truth in Substance," WP, 12/4/03. WADA is the international agency that oversees doping control in Olympic sports. **Pittsburgh cocaine trials:** "Baseball and Cocaine: A Deepening Problem," NYT, 8/19/85. **Webber case:** "Plea Bargain Keeps Webber Out of Prison," *Detroit News,* 7/15/03. **Subpoena baseball's records, outraged reaction:** Four sources with knowledge of the government action. **Baseball worried about perjury:** David Cornwell interview, 2005; another lawyer connected to the case. **Cornwell and Orza phone call:** Cornwell interview, 2005. **Make clients non-valuable:** a lawyer connected to the case. **Rains bio, involvement in case, concerns, impressions:** Rains interview, 2005. **Rains meeting with lawyers:** Interviews with Rains, Rapoport, Ellerman, 2005. **Ellerman on Rains:** Ellerman interview, 2005. **Rains and Nedrow:** Rains interview, 2005. **"Trial balloon":** "Bonds Still Has Some Questions to Answer," LAT, 11/20/03. **Bonds teleconference:** "Bonds Defends Trainer," SFC, 11/19/03. **Bonds pops off:** "Barry Carries Weight of World," NYP, 5/5/04. **Mock cross-examinations:** A source close to Bonds, 2005. **Catlin to grand jury:** Catlin interview, 2005. **First week:** "Grand Jury Hears From 5 Athletes," SFC, 10/31/03. **Montgomery hiding:** "BALCO Athletes Granted Immunity," SFC, 11/7/03. **Wheatley's Karate Chop:** "Wheatley's Photo Op Goes Over the Top," SFC, 11/14/03. **"John Doe:"** "Ex-Giant Estalella Also Testifies," SFC, 11/21/03. **Most athletes admitted:** BALCO GJ testimony; sources familiar with the testimony. **Admissions by Montgomery and Estalella:** GJ testimony.

CHAPTER NINETEEN:

Bonds en route to court, meeting with prosecutors: Michael Rains interview, 2005. **Rains wants Bonds to shut up:** A source familiar with situation. **10:56 arrival:** "Bonds Gives Testimony," WP, 12/5/03. **Bonds testimony:** Bonds GJ testimony. **Ear to the wall:** "Bonds Denies Using Steroids," NYDN, 12/5/03. **Cornwell meets Rains:** David Cornwell interview, 2005. **Nedrow, Bonds reaction:** A source familiar with Bonds's day in court. **"Talk to your client":** Rains interview, 2005. **"Barry didn't do it!":** "Bonds Blows in to Face Grand Jury," CCT, 12/5/03. **Santiago, Montgomery, Jason Giambi testimony:** GJ testimony. **State of the Union:** "In Speech, Bush Calls for Steroid Ban," WP, 1/21/04. **"Two crazy sentences":** A Washington source familiar with BALCO case. **Ashcroft daily briefing:** Mark Corallo interview, 2005. **Ashcroft biography:** "Missouri Getting 'A Straight Arrow' for Governor," NYT, 1/14/85. **Loss to Carnahan:** "Senator Refuses to Challenge Loss," NYT, 11/9/00. **Sports fanatic:** Corallo and Ed McFadden interviews, 2005. **Musial career:** www.baseball-reference.com. **Ashcroft's office, aides, attitude about BALCO:** Corallo and McFadden interviews, 2005. **Indictments announce-**

ment: "Four Charged Over Designer Steroid," CNN.com, 2/12/04.
Names redacted: BALCO court documents.

CHAPTER TWENTY:

Web site: www.snac.com. **"Three BALCO scoops":** "Grand jury probes nutrient company," 10/14/03; "Bonds Subpoenaed, 10/18/03; "Raid uncovered suspected steroids," 10/19/03. **USADA wants to get story out:** Terry Madden interview, 2005. **USADA statement, teleconference:** Notes from teleconference, 10/16/03. **"Awkward . . ."** **Troubled by material:** Madden interview, 2005. **USADA meets with prosecutors:** Madden interview, 2005; A Source familiar with the meeting. **Letter to Madden:** Madden interview, 2005. **USADA meet with Conte:** Madden, Ellerman interview, 2005; a source familiar with the meeting. **Turk Wendell:** "No Masking Suspicion," *Denver Post*, 2/25/04. **Giambi under scrutiny:** "Food for Thought," *Newsday*, 2/24/04; "The Skinny on Giambi's Arrival," *Bergen Record*, 2/24/04. **"Bonds had received The Clear":** "Bonds Got Steroids, Feds Were Told," SFC, 3/2/04. **Sweeney and DuPuy:** "Feds Were Told Bonds, Giambi, Sheffield Received Steroids," AP, 3/3/04. **Reggie Jackson:** "Can't Silence Mr. October About Steroids," *Atlanta Journal-Constitution*, 3/11/04. **Bonds's reaction:** "Bonds Deflects Questions" and "Bonds Embraces Outlaw Status," SFC, 3/3/04. NYT reporter Paul Giblin approached Bonds, prompting Rhodes' comment. *Sports Illustrated:* "Is Baseball in the Asterisk Era?" SI, 3/15/04. **Senate hearing:** "Baseball Receives Steroid Warning," NYT, 3/11/04; transcripts from hearing. **Selig letter to Fehr:** "Fehr May Discuss Steroid Changes," LAT, 3/17/04. **Major League official:** Interview, 2005. **Giants mum:** "Bonds Deflects Questions," SFC, 3/3/04. **Giants see no proof:** A source familiar with team's front office. **BALCO defense lawyers:** "Bonds Did Nothing Wrong," AP, 3/5/04. **DEA at the Arnold:** "New Grand Jury Convened in Iowa," *ESPN the Magazine*, 3/13/04. **Serra attacks case:** "Lawyer for Bonds Coach Tears into Prosecution," SFC, 3/27/04. **Homers 659 and 660:** "Perfect Start for Giants," SFC, 4/6/04; "Family Ties," SFC, 4/13/04; "Bonds Ties Mays," SFC, 4/13/04.

CHAPTER TWENTY-ONE:

USADA point of view and actions: Based on 2005 interviews with Terry Madden, Travis Tygart, Bill Bock, and a source familiar with USADA. **"Non-analytical positive":** World Anti-Doping code. **McCain committee exchanges with Justice Dept.:** BALCO court documents. **USADA meeting with Conte:** Madden and Ellerman interviews, 2005; a source familiar with the meeting. **USADA and prosecutors:** Madden interview, 2005; a source familiar with the meeting. **"Jeff":** a source familiar with Jones's GJ testimony. **Mt. SAC.:** "Jones Discovers She's Not Yet Back on Track," *Orange County Register,* 4/19/04. **"Glossy . . . spin":** Jones/Sekules. **Lehane background:** "Grins and Grenades," *Newsweek,* 1/26/04. *Mercury News* **story:** "Agent's Report Disputed in BALCO Case," SJM, 4/25/04. **Hearing with McCain, release documents:** "Olympic Officials Appeal to Committee," WP, 5/6/04; "Senate Says It Will Release Drug Data to Olympic Officials," AP, 5/7/04. **Tygart gets documents:** Tygart interview, 2005. **Sifting through evidence:** 2005 interviews with Tygart, Madden, Bock, and a source familiar with USADA. **USADA meetings with Kelli White:** 2005 interviews with Bock, Tygart, Madden, and a source familiar with the meetings. **White in Qatar:** "Flop for Top Guns at Qatar Athletics Meet," AP, 5/14/04. **White confession:** "Kelli White suspended," SFC, 5/20/04. **Collins meeting:** 2005 interviews with Madden, Tygart, Brian Getz, and a source familiar with the meeting. **Four athletes charged:** "Doping Agency Accuses 4 Sprinters," SFC, 6/9/04. **Jones warning:** "Jones Will Sue if Barred from Games," NYT, 5/17/04. **USADA meeting:** "Jones Meets with Officials," SFC, 5/25/04. **Conte e-mails:** Sent to SFC. **Senate hearing request:** "Olympian urges Senate to hear her doping case," SFC, 6/17/04. **Selection of BALCO documents:** "Sprinter's camp shows disputed evidence," SJM, and "Jones's Lawyers Challenge Evidence Against Her" NYT, both 5/26/04. **Exonerated:** "Attorney says Olympic star passed lie detector test," SFC, 6/18/04. **"No evidence":** "Attorney Disputes Conte," WP, 6/19/04. **Montgomery's secret testimony:** "Sprinter admitted use of BALCO 'magic potion'" SFC, 6/24/04. **Jones at trials:** "Quick Exit After Jones Fails in 100 Meters," SFC, 7/11/04. **USADA approach to Jones:** Sources familiar with USADA. **BALCO athletes**

don't make it: "Final Factor: It's Results, Not BALCO," SFC, 7/13/04.
Hunter's account: Hunter's statement to Novitzky. *Chronicle* **story on Hunter:** "Olympian Accused of Doping in Sydney," SFC, 7/23/04.

CHAPTER TWENTY-TWO:

Dick Pound: "Pound Takes on Jones, USA Track," SFC, 8/13/04.
Greek scandal: "Top Greek Sprinters Injured . . . ," AP, 8/13/04;
"Greek Icon Facing Fall from Grace," SFC, 8/13/04; "2 Greek Sprinters Quit Games," SFC, 8/19/04. **Greeks and BALCO:** BALCO court documents, Patrick Arnold indictment. **Graham admissions:** "Graham Finally Admits He's Coach Who Turned in THG Syringe," AP, 8/23/04; "Graham Remains in the Spotlight," SFC, 8/28/04. **Jones results:** "Double negative," SFC, 8/28/04. **Doping rumors:** "Rumors Running Rampant as More Athletes Get Caught," SFC, 8/27/04.
Yuliya Nesterenko: "Unheralded Nesterenko Captures 100m Gold Glory," SFC, 8/22/04. **Fani Halkia:** "After Upset, Halkia Must Hurdle Skeptics," *Boston Globe,* 8/26/04. **Record number of cheats:** "Are Cheaters Still Running a Step Ahead of the Law?" SFC, 8/30/04. **Latest outrage:** "Bonds used steroids in 2003, trainer says on secret recording," SFC, 10/16/04. **"Poison ink":** "Defendants assail media leaks," SFC, 12/2/04. **Holley's objections:** Sources familiar with Conte and his defense team. **"Get ready . . .":** Conte e-mail to *Chronicle,* 11/4/04. **December 1 hearing:** "Defendants Assail Media Leaks," SFC, 12/2/04. **Giambi story:** "Giambi Admitted Taking Steroids," SFC, 12/2/04. **Bonds story:** "What Bonds Told the Grand Jury," SFC, 12/3/04. **Reaction to** *Chronicle* **stories:** "Shocked, shocked" by Steve Kettman, Salon.com, 3/24/05. **Gammons:** ESPN.com 12/4/04. **Boswell:** "The truth lies in the numbers," WP, 12/4/04.
Safire: "Judges as Plumbers," NYT, 12/13/04. **McCain reaction:** "McCain Demands Immediate Action to Tighten Drug-Testing Policy," AP, 12/4/04. **Biden:** "Baseball Has to Rid Game of Steroids," *Wilmington News Journal,* 12/12/04. **E-mails to** *Chronicle*: Sampling of correspondence received: "Guess you have nothing else to do in your pathetic lives but hound Bonds . . . You are both parasites and sycophants who crawl out from under the rocks when you have a chance to take a shot at a star . . . Disgusting . . . Shame on you . . .

No morals, no concern for human rights . . . To besmirch the name of the greatest Giants hitter of all time . . . Very irresponsible . . . Your smear campaign . . . You broke the law, or you conspired with someone to break the law. Where are your ethics? That's right—you don't have any ethics! . . . You are as low as one can get . . . You deserve jail time . . . I hope you refuse to reveal your source and I hope you go to jail . . . I bet it won't feel so good when that lawsuit and prison time ruin your lives . . . Reprehensible . . . Despicable." **Ryan after sources:** "Justice Department Probe into Media Leaks Is Sought," SFC, 12/3/04. **Conte admissions:** "BALCO Owner Comes Clean," *ESPN the Magazine,* 12/2/04; *20/20* interview with Bashir, 12/3/04. **"Narcissistic personality disorder":** Source familiar with Holley. **Conte's house raided:** "FBI Raids BALCO Chief's Home," SFC, 1/27/05.

CHAPTER TWENTY-THREE:

Lead-up to hearing: "Baseball Balks at Authority of House," (Baltimore) *Sun,* 3/10/05; "Schilling Is Planning to Testify on Steroids," NYT, 3/12/05. **Underlying fear:** Sources familiar with baseball's negotiations. **The hearing:** "Congress Slams Baseball's Integrity," SFC, 3/18/05; "Baseball on the Hot Seat," LAT, 3/18/03. **Ray and Denise Garibaldi:** Interviews, 2004–2005. **Bonds not subpoenaed:** Government source with knowledge of the hearings. **"Three urgent voice mails":** Kimberly Bell interview, 2004. **Rains's reply:** Bell provided copies of the letters. **Novitzky's visit and Bell at grand jury:** Two sources familiar with the interview and the testimony. **Testicles:** "Bonds sounds off on cheating, parenting, exploitation," ESPN.com 3/4/05. **Bonds hired tax lawyers:** a Giants source. **Semi-coherant monologue:** "It's Time to Move On," SFC, 2/23/05; "Sidestepping steroids spotlight, Bonds lashes out at Media," SJM, 2/23/05. **Press conference with son:** Broadcast by ESPN 3/22/05. **BMW shopping:** "Leah Garchik Column," SFC, 3/31/05. **Collins and Harrison 4-year bans:** "Olympic Star Suspended for Drugs Tied to BALCO," SFC, 10/20/04; "Collins Drops Doping Appeal," SFC, 5/20/05. **Dwain Chambers:** "World-Class Speed," SFC, 8/22/04; "Chambers' Dash to Chabot Tackled by Visa Problem," SFC, 10/1/04; "Chambers Faces U.S. Court Call," (London) *Guardian,* 3/20/04; "Celebrities

Given a Roasting in Kitchen from Hell," (London) *Times*, 5/22/04.
Marion Jones lawsuit, plummeting Q rating: "Second to None
Now Second to Many," CT, 6/3/05. **Jones results:** "Jones Fades to
Last in 400," LAT, 4/18/05; "Marion Jones Comes in Fourth at Mexi-
can Track and Field Event," AP, 6/12/05. **Jones, Montgomery at U.S.
Nationals:** "Embattled Sprinter Montgomery Won't Run at US
Championships," AFP, 6/25/05; "Jones and Montgomery Pull Out of
Their Events," AP, 6/25/05. **Montgomery denial before hearing:**
"Montgomery is Seventh in 100 Meters," *Oregonian,* 6/5/05.
Novitzky and White testify: Sources familiar with the hearings.
Plea deal: "40 of 42 Charges Dropped," SFC, 7/16/05. **Conte vilifies
Novitzky:** E-mail to Chronicle, 9/22/04. **No remorse:** "BALCO
Owner Comes Clean," *ESPN the magazine,* 12/2/04. **Palmeiro sus-
pended:** "Palmeiro Suspended for Steroid Violation," WP, 8/2/05.
Ryan's background and aspirations: A lawyer familiar with Ryan.
Defiant self-promotion: "Conte says he'll plead guilty in BALCO
case," LAT, 7/15/05. **Not asked to name names:** "40 of 42 Charges
Dropped," SFC, 7/16/05. *Daily News* **story:** "BALCO out of Juice,"
Daily News, 7/17/05. **Sentencing:** "Short Prison Terms for BALCO
Defendants," SFC, 10/19/05. **Novitzky's raid on Arnold:** Arnold in-
dictment and affidavit. **Interest in centerfold:** A source familiar with
Novitzky. **First surgery:** "Bonds Has Knee Surgery," SFC, 2/1/05.
Bonds on his own, drainings: A source familiar with his rehab. **Keeps trainer:** "MLB Relents, Bonds Gets His Trainer," SFC,
5/21/04. **The Coneheads:** A team source. **Bonds's aggressive rehab:**
ESPN broadcast, 3/10/05; Pedro Gomez interview; a source familiar
with Bonds's rehab. **Second surgery:** "Bonds Back at Square 1," SFC,
3/18/05. **The gym near BALCO:** "Bonds working with Anderson,"
SFC, 4/9/05. **Ting's problem:** "Bonds's knee surgeon is on medical
probation," SFC, 5/6/05. **Bonds's guaranteed contract:** "Bonds receives guarantee for '06," SFC, 9/22/04. **Club knew little, worried:**
A source familiar with Giants front office. **Another operation:**
"Bonds has Surgery to Clean Out Infection," SFC, 5/4/05. **Urged to
train elsewhere, Shields and Oliver go, too:** A source familiar with
Bonds's rehab, Giants. **Fight:** A team source. **Giants blindsided:**
"Bonds: see you in '06," SFC, 8/2/05. **Can he play?:** A team source.

Bonds versus Nationals: "Bonds handles the boos," Gwen Knapp, SFC, 9/21/05. **Brennan column:** "Bonds Return Not Happy for Many," USAT, 9/8/05. **Larry Baer:** KNBR radio appearance, 9/12/05.

EPILOGUE:

Black Sox: *Eight Men Out,* Eliot Asinof (New York: Pocket Books, 1979). **Steroid questions in Houston:** "Steroid Policy on Hold," SFC, 10/26/05. **New Joint Drug Agreement, Bunning and Sweeney:** "Baseball gets tougher on steroids," SFC, 11/16/05. **Letterman:** 12/14/04, CBS.com. **Leno:** 12/9/04, at www.oregoncomedy.com. **Chris Rock:** "Host Chris Rock Pulled Punches," *Daily News of Los Angeles,* 2/28/05. **Booing Giambi:** "Giambi's Bat and Brown's Back Both Flare Up," NYT, 6/16/05. **Palmeiro's earplugs:** "Palmeiro covers his ears," *Baltimore Sun,* 8/31/05. **Giambi's comeback:** "The Shoe Fits," NYT, 11/5/05. **Aaron's concern:** "Aaron Expresses Dismay," by Terence Moore, *Atlanta Journal and Constitution,* 12/5/04. **"Clean up baseball":** "McCain Roasts Fehr on Steroid Penalties," CT, 9/29/05. **"Found guilty of nothing":** "Aaron foresees Bonds breaking HR record," SFC, 10/27/05. **$191.37:** Team Marketing Report's "Baseball fan cost index" at TMR.com. **"We're entertainers":** "Bonds sounds off on cheating, parenting, exploitation," ESPN.com, 3/4/05.

AFTERWORD:

Bonds as pariah: "Bonds Swings Headlong Into the Storm," *Washington Post,* 4/4/06; "A Frosty Reception for Bonds," LAT, 4/4/06; "Laid-back San Diegans don't hold back on Bonds," SFC, 4/4/06. **Road trips:** "Nothing Dampens Scorn for Bonds," LAT, 4/15/06; "Jeers, not cheers for man who would be king of swat," SFC, 4/23/06; "Fan says his target was steroids, not Bonds," SFC, 4/23/06. **Sports Illustrated excerpt:** "The Truth About Barry Bonds and Steroids," SI, 4/7/06. **"Guilty":** SI source. **Editorial:** "A Baseball Tragedy," NYT, 3/9/06. **Vin Scully:** "Bonds' Bid for Baseball Glory Not Exactly a Solid Hit," LAT, 4/3/06. **Bonds mocked and parodied:** *Late Show with David Letterman,* 3/29/06; "Barry Bonds Took Steroids, Says Everyone Who Ever Watched Him Play," *The Onion,* 3/9/06; SportsCenter skit, *Saturday Night Live,* 3/11/06; "What—Me Barry?" *Mad* magazine, 9/06.

Corporate reluctance: "Bonds' Bid for Baseball Glory Not Exactly a Solid Hit," LAT, 4/3/06. **Angry commissioner:** Source who spoke with Selig. **Mitchell investigation announced:** "Hints of a wider probe," SFC, 3/31/06. **Bonds lawsuit:** "Lawyers for Bonds plan to sue over steroids book," SFC, 3/24/06. **Olbermann:** "Countdown," 3/23/06. **Judge rules on suit:** "S.F. judge refuses to order profits of Bonds book seized," SFC, 3/25/06. **Mercury mocking Bonds on Bonds:** "We watch . . . so you don't have to," SJM, spring 2006. **Magowan in denial:** "Inside Baseball," SI, 4/10/06. **Attendance weak:** "Bonds Remains Stuck on No. 713, WP, 5/12/06. **Homer in Philly:** "Mother's Day comes one Sunday early," SFC, 5/8/06. **Oakland homer:** "No. 714's Catcher is No Fan of Bonds," *Oakland Tribune,* 5/21/06. **Number 715:** "Giants Slugger Now Trails Only Aaron," WP, 5/29/06. **Radio problems:** "Not heard 'round the world," SFC, 5/29/06. **Wayward fan:** "He went for peanuts, and came back with a chance for a fortune," SFC, 5/29/06. **Novitzky and the energized Bonds probe:** Sources with knowledge of the investigation. **Ting subpoena:** "Bonds' doctor subpoenaed," SFC, 4/14/06. **Ting and Anderson talked:** Source with knowledge of the investigation. **Ting went to lab:** BALCO court documents. **Giants' medical records and Giants' employees:** "Prosecutors get Giants' medical records on Bonds," SFC, 7/22/06; "Subpoena for Giants trainer in Bonds case," 6/18/06; source with knowledge of the investigation. **Jersey, shoe, hat sizes:** Jeff Kranz interview, August 2006. **New witnesses:** Sources with knowledge of the investigation. **Government obtains recording, Anderson dilemma:** "Bonds trainer won't testify in perjury probe," SFC 6/30/06. **Anderson plea negotiations:** Court documents in Anderson contempt case. **Jason Grimsley:** Court documents. **Ryan Howard speculation:** "A question of mistrust," Yahoo! Sports, 9/3/06. **Mitchell investigation stalls:** "Feds' steroid investigation trumps baseball's," SFC, 6/10/06; sources with knowledge of government probe. **The airtight case:** Sources with knowledge of the investigation. **Anderson held in contempt:** "Bonds' trainer sent to prison," SFC, 7/6/06. **Rains offensive:** "Speculation mounting on possible Bonds perjury indictment," AP, 7/12/06; "Old friend seen as key witness against Bonds," SFC, 7/14/06; "Bonds' Attorneys Set to

Defend Any Charges," LAT, 7/15/06; Rains interview, The Dan Patrick Show, 3/24/06; Rains interview, KTVU, 7/11/06. **Mountain of evidence:** "Bonds' trainer sent to prison," SFC, 7/6/06. **Ryan won't pull the trigger, lobbying:** Sources with knowledge of the investigation. **No indictment, Anderson new subpoena:** "The Game's Not Over," SFC, 7/21/06. **Anderson back to jail:** "Bonds' trainer back behind bars," SFC, 8/29/06. **Floyd Landis:** "Tour Champ is Suspended After Testing Positive," NYT, 7/28/06. **Gatlin positive:** "Gatlin nailed for doping," SFC, 7/30/06. **Graham's defense:** "I know it was sabotage," ESPN.com, 8/4/06. **Marion Jones:** "Jones Says She's 'Shocked' by Her Positive Drug Test," NYT, 8/22/06; "Second Test Said to Clear Jones," NYT, 9/7/06. **Bonds resurgence:** SFgiants.com; baseballreference.com; "Healthy Bonds is hammerin' the ball," SFC, 9/10/06. **Breaks N.L. record, boos:** "Wild and Crazy," *Milwaukee Journal-Sentinel,* 9/24/06. **Surge no surprise:** Giants source. **Bonds vacillates, Magowan:** "Bonds says he plans to retire after this season," AP, 2/19/06; "Bonds backs off retirement talk after earlier report," AP, 2/19/06; MLB.com, throughout 2006 season; "Magowan's analysis of Bonds in 2006, 2007," SFC, 7/15/06. **Meet the President:** White House Correspondents' Dinner, private reception, 4/30/05. **Subpoenas:** "*Chronicle,* two reporters subpoenaed on BALCO sources," SFC, 5/5/06. **Attorney General:** "Gonzales defends move against BALCO reporters," SFC, 5/20/06. **Mark Corallo:** "Justice Dept. Is Criticized By Ex-Official On Subpoenas," NYT, 6/1/06. **Supporting affidavits:** Court documents, filed 5/31/06. **Rulings by White:** "Judge rules BALCO reporters must name their sources," SFC, 8/16/06; "Silence means prison, judge tells reporters," SFC, 9/22/06.

APPENDIX ONE:

1997 body fat: "Bonds on the Loose," USAT, 4/15/97. **2002 body fat:** "Baseball without Metaphor," *NYT Magazine,* op cit. **Mathematical formula:** "Fat-Free Mass Index in Users and Nonusers of Anabolic-Androgenic Steroids," by Elena M. Kouri, Ph.D., Harrison G. Pope, M.D., David L. Katz, M.D., J.D., and Paul Oliva, B.A., *The Clinical Journal of Sports Medicine,* vol. 5, n4, 1995.

The index is computed as follows:

$$\frac{(\textit{fat-free mass in kilograms})}{(\textit{height in meters})^2} - 6.3 \times (1.8 - \textit{height in meters})$$

APPENDIX TWO:

Sinins's list: There are at least four variants of James's runs-created formula, and thus several variants of the list. Sean Forman's runs-created computation ranks Bonds's 2001 season fourth all time, behind Ruth's 1921 and 1923 seasons, and Lou Gehrig's 1927 season. **Late-in-life power:** This study was done by *Chronicle* intern Frank Bauch. **OPS:** Using OPS, Forman ranked the five best seasons in history as follows: (1) Bonds 2004; (2) Bonds 2002; (3) Ruth 1920; (4) Bonds 2001; (5) Ruth 1921.

Acknowledgments

Game of Shadows began as our project on the investigative reporting team at the San Francisco Chronicle. We are indebted to our newspaper for supporting our efforts to learn the truth about BALCO, and for making it possible for us to write a book. We owe particular thanks to Investigative Editor Steve Cook, who recognized the potential of the BALCO story and guided our pursuit of it. We also are especially grateful to Chronicle Executive Editor Phil Bronstein. His interest in the story was important to our success, and his support was crucial at a time when we were resisting the efforts of the federal prosecutor to compel us to reveal the identity of our sources.

We also received important help from Sports Editor Glenn Schwarz, who assisted in directing our coverage and ensured that his department was ready to help. In addition, we valued the ongoing support of Deputy Managing Editor Stephen R. Proctor, Deputy Editor Narda Zacchino, and Managing Editor Robert Rosenthal. At Hearst Corporation, we appreciated the guidance of General Counsel Eve Burton and Senior Counsel Jonathan Donnellan, our advocates in the dispute over our sources.

Our coverage of BALCO benefited considerably from the help of several colleagues: on the Chronicle's investigative team, Elizabeth Fernandez and Seth Rosenfeld; and in the sports department, John Crumpacker, Gwen Knapp, Ron Kroichick, and John Shea. We owe particular thanks to Giants beat writer Henry Schulman. Chronicle photographers Darryl Bush, Deanne Fitzmaurice, Kurt Rogers, Chris Hardy, Paul Chinn, Frederic Larson, and Mark Costantini did a superb job documenting BALCO and Bonds, and the Chronicle was generous in allowing us to reproduce their work here. Thanks to Gary Fong, Director of Editorial Graphics Technology, for his assistance. For additional photographs, we would like to thank: The Alaska Goldpanners and Todd Dennis of goldpanners.com, for the photo of the young Barry Bonds; David Marasco, baseball blogger at thediamond angle.com, for his Giambi photo; and San Francisco Bay Area sports photographer Brad Mangin for his action shots of Bonds, Jason Giambi, and Gary Sheffield, and for the back jacket photo.

Throughout BALCO, we benefited from the assistance of Patty Hoyt, the *Chronicle*'s director of media public relations, and her staff: Yung Ahn, Kay Phan and Esther Ingrao; we also are thankful for the *Chronicle* library, especially librarian Lois Jermyn.

Washington Post foreign correspondent Steve Fainaru played a critical role in our project. Steve, Mark's older brother, wrote the initial draft of what became our proposal for a BALCO book. He also offered considerable editing and guidance throughout the entire process, even as he dodged mortar shells in Iraq.

Tom Goldstein, Professor of Journalism and Director of the Mass Communications Program at the University of California–Berkeley, gave our manuscript a careful read and made important suggestions. We'd also like to thank our friend Roger Myers, attorney with DLA Piper Rudnick Gray Cary US LLP.

We are grateful to William Shinker, publisher at Gotham Books, for believing in us and providing encouragement. The manuscript benefited considerably from the smart edit of our collegial editor, Brendan Cahill. And our book might never have been written at all but for the efforts of our enterprising agent, Scott Waxman of the Scott Waxman Agency; thanks, also, to Farley Chase of Scott's firm.

Many people were generous with their time and assistance. We particularly would like to thank Kimberly Bell; Jonathan Littman; Terry Madden; Travis Tygart, Larry Bowers, and Bill Bock of USADA; Don Catlin and Caroline Hatton at the UCLA lab; Randy Huntington; attorneys David Cornwell, Mike Rains, Brian Getz, Paula Canny, Bob Holley, Troy Ellerman, Rick Collins, and Howard Jacobs; Mark Lessler of the IRS; and Dr. Steven Ungerleider, Dr. Gary Wadler, and professor Charles Yesalis, experts who never seemed annoyed at our repeated calls.

We are indebted to Ray and Denise Garibaldi for their generosity in sharing the story of their late son Rob.

Finally, we reserve our greatest thanks to the sources who, at considerable risk, provided us with the confidential documents and information that revealed the true scope of the BALCO conspiracy.

Mark Fainaru-Wada

I would like to thank my longtime boss Glenn Schwarz, the best and most unappreciated sports editor in America. I am grateful for the encouragement of my colleagues from the *Chronicle* sports department, notably Ron Kroichick and Ray Ratto, whose constant cynicism was a source of great motivation.

Thanks to the many great sports editors I have worked for over the years, specifically Kevin "Moose" Huhn, Rick Vacek, Tom O'Toole, and Dan McGrath. Additional gratitude goes to Moose for providing lodging (and a hangover) during my trip to Colorado for the book.

I feel most lucky to be working among the talented group of reporters that comprise the *Chronicle*'s I-team. I want to especially thank Steve Cook and Lance Williams for teaching me so much about producing quality journalism.

I am grateful to my dear friends Timothy Davis and Michael Heenan for their unwavering support. I want to thank my mother-in-law, Jocelyne Allard, for her unending availability to care for our children, and to my brothers- and sisters-in-law—Sylvie and Jim Everson, Isae Wada, and Ariel Wada—for their encouragement.

Thanks to my father, Bob Fainaru, for continuing to remind me how lucky I am. I am blessed to have a mother, Ellen Gilbert, who thinks I can do no wrong and whose excitement about the book buoyed me throughout. I was equally fortunate to have a grandmother, Rose, who, sadly, didn't make it to see this book published but whose presence will always be with me. I am indebted to my stunning, smart and loving wife, Nicole; far more than suggesting important edits for our book, she endured two-plus years of BALCO consuming our lives—yet somehow managed to keep our family together and me from going crazy.

Lastly, I owe much more than I can possibly say to my brother Steve Fainaru, my best friend and the finest journalist I know. I'm not part of any of this without him.

Lance Williams

Steve Cook hired me as a reporter at the old *San Francisco Examiner*, and Phil Bronstein decided I should do investigative reporting full-time. Over the years, first at the *Ex* and now at the *San Francisco Chronicle*, they have given me a lot of leeway, while demanding a lot in the way of results. It's been a great arrangement.

My friends Paul G. Rohrdanz, Mark Livingston, Anthony A. Schumacher, and Judy Schumacher gave me aid and comfort while I worked on the book. My parents, Byron and Gayle Williams, were enormously enthusiastic. Thank you all.

I was inspired by the memory of my friends John Jacobs, political columnist at the *Sacramento Bee;* Jeff Fairbanks, editor of the *San Luis Obispo Telegram Tribune;* and Ann Fairbanks, the TT's star reporter. I also recall with fondness two great reporters who were my teachers at the Graduate School of Journalism at UC–Berkeley, Edwin Bayley and Joseph Lyford. I am grateful beyond words to my dear family for their patience, encouragement, and good humor during the writing of *Game of Shadows*. Thank you always to my wife, Barbara E. Williams, our daughter, Claire A. Williams, and our son, Anthony Z. Williams.

Index